The extraordinary photographs depicted throughout this book Calling the Shots: Aboriginal Photographies *touch on the beauty and trauma of Aboriginal lives. From Eastern Arnhem Land to western New South Wales and beyond, the depiction of Aboriginal people from early frontier and settler times to the present day is at once confronting, and then positively liberating! Those who have worked with such conflicting and inspirational photographic archives know the bittersweet pill of how we ask the questions: should we remember, do we want to remember, and how do we make this happen? There is no real fast or true rule for all. But in Lydon's book, there is a way-finder.*

Calling the Shots: Aboriginal Photographies' *cohesive netting of diverse community stories and images parallel international modes of documentation. Australia's own trauma-scape can sit alongside the photographic evidence of the victims of Second World War, Pol Pot, and the disappeared of Chile and Argentina.*

This inspirational book recalls personal and institutional histories and custodianship, collaborations and family passions that keep alive the memories that were systematically eradicated, divided or documented for the global currency of science, romance, fascination and tourism. The photographic evidence of the mostly nameless people originally photographed for nostalgia, is re-visited, re-expressed and re-positioned to re-divert the gaze.

The breath of fresh air in Calling the Shots: Aboriginal Photographies *is the inclusion of historical research of diverse photographic documentary histories told by strong Indigenous voices that provide a curative to the dominant western historical narrative.*

Energised by Lydon's book, we should come together and speak about our histories through photographs, no matter how far and wide we are from our families today, no matter how difficult; it reminds us that we can keep alive important histories — and make action for healing, inspiration and cultural-worth. This book allows us to unpack, re-piece and juxtapose divergent photographic stories about how and why photographs of Aboriginal people were made and kept.

Read on and see, feel and share the unravelling...there has been change in the air, and it just got crisper.

Brook Andrew, Artist

Calling the Shots *is a welcome intervention into an emerging literature on photographies' other histories, an exciting work for those interested in photographic history, visual culture, decolonized history, and indigeneity. The volume draws on remarkable archives of images made of and at times by Indigenous Australians; in all cases, these archives are being reclaimed by those whose images were taken. Readers are invited to reflect with the authors – a robust combination of Indigenous and non-indigenous scholars – on a wide range of work, from the earliest photographic encounters on the continent only two years after the invention of the medium, to more recent collections emerging from family archives and Aboriginal cultural activists. In short, this collection brings us the richness of rarely seen images and rarely heard Indigenous Australian perspectives on photography that engages their past, present, and future with great insight and sensitivity.*

Professor Faye Ginsburg, New York University,
Director, Center for Media, Culture and History

CALLING THE SHOTS

ABORIGINAL PHOTOGRAPHIES

EDITED BY JANE LYDON

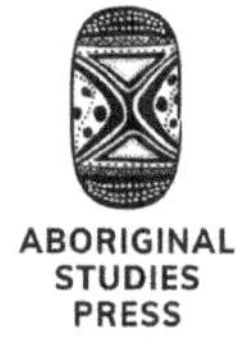

ABORIGINAL
STUDIES
PRESS

First published in 2014 by Aboriginal Studies Press
Reprinted in 2026

Aboriginal Studies Press is the publishing arm of the Australian Institute of Aboriginal and Torres Strait Islander Studies.

GPO Box 553, Canberra, ACT 2601

Phone: (61 2) 6246 1183
Fax: (61 2) 6261 4288
Email: asp@aiatsis.gov.au
Web: www.aiatsis.gov.au/asp/about.html

National Library of Australia Cataloguing-in-Publication

Title: Calling the shots: aboriginal photographies/Jane Lydon, editor and contributor; contributors, Julie Gough, Sari Braithwaite, Shauna Bostock-Smith, Lawrence Bamblett, Michael Aird, Karen Hughes, Aunty Ellen Trevorrow, Donna Oxenham, Laurie Baymarrwangga and Bentley James.

ISBN: 9781922059598 (paperback)
9781922059604 (ebook:pdf)
9781922059611 (ebook:epub)
9781922059628 (ebook:Kindle)

Notes: Includes index.

Subjects: Aboriginal Australians—Australia—History—Pictorial works. Aboriginal Australians—Social life and customs—Pictorial works. Families, Aboriginal Australian—Pictorial works.

Other Authors/Contributors: Lydon, Jane, 1965– editor. Gough, Julie, 1965. Braithwaite, Sari. Bostock-Smith, Shauna. Bamblett, Lawrence. Aird, Michael, 1963–. Hughes, Karen Elizabeth. Trevorrow, Ellen. Oxenham, Donna. Baymarrwangga, Laurie. James, Bentley.

Dewey Number: 305.899150994

Front cover: Aboriginal man of Poonindie. Ambrotype. With the permission of Special Collections, University of Bristol Library, Papers of Mathew Blagden Hale, DM130/239.

CONTENTS

Acknowledgments **vii**
Contributors **viii**
Language and style **xii**

Chapter 1: Introduction: the photographic encounter **1**
Jane Lydon

TASMANIA

Chapter 2: Forgotten lives — the first photographs of Tasmanian Aboriginal people **21**
Julie Gough

NEW SOUTH WALES

Chapter 3: Photographing Indigenous people in New South Wales **55**
Jane Lydon and Sari Braithwaite with Shauna Bostock-Smith

Chapter 4: Picture who we are: representations of identity and the appropriation of photographs into a Wiradjuri oral history tradition **76**
Lawrence Bamblett

VICTORIA

Chapter 5: Photographing Kooris: photography and exchange in Victoria **103**
Jane Lydon

QUEENSLAND

Chapter 6: Aboriginal people and four early Brisbane photographers **133**
Michael Aird

SOUTH AUSTRALIA

Chapter 7: Photographing South Australian Indigenous people: 'far more gentlemanly than many' **157**
Jane Lydon and Sari Braithwaite

Chapter 8: 'It's that reflection': photography as recuperative practice, a Ngarrindjeri perspective **175**
Karen Hughes and Aunty Ellen Trevorrow

WESTERN AUSTRALIA

Chapter 9: Photographing Aboriginal Australians in West Australia **207**
Donna Oxenham

NORTHERN TERRITORY

Chapter 10: Photographing the outback: the last frontier? **233**
Jane Lydon and Sari Braithwaite

Chapter 11: The 'Myalls' ultimatum': photography and Yolŋu in Eastern Arnhem Land, 1917 **254**
Laurie Baymarrwangga, Bentley James and Jane Lydon

Index **273**

ACKNOWLEDGMENTS

This book was funded by a four-year Australian Research Council Discovery Project, titled *Aboriginal Visual Histories,* which explored the role of the camera in mediating colonial exchange and incorporated Indigenous perspectives through collaboration with descendants. We thank several researchers for the *Aboriginal Visual Histories* project between 2008 and 2011, especially Tom Gara for research in South Australia and Sue Stanton for the Northern Territory. Their careful archival research helps form the basis for further work presented here as introductory histories. As co-Chief Investigator, Lynette Russell was a supportive colleague throughout the project. We also thank Rhonda Black of Aboriginal Studies Press for her encouragement and patience. Sari Braithwaite and Megan McKeough obtained image permissions. Many colleagues and friends have provided advice and encouragement throughout the project and we are grateful to them all.

We are grateful to the many institutions and individuals who generously gave us permission to reproduce their photographs, also acknowledged within each separate chapter. We thank the Allport Library and Museum of Fine Arts; the Thomson family and the Museum of Victoria; Bill Nicholson and the Wurundjeri Tribe Land Cultural Heritage Council Inc.; Loraine Padgham, Angela Tenbuuren and the Taungurong; the Tasmanian Museum and Art Gallery; the Trustees of the British Museum; Ronald Briggs and the Mitchell Library at the State Library of New South Wales; the National Library of Australia; Christopher Morton and the Pitt Rivers Museum, Oxford; Les Simon of the Batemans Bay Local Aboriginal Land Council; Tharawal Land Council; Jude McBean and the Grafton Regional Gallery; the Northern Territory Library; Sarah Morgan; Zena Cumpston; Isobel Crombie, Jennie Moloney and Maggie Finch at the National Gallery of Australia; La Trobe Picture Collection at the State Library of Victoria; Gary Murray for the Yung Balug and Dhudhuroa clans; the Dja Dja Wurrung Clans Aboriginal Corporation; Michael Treloar; Doris Yuke Collection; John Oxley Library of the State Library of Queensland; Paul Costigan; Queensland Art Gallery; University of Queensland Anthropology Museum; Queensland Museum; South Australian Museum; Ellen and Tom Trevorrow; Walter Richards; Cynthia Hutchison and the Ngaut Ngaut Mannum Aboriginal Community Association; Ayers House Collection, Adelaide; Jamie Carstairs and Hannah Lowery of the Special Collections, University of Bristol Library; Jackie Johnston and the Mill Cottage Museum Collection, Port Lincoln; State Library of South Australia; State Library of Western Australia; Berndt Museum; Northern Territory Library; National Archives of Australia; Ara Irititja; Royal Geographical Society of South Australia; the Elders of Billiluna Pastoral Company; Jill Braithwaite; and Ian Conway.

CONTRIBUTORS

Jane Lydon is the inaugural Wesfarmers Chair in Australian History and an Australian Research Council Future Fellow (2010–15) at The University of Western Australia. Since 1997 her research has addressed the history and meanings of photographs of Indigenous Australians. Her books include *Eye contact: photographing Indigenous Australians* (Duke University Press, Durham and London, 2005), and *The flash of recognition: photography and the emergence of Indigenous rights* (NewSouth Books, Sydney, 2012), which won the Queensland Literary Awards' University of Southern Queensland History Book Award.

Michael Aird has worked full time in the area of Aboriginal cultural heritage since 1985, graduating in 1990 with a Bachelor of Arts in Anthropology from the University of Queensland. His main interest is urban Aboriginal photographic history, curating several exhibitions, as well as being author of several books and articles. In 1996 he established Keeaira Press, an independent publishing house. For five years Michael was the Curator of Aboriginal Studies at the Queensland Museum and continues to work as a freelance curator and anthropologist.

Lawrence Bamblett is an Education Fellow at the Australian Institute of Aboriginal and Torres Strait Islander Studies and an Adjunct Research Fellow for the Australian National University (at the National Centre for Indigenous Studies). He grew up at Erambie Mission, Cowra, a Wiradjuri community, and worked for various community development programs there before enrolling at university. His doctoral thesis explored cultural continuity through storytelling within his Wiradjuri community. He is Chairperson of Erambie Advancement, a community corporation that develops and administers community education, health and employment programs at Erambie. He was lucky to have been taught by some very talented Koori storytellers and his work today reflects their teaching. Photographs have been a significant part of his learning, teaching and research, as well as his community development work. His academic career has been an extension of his interest in the use of photographs in community storytelling.

Laurie Baymarrwangga is a nonagenarian Yan-nhangu speaker and Aboriginal Traditional Owner of Murrungga, Galiwin'ku, and Bural-Bural Islands, and the seas of Ganatjirri Maramba. Born c. 1920 on Murrungga Island, largest of the outer Crocodile Islands, Baymarrwangga speaks six different languages fluently and understands a further three. Having survived the Japanese bombing of her islands and the missionisation of her kin, she continues to pass on the intimate local knowledge of the islands and to resist neo-colonial settler pressures for normalisation. Striving to save her language and local culture requires a continuing struggle for equitable rights in local natural resources. Baymarrwangga continues to care for her homelands as a base for sustainable livelihood activities on her sea country and a real future for her grandchildren's children. She was winner of the 2011 Northern Territory Innovation and Research Lifetime Achiever Award and Senior Australian of the Year for 2012, and her continuing courage, intelligence and persistence against assimilation policies is a lesson for all.

Shauna Bostock-Smith is a Bundjalung woman whose family descends from northern New South Wales. She has worked as a primary school teacher since graduating from the Australian Catholic University with a Bachelor of Education in 2006. Shauna resigned from full-time teaching to research and write about her family history. She completed her BA (Honours) at Griffith University (2013) and was recently offered a place at the Australian National University (Canberra) to begin a PhD in Indigenous History in 2014.

Sari Braithwaite graduated from the Australian National University with Honours in History in 2007. She has worked as a research assistant on the Australian Research Council-funded Discovery Project *Aboriginal Visual Histories* since 2007, conducting research in the archives, making three short films and *Conversations with Michael Aird* (http://arts.monash.edu.au/mic/research/visual-histories/conversations.php), and writing on a range of key themes. She was the Program Manager of the Human Rights Arts and Film Festival from 2011 to 2013 and is currently working on a range of documentary film projects.

Julie Gough is an artist, curator and writer who lives in Hobart. Her research and art practice involves uncovering and re-presenting often conflicting and subsumed histories, many referring to her own and her family's experiences as Tasmanian Aboriginal people. An Honorary Associate, University of Tasmania, and Adjunct Principal Research Fellow, James Cook University, Townsville, she holds a PhD and BA (Honours) in Visual Arts at the University of Tasmania, a Master's degree (Goldsmiths College, University of London), a BA (Visual Arts; Curtin University) and a BA (Prehistory/ English Literature; The University of Western Australia).

Karen Hughes is a Lecturer in Indigenous Studies at Swinburne University of Technology. She has formerly taught at Monash University and the University of South Australia, and in 2011 was a Visiting Fellow at University Paris 13. She is finishing a book, titled *My grandmother on the other side of the lake*, based on her doctoral research, which weaves a cross-cultural history of intimate and domestic spaces around Lake Alexandrina, from the perspectives of Ngarrindjeri and settler-descended women's stories and lived experiences in the late nineteenth and early twentieth centuries.

Bentley James is a Social and Cultural Anthropologist, Linguist and Educator who has lived on the Crocodile Islands in North East Arnhem Land, in the Northern Territory of Australia, for twenty years. He continues recording language, ritual, social organisation, local knowledges and recent archaeological prehistory of the people of the islands. Since 1993 he has worked in close collaboration with Yan-nhangu elders, including Baymarrwangga, on the Yan-nhangu dictionary and more recently on the Yan-nhangu atlas, an illustrated dictionary of the Crocodile Islands. In 2003 he published the first Yan-nhangu dictionary and has since published on language revitalisation, ethnobiology and local maritime knowledge of the Yan-nhangu. With local collaborators he is leading a multi-disciplinary team recording the 'Intergenerational Transmission of Indigenous Ecological Knowledges' with Charles Darwin University and the North Australian Indigenous Land and Sea Management Alliance. He continues to research how practical local projects like the Yan-nhangu language team's Language Nests project, Crocodile Islands Rangers program, Crocodile Islands Initiative and turtle conservation project can deliver equity in resource governance and a culture-based economy. His doctoral thesis, 'Time and tide in the Crocodile Islands: change and continuity in Yan-nhangu marine identity', explores in detail the hitherto unrecorded ethnography and languages of the Yan-nhangu of Mooroongga (Murrungga) and the Crocodile Islands.

Donna Oxenham is a Yamatji woman and a descendant of the Malgana people of Shark Bay in the north-west of Western Australia. She also has extensive links into the Nyungar community through her grandfather, who was a Wardandi man from the Busselton area in the south-west of Western Australia. In 2006 Donna was a visiting Research Fellow at the Australian Institute of Aboriginal and Torres Strait Islander Studies. In 2008 she was employed as a researcher involved with the Stolen Wages Project facilitated by the Department of Indigenous Affairs. Donna has worked with Indigenous people, groups and organisations throughout Western Australia and the broader Australian Indigenous community, particularly within the field of arts, history, cultural heritage and native title. In 2002–03 Donna was the Cultural Heritage Officer at the Yamatji Marlpa Barna Baba Maaja Aboriginal Corporation, and in 2004 a Policy Officer with the South West Aboriginal Land and Sea Council. Of particular significance, Donna was employed by the Berndt Museum of Anthropology from 2000–02 to facilitate the digitisation, restoration and repatriation of Indigenous photographic collections. Through her positions, tertiary studies and her research fellowship, Donna has gained considerable experience in undertaking a range of research and related tasks on Indigenous children, families and communities.

Ellen Trevorrow is a Ngarrindjeri weaver and educator who has exhibited widely throughout Australia. She regards herself as a 'cultural weaver' and is dedicated to sharing her knowledge of the practice, and Ngarrindjeri culture and ecology. She was born at Point McLeay (Raukkan) in 1955 and raised near Tailem Bend, a small town in the Murraylands region of South Australia. She spent her childhood in fringe dwellers' camps just outside the town with her grandmother, Ellen Brown, from whom she gets her name. She attended primary school in Tailem Bend, and moved South to Bonney Reserve near Meningie when she was eleven, and went on to complete high school. She met her husband to be, Tom Trevorrow, when she was fourteen. They were married in 1976 and had seven children. They have remained in or near Meningie ever since. She and her husband have been foundation members of Camp Coorong Race Relations Cultural Education Centre since 1985. Camp Coorong is located close to Meningie, adjacent to the site of Bonney Reserve. It is situated within the Coorong, a coastal ecosystem of estuaries, lakes and lagoons where the Murray River meets the sea. Trevorrow has a deep sense of attachment to the Murray River, which constitutes part of her Ngarrindjeri Clan Group's Traditional Country.

LANGUAGE AND STYLE

We use both 'Aboriginal people' and 'Indigenous people' to refer to the original inhabitants of this continent. The noun 'Aborigine' has fallen out of favour as being overly determinist, and we use the currently preferred adjective 'Aboriginal', denoting simply one aspect of a person's identity. The use of 'Indigenous' follows the Australian Government's recommendation, which calls for capitalising 'Indigenous' when it refers to the original inhabitants of Australia but no capital when used in a general sense to refer to the original inhabitants of other countries.[1] Where we have reproduced certain historical terms that are now deemed offensive, we have done so in their original context in order to make specific historical arguments. We signify their origin and our distance from them through the use of quotation marks.

Some of the spellings used in this book are historical, although in the present the preferred spellings of living people and current representative organisations are used.

NOTE

1. Australia Parliamentary Council, *Drafting direction no. 2.1: English usage, gender-specific and gender-neutral language, grammar, punctuation and spelling*, Canberra, 2010, p. 6, viewed 10 March 2012, <www.opc.gov.au/about/drafting_series/DD2.1.pdf>.

Chapter 1

INTRODUCTION: THE PHOTOGRAPHIC ENCOUNTER

Jane Lydon

In March 1897 the ethnographer Francis Gillen wrote from Central Australia to his Melbourne-based colleague, Baldwin Spencer, that he had printed a set of photographs of an Arrernte ceremony. He described having 'had a neat shallow tin case made to hold them and they are to be taken and deposited with the churinga [secret sacred boards] in the ertnatulinga [storehouse cave]', to the pleasure of the Arrernte men concerned.[1]

Twenty years later, the murder of two Filipinos was re-enacted by Yolŋu men of eastern Arnhem Land, in the Northern Territory, for visiting photographer Edward Reichenbach. The Yolŋu commissioned 'Ryko' to show how the intruders had been killed in retaliation for their brutality, explicitly calling upon the camera to provide testimony on their behalf. The elders framed the image as a petition to the colonial authorities, asking, 'Why can't strangers coming to our shores give us a square deal?...Where can we lodge complaints against such unscrupulous invaders and abolitionists of our race?'[2]

Although many accounts of colonial photography have emphasised the medium's controlling and destructive effects upon its Indigenous subjects, these two examples — explored further in subsequent chapters — demonstrate considerable evidence for its deployment by and for Aboriginal people themselves. As a medium of exchange, photographs of Aboriginal people have served vastly different purposes within Indigenous and Western knowledge systems, from embodiments of kin and ancestral powers to visual data that actively created scientific knowledge.

This collaborative book explores Indigenous Australian perspectives on photography. Historians of Australian photography have noted that from the medium's inception Indigenous Australians were of great interest to photographers.[3] Yet one aspect of this encounter that has been overlooked, but is evident from the earliest years, is the participation of Aboriginal people themselves. There is no longer any excuse to assume that they were simply passive victims. This is not to dismiss the often enormous power inequalities that shaped colonial relations. However, rather than telling us what 'the white photographer saw', or conceiving of photography as inevitably a means of defining and managing Aboriginal subjects, we simply ask a question: what were the views and experiences of the Indigenous participants? Contributors examine historical interactions between photographer and Indigenous people and the ways that such images can be understood to express the process of cross-cultural exchange, as well as the rich and vital meanings photographs have today. As Indigenous scholar Marcia Langton argued fifteen years ago, 'the problem' with analysis of the visual representation of 'Aborigines lies in the positioning of us as object, and the person behind the camera as subject'.[4] So in contrast to the substantial literature that defines colonial photography simply as the white photographer's view, this study considers the ways that the camera was used in particular places and times to communicate Indigenous views.

Contributions represent diverse views, stemming from the specific, varied histories of each former colony rather than presenting a uniform story across the continent. Where these images subsequently became detached from their local context, sometimes circulating around the globe as 'types' of Australian Aboriginal people, this book aims to restore their cultural and historical specificity, returning them to their Indigenous origins, however transformed.

VISIBILITY AND PHOTOGRAPHY: A BRIEF HISTORY

The history of photographing Indigenous Australians reflects the intersection of photographic technologies with the visibility of Indigenous people within the 'contact zone' — a moving space of encounter and conflict that followed waves of invasion around the continent. The historically specific circumstances of each former colony and its changing relations with Indigenous people, in conjunction with the photographic technology available, largely determined what was photographed and how.

After photography was invented in 1839, practitioners of the new method quickly saw its commercial benefits and transported it around the globe, recording sights of interest for European audiences. The first Australian experiment owed much to French entrepreneurship: the famous first, lost, daguerreotype of Macquarie Street, Sydney, was made by Captain Augustin Lucas, former commander of a French Naval School Expedition supported by the influential Paris organisation *la Société d' Encouragement pour l'Industrie Nationale* in April 1841.[5] This speculative beginning was quickly followed by the arrival of adventurous photographers capitalising on curiosity about foreign sights and peoples, but also catering to local desires for domestic portraits.

Photographers quickly saw the commercial value of taking photographs of Australian Aboriginal people. Ideas about them had been shaped by Western conceptions of progress and civilisation since first contact. Some observers argued that they represented an earlier stage of humankind: for example, in the first decades of settlement, naval surgeon Peter Cunningham pronounced Aboriginal people 'at the very zero of civilisation'.[6] Following the 1859 publication of Charles Darwin's *The origin of species by means of natural selection*, the theory of natural selection quickly became scientific orthodoxy and such ideas only strengthened. Applied to humankind, the social evolutionist paradigm was used to rationalise the ill effects of invasion and dispossession upon Indigenous people. The general public took a great interest in these theories and debates during the nineteenth century, and the market for images of Indigenous people comprised a large general audience, as well as scientists and collectors.

As a result of the growing belief that the Aboriginal race was doomed to extinction, photographers sought to record what was believed to be a disappearing way of life. They followed the 'frontier', seeking Aboriginal people apparently untouched by change — seemingly 'primitive', 'authentic' subjects, stripped of signs of European civilisation (such as clothing). As colonisation spread, such people were harder to find, or paradoxically required greater intervention to appear untouched. As each frontier was opened up, local Indigenous people were represented visually according to settlers' imaginative desires, as well as photographic possibility. This resulted in the development of distinctive visual traditions in each colony, despite the connections and photographers common to all.

During the 1840s photographs in the form of daguerreotypes showed Indigenous people posed in studios, as required by contemporary technology. Some, such as Kilburn's c. 1846–48 portraits of the Kulin confederacy of central-southern Victoria, appeared in traditional dress. Others, such as the c. 1855–60 portraits of Jemima, nanny to the Mortlock family of South Australia, show her in neat and respectable European attire. Rediscovered South Australian collections record prominent members of the Poonindie Mission community during the 1850s, well-dressed and posed as gentlemen. These are tantalising glimpses of the early years of encounter and accommodation.

In the 1850s the invention of the wet-plate collodion process allowed outdoor scenes to be recorded by photographers who were now almost as mobile as their Indigenous subjects. During this decade some of the first photographs of Indigenous people away from white settlements were produced, such as William Stanley Jevons' 1859 group view on the Braidwood goldfields, the first images of New South Wales Aboriginal people.[7] In Victoria several innovative visual projects showed the colony's Indigenous people still living on traditional country, as well as undergoing transformation as they adjusted to white incursion (Chapter 5 explores this further). It is easy to overlook the mobility both of the photographer and his subjects from this time onwards, given their seeming fixity: researchers often work from the place to a people, assuming that those in the photograph were traditional owners of the land depicted. This is a dangerous assumption, however, and may lead to misidentification. Although the connection between Aboriginal people and their country is profound, we are now aware of the mobility and cosmopolitanism of many who travelled for work, adventure or curiosity.[8]

With the emergence of the cheap, palm-sized *carte de visite* in the mid-1850s, portraiture became an international craze, allowing family portraiture across all classes, prompting an international trade in celebrities and permitting collectors to obtain examples, or 'types', of different peoples from around the world. Photographers recorded diverse Indigenous Australians in images that found their way into scientific collections across the globe. During the 1860s many featured portraits from Queensland, which had been made a new colony in 1859 and where local studios were able to record people still leading a noticeably traditional way of life (as Chapter 6 explores further). While officials sought to segregate Indigenous people in farming settlements, such places sometimes became sites of cultural encounter. In Victoria the six major missions and reserves established around 1860 became places of contact and exchange between black and white, and the visual record reflects this process, with sites such as Coranderrk, near Melbourne, generating thousands of photographs. From the 1870s onwards, evolutionist notions of Aboriginality began to predominate, as Darwinism became dogma, and a racial hierarchy was cemented in place. As control tightened in southern Australia over the last decades of the nineteenth century, greater distance between black and white was expressed through images of people living on government institutions, seemingly leading a Europeanised way of life. Northern and north-western Australia remained a 'frontier' and a source of 'authentic', 'primitive' views of tradition.

By the early twentieth century, however, cheap Kodak cameras started to become widely available, allowing Aboriginal people to adopt the medium for their own purposes. As a storekeeper on the Birdsville Track wrote to a friend in 1933, 'Nearly all the young [Aborigines] today go through a Kodak stage. I have three box Brownies left here for repairs by young [Aborigines] who have had the craze.'[9] As Indigenous activists themselves began to campaign for reform, they deplored the power of racist media representations: in 1938 at the first Day of Mourning and Protest, campaigners Jack Patten and Bill Ferguson demanded equal citizenship and attacked media misrepresentation, arguing that 'the Popular Press of Australia makes a joke of us by presenting silly and out-of-date drawings and jokes of "Jacky" or "Binghi", which have educated city-dwellers and young Australians to look upon us as sub-human. Is this not adding insult to injury?'[10] Activists took up photography as a form of witness to past injustice and as the basis of demands for rights in the present.[11]

Following the Second World War, official attempts to promote assimilation relied heavily on visual propaganda, which showed 'model' settlements that were being constructed and 'success stories' that profiled individual Aboriginal people who had 'made it' in mainstream society. However, such narratives clashed with graphic and sometimes shocking documentary imagery deployed in the service of housing and welfare reform, which showed the violation of Aboriginal people's rights as citizens. Such photographs helped to prompt the campaign for constitutional reform that culminated in the 1967 referendum and gave the federal government a mandate to make specific policies for Indigenous people.

Despite its symbolic importance, disillusionment with the effects of the referendum during the 1970s drew a younger generation of Indigenous leaders into activism. This was an especially turbulent phase in the Aboriginal struggle for recognition; the Tent Embassy protest of 1972 occurred in the context of a growing land rights movement and, ultimately, has been credited with contributing to the passing of the *Aboriginal Land Rights (Northern Territory) Act 1976*. As the movement for Indigenous rights gained momentum during the early 1970s, photographers made the activism of these years publicly visible, expanding the visual field to show Aboriginal people's everyday lives and, for the first time, displacing earlier, stereotypical images of romanticised primitives or detribalised fringe-dwellers.

Indigenous and non-Indigenous photographers seized upon the medium as a means for making Aboriginal Australians visible, recording their experiences from an explicitly Indigenous perspective; their political project was frequently driven by an intense desire to counter degrading historical imagery. During the early 1980s a self-consciously Indigenous photography movement began to emerge. Mervyn Bishop, now recognised as the forerunner to this development, worked in the 1970s as Australia's first Koori press photographer. In 1974 Bishop started work at the Department of Aboriginal Affairs in Canberra, a role in which he covered the major developments in Aboriginal communities throughout Australia, including the hand-back of land to the Gurindji on 16 August 1975 at Kalkaringi. Bishop's famous photograph shows then Prime Minister Gough Whitlam pouring a stream of desert sand into Vincent Lingiari's hand, as Whitlam declared, 'I put into your hands part of the earth itself as a sign that this land will be the possession of you and your children forever'.[12] In recording the Australian Government's recognition of Aboriginal land rights, this image has become an icon of the land rights movement, and of Australian photography. Moreover, it stands for restitution and reconciliation between black and white Australia. It has come to represent a particular historical narrative that is broader than the single moment it records, its meaning seemingly exceeding words. When a politicised and self-reflective Indigenous photography movement emerged during the early 1980s, Bishop's Kalkaringi photograph was displayed in the first Indigenous photographic exhibition, the landmark 1986 National Aborigines Day Observance Committee show.

From the early 1980s Indigenous photographers and historians realised that the visual archive offered evidence for their historical experience, and might be framed by Indigenous narratives in order to counter colonial documentary history. In particular, the legal need to demonstrate prior occupation and a continuous history underlay the recognition of rights to land, and so photography was drawn upon as a means of demonstrating this history factually and clearly, in a visual language accessible to all. An Indigenous photography movement emerged that began to represent Aboriginal culture, identity and political claims from an explicitly Aboriginal perspective. A range of mostly young, mostly art-school graduate Aboriginal photographers established public profiles, including now famous artists Tracey Moffatt, Brenda L Croft and Michael Riley.

The bicentennial year was particularly important and focused attention on the nation's unresolved past and Indigenous photographers (for example, an image by Peter McKenzie showed a La Perouse protest against the First Fleet re-enactment of January 1788). Southport-based Michael Aird recorded the wave of protest that countered the celebration of white settlement. His photograph of Vincent Brady, now known as Qawanji Ngurku Jawiyabba, shows the Black Panther and son of radical Pastor Don Brady leading a Brisbane protest against bicentennial celebrations. These oppositional projects took issue with the celebration and rejected the triumphalist tone of most commemorations. The major *After 200 years* bicentennial project, co-ordinated by Penny Taylor and the Australian Institute of Aboriginal and Torres Strait Islander Studies, brought together twenty-one photographers (of whom eight were Indigenous) who visited nineteen Indigenous communities to document the diversity of Indigenous life in Australia. It sought to splinter the binary stereotypes of 'noble savage' versus 'fringe-dweller' by revealing the diversity of everyday lives and 'some of the positive things that were going on'.[13] The project's photographers were guided by Eric Michaels' highly influential essay 'Restrictions on photography in Aboriginal Australia', which, above all else, advocated collaboration with Indigenous people and Indigenous people's control over their own cultural heritage.[14]

Today such procedures are standard ethical practice. As advocated by internationally recognised documentary photographer Ricky Maynard (a Tasmanian Aboriginal man of the Ben Lomond and Cape Portland people), what is crucial is that collaboration with photographic subjects is guided by openness and trust.[15] Curator Keith Munro calls this 'the formation of an Aboriginal photographic practice', and it centres upon 'co-authorship between image-maker and subject'.[16]

PHOTOGRAPHS TODAY: INDIGENOUS CULTURAL HERITAGE

Many cultural institutions across Australia and overseas now house large collections of photographs documenting Aboriginal lives and history. Since the 1970s, Indigenous demands for restitution and return of cultural heritage have signalled a shift to acknowledge Indigenous rights in a wide range of objects and practices that constitute cultural heritage. Originally focused on the repatriation of skeletal remains and secret/sacred items, such recognition has now broadened to include a wider range of material and intangible culture, and, by extension, photographs.[17]

An emergent international literature examines the process and effects of returning photographs to source communities; however, the intersection of new digital technologies and traditional Aboriginal visual practices remains a challenge for Australian curators, scholars and Indigenous descendants, even as it offers exciting new possibilities for returning photographs to descendants.[18] Many cultural institutions define photographs as Indigenous intellectual property and have developed protocols to manage collections of historical materials, including photographs.[19] In acknowledgment of Indigenous demands for control over their heritage and representation, such Australian Indigenous protocols emphasise the need for consultation by researchers.

Many projects have established digital points of contact between communities and photographic archives — notably, the A_ra Irititja Project, which means 'stories from a long time ago' in the language of Anangu (Pitjantjatjara and Yankunytjatjara people) of Central Australia. This much-loved project, mounted in 1994 by Anangu in partnership with a team led by John Dallwitz, has transformed records of the past into valuable cultural heritage for descendants by returning 'lost' material, including photographs, films, sound recordings and documents. A_ra Irititja has designed a purpose-built computer archive that digitally stores repatriated materials and other contemporary items, and this model has now been adopted by other communities and government departments across Australia. In 2005 Wilton Foster, Chairman of the Pitjantjatjara Council, explained the rationale for A_ra Irititja:

> It is important for all our people, throughout the west, east, north and south to see their own history — for children, teenagers, young and old people, men and women to see and hear about their past.
>
> Missionaries, explorers and others recorded and photographed the lives of the people and took these records away. A_ra Irititja makes it possible to bring the history back home where it belongs. To have A_ra Irititja in our communities helps keep the past in the present and helps keep our culture strong. It is important to link future generations through A_ra Irititja to generations past.[20]

The project aims to transmit culture and language in an age of globalisation, using contemporary technology to provide a central storage 'forever'. As the project's website states, 'These are the cultural sources for the stories of land, of self, of the present, the past and the future. They provide for the celebration of cultural identity, and allow also for focus on family and kinship.'[21] The project also serves to safeguard language, and has developed cultural protocols to guide access to its resources.

The Aṟa Irititja Project officially commenced in 1994 to identify, copy and electronically record history and culture, and to offer access along such axes as gender, seniority and 'sorrow' (mourning). With increasingly sophisticated capabilities, it remains a model for respectful digital return.[22]

However, as Indigenous leaders Martin Nakata and Marcia Langton have argued regarding Indigenous intellectual property, 'the path to developing clear and high standards of practice in this area rests on *building a strong foundation for understanding what informs the concerns of Indigenous people* about the intersection of our knowledge and cultural materials with library and archival systems'.[23] While the issues surrounding Indigenous intellectual and cultural property rightly remain a focus of scholarly analysis and provide the socio-political context for our study, this book instead explores the cultural and historical foundations of current Indigenous views and the social meanings of these images to Aboriginal descendants, and aims to improve our understanding of this important Indigenous field. Historical photographs are crucially important to Aboriginal communities: such images represent otherwise unknown ancestors and relatives, often lost as a result of official processes, as well as information about places, history, culture and relationships. They also represent a range of other meanings that this book sets out to examine. In addition, while Indigenous people remained a popular and scientific subject of photography well into the twentieth century, they increasingly obtained the means to use the medium for their own purposes when cheap cameras made private photography widely available. As Michael Aird shows (Chapter 6), from this time onwards, private, familial collections were amassed, shaped by Indigenous views.

Previous studies of Indigenous (re)evaluations of photography suggest the distinctive ways the medium is deployed within Indigenous social relations and histories. For many Australian Aboriginal people photographs are not merely representations, as in the Western tradition; within Indigenous cultures they may assume the powers of the ancestors, embedded within social relationships with both the living and the dead. Such analyses suggest that Aboriginal descendants treat photographic portraits within traditional visual conventions as embodiments of kin to create 'extended personhood'.[24]

However, such studies have also shown that photographs have assumed new values in the context of colonial dispossession and loss, revealing unknown ancestors and substantiating Indigenous stories and experiences formerly hidden from view. In this way, as anthropologist Gaynor Macdonald has suggested of Wiradjuri practices, they serve as an important means of countering 'the non-writing of the past, the secret and silent histories, and the past distorted by imperial histories'.[25] Beyond tradition, in a context of transformation and continuity, photographs may also serve a range of purposes — telling stories, connecting families and countering colonial amnesia.

Lawrence Bamblett grew up in the Wiradjuri community of Erambie Mission at Cowra and completed a doctorate that explored cultural continuity through storytelling within his community. In the course of his research, he observed how photographs are an integral part of the community's oral history tradition and are used as memory aids (for example, in recording sporting prowess). He notes the reluctance of some owners of photographs to share their collections, due to their fear of theft: 'When I did ask for access I was often confronted by angry older women who jealously guarded their tins full of treasured "old photos"' (Lawrence Bamblett, pers. comm., 2012). Such attitudes express tensions within communities, as well as commonalities, and the status of photographs as often people's 'most treasured material possession'. In response, Bamblett developed a number of strategies for looking at these precious images that were designed to create trust, such as ensuring credit for ownership and a process of rapid copying and return. These tactics were based upon his personal relationships through kinship and community membership, as well as by establishing his good intentions and ethical approach through demonstration, ongoing relationships and informed consent. Bamblett concludes that 'The most enjoyable part of having this large collection is that it encourages people to gather at my home and talk about the past'.

In 1993, at a time when only a few scholars around the world had begun to realise the value of such photographs as a means of exploring culture and history, Indigenous researcher Michael Aird was invited to curate an exhibition by the Queensland Museum, for which he produced a landmark book, *Portraits of our elders*.[26] As he remembers:

> What was remarkable about this offer was that I was given the opportunity to present a concept of an exhibition without any parameters...Prior to this a few major galleries and museums had involved Aboriginal people in curatorial teams but always in projects that had been initiated and controlled by non-Aboriginal curators. (M Aird, pers. comm., 11 November 2012)

Aird chose to assemble studio photographs of Queensland Aboriginal people that reveal the transition they experienced between the 1860s and the 1920s.[27] Against the prevailing interpretative orthodoxy of the 1980s, which cast photography as an inevitable tool of oppression, Aird noted, if 'you look past the props and awkward poses, the personality and strength of the individuals emerge. Regardless of the props and stereotypes, they look beyond the situation they are in — they are looking at us.'[28] Of family portraits commissioned during the 1920s, he comments:

> The more recent photographs are obviously of paying customers with total control over the situation. They display absolute confidence and dignity of people who have succeeded, who have earned the respect of the community. Aborigines felt a very real need to state their successes in the European community to ensure protection from the oppressive 'protection' policies.[29]

Finally, he suggested that, 'Through these photographs you can look into the eyes of these elders and ask yourself about the lives they may have lived. These photographs give an insight into the changes in Europeans' perceptions of Aborigines and of Aborigines' perceptions of themselves.'[30] This points towards a way of seeing these photographs that is often difficult for non-Indigenous viewers to understand: that is, the healing power of images of kin and culture, as they are enfolded into living families and worlds. According to Donna Oxenham, a Western Australian Yamatji woman, when descendants look at images they see past the sometimes degrading context to their relatives recorded within the photographs. Oxenham states that through photographs 'our pasts, present and futures are intrinsically linked — so that they no longer remain in the past, but are a part of who we are today'.[31]

As this book explores, it is clear that for many Indigenous Australians, a major role of photographs is to reveal family and social worlds. Although such uses may appear more or less 'traditional' or transformed, it is clear that their significance resides in how they may stand in for *people*. In the case of Gillen's 1897 gift, to the Arrernte these images recorded the performance of sacred ceremonies that reunite participants with the powers of the ancestors. Recent analyses of family photography have challenged orthodox interpretations that suggest such images are merely an expression of capitalist consumption and a celebration of the nuclear middle-class family.[32] We show that how photographs are used and the emotional response they prompt transcends these reductive approaches. In many ways, these domestic uses

Aboriginal people make of photographs, to assert and remember family relationships, are largely shared with the practices of non-Indigenous Australians.

What *is* specific is their deployment within cultures, constituted by remembered traditions, but also historical experience and its forces. The historical understanding imparted by such photographs provides a perspective on the past that is fundamentally different to that provided by textual sources. As history, they may prove or generate Indigenous narratives, and assert a historical presence. They reveal Indigenous experience — including change, strength, dignity and worth. Enmeshed within Indigenous narratives, identified as relatives and as historical actors with biographies and objectives, recent analysis has suggested that photography stands 'at the crossroads of history and memory', providing an essential resource for 'critical black memory'.[33] In the aftermath of colonialism, these images may also serve recuperative purposes; for example, by destabilising the 'structures of forgetting' that excised Aboriginal people from the national story and by confirming the truth of a history otherwise known only through family stories.

INDIGENOUS ARTISTS

As well as these domestic and historical uses of photographs, Indigenous artists have long understood the power of old photographs; some artists — such as Brook Andrew — draw directly from the archive to literally re-work or re-frame them. Others have chosen to re-create or re-imagine historical photographs — and even to cast themselves as re-imagined subjects or heroes and heroines.[34] One such imaginative engagement with the colonial photographic collection is Christian Thompson's 2012 series *We bury our own*, in which he has engaged with the colonial archive held in the Pitt Rivers Museum at Oxford University, where he is one of the first recipients of the Charlie Perkins Scholarship. In reflecting upon Thompson's 2008 show *Australian graffiti*, art critic Rex Butler terms his work an exercise in 'cultural cross-dressing'[35]: in the series he turned to native plants for inspiration, his trademark self-portraits showing him wearing a black hoodie, for example, with his face replaced by red-flowering gum blossoms. These images evoke Margaret Preston's 1920s 'national' still life paintings of Indigenous flowers. As Butler notes, 'Thompson is making the point that these flowers are arranged on the otherwise invisible face of the Aborigine, or even as a way of covering up an Aboriginal gaze', with the effect of reminding us that 'there is nothing less natural than nature itself'.[36] This goes to the heart of the way that Indigenous Australians have been represented by white settlers: a range of colonial visual strategies have sought to construct Aboriginal people as part of nature, for example, or as naturally 'different' or 'other' on biological grounds.

In his new *We bury our own* series, Thompson has again displaced the historical markers of identity central to colonial photography — especially the anthropometric mug shot. Here *he* is the photographer who chooses how to see the Indigenous subject. Instead of the Australian flora of his earlier work, he has replaced red-flowering gum blossoms with roses and chrysanthemums, alluding to his new environment, the domestic flower gardens of England. He wears the formal dress of an Oxford student.

In other self-portraits a scatter of crystals is arranged carefully across his eyes, or forms a tiara — perhaps a means of connecting the spiritual with the corporeal, as suggested by Christopher Morton, Senior Curator of Photography at the Pitt Rivers Museum. Morton's perceptive catalogue essay picks up Thompson's own phrase, 'spiritual repatriation', to refer to a process of engaging with these images' colonial heritage in ways that are not concrete and direct but, rather, imaginative and allusive; instead of returning the bodies of war victims, as the term 'repatriation' originally denoted, Thompson transcends the meanings once attached to the material photographic object — its code — and holds on to its affect. During the nineteenth century, Indigenous bodies were, in a sense, captured by photographs that sought to reduce their humanity to an essential corporeal truth. Thompson, by contrast, shows us new forms of a cosmopolitan, hybrid Indigenous identity that transcends this literalism. The beauty, clarity and formality of these portraits convey a sacred process of acknowledgment and engagement with ancestral forces with great dignity and emotion.

Contributors to this volume elaborate these issues, with historical overviews that detail the specific experiences and visual record of each former colony. Julie Gough re-examines photographs of the 'last of the Tasmanian Aborigines', among the most famous images of Indigenous people in the world during the late nineteenth century (Chapter 2). More recently, they have been publicly recognised as deeply disturbing for many surviving Indigenous Tasmanians. Examining these iconic yet little-researched images, Gough re-tells the almost mythical experience of Indigenous Tasmanians, known throughout the world from the late nineteenth century as an extinct people. Within an evolutionary framework, these famous photographs circulated around the world through exhibitions, books and scientific journals in a narrative of extinction now vehemently refuted by descendants. Gough brings lives to light, showing how photographic portraits, made to generalise the subject and 'prove' diverse scientific arguments, can now be seen as a means of acknowledgment and engagement in the present. She reminds us that these images do not show one family or coherent group, but members of nations from around the island, forced together by circumstance, and that Oyster Cove was a cosmopolitan place of diverse languages and cultures.

Lydon and Sari Braithwaite with Shauna Bostock-Smith trace a similar yet distinct process for New South Wales, where the famous Clarence River series made by JW Lindt has become a treasured resource for descendants — a story that Bostock-Smith tells with vivid life (Chapter 3).

Lawrence Bamblett explores the uses of photography in constructing identity for Wiradjuri people living at Erambie, in western New South Wales (Chapter 4). Bamblett describes how he became determined to prove that a senior, cherished woman was Koori, although she had been called a 'negress'. He also explores how a wonderful family photograph — taken by a newspaper journalist investigating housing reform — has been used to tell a range of stories and to remember the leadership of a senior man named Doolan, and he examines the importance of photographs in creating relationships with the 'idolised' men and women whose exploits are remembered by the community. Bamblett traces attempts to denigrate Wiradjuri people in their daily lives through newspaper representations, and the resistance and strength shown by figures, and he uses photographs to assert their dignity and achievements. Bamblett notes that, as his aunties 'both often say, photographs are proof not only of their connection to Erambie, but also of the special place their grandparents hold as leaders and representatives of Wiradjuri people'.

Jane Lydon draws from many years spent working with the Koori people of Victoria to trace the history of Indigenous–white photographic exchange in the former Port Phillip district (Chapter 5). The camera arrived in Melbourne shortly after white settlers, and recorded the response of members of the Kulin nations to invasion and dispossession. These images also tell a story of mutual interest and exchange, testifying to the power of photographs to record kin and define identity.

Michael Aird examines the history of photographing Indigenous people in Queensland, which separated from New South Wales in 1859 (Chapter 6). He reviews the early images produced on what was, during the 1860s, the latest frontier, showing Indigenous Australians still leading a traditional way of life.

Thanks to the newly available *carte de visite*, these Queensland images were uniquely collectable. They found their way around the world and now constitute a prominent feature of some of the oldest European collections.

As Aird argues, the viewer is often struck by the huge changes that have taken place in Aboriginal culture and the landscape. But through developing his own forensic method over decades of research, he argues that identifying specific photographers and their output, in conjunction with contextual cultural and genealogical information, provides important clues towards identifying the images' subjects and where they were produced.

Jane Lydon and Sari Braithwaite explore the historical story of photography and Indigenous people in South Australia, reviewing recently recovered evidence for the work of the Anglican Church in the former colony (Chapter 7). Commissioning photographs to record achievements in transforming Indigenous people into 'gentlemen', the Church's belief that black and white were of 'one blood' underlay a vision of inclusion that was unique in Australia in the mid-nineteenth century.

Karen Hughes and Ngarrindjeri Elder Ellen Trevorrow talk together about the meanings of photography and history in the present, exploring the complex and sometimes poignant uses of family collections of photographs (Chapter 8). For Ngarrindjeri people, photographs evoke stories of colonial fragmentation, but may also be a means of reconnection for descendants. They share some of the Trevorrow family's photographic archives, sometimes produced by Indigenous photographers, which reflect a private world of life away from official or public scrutiny.

Donna Oxenham provides a wide-ranging overview of photography in the colony of Swan River, established in 1829 (Chapter 9). She traces the difficult and often destructive history of settler relations with Noongar, and the role of photographers in recording, engaging with or making this story, and she reviews the history of Western Australia's notoriously racialist policies, as well as the story of institutional life at missions such as New Norcia. But Oxenham reflects generously on the meanings of this archive, explaining how photographic images are enfolded into an Indigenous oral tradition, so that 'the past, present and future co-exist in the here and now'. Tracing a range of key historical processes, and the resulting photographic archives, she explores the significance of photography to Aboriginal people in the present.

Laurie Baymarrwangga, Bentley James and Jane Lydon examine a remarkable photograph made in 1917 by the travelling photographer Edward Reichenbach (Ryko) in north-eastern Arnhem Land on Rabuma Island (Chapter 11). The image records a re-enactment of the murder of two visiting trepangers at Rabuma Island in the Crocodile Islands. This photograph was one of a series he produced along the Territory's northern coast in collaboration with his Indigenous subjects, often commemorating conflict with outsiders. These images served as a mediated form of Indigenous testimony: at Rabuma, Ryko told how he had taken his photograph after 'the witnesses...voluntarily dramatised the whole affair over in detail for us, on the exact ground of the onslaught'.[37] The image was framed by Ryko's publication of 'The Myalls' ultimatum', the outcome of a Gurryindi Elders' Council, which was 'carried unanimously [and] which was carefully translated and verified by witnesses and murderers and friends to the writer personally'; the ultimatum concluded, 'let us go and punish by death according to our own law'. This event took place between the official end of the trepang trade in 1907 and the establishment of the mission at Milingimbi in 1922. If we look closely at the Gurryindi context for this event, particularly the long and frequently violent history of trade and communication with Macassans, as well as the 'ultimatum' itself, we may see the photograph and its narration as a complex assertion of Indigenous ownership, law and autonomy that reveals the continuities of Yolŋu law and identity from the early twentieth century to the present, and its translation across media, from photographs to oral histories. As a ninety-six-year-old elder, Baymarrwangga's perspective provides a powerful living link with Ryko's 1907 photograph of men from the Crocodile Islands.

NOTES

1. J Mulvaney, H Morphy & A Petch (eds), *My dear Spencer: the letters of F.J. Gillen to Baldwin Spencer*, Hyland House, Melbourne, 1997, p. 157 (letter of 23 March 1897).
2. Ryko, 'Territory jottings: primeval justice in the N.T.'s "top-knot": the crocodile massacre', *Northern Territory Times and Gazette*, Darwin, 1 February 1917, p. 17.
3. Several excellent overview histories of Australian photography include images of Aboriginal people, especially Helen Ennis, *Photography and Australia*, Reaktion Books, London, 2007; Anne-Marie Willis, *Picturing Australia: a history of photography*, Angus and Robertson, Sydney, 1988; Gael Newton, *Shades of light: photography and Australia 1839–1988*, Australian National Gallery, Collins, Canberra, 1988 (available with updates online at photoweb, <www.photo-web.com.au/ShadesofLight/default.htm>). For discussions of the history of photography and Aboriginal people, see especially Catherine de Lorenzo, 'Ethnophotography: photographic images of Aboriginal Australians', PhD thesis, University of Sydney, 1993; Catherine de Lorenzo, 'Appropriating anthropology? Document and rhetoric', *Journal of Material Culture*, 5(1):91–113, 2000.
4. M Langton & Australian Film Commission, *'Well, I heard it on the radio and I saw it on the television': an essay for the Australian Film Commission on the politics and aesthetics of filmmaking by and about Aboriginal people and things*, Australian Film Commission, Sydney, 1993, p. 39.
5. RD Wood, 'The voyage of Captain Lucas and the daguerreotype to Sydney' in A Foucrier (ed.),

The French and the Pacific World, 17th–19th centuries: explorations, migrations and cultural exchanges, Ashgate Publishing Ltd/Variorum, Aldershot, England, and Burlington, VT, March 2005, pp. 69–79.

6. P Cunningham, *Two years in New South Wales*, Henry Colburn, London, 1827, p. 46.
7. L Barrett, 'The utilitarian photographer', *Scan: Journal of Media Arts Culture*, n.d., viewed 30 October 2013, <http://scan.net.au/scan/journal/display.php?journal_id=62>.
8. J Carey & J Lydon (eds), *Indigenous networks: transnational mobility, connections and exchange*, Routledge, London and New York, in press.
9. George Aiston to WH Gill, 15 December 1933, ML A2535-2537, Mitchell Library, Sydney. George Aiston (1879–1943) became a 'Subprotector' of Aborigines, developing a keen interest in documenting Indigenous culture through photography; see P Jones, *Images of the interior*, Wakefield Press, Kent Town, SA, 2011, pp. 48–69.
10. J Patten & B Ferguson 'To all Aborigines!', *Australian Abo Call: The Voice of the Aborigines*, vol. 1, 1938, p. 1. For the 1920s, see especially J Maynard, *Fight for liberty and freedom: the origins of Australian Aboriginal activism*, Aboriginal Studies Press, Canberra, 2007.
11. J Lydon, *The flash of recognition: photography and the emergence of Indigenous rights*, NewSouth Books, Sydney, 2012.
12. J Hocking, *Gough Whitlam, his time*, Melbourne University Publishing, Melbourne, 2013, p. 10.
13. P Taylor, 'Introduction' in *After 200 years: photographic essays of Aboriginal and Islander Australia today*, Australian Institute of Aboriginal Studies, Canberra, 1988, pp. xv–xix.
14. E Michaels, 'A primer of restrictions on picture taking in traditional areas of Aboriginal Australia', *Visual Anthropology*, 4(3–4), 1991[1988]; reprinted in *Bad Aboriginal art: tradition, media and technological horizons*, University of Minnesota Press, MN, 1994.
15. R Maynard, 'Ricky Maynard' in H Perkins & J Jones (eds), *Half light: portraits from black Australia*, Art Gallery of New South Wales, Sydney, 2008, p. 91.
16. K Munro, 'Portrait of a distant land' in K Munro et al. (eds), *Ricky Maynard: portrait of a distant land*, Museum of Contemporary Art, Sydney, 2008, p. 18.
17. For a seminal statement see R Langford, 'Our heritage — your play-ground', *Australian Archaeology*, 16:1–6, 1983; for a recent overview of repatriation in Australia, *see* M Green & P Gordon, 'Repatriation: Australian perspectives' in U Rizvi & J Lydon (eds), *Handbook on postcolonialism and archaeology*, World Archaeological Congress, LeftCoast Press, Walnut Creek, CA, 2010; for an overview with respect to photography, see J Lydon, 'Return: the photographic archive and technologies of Indigenous memory', *Photographies*, 3(2):173–87, 2010.
18. E Edwards & J Hart (eds), *Photographs, objects, histories: on the materiality of images*, Routledge, London and New York, 2004; L Peers & AK Brown (eds), *Museums and source communities: a Routledge reader*, Routledge, New York, 2003; DA Smith, 'From Nunavut to Micronesia: feedback and description, visual repatriation and online photographs of Indigenous peoples', *Partnership: The Canadian Journal of Library and Information Practice and Research*, 3(1), 2008; AK Brown & L Peers with members of the Kainai Nation, *Pictures bring us messages: Sinaakssiiksi aohtsimaahpihk ookiyaawa: photographs and histories from the Kainai Nation*, University of Toronto Press, Toronto, 2006.
19. For example, Aboriginal and Torres Strait Islander Library, Information and Resource Network (ATSILIRN), *ATSILIRN protocols for libraries, archives and information services*, ATSILIRN, Canberra, 2012, viewed 28 October 2013, <www1.aiatsis.gov.au/atsilirn/protocols.atsilirn.asn.au/index0c51.html?option=com_frontpage&Itemid=1>.
20. Ara Irititja Project, 'About Ara Irititja', n.d., viewed 28 October 2013, <www.irititja.com/about_ara_irititja/>.
21. Ara Irititja Project, 'Challenges', n.d., viewed 28 October 2013, <www.irititja.com/challenges/index.html>.
22. J Anderson, *Access and control of Indigenous knowledge in libraries and archives: ownership and future use*, American Library Association and The MacArthur Foundation, Columbia University, New York, 2005, pp. 34–5; M Hughes

& J Dallwitz, 'Ara Irititja: towards culturally appropriate best practice in remote Indigenous Australia' in LE Dyson, M Hendriks & S Grant (eds), *Information technology and Indigenous people*, Information Science Publishers, Hershey, PA, pp. 146–58; S Thorner, 'Imagining an indigital interface: Ara Irititja indigenizes the technologies of knowledge management', *Collections: A Journal for Museum and Archives Professionals*, 6(3):125–46, 2010.

23. M Nakata & M Langton (eds), *Australian Indigenous knowledge and libraries*, UTSePress, Sydney, 2007, p. 3.

24. See, for example, G Macdonald, 'Photos in Wiradjuri biscuit tins: negotiating relatedness and validating colonial histories', *Oceania*, 73(4): 225–42, 2003; BR Smith, 'Images, selves, and the visual record: photography and ethnographic complexity in central Cape York Peninsula', *Social Analysis (Adelaide)*, 47(3):8–26, 2003; J Deger, *Shimmering screens: making media in an Aboriginal community*, University of Minnesota Press, MN, 2006; R Poignant & A Poignant, *Encounter at Nagalarramba*, National Library of Australia, Canberra, 1996.

25. Macdonald, above n 24, p. 239.

26. M Aird, *Portraits of our elders*, Queensland Museum, Brisbane, 1993. At this time, only the pioneering collection edited by Elizabeth Edwards had been published: *Anthropology and photography, 1860–1920*, Yale University Press, New Haven, 1992.

27. M Aird, *Brisbane blacks*, Keeaira Press, Queensland, 2001; M Aird, 'Defining who we are', presented at Campbelltown Art Gallery, NSW, July 2007.

28. Aird, above n 26, p. vii.

29. ibid.

30. Aird, above n 26, cover; see also, for example, M Aird in C Pinney & N Peterson (eds), *Photography's other histories*, Duke University Press, North Carolina, 2001.

31. D Oxenham in Lydon, above n 17, p. 180.

32. Classic accounts that reduce their significance in this way include P Bourdieu, *Photography, a middle-brow art*, Stanford University Press, CA, 1996. Through a study of the culture created by middle-class white British mothers, Rose provides a review of this interpretive tradition and proposes an analysis that focuses on how family photographs are used and their emotional effects, rather than their visual content; G Rose, *Doing family photography: the domestic, the public and the politics of sentiment*, Ashgate Publishing, Burlington and Farnham, 2010.

33. L Raiford, *Imprisoned in a luminous glare*, UNC Press, North Carolina, 2009, p. 119.

34. For a review that places Christian Thompson within this context, see C Parsley, 'Christian Thompson and the art of indigeneity', *Discipline*, 1(1), 2011, viewed 30 May 2012, <http://discipline.net.au/Discipline/Issue_1_files/Connal%20Parsley%20-%20Christian%20Thompson.pdf>.

35. R Butler, 'Margaret Preston and the history wars', catalogue essay for *Australian graffiti by Indigenous artist Christian Thompson*, Gallery Gabrielle Pizzi, Fitzroy, Vic., 4 March – April 5 2008, p. 1.

36. As he notes, Thompson typically creates a feminised space: 'It is in fact a form of drag that Thompson is engaged in here, but it is not Tracy Moffatt he is playing...but Margaret Preston'; Butler, above n 35, p. 1.

37. Ryko, above n 2.

TASMANIA

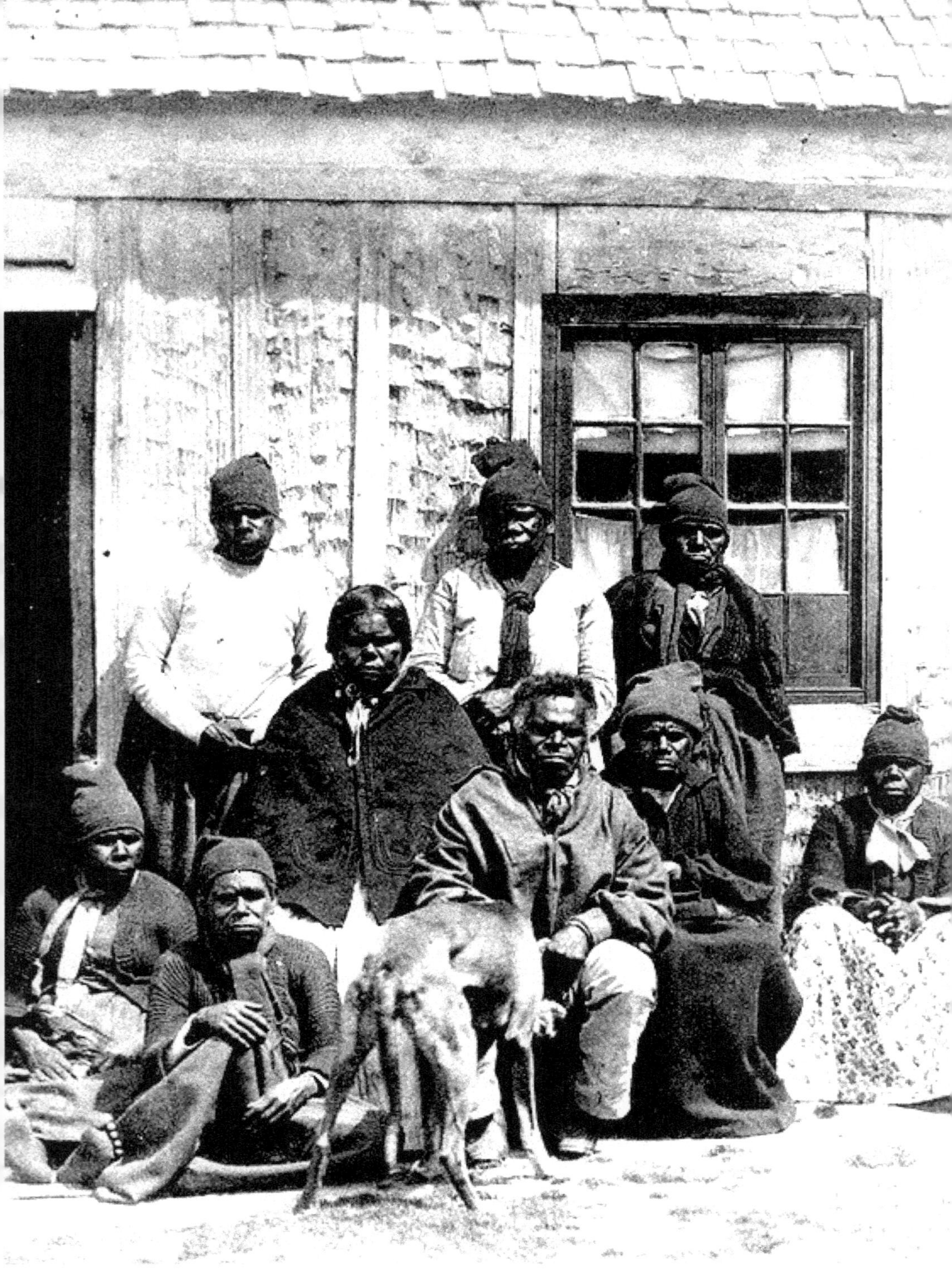

FIGURE 1: (Back row left to right) Drayduric (Sophia), Coonia (Patty), Drunameliyer (Caroline); (front row left to right): Wapperty, Meethecaratheeanna (Emma), Mary Ann Arthur, Calamarowenye (Tippo Saib), Plowneme (Flora), Truganini (Lalla Rookh). Inscribed 'Aborigines of Tasmania' in FR Nixon, *The cruise of the Beacon: a narrative of a visit to the islands in Bass's Straits with extra illustrations and photographs by the author – 1854*, Bell and Daldy, London, 1857; inserted between pp. 18–19 (copy from Nixon to his wife 'AM' (Anna Maria) held in Allport Library and Museum of Fine Arts, Hobart).

Chapter 2

FORGOTTEN LIVES – THE FIRST PHOTOGRAPHS OF TASMANIAN ABORIGINAL PEOPLE

Julie Gough

THE LEGACY

A certain number of the Blacks must inevitably be caught, and being afterwards placed in a state of security though comparative liberty, their comfortable condition will gradually spread and become known to the others still at large, until they are all induced at last to surrender themselves and be domesticated.[1]

The stare of most of the Old People, our Tasmanian Aboriginal forebears, is relentless, accusatory, unwavering.[2] Captured in the nineteenth century lenses of at least eight colonial photographers, permanently present, their gaze is more than only fixed forever at a time, amidst events they should not have experienced. It is something uncanny and uncomfortable, downright painful to be subjected to. While not direct ancestors, these people are kin and compatriots. When I look at their faces I see family and feel a lot more than I want to.[3]

Understanding these photographs requires spending time in the space of invasion, removal, loss, despair, death. Today there are tens of thousands of descendants. We come from two Aboriginal people who lived at Oyster Cove, and from less than fifteen of their contemporaries who survived government control long enough to bear descendants during the harshest times.[4] We live on and these images seem to find us, like some kind of episodic haunting, we face them and remember.

It is hard to *remember*, given the rush of invasion and its aftermath coming so soon after the first ships; for most it was a span of one generation until nigh near genocide. The British officially arrived in 1803 when they set up camp at Risdon Cove, near today's state capital, Hobart. Within months the first fatalities of Aboriginal people were recorded: carronades were fired at a party of men, women and children, likely hunting kangaroo. An unknown number of Aboriginal people were killed. This collision of cultures typified our meetings for the next forty years, by which time an estimated five thousand Aboriginal people were reduced to fifty.

The rapidity of many of our ancestors' dispersal and deaths is cruelly countered by the impossible longevity of these images. Why did these Old People sit for more than fifty photographs over two decades, if not to be seen forever and remembered specifically and differently than by the innumerable etchings and sketches, paintings and casts they had also been subjects of, subjected to over previous decades by British, French and German colonists and voyagers? This chapter considers the practically forgotten lives of some of the fourteen Tasmanian Aboriginal people who were captured by early amateur and professional photographers in Van Diemen's Land. It attempts to answer why the prior lives, identities and activities of these Tasmanian Aboriginal people became practically unknown after their return in 1847 from island exile to mainland Tasmania. But, first, I begin with a rediscovered photograph from 1847.

THE FIRST PHOTOGRAPH

> *I wish to be a good Man and to learn to love God & Jesus Christ, so that when I die I may be happy.*
>
> (David Brune, Aborigine, Flinders Island[5])

In 2012 I was first shown a startling photograph by my former archaeology lecturer, Sandra Bowdler, while she was visiting Tasmania (Figure 2). It seems

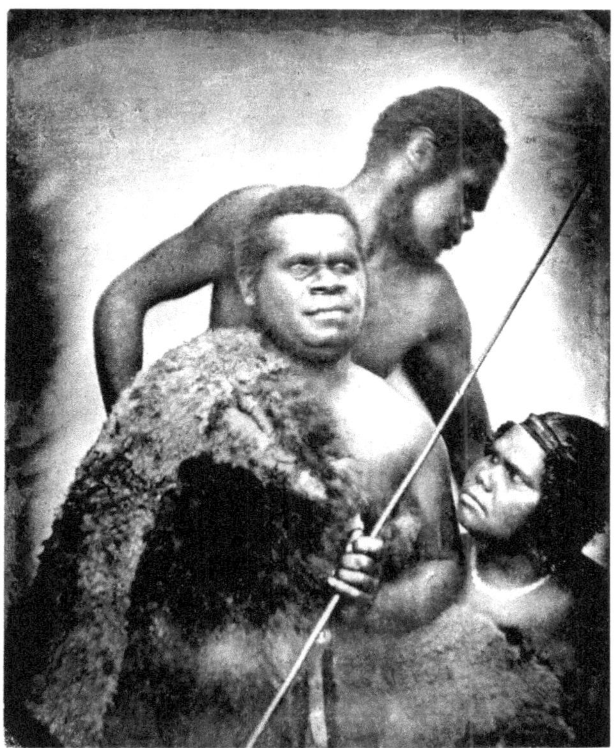

FIGURE 2: Thomas Browne (1816–70). *Walter George Arthur, Maryann and David Bruny, 1847–48* (left to right). Hand-coloured photograph, c. 1930, from unlocated daguerreotype. Museum of Victoria, XP22674.

a miracle this image was found, reprinted, buried in a book about Victorian Aborigines. How exciting, and how amazed I still feel about it. How pleased and grateful I feel that it was shared with me. The photo, so unexpected, has made me ponder the unique way Tasmanian Aboriginal people were first represented in the new photographic medium. The poses and apparel worn by the three people are unlike any subsequent photographs of Aboriginal people in Tasmania, and it is the first known photograph of our people.

Incongruously published, unreferenced, in monochrome in Aldo Massola's 1969 book *Journey to Aboriginal Victoria*, the sitters are captioned 'Tasmanian Aborigines: Walter, his wife Maryann and David'.[6] I subsequently remembered seeing this image before, cropped, on the cover of Sally Dammery's publication *Walter George Arthur — a free Tasmanian?*[7] However, due to its strangeness I had never believed that the image was of Walter George Arthur, or any Tasmanian Aboriginal person.

To understand the representation of Tasmanian Aboriginal people in early photography we must start with this image. Despite its incongruity in the photographic record, who, where and what it represents offers some insight into Tasmanian Aboriginal life in colonial times during the second, post-Black War, period of great change. Mary Ann, Walter and David were three of the fourteen Tasmanian Aboriginal people who George Augustus Robinson, government-appointed conciliator of the Aborigines in Van Diemen's Land, took to Victoria when he commenced a position in the Port Phillip Protectorate in February 1839. They spent almost three years at Port Phillip before returning to Flinders Island in 1842.[8] David Bruney died in October 1848, so we may date this photograph to before this time, and assume that it would have been a daguerreotype. This makes it closely concurrent with the earliest daguerreotypes of Aboriginal people in Australia made by Douglas Kilburn in Victoria in 1847 (see Chapter 5).

When I first encountered this image, it struck me as structurally mirroring a major painting, *The conciliation* (1840), by Benjamin Duterrau, referred to as 'Australia's first history painting'.[9] Three Tasmanian Aborigines in Duterrau's painting are reversed by the daguerreotype process. I propose that the new chemical medium of photography entered Tasmania as a demonstrable apprentice and extension to the established fine arts representations of Aboriginal Tasmanians.

The 1847–48 daguerreotype of Walter, Mary Ann and David, it can be argued, contains more power, promise and politics than the painting by Duterrau from which it is ostensibly derived. This amplification is due to the photograph carrying both the history and meanings of the 1840 painting while also incorporating fresh meaning from the new medium, its different sitters, and the motives for and period of its creation. By documenting 'real', living people, in a pose recognisable from the 1840 painting, the image is embedded within the narrative of conciliation from the earlier, fictional painting. When the photograph was made some seven years later, in December 1847/January 1848, only Trucanini[10] and Robinson (the government-employed 'conciliator' responsible for the removal of most Aboriginal people from mainland Tasmania) were still alive; Robinson was in Port Phillip, and Trucanini was apparently absent from the gathering during which the photograph was taken, as I explore further.

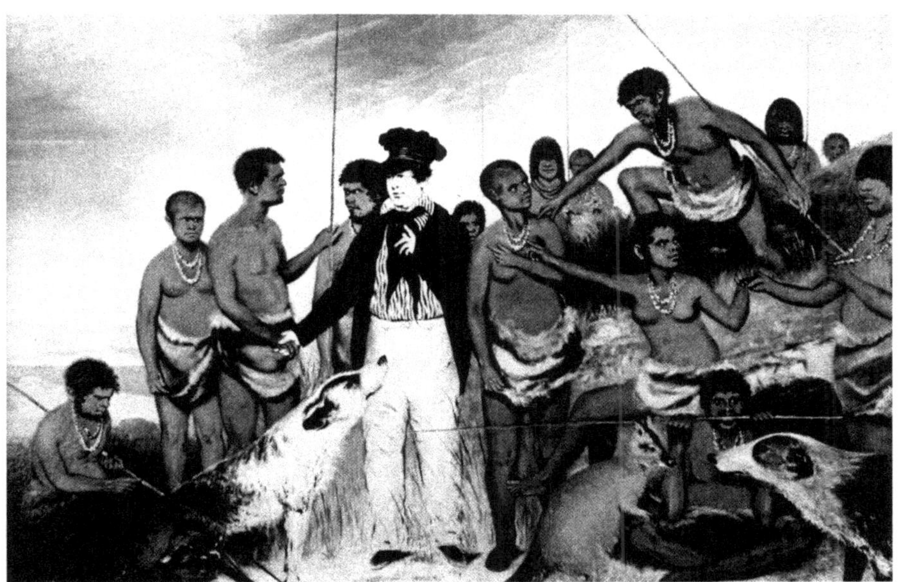

FIGURE 3: Benjamin Duterrau (1767–1851). *The conciliation*, 1840. Oil on canvas. Tasmanian Museum and Art Gallery, Hobart.

The photograph promises more than it delivers. It appears as a detail from the centre of *The conciliation,* which consists of fifteen Aboriginal people, George Augustus Robinson, three dogs and a wallaby. By focusing on a detail, the image seems to lend an uncanny veracity to the greater story of the supposedly willing exile of Tasmanian Aborigines. Made from the new medium taking Hobart gentry by storm, this photograph would remind settler society of frontier history while making present the proximity of Tasmanian Aborigines.

It appears the image was made by Thomas Browne, who operated one of only two permanent daguerreotype studios in Hobart before David Bruney's death. This attribution can be made on the basis of his linkages with Aboriginal people by association, his early portraiture work, on technical grounds and on direct historical documentation. By October 1847 Browne was busy between Hobart and Launceston increasing his photographic business.[11] In Launceston Browne had worked nine years for stationer Henry Dowling (1835–44), elder brother of artist-to-be Robert Dowling, both sons of Henry Dowling Senior, a preacher whom Robinson encountered on various occasions.[12] In 1837 Henry Dowling Junior commissioned Thomas Bock to make a set of watercolour portraits of Tasmanian Aborigines for him following the set Bock had previously made for Lady Jane Franklin, the wife of Governor John Franklin. This became the reference set on which Robert Dowling based his single portraits, studies, and three epic paintings of groups of Tasmanian Aborigines between 1853 and 1860.[13] These were publicly acclaimed – unlike the less derivative and more topical *The conciliation* by Duterrau, which unceremoniously went to auction with the rest of his works and library upon his death in Hobart in 1851.[14] Dowling's works significantly did not include self-proclaimed conciliator Robinson, and situated the Aboriginal people in an outdoor pre-colonial state.[15] In addition, the triangulated darkened corners of the print are indicative of Browne's work.[16]

Unequivocal evidence that Thomas Browne made this image comes from a letter written by Robinson on 16 March 1848 to the artist John Skinner Prout (1805–1876) to say that he was sending him some articles relating to the Tasmanian and Australian Aborigines. In this letter Robinson also says, 'I should much like Mr Brown's dgt. [daguerreotype] group of Walter, Mary Ann & David Brune'.[17] Historian NJB Plomley points out that '1 daguerreotype of 3 Tasmanians' is included in a 'List of Ethnological objects collected by the late Geo. Augustus Robinson, and purchased of (from) his widow, Mar 29 1867' by Joseph Barnard Davis, catalogued in the Royal Anthropological Institute Library, London. It appears that the original daguerreotype returned to England with Robinson in 1851.[18]

David Bruney (Myyungge) died in October 1848, one year after he and forty-six other Aboriginal people who had been exiled on Flinders Island were relocated to Oyster Cove Aboriginal Station, south of Hobart. He was about twenty-eight years of age in 1848, and there is no reason to doubt this is his image. He was a son of Woorrady (c. 1790–1842), leader of the Nuenone of Bruny Island in south-east Tasmania.[19]

Browne may have had the opportunity to photograph Walter, Mary Ann and David Bruney, most probably at either Government House cottage, New Norfolk, on 27 December 1847 or sometime between then and 31 January 1848 in Hobart Town. The image was made during the governorship of William Denison, which commenced in January 1847, and prior to David Bruney's death near the end of 1848. Denison's reminiscences note that in December 1847 he hosted a placatory Christmas meal for fourteen Aborigines who had been brought from Oyster Cove. Their children were to be sent the following day to the orphan school.[20] Denison, one year into his eight-year term, could hardly have been more provocative to his non-Aboriginal constituency. Only two months earlier, in October 1847, against great mainstream opposition, Denison had returned the remainder of the subjugated black 'savages' to mainland Tasmania.[21] This image can be viewed in the context of Denison's challenge to the colonising culture, in distancing himself from — if not denouncing — the treatment of Aboriginal people by previous governments and the Tasmanian populace.

This photograph makes more 'real' the conciliation event that Duterrau introduced, which never took place, at least in the way Duterrau conceived it. By re-staging this meeting photographically, what had previously seemed classically staged and fictional becomes more historical, and is brought closer, within living memory, to Van Diemen's Land colonial culture. Both representations endorse the 'successful' outcome of the supposed conciliation of the tribal population to their white conquerors. These works are propaganda from different eras — the photograph reinforced the painting's version of Aboriginal willingness to submit to one man, by implying that the sitters were in tacit agreement with this version of history.

However, there are indications that the peculiar staging of this daguerreotype closely involved not only the direction of a photographer with perhaps an artist's assistance but members of the Denison family themselves. At this time the Denisons had six children, and entertaining the family became a preoccupation for Lady Denison. In 1847 Caroline Denison wrote to her mother of her husband's suggestion for relieving the tedium of vice-regal life, to try and get up a few 'tableaux vivants from some of our prints'.[22] *Tableaux vivants*, or a scene presented by actors who remain still as if in a picture, quickly became popular among professional entertainers in Hobart.[23]

Although the staging of the December 1847 – January 1848 daguerreotype appears to closely reference *The conciliation*, there is a broader question regarding the extent to which the structure of this daguerreotype was also influenced by the Denisons' own knowledge of fine art and staging of *tableaux vivants* at home, as well as in public. The Denisons may have seen Benjamin Duterrau's widely distributed etching of his work *The conciliation*, or even the now-missing version of *The conciliation* on a grander scale, titled *The national picture* (1843).[24] There is an intriguing confluence of local art history, European art history, private and public performance, and colonial cross-cultural history at work in the production of this daguerreotype that renders it momentously complex alongside parallel questions about the people who are depicted, what the subjects of the image believed they were undertaking, and why.

On 5 January 1848 the *Launceston Examiner* announced that 'a *tableau vivant* has even been established at government house'.[25] This setting, no doubt with props, seemed to be waiting for the photographic event to take place. On 31 January 1848, a month after the Christmas gaieties, the Denisons, back at Government House in Hobart, were visited by a group of Tasmanian Aboriginal men. Lady Denison recounted how:

> On Saturday morning we had a visit from a party of natives, six men, who have come up here with their boat, and a very respectable-looking crew they make...We led them into the housekeeper's room, and made the children hand them some fruit and cakes, to which they took cordially. As far as I have yet seen, the men are not nearly as lively as the women, and this to my mind, gives them an appearance of less intelligence, as their silence and gravity wear rather an aspect of apathy and stupidity, than of attempted dignity. *The only thing that moved these men to laughter, was our showing them some daguerreotype likenesses of those of their country men who were up here at Christmas. None of those who came yesterday were the same, but they recognised the individual likenesses very cleverly, and were much amused with them.*[26] (author's emphasis)

Lady Denison named thirteen Aboriginal people who attended her luncheon in December 1847.[27] David Bruney was not identified as present, which raises the question of whether he was there, and, if not, when and where was the photograph made?

Significantly, artist John Skinner Prout was present at the critical Christmas events of 1847.[28] It is likely that Prout's connection with Tasmanian Aborigines and their representation extended beyond his own work, such as his previous portraits of Tasmanian Aboriginal people, including Mary Ann (Figure 4) on Flinders Island in 1845. It seems probable that Prout assisted Browne to stage the photographic session with Walter, Mary Ann and David Bruney, and mediated the transfer of this early daguerreotype of Aboriginal Tasmanians to Robinson. If the daguerreotype session did not take place at Government cottage, New Norfolk, on 27 December, it possibly took place in the weeks before

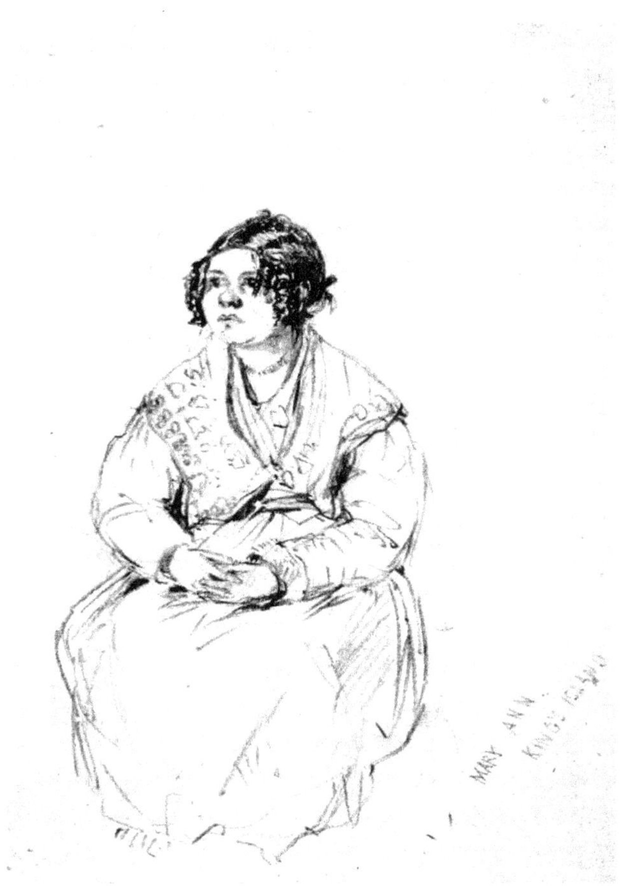

FIGURE 4: John Skinner Prout. *Mary Ann, Kings Island,* March 1845, Wybalenna, Flinders Island. Pencil on paper, Oc2006, Drg.22, collection of the Trustees of the British Museum.

Robinson's request for it on 16 March, at Browne's Hobart photographic studio in Macquarie Street, near Government House.

And what of the coloured version of Browne's daguerreotype, now held by Museum Victoria? It was acquired from colonial official and botanist Ronald Campbell Gunn's (1808–81) sale of unknown date before being donated in 1937 by Roy Michaelis.[29] Gunn was an associate of Browne's and a close friend of Joseph Milligan (1807–84), also a field naturalist, who was engaged intermittently between 1844 and 1847 as the Superintendent of the Aborigines at Wybalenna,

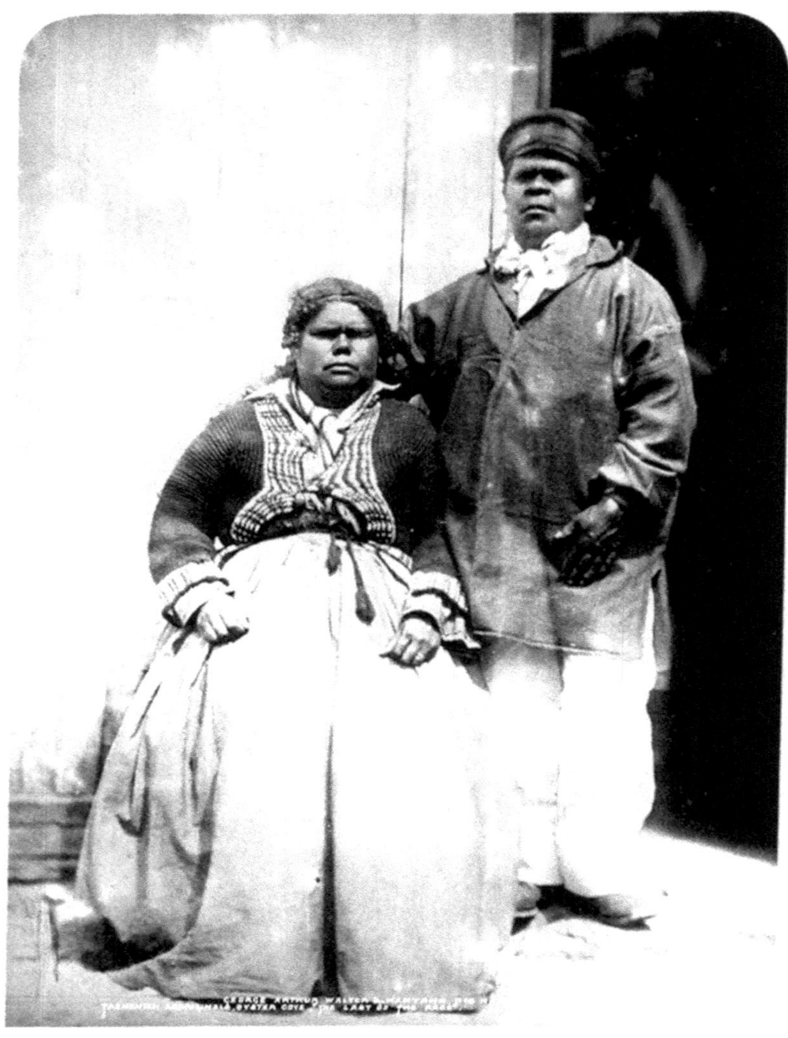

FIGURE 5: Francis Russell Nixon. *Mary Ann and Walter George Arthur*, c.1858. Albumen print, c. 1890. JW Beattie Album, PXD 571, Vol. 1, Mitchell Library, State Library of New South Wales, Image: a1897008.

Flinders Island, and between 1847 and 1854 at Oyster Cove.[30] Milligan also took part in the 1847 Christmas festivities with Governor Denison and his family. It appears that Gunn, late in life, was concerned and even sentimental about Tasmanian Aborigines.[31]

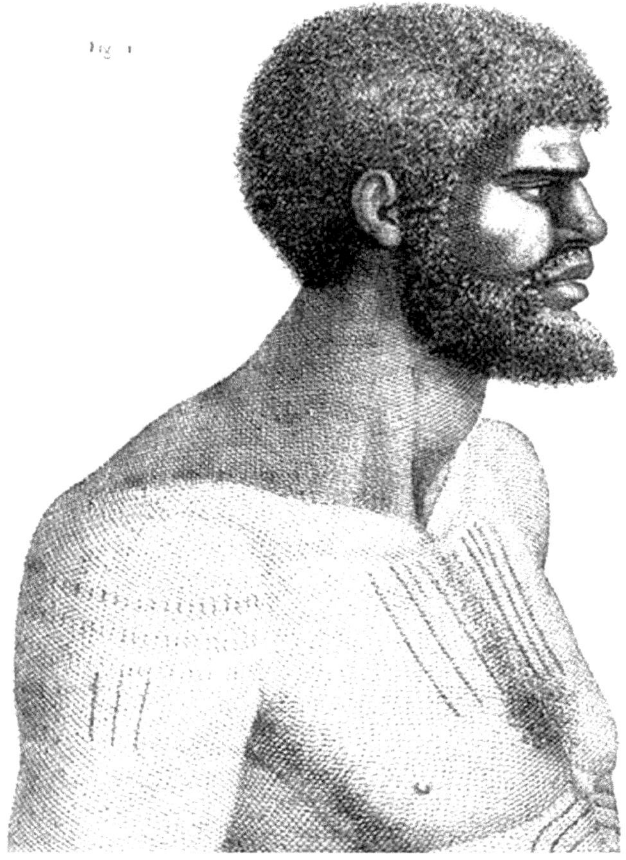

FIGURE 6: Jacques Louis Copia (1764–1799). *Homme du Cap de Diemen; Enfant du Cap de Diemen*, engraving, Chez Dabo, Paris, 1817. National Library of Australia, nla.pic-an20973426-2.

The three subjects in Browne's photograph had a record of agitation against unreasonable white authority, so the structural resemblance of Browne's daguerreotype to Duterrau's work appears to fail in its political intent. Three key strategists of Aboriginal rights form this image and were well known to Denison by reputation by the time they arrived back in southern Tasmania.[32] Plomley shows how pivotal Walter George Arthur was in arousing fellow Aborigines to mount a substantial series of written attacks against unpopular commandant Dr Henry Jeanneret; he was successful not only in having him dismissed, but also played a part in Denison's decision to close Wybalenna and return the remaining Aboriginal people to mainland Tasmania.[33] They had witnessed colonial injustice up close not only in Van Diemen's Land but in Port Phillip, during which time two of their close companions, Tunnerminnerwait (Jack) and Maulboyheener (Robert), were executed, the first two people hanged in Victoria.[34]

Both the painting and daguerreotype invent and reinvent a re-imagined colonial history episode. What is most notable, beyond the arresting poses in this image, and the appearance of these three people in pseudo-tribal garb in an era when they were accustomed to wearing European dress, is that Walter George Arthur's left arm reveals what appears to be cicatrice markings.

These scarifications support the theory that Walter's status changed early in 1837 at about seventeen years of age from that of a child to an initiated man — a leader of the Ben Lomond Tribe — as he began to refer to himself while increasingly protesting the treatment of Aboriginal people on Flinders Island.[35] This would make sense of the noted changes in his personality and refusal to attend school soon after his return from his bush absence. The significance of the kangaroo to Tasmanian Aboriginal people, as an inherent part of life immemorial and as a key being in Creation Stories across the island, raises the possibility that these marks are made as though by a kangaroo, upon the bodies of youths, embodying them as hunter/hunted in an alliance with the creation Ancestor. By the action of receiving this scoring upon his body, Walter can be seen as having been given a future by and for Aboriginal people while on Flinders Island.[36] These markings, in this reading, would have been a constant reminder of his duty and eventually his failure to achieve what Aboriginal people needed — freedom, equality, Country. Walter lived in a post-apocalyptic Aboriginal Tasmania demarcated by unstable relationships with unreliable British administrators who were continually departing. He was eventually, in frustration, to take to alcohol, and to the sea, seeking employment on what was perhaps the only space operating relatively equitably in terms of race relations. The impossibility of living on, off or with the land for Aboriginal Tasmanians returning to their mainland homeland of more than 40,000 years was to force them into an inactive, dissolute despair, explicit in the photographs that were made over following years at Oyster Cove.

CONTROL AND CONTAINMENT

The Photos
The horror
Makes me angry
No, they're not for you
Not to feed your white guilt
Not to trap them and us in your endless net of conquest
These are not for you
They sat for you but watch out at us
Everyday, forever, fixed
They look out into the future they wouldn't live
Knowing of all that had been lost
They remind us of who we are
They are our blood
They remind us of why we are
They are our memories.[37]

THE PEOPLE WHO WENT TO OYSTER COVE

On 18 October 1847 a likely forty-seven Tasmanian Aboriginal people who had been incarcerated for fifteen years at Wybalenna on Flinders Island arrived to take up forced residency at Oyster Cove station, an ex-convict government settlement thirty-five miles south of Hobart.[38] Their Aboriginal names and their European (c. 1836) 'given' names are provided in the following list, and their territory is given in brackets.[39] They came from 'no less than 10 tribes' that were inconsistently notated and usually confused by the colonisers' alien geographic logic.[40] Fourteen of these people are known to have been depicted in photographs between 1847 and 1876. Those photographed are listed in bold font. Twenty people, in italics, were sketched by John Skinner Prout on Flinders Island in 1845, seven of whom were later photographed.

1. *Barney/Barnaby Rudge* (North West), died pre-April 1851.
2. **Myyunnge/David Bruny/Brune/Bruney** (Bruny Island, South East), born c. 1820, died 11–17 October 1848.
3. *Drueretattenananne/Cranky Dick* (Ben Lomond), m. *Louisa,* died October 1848.
4. Nicermenic/Eugene (North West), died 27/28 May 1849.
5. Nannie/Nancy (girl) McSweeney? (South West?), died 25 April 1849 in Orphan Asylum, mother Henrietta/Thielewanna.
6. Narrucer/Catherine (North West), died 29 November 1849.
7. Martha (girl) (North West), mother Catherine, died 2 February 1851.
8. *Pignacommiana?/Wild Mary/Wilhelmina?* (Big River?/Hampshire Hills?), died 15 February 1851.
9. *Drinene/Neptune* (North West), died 21 March 1851.
10. Tooernac/Edmund (Pieman River), died 26 March 1851.
11. *Drummernerlooner/Louisa* (North East), m. Dick, m. *Tippo,* died between 18 October 1847 and 26 April 1851.
12. Hannah (McSweeney?) (South West), mother Thielewanna?/Henrietta sent 1850 to Malcolm Laing Smith, Flinders Island.
13. Charley? (Lanne?) (child) (North West) or Charley? [Clark] (South West), mother Toindeburer?, unknown date of death.
14. George (child) (whose?) (North West), unknown date of death.
15. Cuish/Gooseberry/Parthemeena (Swanport), unknown date of death.
16. *Parateer/Daphne* (*Swanport*?) (b. 1803), husband Buonaparte, unknown date of death.
17. Fanny (Planobeena?) (George Town or Piper's River, North East), partner Pevay/Jack/Tunnerminerwait, unknown date of death.
18. Henrietta?/Thielewanna (South West Port Davey) daughters Nancy (Nannie?) McSweeney and Hannah McSweeney? any other Port Dalrymple woman with sealers? unknown date of death.
19. Matilda/New Maria (Swanport), partner Davy Bruney, unknown date of death after April 1851.
20. *Moomereriner/Alexander* (Big River), wife *Caroline* (Alexander, Washington, Nomie or Frederick, died on 24 June 1851 — unknown date of death).
21. Frederick/Pallooruc (North West) (Alexander, Washington, Nomie or Frederick died on 24 June 1851 — unknown date of death).

22. Nomie/Boneneveveve (West Coast), wife Parpeder (Alexander, Washington, Nomie or Frederick died on 24 June 1851 — unknown date of death).
23. Maccame/Washington (Big River?) (Alexander, Washington, Nomie or Frederick, died on 24 June 1851 — unknown date of death).
24. Unknown person — possibly the man who died on 24 June 1851.
25. *Kittewa/Amelia* (North West), husband *Neptune*, died after 26 April 1851.
26. *Warrameenaloo/Juliet/Julia?* (Cape Portland), husband *Washington*, died after 26 April 1851.
27. Thinginoop (South West), died after 26 April 1851.
28. *Moriarty* (child) (North West), died 5 March 1852.
29. *Arwenia/Mathinna* (girl) (South West), died 1 September 1852.
30. Wottecowidger/Harriet (North East), died 27 September 1855.
31. Adam, mother *Tairenootairer/Tanganutara/Sarah* (North East), father Nicermenic (North West), died 28 October 1857.
32. *Tairenootairer/Tanganutara/Sarah* (North East), died 3 October 1858.
33. ***Drunameliyer/Gunneyanner?/Caroline*** (Big River?), born c. 1799, m. Alexander, died c. 12 July 1860.
34. ***Plowneme/Flora/Banghum/Pelonamena*** (Ben Lomond, North East), born c. 1807, died 27 August 1860.
35. ***Thermanope/Toyenroun/Augustus*** (South West), born c. 1821, died 28 August 1860. *Possibly in image SLNSW.*
36. ***Calamarowenye/Tippo Saib*** (Kangaroo Point Hobart?/was with Big River people), born c. 1803, died 2 September 1860.
37. **Walter George Arthur** (Ben Lomond), born c. 1823, died 11 May 1861.
38. **Drayduric /Sophia** (South West), born c. 1798, died 29 August 1861.
39. ***Meethecaratheeanna/Emma*** (Big River), husband Rolepa/King George, born c.1809, died 27 May 1863.
40. **Lennimenna /Tillarbunner/Jack Allen** (Ben Lomond), born c.1824, died 10 February 1864.
41. ***Pangernowidedic/Bessy Clark*** (South West), mother Thingernoop, born c.1822, died 12 February 1867.
42. **Coonia/Patty Clark** (North West), born c. 1814, died 8 July 1867.
43. **Wapperty** (North East), born c. 1799, died 12 August 1867.

44. **Billy/William Lanne** (North West), born c. 1838, died 3 March 1869.

45. ***Mary Ann*** (North East), born c. 1825, died 25 July 1871.

46. ***Truganini/Lalla Rookh*** (South/Recherche Bay), born c. 1812, died 8 May 1876, Hobart.

47. Fanny Cochrane (girl), born 1834 Flinders Island, mother *Tairenootairer/Tanganutara/Sarah*, died 1905, Nicholls Rivulet.

This list reveals that only twelve people were repeatedly photographed (plus two — David Brune and Lennimenna (Jack Allen), who were each photographed at least once, and unknown others also photographed by Browne in 1847/48). These twelve were the post-1857 survivors at the Oyster Cove settlement. To this day their portraits continually resurface, purportedly representing Tasmanian Aborigines and Aboriginality.

Scrutinising the first fifty early photographic works depicting Tasmanian Aboriginal people reveals an abrupt and dehumanising shift from photography as 'art' to photography as a tool of science and a means of recording otherness within a frame of 'decline' and supremacy of Empire. This shift became evident in Tasmania with the onset of the Great Exhibitions to which colonies sent exhibits to demonstrate their wealth, worth and 'civilisation'. Concurrent with the growth and popularity of Great Exhibitions was intensified interest in Tasmanian Aboriginal human remains by European science; an 1899 report listed the remains of seventy-seven Tasmanian Aboriginal people held in collections in Britain.[41] This was followed by the collection of Tasmanian Aboriginal stone artefacts, as apparent exemplars of a still living, but near lost, stone-age culture. Tasmanian Aboriginal people at Oyster Cove were staged as living curiosities, intermittently brought to Government House and Hobart Town over the following two decades, dressed to mark special occasions and there photographed by Samuel Clifford (1861), Henry Albert Frith (1864), Charles H Woolley (1866), Henry Hall Baily (c. 1870, c. 1873, c. 1874) and Alfred Winter (c. 1874). Simultaneously, their friends and family members were being disinterred from Oyster Cove and Wybalenna and sent overseas by key figures in colonial Tasmanian society seeking status in scientific circles.[42]

The controlled isolation of Aboriginal people at Oyster Cove who were segregated from the increasing Aboriginal community in Bass Strait and isolated family groups on mainland Tasmania can be viewed as part of a future-oriented agenda. The official determination to *not* recognise Aboriginal people *not* at Oyster Cove as legitimate Aborigines has had ramifications to this day, as the mainstream populace has misunderstood Aboriginality, Aboriginal history and cultural continuance in Tasmania.

In April 1851, four years after the establishment of the Oyster Cove Aboriginal settlement, Robinson visited the inhabitants and noted that 'The natives want to return to Flinders Island. The Brune [sic] Islands excepted. All agree that OC [Oyster Cove] place is unhealthy too low. Damp. Like a funnel all wind out of Mountain.'[43] Official documents that were next produced reveal an alternative future was then possible for many Aboriginal people at Oyster Cove to return to Bass Strait and reunite with extended family across the islands. In 1853 Superintendent Milligan reported on the residents, including the desire by Wapperty (b. 1798–d. 1867 at Oyster Cove) and Emma (d. 1863 at Oyster Cove) to rejoin their families in Bass Strait (see Figure 1, p. 20).[44] Milligan also proposed the abandonment of Oyster Cove by the remaining sixteen people, suggesting that seven could run a farm together at Brown's River and that the remaining nine, 'of dissolute habits', be sent back to Bass Strait, either to Clarke Island under the care of Dr James Allen, formerly at Wybalenna, whose wife Maria Allen was Robinson's daughter, or to Flinders Island.[45]

Wapperty was a daughter of Mannalargenna, a leader of the east coast, father of at least four daughters and two sons. Many Tasmanian Aboriginal people are descendants of Wapperty. Her daughter Bessy Myetye married John Mira, a Māori sealer, in March 1847, which removed Bessy from Wybalenna seven months before the fate that awaited those held there, their removal to Oyster Cove. But Bessy's marriage also led to great heartache for mother and daughter who were separated and never reunited.[46] Wapperty could have easily been relocated back to the islands, where she had been living for thirty years before being taken to Oyster Cove. The official reports of 1853 and Robinson's earlier account in 1851 both state she could return.[47] This recommendation by Milligan has been overlooked in recent history, and yet it was written with careful consideration of the futures, desires and tribal affiliations of those eighteen people still alive at Oyster Cove. The government reply dated 9 March 1854 was open to Milligan's proposals yet he did not act.[48]

Implementing these repeated requests would have changed history significantly for Aboriginal Tasmanians. We would not have Bishop Nixon's images of thirteen desperate, hopeless people, still at Oyster Cove in 1858, whose wants were never met. We would, instead, have histories of extended families who were reunited in Bass Strait, while others would have had the opportunity to run their own viable farm near Hobart. We would, instead, have memories of these people, rather than their aggrieved faces on paper.

THE VISITING BISHOP AND TOO LITTLE, TOO LATE

Here for several years they were under no other supervision than that of a petty constable or two, and menials, while their paid superintendent was pursuing his elegant studies and follies in Hobart Town, 20 miles off. He was removed from his office, or probably retired, in 1855, but not until the demoralization of the natives was completed.[49]

The death rate at Oyster Cove from the onset had been horrendous. Eight of ten children had died by 1852, their plight exacerbated surely by the early decision to remove them to the Orphan Asylum in Hobart rather than allow them to live amidst their families and community. The figures for deaths at Oyster Cove that Superintendent Joseph Milligan provided in 1853 under duress to the government show the rapid decimation of the Aboriginal population under his authority. Milligan claimed that forty-five people arrived in October 1847 at Oyster Cove: thirteen men, five boys, twenty-two women and five girls. By December 1853 there remained only eighteen people: four men, two boys, twelve women and no girls.[50] He did not account for the deaths of so many so quickly. In fact, there are no dates or causes recorded for the deaths of seventeen Aboriginal people at Oyster Cove. Milligan had refused to live there, instead staying in Hobart. By 1855 there were only seventeen people remaining, thereafter under the care of live-in Superintendent John S Dandridge and his wife Matilda, the daughter of John Skinner Prout. For the next twenty-one years the Dandridges dedicated themselves to the Aborigines. However, bad habits and declining health in a damp, cold setting were not conducive to a long life. When, in 1871, Mary Ann Arthur died, Trucanini was alone, the last of the survivors of Oyster Cove. Thereafter she lived with the Dandridge family.

The infamous photographs taken from 1858, attributed to the First Bishop of Tasmania, Francis Russell Nixon (1803–79), suggest these circumstances. There is no mention of photography having taken place during Nixon's first recorded visit to Oyster Cove in April 1858, — however, with a friend's assistance it is probable that the first photographs made by Nixon were achieved that day because April 1858 is inscribed on three contemporaneous photographs.[51] Bishop Nixon had arrived in Van Diemen's Land in 1843, and soon after visited Wybalenna Aboriginal Establishment with the outgoing Lieutenant Governor Sir John Franklin and his wife. Nixon managed the affairs of the Anglican Church with controversy. He was critical of the treatment of convicts and Aborigines, and disapproved of the government not giving precedence to his church. He also managed a busy social life; a keen sketcher, he kept company with the colony's most renowned artists.[52]

By this period the 'savage natives' were viewed as tamed early tourist attractions in their hardly model village of Oyster Cove.[53] Uninterested, thirteen different people sat outside their huts holding poses that they surely knew marked an end point for those bringing the photographic apparatus.

One photograph shows Trucanini, Calamarowenye (Tippo), William Lanne(?) and Plowneme (Flora).[54] Another image, widely distributed, shows Plowneme alone[55] and a third image is a stereoscopic photograph showing three women, Plowneme, Trucanini and Bessy Clark[e].[56] Less than three months later, on 13 July 1858, Nixon donated the first two of these photographs to the Royal Society of Tasmania, where they were recorded as:

> Two Photographs, one a portrait of an aboriginal woman of Tasmania, the other representing a group of aborigines of both sexes as they now present themselves upon the Government Establishment at Oyster Cove. Presented by the author, the Right Rev. the Lord Bishop of Tasmania. These are finely executed specimens of the art, and render accordingly with striking fidelity the characteristic features and aspect of the aboriginal inhabitants of the island.[57]

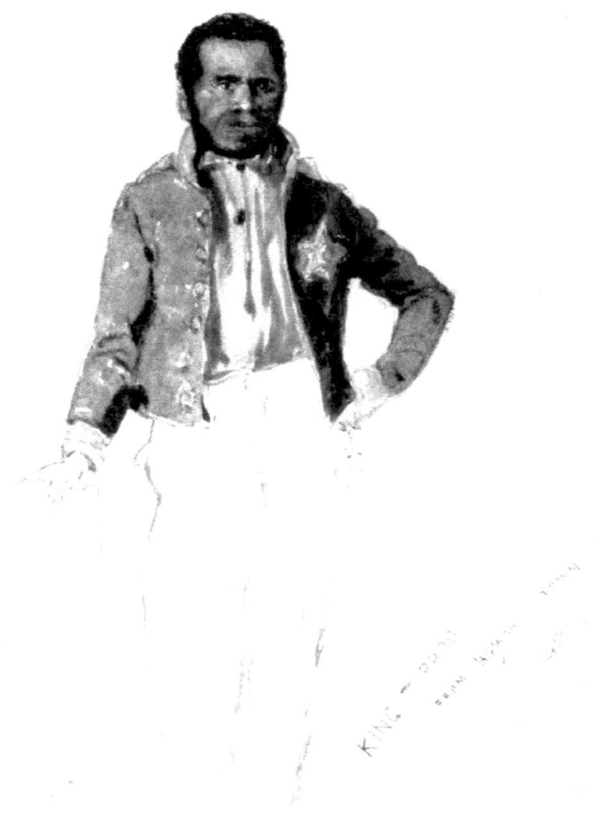

FIGURE 7: John Skinner Prout. *King Tippoo from Hobart Town V.D.L.* [*Van Diemen's Land*], 1845. Collection of the Trustees of the British Museum, Oc2006, Drg.18. Accompanying description: 'King Tippoo from Hobart Town V.D.L. Feby 27. 45'; 'Tippoo born at Kangaroo Point – when the White men settled at Hobart he left with his tribe for Lovelybanks – remained there several years, and when the White Settlers came, the Tribe again fled – Mr Robinson's party induced him to go to Launceston and from thence to Flinder's – he has seen a great number of his people killed by the White men at Lovelybanks' – from notes given to Prout in 1845 by Robert Clark, Catechist at Wybalenna, Flinders Island[60]

Tippo, a subject in what appears to be Nixon's first photograph series of Aboriginal people (Figure 8), was one of more than one hundred Aboriginal people who Robinson renamed, most in a ceremony on 15 January 1836 on Flinders Island.[58] Calamarowenye was to be publicly known as 'Tippo Saib', the name of a fearsome leader of a recent failed Indian uprising. Tippo

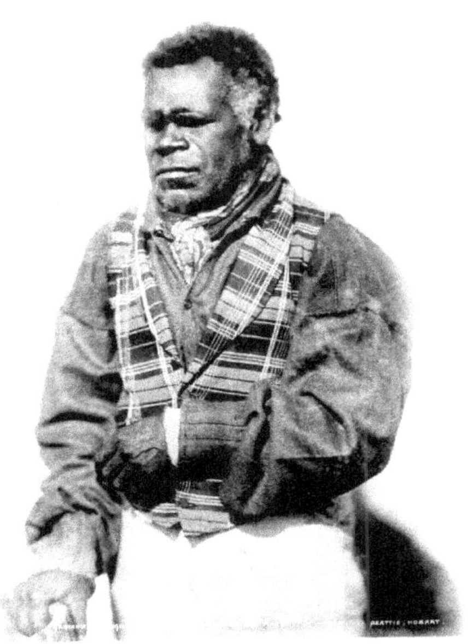

FIGURE 8: Francis Russell Nixon. *Tippo, Tasmanian Aboriginals, Oyster Cove, the last of the race, Beattie, Hobart*, c. 1858. Albumen print, c. 1890, JW Beattie Album, PXD 571, Vol. 1, Mitchell Library, State Library of New South Wales, Image: a1897001.

was photographed thirteen times between 1858 and his death in September 1860, and also sketched by John Skinner Prout (1845, Figure 7), Francis Guillemard Simpkinson De Wesselow (1845), John Glover (1831) and Ludwig Becker (1852). His participation in the once notorious events at Port Sorell, where he was one of three men charged with the murder of affluent landholder BB Thomas and his overseer James Parker in 1831, apparently quickly faded from public view.[59]

Study of the people represented in the Oyster Cove images, their clothing and appearance, and the impossibility of all known photographs of Aboriginal people at Oyster Cove having been taken on one day, has assisted in determining that seven photographic episodes took place at Oyster Cove. Further, it is suggested that only the images from the first three visits were definitely made by Bishop Nixon, with six photographs from the accumulated sixteen images from these three visits selected and inserted into Nixon's author's copy of his book, *The cruise of the Beacon*, which he presented as a gift to his wife 'AM' (Anna Maria).

Nixon's careful insertion of his images in this book is important. It made a clear, and for that period, radical link between geographically separate populations that the government refused to view as one people. This action of placing later photographs of people at Oyster Cove within his textual account of journeying to meet Aboriginal people across Bass Strait in 1854 is evidence of Nixon's instinctive understanding that the people in Bass Strait *were* the same people as those at Oyster Cove, and therefore all *were* Aboriginal. Between pages 17–19 in his book there are images of eight Aboriginal people, and nine of Aboriginal people from Oyster Cove dated 1858 to 1860. Between pages 20–4, the section dedicated to explaining the Black War, he includes two images of four women and a dog, and another image of four women. Finally, within a dense section about Tasmanian Aboriginal history between pages 24–5 dedicated to chronologically explicating the move from the Black War to Wybalenna to Oyster Cove, Nixon inserted images of Plowneme (Flora) and another image depicting eight people. However, Nixon does not insert the photographs of people at Oyster Cove amidst pages 34–50, where he described spending time with the contemporary Aboriginal community of the islands, who he determinedly called 'half caste', not Aboriginal, except for Judy (sister of Emma, whom he later photographed at Oyster Cove), who he called 'an aboriginal woman'. This section lacks photographs and reveals Nixon's fluctuating notion of Aboriginality. All the more surprising, then, that once back in England he strenuously supported the missions to the 'half-castes' on the islands.

It appears that Nixon made two further photographic trips to Oyster Cove at unknown times — but one would have been between April 1858 and 10 July 1860 (when Drunameliyer (Caroline) died). Nine images are in circulation, taken on that one- or two-day trip, including Figure 1. The third photographic visit was probably after early July 1860 and before 2 September 1860 (when Calamarowenye (Tippo) died). It is suggested that four photographs were made on that visit, also in wide distribution today.[61] In the 1890s, JW Beattie commenced mass reproduction in Hobart Town of these and other photographers' images of Tasmanian Aboriginal people dating from the 1850s, 1860s and 1870s, and somehow, four decades later, all of these images of Oyster Cove were attributed to Bishop Nixon.

A fifth visit by an unknown photographer, possibly Nixon, resulted in two images. One is out of focus and disjointed, showing Mary Ann, Walter (or Calamarowenye) (sitting on a roof), Coonia (Patty), Plowneme and Drunameliyer (Caroline).[62] The second photograph depicts Drunameliyer, Coonia, Plowneme, Trucanini and Wapperty. The women appear uncomfortable in both images, in new floral dresses possibly worn over their regular clothes and perhaps gifted that day to these women. This image is included in the Beattie Albums, attributed to Bishop Nixon, and these two photographs would have been taken before 2 September 1860.[63]

Another image from a sixth trip made by an unknown photographer, but also attributed to Nixon and in the Beattie Albums, shows Meethecaratheeanna (Emma), Calamarowenye and Pangernowidedic (Bessy Clark). This image shows these three people as unwilling subjects; the women are wearing peculiar dresses with flowers attached to their headwear. Calamarowenye is barefoot and dishevelled. Bonwick outlines an episode that explains how women were quickly attired when visitors approached the station.[64] Sketches from memory in c. 1905 by Annie Benbow, resident at Oyster Cove in the 1840s–50s, suggest that Western clothing was worn in practical but unconventional ways at Oyster Cove, particularly when outsiders were not present.[65]

A final anomalous image of people at Oyster Cove produced before Nixon left Tasmania shows Trucanini, William Lanne, Pangernowidedic (Bessy) and Wapperty. Pangernowidedic apparently had a broken arm, as she also did during a different visit, shown in the second series of photographs. This image might relate to the period when Official Visitor to the Station, Edward Walpole, noted in the Visitor's Book on 24 February 1861 that 'Betsy [sic] is not recovering from a broken arm'.[66]

In January 1862 Bishop Nixon, suffering ill health, departed for England and never returned. His family followed. Their belongings were auctioned, including camera equipment.[67] His photographic glass plate negatives possibly remained in Hobart, perhaps with the Royal Society, later with Beattie's Studio. His photographs were slowly disseminated across a range of media. They appeared in the Hobart Hull's Royal Kalendar, and were exhibited in the 1862 Great Exhibition in London.[68]

After Nixon left Tasmania, Archdeacon Thomas Reibey went on two mission visits to the islands. His reports reiterated what had been requested by Aboriginal people for at least twelve years:

> When the present Session of Parliament has closed, it may, perhaps, be desirable for the Governor in Council to consider if it would not be advisable to send the six Aborigines still remaining at Oyster Cove to their relatives at these Islands. I am informed that they are anxious to go, and their friends willing to receive them.[69]

These six were Trucanini, William Lanne, Bessy Clark, Wapperty, Mary Ann and Walter George Arthur. Emma, who had repeatedly asked to return to the islands and live with her sister Judy, had died in May 1863. Reibey continued:

> In the working of the laws of God's providence, we have dispossessed these poor people of this fair land. In that, we may hope, there was no sin: but surely sin will lie heavy at our doors, if we, blessed with civilization and Christianity, neglect to fulfil to them the simplest duties laid upon us by the requirements of Christian charity.[70]

Nixon continued his apparent interest in Aboriginal welfare from England, but he tellingly ignored the Aboriginal people at Oyster Cove, instead beginning an intensive fundraising campaign towards an able-bodied vessel and annual visits by Archdeacon Reibey to minister to the 'half-castes' on the islands.[71] Nixon never referred to those living on the Bass Strait Islands as Aboriginal people. He hence supported the mainstream agenda, which saw the (Oyster Cove) Aboriginal race as doomed, obviating any redress and compensation for the ongoing Aboriginal communities in Bass Strait and extended families based at Nicholls Rivulet and Latrobe on mainland Tasmania.

In January 1877 Nixon, retired and living in northern Italy, received JE Calder's book *The native tribes of Tasmania* and wrote his thanks, in which he revealed his attitude towards the people he so assiduously photographed in the late 1850s. He wrote of his surprise at 'those portions, which spoke of their intellectual qualities and readiness to receive instruction. I confess that from all that I had seen and heard of them I have formed a far lower estimate...'[72]

After Nixon's departure at least one other photographic visit was made to Oyster Cove. Two images resulted, one of two women, another of three women (Wapperty, Pangernowidedic and Mary Ann), here reattributed to Mrs Davidson. These images are especially significant because Davidson was a very early female photographer in Australia, and her subjects were also women. The authorship of these images to Davidson was seemingly 'lost' once JW Beattie compiled and marketed his own

'Nixon'-attributed albums of Tasmanian Aborigines from the 1890s.[73] Mrs Davidson was the sister of Henry Albert Frith, and his photographic hand colourist. One of Frith's last Hobart commissions was his famous August 1864 sennotype of William Lanne, Mary Ann, Trucanini and Pangernowidedic at Government House, which was mass produced and also popular as a glass lantern slide. When Frith departed Hobart soon after, it was his sister, Davidson, who applied to the Royal Society, along with Samuel Clifford, Charles Woolley and Alfred Bock, to be commissioned to make photographs of the Tasmanian Aborigines (by which was meant those living at Oyster Cove) for the 1866 Intercolonial Exhibition in Melbourne. Charles Woolley was awarded the commission, given his influential connections.[74] The other applicants planned to visit Oyster Cove to take their photographs, whereas Woolley's resultant early examples of anthropological photography were indoor studio works.[75] Davidson, it is presumed, not to be deterred, did visit Oyster Cove and made photographs that were exhibited along with Woolley's in Melbourne.[76]

By the 1870s Bishop Nixon's c. 1858 photographs of Tasmanian Aborigines were being increasingly reproduced as etchings in books such as James Bonwick's (1817–1906) *The last of the Tasmanians* (1870) and *The daily life and origins of the Tasmanians* (1870), and as photographs in books, postcards and albums from the 1890s, such as Henry Ling Roth's (1855–1925) *The Aborigines of Tasmania* (1890, 1899) and John Watt Beattie's (1859–1930) souvenir photographic albums.[77] The daguerreotype of 1847–8 was not publicly reproduced until 1969.[78] During the mid to late nineteenth century, paintings and drawings depicting Aborigines, such as those by Bock, Skinner, Prout and Simpkinson De Wesselow (1819–1906), remained in the realm of privately held fine art. The absence of these works ensured the increasing primacy of photographic portraits as *the* public representation of Aboriginal people. Through their accessibility and mechanical reproducibility they became the enduring face of Aboriginal Tasmania for more than a century.

The sympathetic intentions of contemporaries Prout and Bass Strait voyager and amateur photographer Nixon contrast significantly with the government adoption of specific photographic works by Woolley and Frith as the official visual endpoint of Tasmanian Aborigines. However, by following Prout and Nixon, in particular their pictorial work, meetings with Aboriginal people, colonial relationships and early departures from Tasmania, we can find a pattern that explicates how the Tasmanian Aboriginal people they encountered

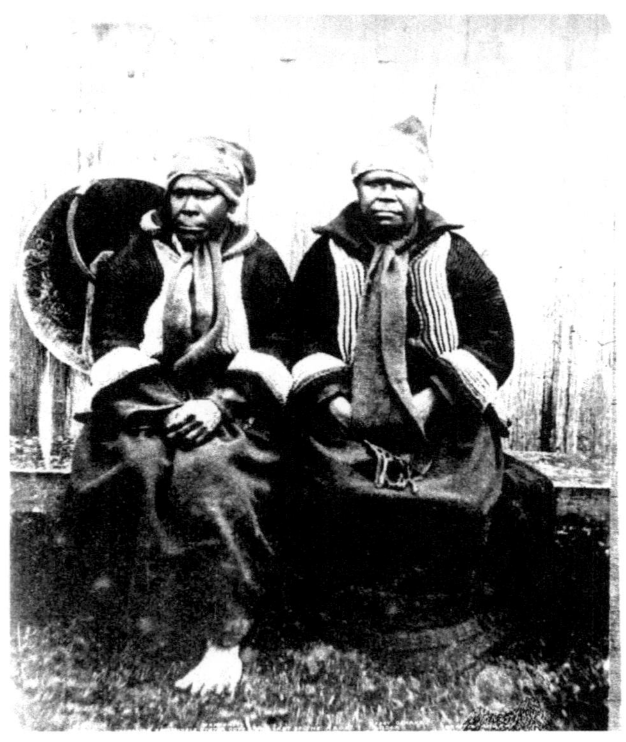

FIGURE 9: Mrs Letitia Davidson (attributed by the author). *Two women* (Wapperty and Bessy Clarke [Clark]), 1866. Silver albumen reprint. JW Beattie Album, State Library of New South Wales, PXD 571, Vol. 1, Image: a1897002h.

and represented by pencil, brush and lens in the mid-1800s had, within three decades, become all but anonymous. Many colonists who had depicted or known, worked with or fought against Tasmanian Aboriginal people in the first half of the nineteenth century died or departed, leaving an information and relationship vacuum that others were unwilling to fill. These included Thomas Bock (died 1855), Bishop Nixon (departed 1862), Benjamin Duterrau (died 1851), Governor Denison (departed 1855), John Glover (died 1849), Sir John and Lady Jane Franklin (departed 1843), George Augustus Robinson (departed 1851), Joseph Milligan (departed 1860) and John Skinner Prout (departed 1848).

The uncontrollability of digital reproduction has led to innumerable images of the fourteen of the forty-seven people photographed who were sent to Oyster Cove being continually and increasingly misidentified, despite each person looking completely, distinctively, different. The, to-date, lack of knowledge, of care, by institutions that manage these photographs about their identities and often distressing but historically important lives led by each of these people is tellingly suggestive of an ongoing determination to avoid connecting those photographed with the Aboriginal community of today — because then, indeed, Aboriginal history is not past, but alive, in us.

ACKNOWLEDGMENTS

The author thanks Jane Lydon for her generosity of spirit and patience awaiting the well overdue completion of this essay. Also, thanks to Vicki Farmery, Curator of Photography at the Tasmanian Museum and Art Gallery, who is always willing to discuss nineteenth century photography with me and kindly shared the photo showing Lennimenna (Jack Allen). Sincere thanks to Sandra Bowdler, who first shared with me the image of David Bruney, Walter George Arthur and Mary Ann in Aldo Massola's *Journey to Aboriginal Victoria*. My extreme excitement in seeing this image motivated me to complete this essay. Thanks to James Tylor, whose inspirational artwork making images with nineteenth century photographic methods of his own beautifully constructed cross-cultural artefacts also made this past year an exciting time to reflect on the past. Thanks also to Warwick Oakman, who was also generous with his time and ideas. Many thanks also to my family, close and extended, in supporting creative thinking, writing and making.

NOTES

1. *Hobart Town Courier*, 9 October 1830, p. 2.
2. Photographers from the 1840s to the 1870s included Thomas Browne, the Bishop of Tasmania (Francis Russell Nixon), Mrs Letitia Davidson, Charles Alfred Woolley, Henry Albert Frith, Henry Hall Baily, Alfred Winter, Samuel Clifford and Reverend John Fereday.
3. I have located fifty-three different images of fourteen Tasmanian Aboriginal people taken between 1847 and 1876, apparently on fifteen different occasions. Twenty-three images were made at Oyster Cove station. These were likely taken on six different occasions between 1858 and 1866 by at least two, and possibly four, different photographers. The remaining thirty images are likely to have been taken in Hobart, New Norfolk and on Sable Island, D'Entrecasteaux Channel, south of Hobart. Eighteen images, commissioned by the Tasmanian Government for the 1866 Intercolonial Exhibition in Melbourne, were taken in Hobart in August 1866 by Charles Woolley.
4. Among them, Wapperty and Tanganutara/Tairenootairer.
5. David Bruney's surname is spelled variously as Brune, Bruny, and Bruney. Text of notes by Tasmanian Aborigines obtained by John Skinner

Prout during his visit to Flinders Island, 1845. British Museum Ethno. doc. 915.

6. A Massola, *Journey to Aboriginal Victoria*, Rigby, Adelaide, 1969, facing p. 165.
7. S Dammery, *Walter George Arthur: a free Tasmanian?,* Monash Publications in History, Monash University, Melbourne, 2001.
8. L Stevens, 'The phenomenal coolness of Tunnerminnerwait', *Victorian Historical Journal,* 8(1):18–40, 2010, viewed 29 October 2013, <www.academia.edu/1472475/_The_Phenomenal_Coolness_of_Tunnerminnerwait_Victorian_Historical_Journal_Vol_8_No_1_June_2010_pp.18-40>.
9. T Bonyhady, 'To quit barbarous for civilized life: Benjamin Duterrau' in D Thomas (ed.), *Creating Australia 200 years of art 1788–1988,* Art Gallery of South Australia, Adelaide, 1988, pp. 76–7.
10. Also spelled Truganini.
11. C Long, *Tasmanian photographers 1840–1940: a directory*, Tasmanian Historical Research Association, Tasmanian Museum and Art Gallery, Hobart, 1995, p. 24; *Launceston Examiner*, 13 October 1847 (afternoon edition), p. 2, viewed 24 November 2013, <http://nla.gov.au/nla.news-page3612311>.
12. Design & Art Australia Online, 'Thomas Browne', 2011, viewed 29 October 2013, <www.daao.org.au/bio/thomas-browne/biography/?>. GA Robinson, for example, attended Dowling's service on 1 May 1836. NJB Plomley (ed.), *Weep in silence: a history of the Flinders Island Aboriginal settlement,* Blubber Head Press, Hobart, 1987, p. 352.
13. J Jones & National Gallery of Australia, *Robert Dowling: Tasmanian son of empire*, National Gallery of Australia, Canberra, 2010, pp. 81–6; *The Mercury*, Hobart, 21 August, 1884, p. 3, viewed 25 November 2013, <http://nla.gov.au/nla.news-page816377>.
14. Classified advertising, *The Courier,* Hobart, 27 August 1851, p. 1, viewed 24 November 2013, <http://nla.gov.au/nla.news-article2960340>.
15. Henry Dowling to Hon. Sec. Mr Barnard, Royal Society of Tasmania, 6 March 1882, RSA/b/18 (Royal Society).
16. Long, above n 11, p. 24 states, 'All daguerreotypes attributed to Browne possess an oval matte and have no backdrop painting'.
17. Quoted in NJB Plomley, 'A list of Tasmanian Aboriginal material in collections in Europe' in *Records of the Queen Victoria Museum*, New Series, No. 15, Queen Victoria Museum, Launceston, Tas., 1962, p. 4. See also NJB Plomley, 'Tasmanian Aboriginal material in collections in Europe', *Journal of the Royal Anthropological Institute of Great Britain and Ireland*, 91(2):221–7, 1961. Prout's influence on Aboriginal portraiture in the colonies within the expanding field of visual arts, including photography, cannot be underestimated. Prout was a catalyst, forming bonds with and between the earliest photographers of Tasmanian Aboriginal people, such as Francis Russell Nixon, Thomas Browne, Mrs Letitia Davidson, Charles Alfred Woolley, Henry Albert Frith, Henry Hall Baily, Alfred Winter, Samuel Clifford and Reverend John Fereday and other artist contemporaries, including Benjamin Duterrau, Robert Dowling, Thomas Bock, Benjamin Law, John Glover, Francis Simpkinson, Ludwig Becker and Owen Stanley.
18. Royal Anthropological Institute, London, MS145, and Plomley, 'A list', above n 17, pp. 3–5. Unfortunately, the usually meticulous Plomley did not reference the location of the 1848 letter from Robinson. The greater mystery is the location of the original daguerreotype today, if indeed it survives. Perhaps it is buried deep inside the British Museum, which acquired some of Robinson's collections after Barnard Davis' death in the 1880s.
19. See Plomley, *Weep in Silence* above n 12, p. 471, 14 August 1837.
20. Lady Caroline Denison in Sir William Denison & Richard P Davis, 1935– & Sir Guy Green, 1937– & Stefan Petrow & Lady Caroline Denison et al. 2004, *Varieties of vice-regal life (Van Diemen's Land section),* Tasmanian Historical Research Association, Hobart, pp. 72–3. 'Aborigines', *Launceston Examiner*, 1 January 1848 (afternoon edition), p. 5, viewed 25 November 2013, < http://nla.gov.au/nla.news-page3641328>.
21. Lady Caroline Denison in Denison, above n 20, pp. 73–4.

22. W Denison, *Varieties of vice-regal life, vol. 1*, Longmans, Green & Co., London, 1870, p. 60, viewed 17 April 2013, <www.archive.org/stream/cu31924087994202/cu31924087994202_djvu.txt>.

23. Royal Albert Theatre advertisement, *Colonial Times*, Hobart, 10 September 1847, p. 2, viewed 27 April 2013, <http://nla.gov.au/nla.news-page672641>.

24. S Scheding, *The national picture*, Random House Australia, Milsons Point, NSW, 2002. Neo-classical influences such as Raphael and Jacques-Louis David (in particular, his painting *The intervention of the Sabine women* (1799)) strongly influenced Duterrau's painting, which remained in his possession in Hobart until his death in 1851. See J Gough, 'The conciliation (etching)' in A Bunbury (ed.), *This wondrous land: colonial art on paper*, National Gallery of Victoria, Melbourne, 2011. For an image of the work, see Louvre, *The intervention of the Sabine women*, viewed 27 April 2013, <www.louvre.fr/en/oeuvre-notices/intervention-sabine-women>. Duterrau proudly holds Raphael's bound collection, *Cartoons and School of Athens*, in his self-portrait in the collection of the Tasmanian Museum and Art Gallery. Scheding explicates Duterrau's classical influences, which included Raphael.

25. *Launceston Examiner*, 5 January 1848 (afternoon edition), p. 3, viewed 27 April 2013, <http://nla.gov.au/nla.news-page3641871>.

26. Denison, above n 20, pp. 84–5.

27. Denison, above n 20, pp. 76–7.

28. *The Courier*, Hobart, 29 December 1847, p. 2, viewed 27 April 2013, <http://nla.gov.au/nla.news-page637183>.

29. Gunn's library was catalogued in 1921, Tasmanian Permanent Executors and Trustees Association, *Catalogue of library of the late Ronald Campbell Gunn, at Newstead House, Launceston, Tas*, Daily Telegraph [printer], Launceston, Tas., 1921; the daguerreotype was not listed. Gunn's collection was auctioned posthumously in 1926 in Melbourne, at which it is possible the photograph of the daguerreotype was purchased by Ridges of Launceston and later acquired by Roy Michaelis, Leonard Joel (firm) and Fine Art Society (Melbourne); *Auction sale of the most important and comprehensive library of books of the late Robert [i.e. Ronald] Campbell Gunn of Newstead House, Launceston, Tasmania: Tuesday, November 9th, at eleven o'clock, at Leonard Joel's auction rooms, 362 Little Collins Street*, Leonard Joel in conjunction with the Fine Art Society: Haase & Sons [printer], Melbourne, Vic., 1926.

30. Gunn was Superintendent of Convicts in Launceston in 1830, Police Magistrate at Circular Head in 1836, and private Secretary to Governor Sir John Franklin by 1840, and is remembered for his extensive botanical work. He was also a member of the inquest committee into the infamous deaths of key colonists Bartholemew Boyle Thomas and his overseer James Parker at the hands of the Aborigines in 1831, along with Henry Dowling Junior, who employed Thomas Browne, the creator of the daguerreotype. In 1838 Gunn accompanied the Governor of Tasmania, Sir John Franklin, and his wife, Lady Jane Franklin, on a tour to Flinders Island Aboriginal Establishment. He concluded that 'They are an interesting race and in my opinion far from so low in the scale of being as many endeavour to urge'; 'RC Gunn to Sir WJ Hooker, 15 Feby 1838' in TE Burns & JR Skemp (eds), *Van Diemen's Land correspondents: letters from RC Gunn, RW Lawrence, Jorgen Jorgenson, Sir John Franklin and others to Sir William J Hooker 1827–1849*, Queen Victoria Museum, Launceston, Tas., 1961, p. 70.

31. Joseph Milligan, in his role as Secretary of the Royal Society, sent many items to international exhibitions. The National Library of Australia holds a copy of *The story of Mathinna* by Old Boomer, Mercury Steam Press Office, Hobart, 1871, that is inscribed 'ex-Ronald C. Gunn', viewed 3 May 2013, <www.utas.edu.au/library/companion_to_tasmanian_history/M/Mathinna.htm>.

32. Plomley, *Weep in silence*, above n 12, pp. 150–5.

33. ibid., p. 148.

34. ibid., pp. 786–7.

35. Clark 1988 cited in Dammery, above n 7, pp. 11–12; Plomley, *Weep in silence*, above n 12, p. 679.

36. It is likely Walter's father was Rolepa (King George) from Plangermaireener Country (Ben

Lomond), who passed away in June 1840; Plomley, *Weep in silence*, above n 12, p. 851.

37. Julie Gough, 2012.

38. See Plomley, *Weep in silence*, above n 12, pp. 193–201.

39. The spelling of Aboriginal names in this paper and the associated English names are those used by NJB Plomley in his publications. On 15 January 1836 Robinson registered more than one hundred new, often classical European names for Aboriginal people (Plomley, *Weep in silence*, above n 12, p. 878–81). For detailed information, see Plomley, *Weep in silence*, above n 12, pp. 194–5, 944–5.

40. See John S Dandridge, *Report from Oyster Cove Station from 1 January 1858 – 28 May 1859*, dated 25 May 1859, CO 284, Tasmanian Archives and Heritage Office, Hobart, pp. 1–5. One Aboriginal person, Meemelunneener (Hannah), was sent from Hobart to Flinders Island in May 1850. Her subsequent whereabouts are unknown. Plomley, above n 12, p. 194.

41. JG Garson, 'Osteology' in H Ling Roth, *The Aborigines of Tasmania*, Fullers Bookshop, Hobart, facsimile of the second revised and enlarged edition with map, Halifax, England, 1972[1899], pp. 191–220.

42. HP MacDonald, *Human remains: episodes in human dissection*, Melbourne University Press, Carlton, Vic., 2005.

43. George Augustus Robinson's visit to Oyster Cove, Sunday 27 April 1851, George Augustus Robinson papers, 1818–1924 [A 7022–A 7092], State Library of New South Wales, pp. 4–5, viewed 21 March 2013, <http://acms.sl.nsw.gov.au/album/albumView.aspx?acmsID=825586&itemID=823443>.

44. J Milligan, *Report to Colonial Secretary on the condition of the Aborigines at Oyster Cove*, December 28, CSO 24/241/9498 (Z857), Tasmanian Archives and Heritage Office, Hobart, 1853, p. (140) 11–13.

45. Those nine people were likely to be Thielewanna (Henrietta, d. unknown date), Wottecowidger (Harriet, d. 1855), Lennimenna (Jack Allen, d. 1864), Coonia (Patty, d. 1867), Toyenroun (Augustus, d. 1860), Drunameliyer (Caroline, d. 1860), Plowneme (Flora, d. 1860), Calamarowenye (Tippo Saib, d. 1860) and Pangernowidedic (Bessy, d. 1867). Plomley, *Weep in silence*, above n 12, p. 950. James and Maria Allen (nee Robinson) raised eight children and lived on Clarke Island from 1846 until Allen drowned in 1856. See also FR Nixon, *Cruise of the Beacon: a narrative of a visit to the Islands in Bass's Straits – 1854*, Bell and Daldy, London, 1857, author's presentation copy to his wife, Allport Library and Museum of Fine Arts, Hobart, pp. 52–3, viewed 29 October 2013, <http://catalogue.statelibrary.tas.gov.au/item/?id=658648>.

46. Bessy was remarried as a widow in May 1856 to James Everett, when she was twenty-five and he was sixty-one. Bessy had two children to James: Robert, born 1861 (who died of tetanus in 1875) and Gertrude, born 1864, who died in December 1913. James died in June 1876 aged 82. Bessy Everett (nee Myetye, stepfather Rew, ex-Miri) died on 12 March 1891, age 58, on Flinders Island. Her mother, Wapperty, died at Oyster Cove on 12 August 1867.

47. See MacDonald n 42. Wapperty was also known as Wonoteah Cootamena (Thunder and Lightning). On Cape Barren Island, Bass Strait, there is a place called Thunder and Lightning Bay (where she never returned from Oyster Cove). There is also a beach called Bungs Beach on Cape Barren Island. Bung was another name for Wapperty's sister, Woretemoeteyenner, an ancestor of the author. Woretemoeteyenner's daughter Dalrymple Johnson (nee Briggs) petitioned the government in 1841 for her mother to leave Wybalenna and live with her family in Perth in northern Tasmania, which, remarkably, was granted. Woretemoeteyenner lived until 1847 with her daughter, son-in-law and grandchildren. Judy Thomas was the sister of Meethecaratheeanna (Emma), who had made a request to Robinson in 1851 and Milligan in 1853 that she wished to join her other sister, Judy (Pollerrelberner, also known as Julia), in Bass Strait. Pollerrelberner had been abducted by sealers. She had lived with John Thomas, who apparently sold her to Edward Mansell decades earlier. Meethecaratheeanna died at Oyster Cove on 27 May 1863, having not been reunited with her sister Julia. Widow 'Mrs Julia Mansell', aged about sixty, died on Sea Lion Island in August 1867; *Mercury*, Hobart, 24 August 1867, viewed

26 November 2013, <http://nla.gov.au/nla.news-article8847672>, p. 3 (Wapperty), p. 4 (Julia Mansell).

48. 'With regard to them who are anxious to join their relatives in the Straits I do not see any objection to comply with their wishes provided of course thus their relatives are willing to receive them, and it might be as well to communicate with them for the purposes of ascertaining this when the Beacon goes down to the Straits', WD 20 Feb 1854 (Governor William Denison) in Milligan, above n 44.

49. JE Calder, *Some account of the wars, extirpation, habits etc. of the native tribes of Tasmania, by J.E. Calder*, facsimile of the original edition, Fullers Bookshop, Hobart, 1972 [1875], p. 42.

50. Milligan, above n 44; Dandridge, above n 40.

51. See Flora (inscribed April 1858), *Abbott album*, Alfred Abbott (1838–1872), Item 3, WL Crowther Library, Tasmanian Archives and Heritage Office, ADRI: AUTAS001136186772, viewed 26 November 2013, <http://rhdtprod.education.tas.gov.au/view/action/singleViewer.do?dvs=13853 905013 59~271&locale=en_US&VIEWER_URL=/view/action/singleViewer.do?&preferred_usage_type=VIEW_MAIN&preferred_extension=jp2&DELIVERY_RULE_ID=16&frameId=1&usePid1=true&use Pid2=true>.

52. In September 1854 Bishop Nixon set sail to meet his unknown Bass Strait congregation. He worked his way around the islands, holding church services and baptisms, leaving Bass Strait having more successfully brought God to Aboriginal people than Anglo settlers; *Oyster Cove official visitor's book 1855–1868*, CSO 89, Tasmanian Archives and Heritage Office, Hobart.

53. Day trips to visit the Aborigines became popular from Hobart Town; 'Miscellaneous shipping', *Hobart Town Daily Mercury*, 25 November 1859, p. 2, viewed 27 April 2013, <http://nla.gov.au/nla.news-article3259337>.

54. Copies of this image are held in various collections, including Pitt Rivers Museum, Oxford; the Abbott Album, Tasmanian Archives and Heritage Office, Hobart; JW Beattie Album, PXD 571, Vol. 1, Image: a1897004h, State Library of New South Wales, viewed 29 October 2013, <http://catalogue.statelibrary.tas.gov.au/item/?id=131145>.

55. Copies of this image are held in many collections, including Pitt Rivers Museum, Oxford; the Abbott Album, in which it is inscribed 'April 1858', Tasmanian Archives and Heritage Office, Hobart, viewed 29 October 2013, <http://catalogue.statelibrary.tas.gov.au/item/?id=131195>; JW Beattie Album, PXD 571, State Library of New South Wales; also in Bishop Nixon's author's copy, presented to 'AM' (Anna Maria Nixon, his wife), above n 40. Also, the image is pasted in the Samuel Wilberforce Album #2, Album 47, National Portrait Gallery, London.

56. A unique photograph from the Abbott Album, Allport Library and Museum, Hobart, viewed 29 October 2013, <http://catalogue.statelibrary.tas.gov.au/item/?id=131198>.

57. Royal Society of Tasmania, *The Courier*, Hobart, 21 July 1858, p. 2, viewed 18 March 2013, <http://nla.gov.au/nla.news-article24633155>.

58. Plomley, *Weep in silence*, above n 12, p. 792.

59. 'Manuscript 3251: Van Diemen's Land 1821–1862', viewed 26 November 2013, <http://manuscript3251.wordpress.com/2009/10/24/ms-3251-1825-31-black-natives-also-paton-vs-gregson>.

60. British Museum, Ethdoc. 915.

61. There are a further three anomalous photographic trips to Oyster Cove by unknown photographers, plus one by a female photographer.

62. Found to date only to be in the State Library of Victoria, Image ref: SLVa04986.

63. JW Beattie Album, PXD 571, Vol. 1, Image: a1897015h, State Library of New South Wales.

64. J Bonwick, *The last of the Tasmanians; or, the Black War of Van Diemen's Land*, Sampson, Low, Son and Marston, London, 1870; republished by the State Library of South Australia, Adelaide, 1969, p. 281.

65. Held in the Tasmanian Museum and Art Gallery and Tasmanian Archives and Heritage Office.

66. Dandridge in *Oyster Cove official visitor's book 1855–1868*, CSO 89, Tasmanian Archives and Heritage Office, Hobart; Dandridge, above n 40; Milligan, above n 44.

67. *The Mercury*, Hobart, 14 November 1863, p. 4.

68. 'Dr Nixon has sent a set also — "Groups, of Tasmanian Aborigines." The photographs are very fine, the subjects, hideous. Thankful was I to say, in answer to enquiries, that all we possessed are represented here', 'The Great Exhibition', *Launceston Examiner*, Tuesday 15 July 1862 (morning edition), viewed 5 December 2012, <http://nla.gov.au/nla.news-article41454413>.

69. 'Half-Caste islanders in Bass Strait', Report of the Venerable Archdeacon Reibey, No. 48, Tasmania Legislative Council, Tasmanian Archives and Heritage Office, Hobart, TSA NS 585/1, Aug 26, 1863.

70. Reibey, above n 68; see also S Murray Smith, 'Beyond the pale: the islander community of Bass Strait in the nineteenth century', *Tasmanian Historical Research Association: Papers and Proceedings*, 20(4):167–200, 1973.

71. 'Furneaux Islands' Mission', *The Mercury*, Hobart, 12 April 1865, p. 2, viewed 14 December 2012, <http://nla.gov.au/nla.news-article8832142>.

72. Letter from Bishop Francis Russell Nixon to James Erskine Calder, 16 January 1877, Royal Society of Tasmania Library, University of Tasmania, RS19/1, viewed 12 December 2012, <http://eprints.utas.edu.au/10659/>.

73. JW Beattie Album, PXD 571, Vol. 1, Images: a1897011, 1897002, State Library of New South Wales.

74. 'Intercolonial Exhibition', *The Mercury*, Hobart, 6 June 1866, p. 3, viewed 24 November 2013, <http://nla.gov.au/nla.news-article8839726>.

75. *The Mercury*, Hobart, 12 September 1866, p. 2, viewed 24 November 2013, <http://nla.gov.au/nla.news-article8841544>.

76. P Edmonds, '"We think that this subject of the native races should be thoroughly gone into at the forthcoming Exhibition": the 1866–67 Intercolonial Exhibition' in K Darian-Smith, R Gillespie, C Jordan & E Willis (eds), *Seize the day: exhibitions, Australia and the world*, Monash University Press, Melbourne, 2008, viewed 24 April 2013, <http://books.publishing.monash.edu/apps/bookworm/view/SEIZE+THE+DAY/123/xhtml/chapter4.html>.

77. Bonwick, above n 63; J Bonwick, *The daily life and origins of the Tasmanians*, 1870; Roth, above n 41. Beattie Albums are held in collections including the State Library of New South Wales and Pitt Rivers Museum, Oxford University.

78. Massola, above n 6.

NEW SOUTH WALES

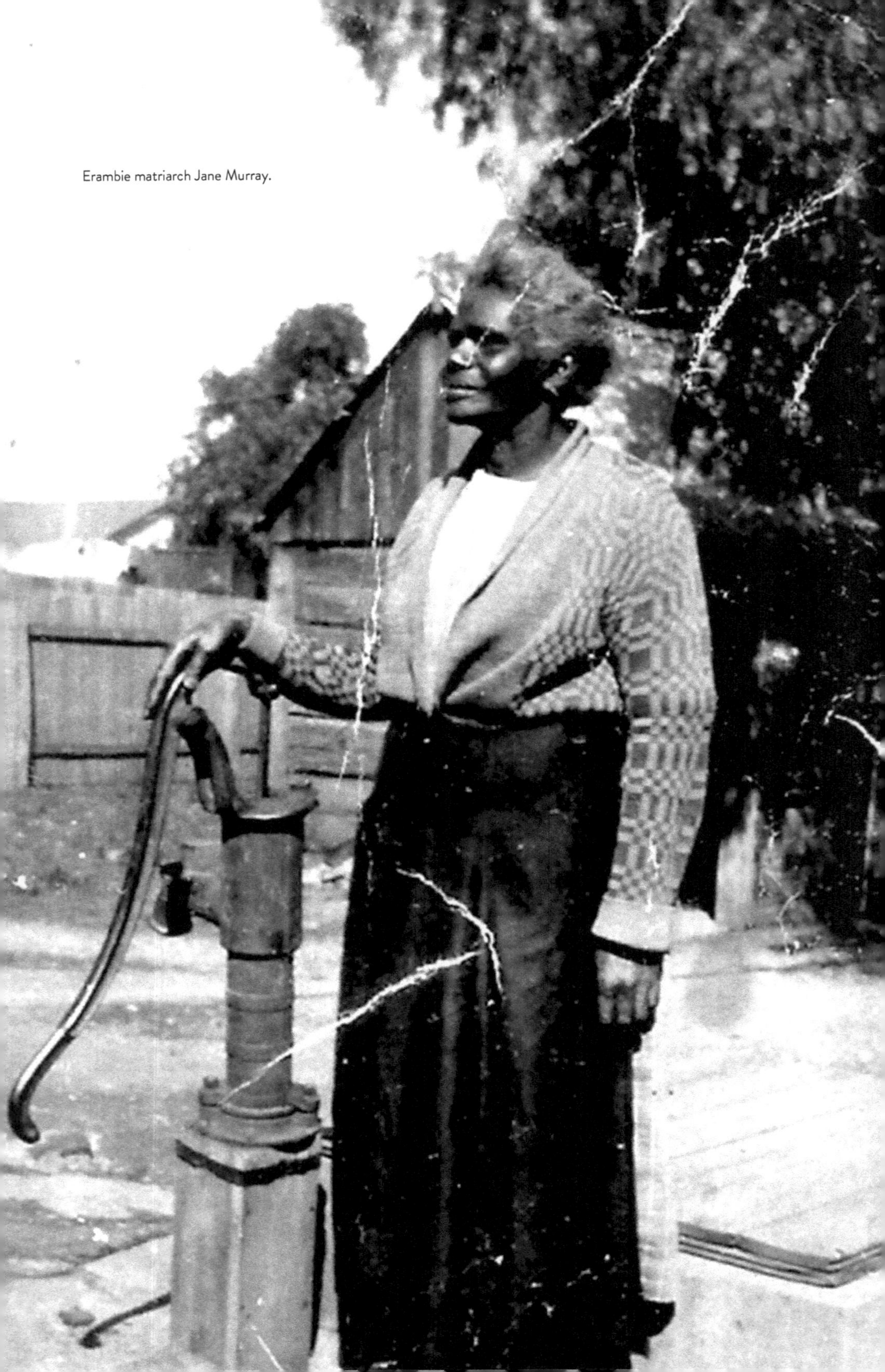

Erambie matriarch Jane Murray.

Chapter 3

PHOTOGRAPHING INDIGENOUS PEOPLE IN NEW SOUTH WALES

Jane Lydon and Sari Braithwaite with Shauna Bostock-Smith

Sydney was the first permanent British colony in Australia. It was established, in 1788, on the traditional land of the Cadigal band of the coastal Eora people.[1] By the time the camera arrived in Sydney in 1841, the Eora had undergone more than fifty years of invasion and dispossession and many had moved to places such as La Perouse on Botany Bay, south of the city.[2] An inquiry in 1846 wrongly concluded that all the local Aboriginal people had died, although families were reported at places such as Wiseman's Ferry to the west.

Therefore, when photographers began to record Sydney, there were few Eora people to be seen on its streets. More importantly, those who remained did not conform to expectations of authentic Indigenous culture and identity. In a pattern followed everywhere across the Australian colonies, the camera followed the frontier, as photographers sought out Aboriginal people still leading traditional ways of life, with their distinctive material culture. The medium was taken up as a hobby by members of the colony's elite, and photographs were produced on the fringes of settlement during the late 1850s. So it was not until 1859 that the young polymath William Stanley Jevons, not yet famous as an economist, wrote to his sister Lucy of the goldfields of Jembaicumbene, near Braidwood, to the south, that he had encountered some Yuin (dialect Walbunja) people:

> I have only just returned from a rough, hard-working, but fine excursion to the southern diggings...I have about twenty pictures, many of which are almost professionally perfect, exhibiting not only general scenery, but all the principal operations of gold-digging and washing and incidents of

> tent life. The diggers were highly amused at being taken, and only required a hint to stand in any desirable attitude, so that my pictures seem almost alive with real diggers. I even got an aboriginal black with two black gins or wives, who sat still in the sun while I made four or five attempts at their portraits before I succeeded.[3]

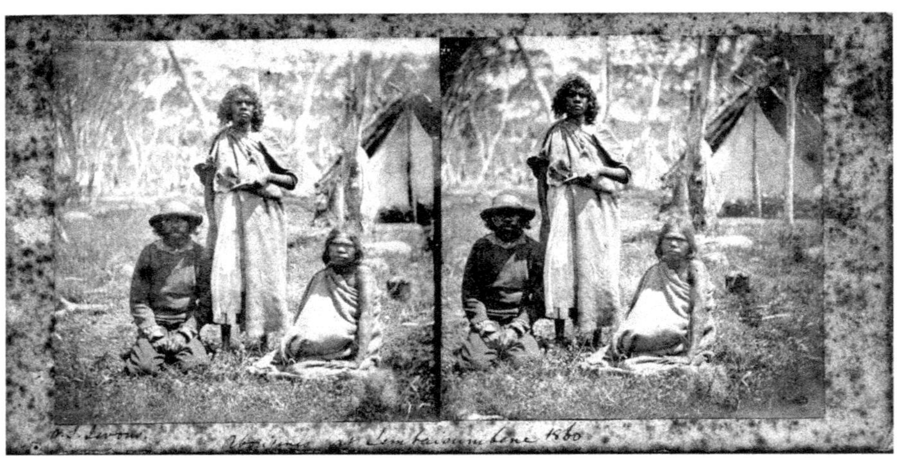

FIGURE 1: WS Jevons. Group of three Aboriginal people at Jembaicumbene, a goldmining settlement near Braidwood, New South Wales. Stereoscopic albumen print, 1859. Macleay Museum, University of Sydney (HP81.106.420). Moral permission Les Simon of the Batemans Bay Local Aboriginal Land Council.

Although Jevons clearly did not communicate very well with the Walbunja, his portrait reveals that, as for the goldfields of central Victoria, Aboriginal people were an integral element of the industry, taking advantage of the economic opportunities it offered, and getting to know the diggers.[4] The image reflects a certain mutual curiosity as white photographer and Walbunja encountered one another in these early years.

About this time, a group of Dharawal people was photographed west of Sydney, probably on the sheep station of pastoralist John Macarthur (1767–1834), at Camden Park.[5]

The Dharawal had endured decades of often violent conflict with the invaders, and after a massacre in 1816 had been granted safe refuge at Camden, their own traditional country, by Elizabeth Macarthur.[6] This photograph is preserved within the Macarthur family albums at the Mitchell Library, and

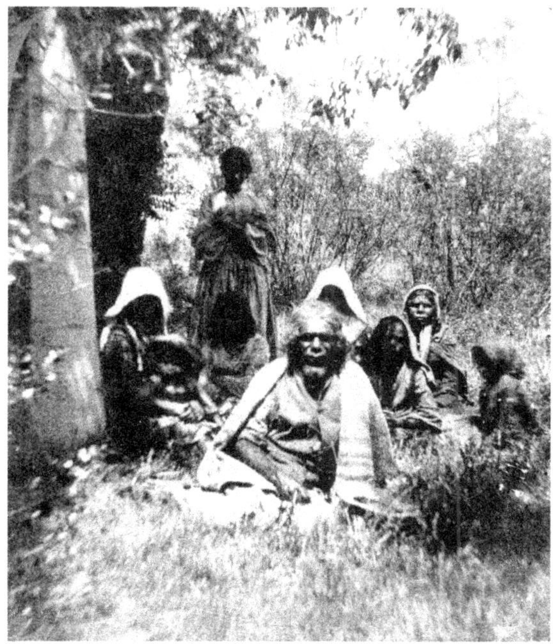

FIGURE 2: W Hetzer. Group of Aboriginal people [Dharawal language speakers], near Camden. Photograph, late 1850s, in 'Album of views, illustrations and Macarthur family photographs, 1857–66 & 1879' by various photographers. Mitchell Library, PXA 4358, Vol. 1, digital order no. Album ID: 824195. Moral/cultural permission of the Tharawal Land Council.

for this prominent settler family it was no doubt a salutary counterpoint to the views, colonial buildings and other evidence for colonial progress that the albums contained.[7] It is difficult to understand what the subjects thought of the encounter, yet the camera records their altered lifestyle and details such as their blankets and European dress.

By this time such records were of international scientific interest, and in 1862 Edwin (or Edward) Dalton and Frank Gale sent portraits of Aboriginal people to an exhibition in Sydney, where they both won medals (Dalton 'for excellent photographic portraits of aborigines', and Gale for ambrotype group portraits of a group of Aboriginal people from Queanbeyan); when forwarded to the 1862 London International Exhibition, Gale's were awarded an honourable mention.[8] Charles Darwin's theory of evolution became scientific orthodoxy during the decades following the 1859 publication of *The origin of species by means of natural selection*, and was applied to humankind. Images of Indigenous Australians were seen as 'data' in these debates, and circulated through international scientific networks. For example, one series of outdoor views of Richmond River (Bandjalung) people may have been taken by Grafton-based Conrad Wagner, and was collected by Henry Nottidge Moseley (1844–91) of the *Challenger* expedition in 1874, and ended up in Oxford.[9]

The social evolutionist paradigm was used to rationalise Indigenous dispossession, and ideas of Aboriginal difference, primitivism and eventual extinction took hold of the popular imagination. In response to the growing belief that the Aboriginal race was doomed to disappear, photographers sought to record what was believed to be a disappearing way of life, their market now comprising a large general audience, as well as scientists and collectors.

JOHN WILLIAM LINDT (1845–1926): STILL LIVES

Australia's most famous nineteenth century photographer, John William Lindt, was to make his name through such imagery, following the release of his acclaimed 1872–73 series *Australian Aboriginals*, which showed portraits of people of the lower Clarence River of the Gumbaynggirr and Bandjalung peoples.[10] These tableaux perfectly captured contemporary taste, and as a result have become some of the most reproduced photographs of Australian Aboriginal people ever, spiralling out and away from their birthplace to lie within major museum collections across the world.[11] In 1872 he began the series, which ultimately comprised around fifty images: these showed carefully posed men, women and children against a studio backdrop, surrounded by items of material culture such as spears, tools, nets and ornaments.[12] In November 1874 a Sydney newspaper announced that:

> Mr. J. W. Lindt, a photographer from Grafton, has this week published in neat album form, a series of twelve photographic views of aboriginals, the choice subjects of a very large collection which he has during three years' residence on the Clarence, laboured strenuously to obtain.[13]

It suggested that Lindt's series would make excellent Australian mementoes for tourists and curious Europeans, and while the portraits seem ludicrously posed and artificial to us now, they were described as 'the first successful attempt at representing the native blacks truthfully as well as artistically':

> Unlike what we have been used to seeing in photographs of blacks, these pictures have been treated, with great skill and artistic judgment. They represent blacks of both sexes and all ages in various groups and positions. Especial care seems to have been taken by the artist to portray his subjects in their natural positions, and with their natural surroundings; and the groups in these pictures would strike anyone that has travelled in the wilds of Australia, as most characteristic and truthful, while the recollection would not fail to give friends in other countries a faithful idea of the appearance of a race fast passing away.[14]

In expressing nostalgia for the supposedly 'disappearing race', the *Sydney Morning Herald* perhaps defined what was so appealing about the images for contemporary viewers, noting:

> There is no settled portion of our colony which affords a better field for the study of aboriginal bush life than that presented by our northern rivers, for there — although decreasing yearly in numbers as their territories become more settled upon by white population — the blacks preserve their customs and traditions, adhering more closely to true aboriginal life than tribes in other districts of New South Wales, and Mr Lindt can be complimented upon the artistic use he has made of the rugged subjects he has had at his disposal.[15]

Lindt was therefore typical in following the frontier to produce records of seemingly pristine, but doomed, subjects, but he also cleverly manipulated his elaborate studio sets to create images of Aboriginality that would satisfy popular and scientific taste. In this he had truly mastered the medium's twin objectives — truth and beauty — in conventional visual terms. In their artifice and elaborate attention to the detail and texture of the subjects' clothes, skin and artefacts, they resemble still lives. In September 1875, the *Sydney Morning Herald* reported that:

> Copies of this album have been sent by the government of this colony to various scientific institutions in the old country, and a number of letters of acknowledgment, appearing in flattering terms of the excellence of this work have been received at the Colonial Secretary's office.[16]

The series was acclaimed at several international exhibitions, such as the 1876 Philadelphia Exhibition, where it was reported that Lindt's 'photos of aborigines, around which are grouped boomerangs and other aboriginal implements, weapons, and fishing nets, command a good deal of attention, and are the best pictures of the kind on view'.[17] By the time of the Amsterdam Exhibition in 1883 his images were as popular as ever, but the *Clarence and Richmond Examiner* noted that 'although but a few years ago when this was done, many of those whose features and characteristics Mr Lindt has thus preserved, have one by one passed away, one of the last, if we mistake not, being "Larrigo"'.[18]

Lindt's series became valuable currency in global scientific networks, and was used as an item of exchange by the Australian Museum in Sydney for decades, and today his images can be found in every major scientific photographic collection in Europe.[19] In 1875, for example, nine tableaux were sent to Italian zoologist and Darwinist Enrico Giglioli by surgeon and trustee of the Australian Museum, Alfred Roberts (1823–98). In 1877 the young Austrian aristocrat Anatole von Hügel offered the museum several Fijian and Solomon Islands artefacts, for which he received two birds for dissection and at least nine Lindt photographs.[20] As many have pointed out, in many ways Lindt's photographs tell us much more about European culture in Australia and the empire than the Aboriginal people that are framed within these photographs.[21]

LINKS TO TODAY

Today, Gumbaynggirr and Bandjalung people have reclaimed the portraits as their heritage, largely thanks to the work of the Grafton Regional Gallery, which was given substantial collections of Lindt portraits by the Cullen family, by the Friends of the Gallery, and by Ian and Florence Robinson. More than 130 years after the photographs were taken, some members of the Indigenous community feel a deep connection to the images: they personify relatives and family histories only now being reconstructed; they also represent a link to country. Indigenous scholar Shauna Bostock-Smith tells the story of her encounter with Lindt's famous image of 'Mary Ann of Ulmarra'.

CONNECTING WITH THE COWANS

Shauna Bostock-Smith

A phone call out of the blue from my father, insisting that I watch a documentary on the ABC because 'it's all about your research!', instantly piqued my curiosity. I quickly changed channels and was able to catch the last half of an *Australian story* documentary called 'The light of day'.[22] 'The light of day' told the story of Sam and Janet Cullen who purchased a collection of thirty-seven albumen paper photographs by John William Lindt (1845–1926) through auction in London in 2004, and gave the collection as a gift to the Grafton Regional Gallery. The historic photographs, taken in the 1870s, were of the Aboriginal people of the Clarence River and surrounding areas. The Cullen family's gift and the subsequent search for the descendants of the (nameless) people in the Lindt photographs has brought about an extraordinary connection between the Aboriginal community of the Clarence Valley, the North Coast, and the descendants of the Bandjalung, Gumbaynggirr and Yaegl countries.

In the collection was a photograph taken in 1873 of a young Aboriginal woman called 'Mary Ann of Ulmarra' (Figure 3). Extensive research carried out by the *Australian story* crew and the Aboriginal community in Grafton has revealed that 'Mary Ann of Ulmarra' had the likely identity of Mary Ann Cowan.

I gasped aloud when I heard this. I have been researching my family history for the past few years, and I knew that Mary Ann Cowan was my great-great-grand-aunt. This exciting news had a profound effect on me. It is as though this lovely photograph has spiritually reached through time and altered my perception of her today. She has now magically transformed from an abstract entity — a name on her marriage and death certificates — into a real life, flesh and blood, beautiful young woman.

Placing the photograph beside my collection of family history records, I can now build a better idea of her life. It can be assumed that her approximate year of birth was 1849.[23] When I look at the photograph I can see the scarification marks on her chest and these lead me to believe she lived a more traditional life than I had previously imagined. Mary Ann had her first child, Herbert, in 1872 when she was twenty-three years old.[24] When the Lindt photograph was taken, Herbert was about one year old, and Mary Ann was approximately twenty-four. She married

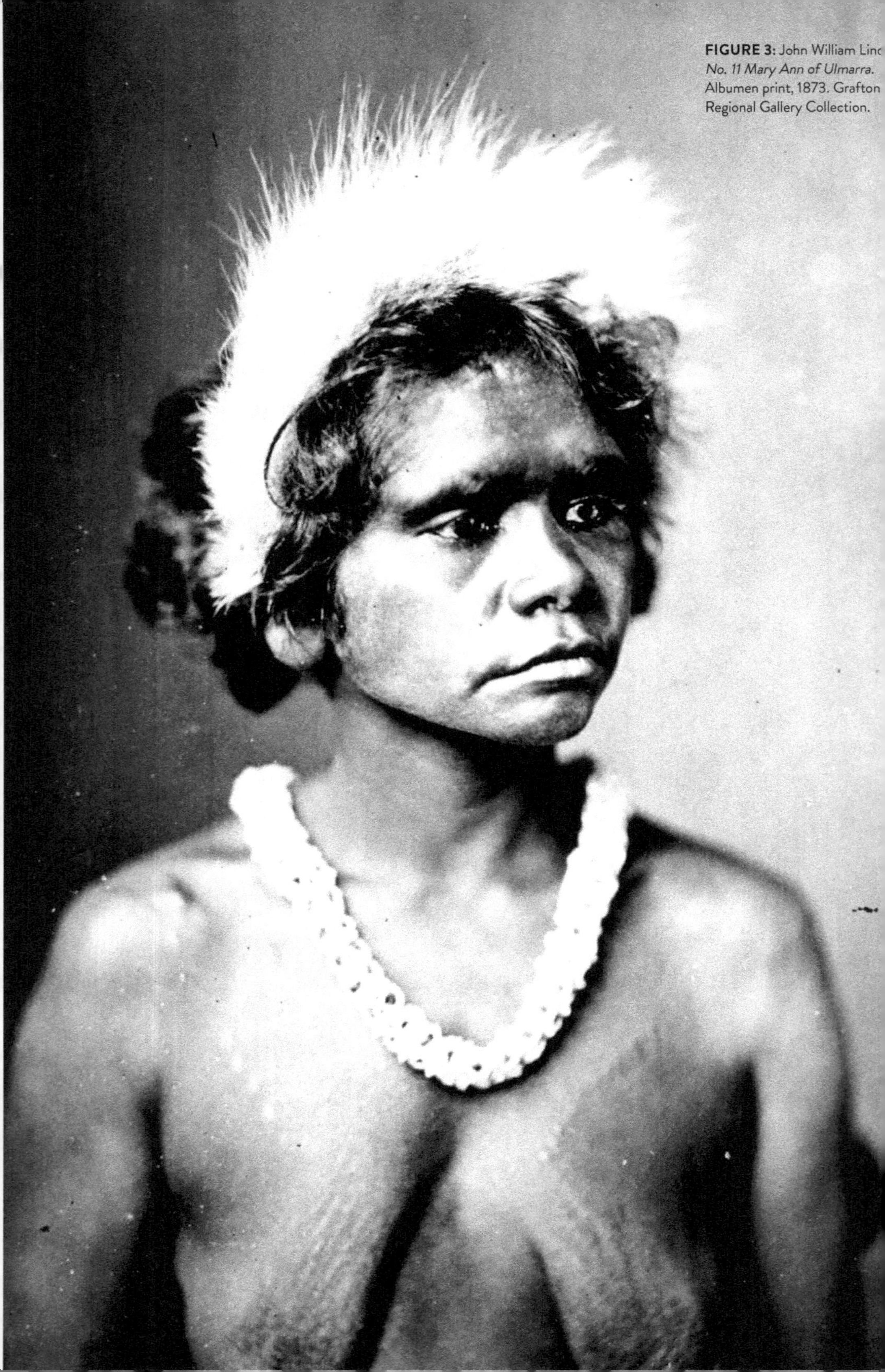

FIGURE 3: John William Linc
No. 11 Mary Ann of Ulmarra.
Albumen print, 1873. Grafton
Regional Gallery Collection.

Leonard Williams in 1877 at the age of twenty-eight, the same year her second child was born.[25] Mary Ann gave birth to five children between 1872 and 1885. My great-great grandfather Jonathon Cowan was Mary Ann's younger brother.

Jonathon Cowan is as far back as I can go in the historic record for my grandmother's family. He was born about 1857 and died on 22 February 1900 at the age of forty-three.[26] His widow, Elizabeth, was left with seven children; Alice, John Thomas, Edith, Walter, Aileen, Harold Arthur and Roy. The children's ages at the time of their father's death ranged from nine months to fifteen years. My family descends from John Thomas.

During the making of the documentary, the descendants of Jonathon's oldest daughter, Alice, discovered their connection to the Lindt photograph of Mary Ann. Many of Alice Cowan's descendants still reside in Grafton. At the end of the documentary there was a plea for anyone who had information to come forward, so I immediately contacted the ABC. The program's producer, Jennifer Feller, gave my phone number to Sam Cullen. He was very interested in my family connection and when I told him about the research I had accumulated over the years, it was apparent that he did not know very much about Mary Ann, or the incredible number of descendants related to her.

Since the gifting of the Lindt photographs to the Grafton Regional Gallery, representatives from the Clarence Valley Aboriginal community have formed the Lindt Research Project to identify descendants of the people photographed. My family and many of the descendants who live outside the Grafton area were unaware of the project until the *Australian story* documentary aired.

The interest generated by the documentary was phenomenal. Many Aboriginal people from northern New South Wales and south-east Queensland made contact with Sam Cullen and the Grafton Regional Gallery. The Lindt Research Project group was bombarded with family history information and genealogies, so it was decided that an opportunity needed to be organised for all the descendants to come together. The gallery organised a special screening of 'The light of day' in March 2013 to gather the descendants together to share family history information.

About two years ago my family history research enabled me to find Pat and Esmay, two elderly women who are the granddaughters of Edith Cowan. We have kept in touch and have shared our family tree information, so as soon as

I heard about the gathering I asked my father, Pat and Esmay if they would like to join me on a road trip to Grafton. They accepted without hesitation.

On the long drive from Brisbane to Grafton we had wonderful conversations, and I began to realise the significance of this journey to the Cowan family elders in my car. It wasn't just a fun, nostalgic road trip to Grafton, where my father was born and where Pat and Esmay had lived in their childhood. It was so much more. These dear souls had a burning desire to connect with *their country* before they died. Figures 4, 5, 6 and 7 show us standing in front of the photograph of Mary Ann.

My father, who is a Vietnam Veteran, made it very clear to my sisters and I that he wants his ashes to be scattered on the banks of the Clarence River, in a particular spot where he 'has a view' of the Clarence Valley Vietnam Veterans Association's memorial for returned servicemen from Grafton (Figure 8 and 9). He has sought permission from the Association, and has been assured of his eligibility, to have a plaque mounted on the memorial in the event of his death. He has specifically asked us to make sure it happens.

After slowly talking through the steps necessary for the computer-illiterate Esmay to watch 'The light of day' documentary online, I asked her to call me back for a chat after she had seen it. I was surprised by her response when she returned the call. She was crying, and through her sobs I was able to hear that this connection to Grafton reminded her of her happy childhood 'being raised by Grandma' (Edith Cowan Senior). It was extremely important to all three elders that the Aboriginal relatives in Grafton knew that although their lives had taken them away from there, in their hearts Grafton and the Clarence River will always be their country.

I wonder if Sam and Janet Cullen realise the enormity of what they have done. The return of these photographs to their rightful place turned out to be more than just a great gesture of goodwill from truly altruistic people. It has brought about the connection of Aboriginal people to their ancestors, to their relatives and to their country.

OPPOSITE PAGE:
FIGURE 4: Shauna Bostock-Smith in front of *Mary Ann of Ulmarra* in the Grafton Regional Gallery.
FIGURE 5: Esmay Monaghan, granddaughter of Edith Cowan Senior (Edith was Mary Ann's niece).
FIGURE 6: Pat Mason, granddaughter of Edith Cowan Senior (Edith was Mary Ann's niece).
FIGURE 7: George Bostock (my father), grandson of John Thomas Cowan (John Thomas was Mary Ann's nephew).
FIGURE 8: George Bostock, standing in front of the Clarence Valley Vietnam Veterans Association memorial in Grafton. The plaque closest to him commemorates his cousin, Jeffery Duroux, another Grafton soldier who served in Vietnam.
FIGURE 9: George Bostock at the Clarence Valley Vietnam Veterans Association memorial.

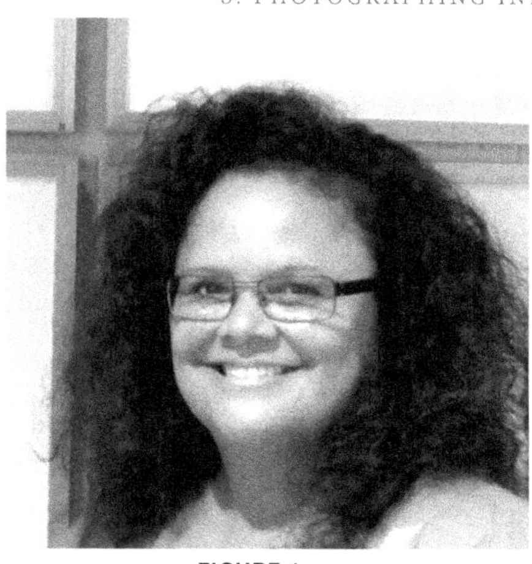

FIGURE 4

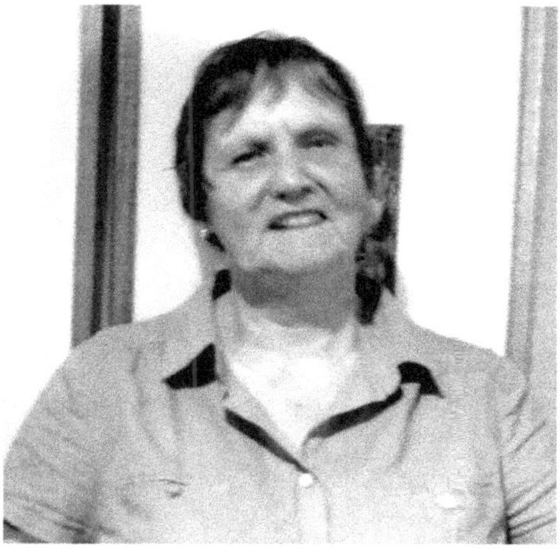

FIGURE 5

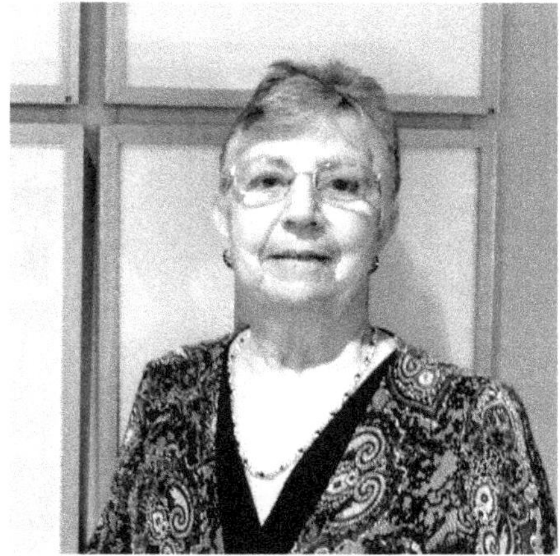

FIGURE 6

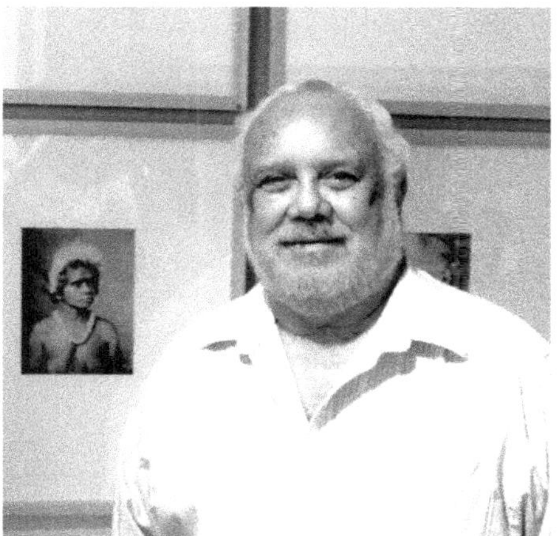

FIGURE 7

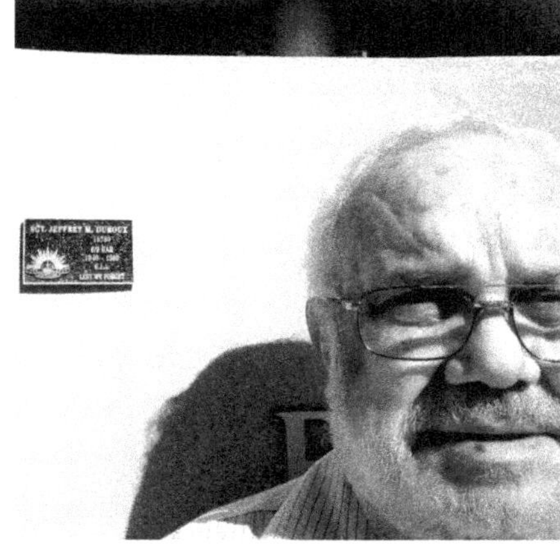

FIGURE 8

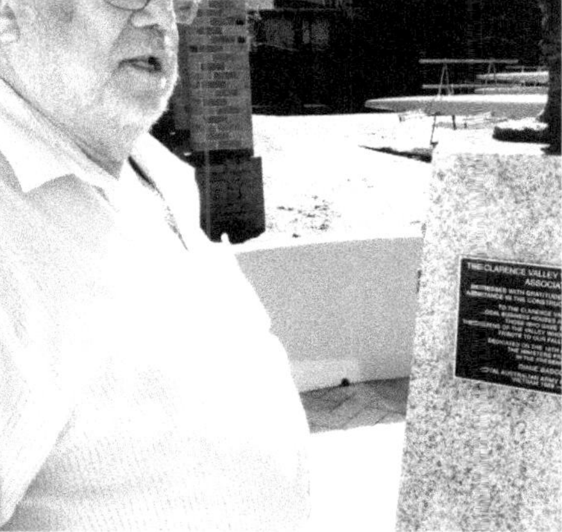

FIGURE 9

TRICKERY AND ARTIFICE

Other photographers of the late nineteenth century also experimented with highly staged visual narratives, but these are sometimes difficult to recuperate. The photographer Thomas Cleary's manipulative tableaux of the 1890s attempted a jocular tone, satirising miscegenation or the Indigenous misrecognition of Western modernity. The Indigenous actors in these narratives — such as Kate Friday and her husband John Friday of Corowa — are lampooned for their inability to lace a corset or soap themselves white. It is interesting to contrast Cleary's ugly vignettes with the delicate drawings of local Kwat Kwat artist Yakaduna (c. 1842–1901, also known as Tommy McRae, or Barnes), which, as art historian Mary Eagle notes, 'showed Aboriginal people in charge of events, their every action graceful and assured, by comparison with which the colonists and the Chinese were inferior, slightly comic types'.[27] Cleary and Yakaduna crossed paths in Corowa in 1897, when Yakaduna and the Fridays agreed to pose for a studio session with Cleary for a fee of £10. The shoot took place in Victoria (at Lake Moodemere, where Yakaduna had managed to establish an Aboriginal reserve at his home, on a traditional camping site). When Cleary reneged on the deal, Friday and Yakaduna sued him in Corowa's Small Debts Court. Cleary claimed that the models — including Yakaduna, a well-known teetotaller — were drunk, and that he had been unable to take the photographs he wished. Cleary also successfully argued that the New South Wales courts had no jurisdiction over activities in Victoria.[28]

Despite this setback, Yakaduna was a canny negotiator, successfully engaging in several legal proceedings during the 1890s.[29] His loss to Cleary pales by comparison with his plight in the larger colonial legal web: as the Victorian Government tightened its control over Kooris during the last decade of the nineteenth century, it adopted a program of assimilation that was designed to 'absorb' the Indigenous population. In 1890 regulations were gazetted that empowered the Board for the Protection of Aborigines to commit Aboriginal children to institutions without their parents' consent. Two of Yakaduna's children were taken in 1891, and to prevent the loss of their remaining two they moved across the Murray to Corowa in 1893. When they returned later that year, another of their children was taken. They went back to Corowa until 1897 but when they returned to Lake Moodemere their remaining child was seized.[30]

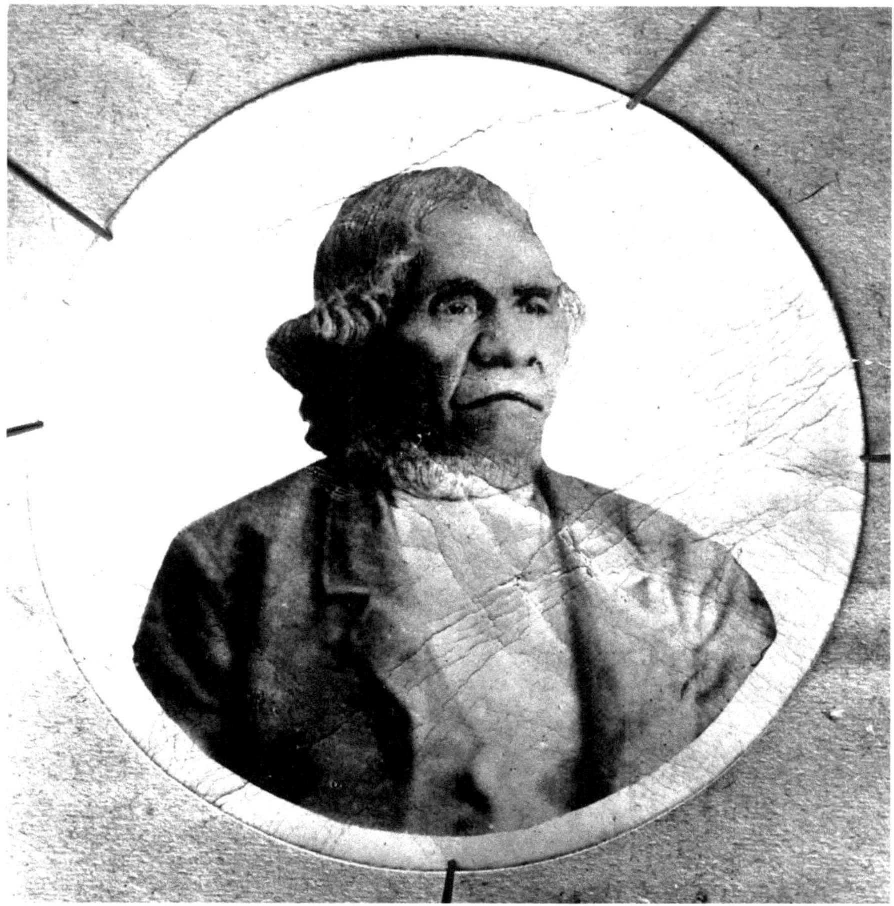

FIGURE 10: Photographer unknown. *Tommy McRae*. Northern Territory Library, Charles Barrett Collection PH0741/0009. Moral permission Sarah Morgan.

Yakaduna sought support from a white ally, Justice J Kilborn, who was unable to help. His daughter later wrote:

> I remember how broken-hearted Tommy was when his children were sent to Koondrook. He came to the house, and, with tears, begged my father to use his influence to allow him to keep the children. Father, of course, did his best, but they had to go, and I think Tommy was rather disappointed with my father in this matter, as he had always been able

> to provide all their other wants. My father was most indignant over this affair, and all the family's sympathies were with Tommy, as it seemed unnecessarily cruel.[31]

When we know this terrible story, we cannot look at Cleary's mocking images with indulgence or humour. The predominant settler view of Indigenous people as childlike and incapable underlay both visual tableaux and official policy.

COMMERCIAL MARKETS

During the last decades of the nineteenth century large collections of photographs of Aboriginal people from New South Wales were assembled by the Sydney studios of professional photographers Charles Kerry (1857–1928) and Henry King (1855–1923).[32] These prosperous enterprises acquired photographs from varied sources that were recycled over and over again in newspapers, postcards and magazines, framed by increasingly predictable and stereotypical narratives about the presumed disappearance of the race. Such representations clearly had commercial value, although, by now, many Indigenous people were living in 'fringe' settlements, and there was a considerable distance between black and white populations, which such imagery purported to fill. In 1898 Kerry wrote an article for the *Town and Country Journal*, titled 'New South Wales Aborigines: scenes at a recent corroborree', which began:

> The decadence of our aboriginal races and the absolute certainty of their utter extinction — as far as New South Wales is concerned — at an early date lends a mournful and pathetic interest to the movements of the few scattered remnants who are all that now remain to tell of the powerful tribes who ruled this continent until the advent of the pale face, a few generations back.[33]

To the modern reader, this sentence seems almost comical, knowing as we do of a growing Indigenous population over recent decades and the vital cultural presence in our own time. It musters as many stereotypes as possible and delivers them with what now seems an excessive, almost anxious, emphasis. However, in a broad sense such accounts were powerful in reassuring mainstream Australians of the unimportance of Indigenous people. Like Lindt's tableaux, the viewer was directed to see these varied assemblages spanning many places and cultural groups as 'mournful and pathetic', a nostalgia that supposedly marked the end of a living Indigenous presence.

Yet, while framed by assumptions of racial superiority, images could also express closer relationships founded on trust and mutuality. Photographs are 'excessive' in capturing more than their maker intends: as historian Carlo Ginzburg has argued, they provide 'clues' that transcend their initial purpose and allow us to observe for ourselves the worlds they contain.[34]

Kerry himself described how in 1898 he had visited Quambone, on Wailwan country between the Macquarie and Castlereagh Rivers of western New South Wales, to photograph a Bora ceremony. He explained that he owed this unique opportunity to the relationship of trust between the white owner Fitz W Hill and the Wailwan, a relationship that was founded on 'a long and systematic course of humane treatment', which had 'endeared him' to the Wailwan.[35] Their 'obligation' did not, however, include unfettered access, and Kerry was required to leave during specific sacred portions of the ceremony. These images were returned to descendants in the late 1990s by Joe Flick, a Yuwaalaraay man whose traditional country borders Wailwan land, and he described the power the images have to reassert culture and connections to country. Elders of the community are proud of their heritage and recognised the images as an enduring record.[36]

INTIMACY AND RECLAMATION

The interpretation of assemblages of Indigenous people may move ambivalently between their commercial or scientific uses and their meanings as records of familiar encounters between photographers and Indigenous people: sometimes these resulted from an ethnographic interest — often regarded as distancing and evolutionist, but also embodying curiosity and a liking and appreciation that cannot be dismissed. In this way, a remarkable series has survived of Paakantyi (or Barkindji) people of far western New South Wales, produced between 1865 and 1880 by Frederic Bonney at Momba Station on the Paroo River. Momba Station now forms part of the Paroo–Darling National Park, and the Momba people of the 1870s are direct ancestors of the Bates, Hunter, Quayle, Barlow and Dutton families, who still live in western New South Wales today. From the late 1820s, colonists began to push along the Darling River system, and the images show both traditional and pastoral activities, such as wool washing and pressing, and many named individuals. Despite the period's typically paternalistic views, Bonney wrote that the Paakantyi were 'naturally honest, truthful and kind-hearted. Their manner is remarkably courteous and to little children they are very kind. Affectionate and faithful to chosen companions, also showing exceeding respect to aged persons and willingly attending to their wants.'[37] Included within his detailed language records and ethnographic notes are many Aboriginal subjects' names, and sometimes stories and other information. Bonney was an unusually sympathetic observer, arguing that:

> White men are the intruders...[Aboriginal people] are open to good treatment everywhere and the behaviour of the blackfellow towards the white man very much depends upon the manner in which he is first approached. It is only natural that they should resent when their women and children are interfered with or themselves ill treated.[38]

Such relationships show us that respect and appreciation existed alongside paternalism. Although his photographs were made possible by the process of displacing Aboriginal people from their land, Bonney's sustained interest produced an important heritage resource for descendants today.[39]

Zena Cumpston is a young Barkindji woman who finds the Bonney photographs 'amazing'. She remembers:

> [I] was utterly entranced the first time I saw them...I knew that it was very likely that some of the people I was looking at are my ancestors and I immediately recognised them as my people — they lived long ago but look familiar to me now. I have only ever seen one old photograph of my Barkindji family — my great-grandmother Mary Eileen Payne. To see so many Barkindji people from so long ago was a joy. Most especially I have a great respect for Bonney because he did document so many names of people and their relationships to each other. So few photographers in this early period showed such respect and care for their subjects, it is obvious to me he felt genuine respect for our people. (Zena Cumpston, pers. comm., 31 August 2012)

As Zena notes, the social context that was recorded — identifying names, relationships and vocabulary — remains precious to descendants. She writes:

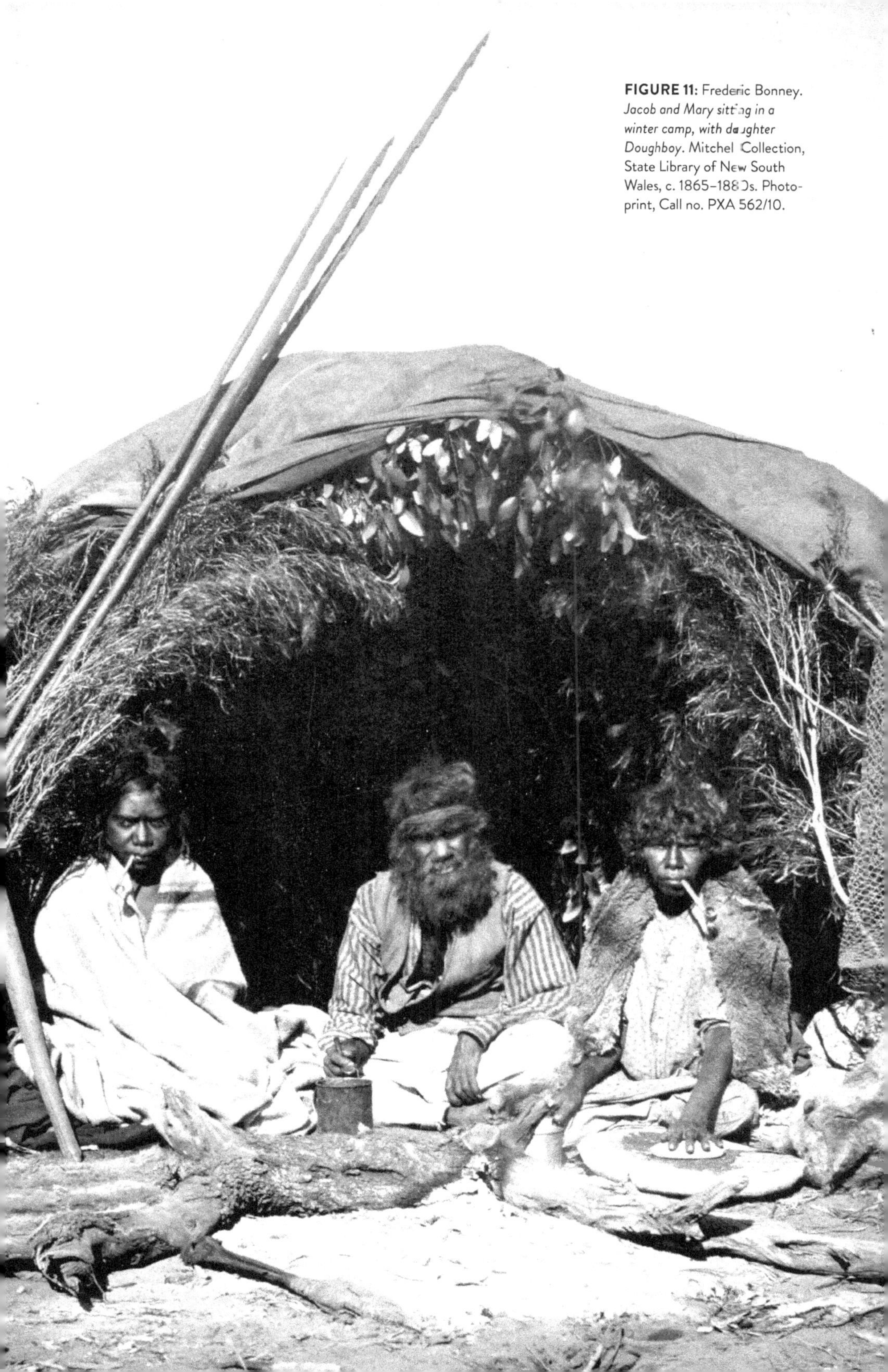

FIGURE 11: Frederic Bonney. *Jacob and Mary sitting in a winter camp, with daughter Doughboy*. Mitchell Collection, State Library of New South Wales, c. 1865–1880s. Photo-print, Call no. PXA 562/10.

> So many thousands of photos of Aboriginal people exist in archives and yet so very few of them give any indication of the subject or their country or how they relate to each other. These people live as ghosts — between worlds, as without their names we cannot let them rest in the past or our present, we cannot reassign their dignity by claiming them as ours. Worse still, so many of these photographs are 'set up' like those of Lindt in his studio, with stock-standard Aboriginal implements and cultural artifacts literally thrown in. Compare this with the amazing photo [Figure 11], the wealth of cultural information available here and I am sure *not* set up! A clean and crisp image showing an incredible array of beautifully made weapons and implements — spears, digging sticks, boomerangs, a grinding stone, a coolamon, a water bag made from roo — there is an emu leg in the fire, Mary is preparing damper in one hand, Jacob makes tea in a billy and their daughter Doughboy smokes a pipe, their mixture of European and traditional paraphernalia captures a moment in time, we can see the shifting frontier, as Aboriginal people today we can try to imagine what it was like for them not from the singular European voice, but this time with our own eyes. In terms of cultural information the Bonney photos are incredible because they show people painted up for ceremony, they show the mourning kopi, the beautifully made loin cloths and bags and sometimes even their manufacture. (Zena Cumpston, pers. comm., 31 August 2012)

Zena defines with great clarity how different kinds of colonial photographs may be understood by Indigenous descendants:

> Bonney's photographs don't give me a cold, sad feeling like almost all other early photos of Aboriginal people I have seen. Perhaps this is because I know these people to be my people, but perhaps much more than that — these people are not lost, they are not ghosts, or continually passively posing in a way that foregrounds unequal power relationships — we can place them, watch them living in their time, we can know who they are, we can claim them and with them a part of ourselves, our culture and survival. (Zena Cumpston, pers. comm., 31 August 2012)

ACKNOWLEDGMENTS

Thanks to Les Simon of the Batemans Bay Local Aboriginal Land Council; Elwyn Brown of the Tharawal Land Council, Picton; Sarah Morgan; Jude McBean of the Grafton Regional Art Gallery; and Ronald Briggs, State Library of New South Wales. Thanks to Jennifer Feller, *Australian story*, ABC, for supplying information.

NOTES

1. They were Darug language speakers. For discussion of the cultural and historical background to settlement, see especially V Attenbrow, *Sydney's Aboriginal past: investigating the archaeological and historical records*, UNSW Press, Sydney, 2002; and G Karskens, *The colony: a history of early Sydney*, Allen & Unwin, Sydney, 2009.
2. City of Sydney, 'Barani: Sydney's Aboriginal history', n.d., viewed 25 August 2012, <www.cityofsydney.nsw.gov.au/barani/themes/theme1.htm#p_1>.
3. L Barrett, 'The utilitarian photographer', *Scan: Journal of Media, Arts, Culture*, viewed 30 October 2013, <http://scan.net.au/scan/journal/display.php?journal_id=62>. C Black (ed.), *Papers and correspondence of William Stanley Jevons*, Royal Economic Society, London, 1972–81, pp. 364–5; HA Jevons (ed.), *Letters and journal of W. Stanley Jevons*, Online Library of Liberty, n.d. [Macmillan and Co., London, 1886], viewed 30 October 2013, <http://oll.libertyfund.org/?option=com_staticxt&staticfile=show.php%3Ftitle=2079&chapter=157872&layout=html&Itemid=27>.
4. F Cahir, 'Are you off to the diggings?', *La Trobe Journal*, 85, State Library of Victoria Foundation, Melbourne, 2010.
5. The town of Campbelltown was formally established by Governor Macquarie in 1820 and, until the mid-1820s, was the southern limit of European settlement. The Aboriginal people who lived in the area were referred to as the Cowpastures tribe by Europeans. C Liston, 'The Dharawal and Gandangara in colonial Campbelltown, New South Wales, 1788–1830', *Aboriginal History*, 12(1 & 2), 1988.
6. Lachlan Macquarie to Lord Bathurst, 4 April 1817, *Historical records of Australia*, series 1, vol. 9, p. 342.
7. The albums contain work by a number of photographers, including professionals such as Edwin Dalton and William Hetzer, who formed part of the Macarthurs' social circle and assisted the 'gentlemen amateurs' with their work. Previously attributed to William Macarthur (1800–82).
8. The Great Exhibition, Awards for New South Wales, from a special correspondent, New South Wales Court, 26 July 1862; *Empire*, Sydney, 12 September 1862, p. 4; 'The International Exhibition', *Sydney Morning Herald*, 10 June 1863, p. 5; Design & Art Australia Online, 'Edwin Dalton', 2011, viewed 25 November 2013, <www.daao.org.au/bio/edwin-dalton/#artist_biography>.
9. CW Thomson & J Murray, 'Report of the scientific results of the exploring voyage of H.M.S. Challenger during the years 1873–76', *Zoology*, 1, 1911.
10. JW Lindt, *The John William Lindt collection: Grafton Regional Gallery*, Grafton Regional Gallery, Grafton, NSW, 2005, p. 4. His 'Australian Aboriginal series' portrait albums have been examined for ways in which the ethnographic image was aestheticised for commercial distribution; C De Lorenzo, 'Ethnophotography: photographic images of Aboriginal Australians', PhD thesis, University of Sydney, 1993, pp. 115–24.
11. *Clarence and Richmond Examiner*, 18 March 1873, p. 3. Conrad Wagner also took photographs of Aboriginal people throughout the 1860s; S Jones, *J.W. Lindt, master photographer*,

Currey O'Neil Ross on behalf of Library Council of Victoria, South Yarra, 1985, p. 3; K Orchard, 'J.W. Lindt's Australian Aboriginals (1973–74)', *History of Photography*, 23(2):163–70, 1999.

12. In August 1873 the *Grafton and Richmond Examiner* announced the series, stating that it had been produced for the flamboyant Italian ornithologist and explorer Luigi Maria D'Albertis, who had travelled to Grafton during a convalescence; *Grafton and Richmond Examiner*, 12 August 1873.

13. 'They represent very faithfully aboriginals, male and female, of all ages, as the traveller finds them in the wilds, and not as if just prepared for portraiture. They are surrounded by back scenery. As a souvenir from Australia to friends in Europe Mr. Lindt's album will be acceptable to many'; 'Aboriginals: an interesting photographic album', *Sydney Morning Herald*, 24 November 1874, p. 5.

14. *Australian Town and Country Journal*, Sydney, 5 December 1874, p. 21.

15. 'Aboriginals: an interesting photographic album', *Sydney Morning Herald*, 24 November 1874, p. 5.

16. 'Photographs for the Philadelphia Exhibition', *Sydney Morning Herald*, 28 September 1875, p .5.

17. *Sydney Morning Herald*, 27 July 1876, p. 7.

18. At Amsterdam in 1883, Lindt's series 'attract[ed] the same attention they have done in all museums and exhibitions where shown'; it was reported that Her Majesty (the Queen of Netherlands) was 'much struck with the portraits' and that 'copies grace the collections of many continental museums. The next generation will probably also have to depend on Mr Lindt's happy thought while among us, to show them what the aboriginals of the Clarence were like'; *Clarence and Richmond Examiner and New England Advertiser*, Grafton, 30 June 1883, p. 3.

19. For example, the Ethnologisches Museum in Berlin.

20. Von Hügel to Australian Museum, 10 December 1877, Museum of Archaeology and Anthropology Archives, University of Cambridge.

21. Orchard, above n 11; Jones, above n 11.

22. 'The light of day', *Australian story*, ABC Television, documentary, 4 February 2013, viewed 30 October 2013, <www.abc.net.au/austory/specials/thelightofday/default.htm>.

23. Mary Ann Williams, Certified Copy of NSW Death Certificate No. D108716. Age at death was subtracted from 1935 to arrive at an approximate birth year of 1849.

24. The death certificate lists the names and ages of her three surviving children at the time of her death; Herbert, sixty-three; Leonard C, fifty-six; and Elizabeth, fifty. Taking the age of each child off the year 1935 gives us a birth year for the children. The death certificate also records that there were two females deceased.

25. Mary Ann Cowan and Leonard Williams, Certified Copy of Marriage Certificate M40527, 26 January 1877.

26. The NSW Birth, Deaths and Marriages online register records two daughters; Barbara, born 1877, and Edith, born 1881, to parents Mary Ann and Leonard Williams of Grafton.

27. M Eagle, 'Tommy McCrae', *Dictionary of Australian artists online*, 2011, viewed 30 October 2013, <www.daao.org.au/main/read/7374>. Also see A Sayers (ed.), *Aboriginal artists of the nineteenth century*, Oxford University Press, Melbourne, 1994. His clan was the Warra-euea, or Whroo, of the southernmost Wiradjuri nation, sometimes referred to collectively as the Waveroo. He was born at Albury, in New South Wales, but was to spend his life moving throughout the Murray River district, crossing the border for work and to escape control. As a young man he worked as a stockman on pastoral stations.

28. 'Tommy McRae...gave evidence that the arrangement was made near the Corowa post office. They were to get 10 pounds, and had been promised a cheque when the work was done. They had not received the money'; 'Corowa Small Debts Court — John Friday and Thomas Mcrae (two aboriginals) v. Thomas Cleary', *Corowa Free Press*, 4 June 1897, p. 3.

29. His father lived at Coranderrk during the 1860s and McCrae received various Aboriginal messengers from the Victorian and New South Wales sites of Indigenous settlement, including Tommy Smyth, Tommy 'Punch' Banfield, John

Friday and Neddy Wheeler. C Barrett, 'Tommy McCrae, Aboriginal artist', *Victoria Naturalist*, 52(5), 1935.

30. C Cooper & J Urry, 'Art, Aborigines and Chinese: a nineteenth century drawing by the Kwatkwat artist Tommy McRae', *Aboriginal History*, 5:81–8, 1981.
31. Mrs JA Foord of Rochester, daughter of R Kilborn, cited in C Barrett, above n 29.
32. The Tyrrell Collection at the Powerhouse Museum consists of 7903 glass-plate negatives from the studios of Kerry and King, who had two of Sydney's principal photographic studios in the late 1800s and early 1900s. The collection — an important record of city and country life — was bought by James R Tyrrell in 1929 and sold in 1980 to Australian Consolidated Press, which donated it to the Powerhouse Museum in 1985.
33. C Kerry, 'New South Wales Aborigines: scenes at a recent corroborree', *Town and Country Journal*, 3 December 1898, pp. 30–2.
34. C Ginzburg, 'Clues: roots of an evidential paradigm' in C Ginzburg, *Clues, myths, and the historical method*, John Hopkins University Press, Baltimore, 1992 (paperback edition), pp. 96–125.
35. Kerry, above n 33.
36. A Stephen, 'Reclaiming Wailwan culture' in S Kleinert & M Neale (eds), *Oxford companion to Aboriginal art and culture*, Oxford University Press, South Melbourne, 2005, pp. 251–4.
37. J Hope & R Lindsay, *The people of the Paroo River: Frederic Bonney's photographs*, Department of Environment, Climate Change and Water, Sydney, 2010, p. 83.
38. ibid.
39. ibid.

Chapter 4

PICTURE WHO WE ARE: REPRESENTATIONS OF IDENTITY AND THE APPROPRIATION OF PHOTOGRAPHS INTO A WIRADJURI ORAL HISTORY TRADITION

Lawrence Bamblett

[She] had photos of everybody, and them photos we'd just look at, she'd never leave you on your own to look at them, she'd be there watching making sure you didn't take any. And she had photos of everybody, that's how we knew who was who, you know right back to Grandfather Murray and Gran. Because I just used to ask, '[W]ho's that?', '[O]h that's so and so, yes it's your great-grandmother'. And I think that's probably why I like to keep my photos to show the family, it goes from generations to generations, and they keep them, but I hope they keep my photos that I've got, I've got about two big port loads, you know to show the kids and that. And when I had the camera be everlasting taking photos, kids get their photos, school photos, I keep all that. But I tell you what some of them come along and grab them, take them and then you look for the photos, wonder where this one got to, where that one got to, and you're searching for them and you find they're missing. That's why I think she used to make sure she was there when we were going through the photos. So like I say, it's just like a book, you go through and show them and tell them, the kids and they're good memories.

(Margaret Murray)[1]

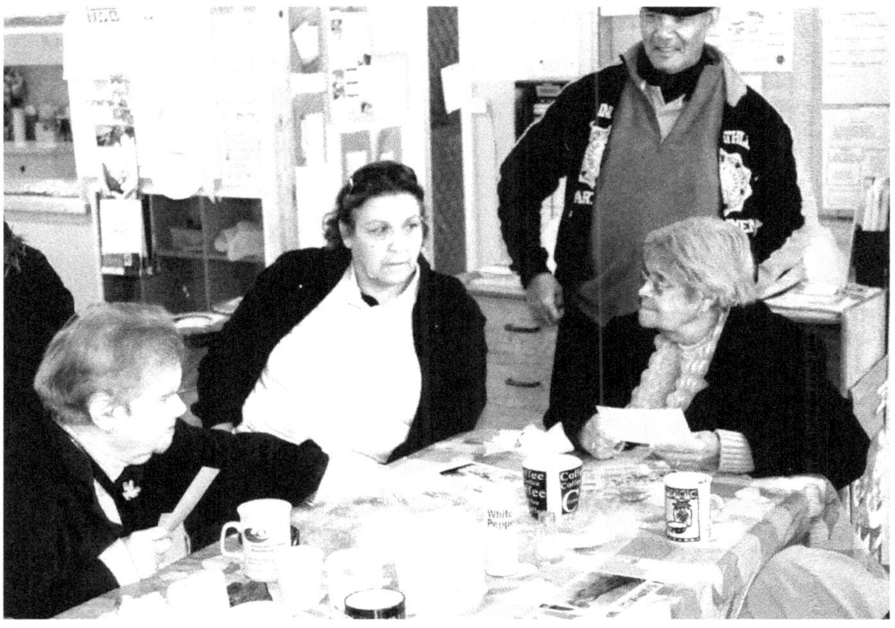

FIGURE 1: Margaret (left) and June Murray (right) reading photographs to relatives at Erambie, 2011.

INTRODUCTION

There is a joyous scene of storytelling that is a constant and reassuring part of everyday life for Erambie Wiradjuri. The scene involves a group of senior Wiradjuri women and men sitting at a kitchen table, poring over and reading photographs. They often spend entire days sharing stories over cups of tea and informal meals. They find much enjoyment in group storytelling, and delight in back and forth banter and the reaffirming discovery of memories of the past. Interested young people are welcomed into the group to share the warmth and humour, and to observe and participate as the history of a whole community is told. Interest in community history and photographs grows out of these happy times in the company of gifted storytellers. Good memories are created as old memories are shared across generations. By returning to, and at times recreating storytelling, we are able to reflect on the ways that Erambie Wiradjuri have incorporated photographs into the oral history tradition of the community.[2]

APPROPRIATING REPRESENTATIONS

The ancient Wiradjuri words for 'teacher' (*muyulung*) and 'story' (*giilang*) are no longer in everyday use at Erambie. However, these words falling into disuse does not mean that the role of teacher/storyteller does not persist in contemporary Wiradjuri life. Erambie people love nothing more than taking time to sit and yarn. A few years ago I was walking the streets at Erambie when I noticed that every home had a lounge suite or table and chairs in the front yard. In the evening people filled the chairs and lounges and it seemed like everyone in the community was having a yarn with someone. At my mother's house a group of women were talking about their memories of childhood. An open tin of photographs sat in the middle of the table and the women looked through them as they spoke. June Murray (Figure 2) explains their use of photographs as something that was appropriated into what they were doing:

> Photos fitted in there. We've done a lot of storytelling with our photos. If you can look at photos, that seems to bring back those memories. To me it brings my memories back more brighter in what happened. It does certainly prompt it...When you lose them, you lose a lot of your memories.

The use of photographs in storytelling among Erambie women has developed over time. Macdonald writes that Wiradjuri women have incorporated photographs into their storytelling for more than a century. She adds that Wiradjuri people altered their ideas and rituals about death and grief in order to include them.[3] In the quote that opens this chapter, Margaret refers to photographs being used by 'generations to generations'. She remembers seeing older people with photographs, but can only say earlier generations 'must have' used them in storytelling because she remembers being introduced to older people through photographs. June adds that 'They all had their own photos, especially the real old ones and a lot of those we lost down the track.' June recalls photographs being special to her parents because it was 'their family they were collecting' on their walls and in reused biscuit tins. Even though photograph collections started at the very least with her grandparents' generation (born during the 1870s), June considers the use of photographs in storytelling to be something that was developed more by her generation.

Why do Margaret, June and their peers invest in photographs to the point that Margaret estimates that her 'port loads' of photographs number in the

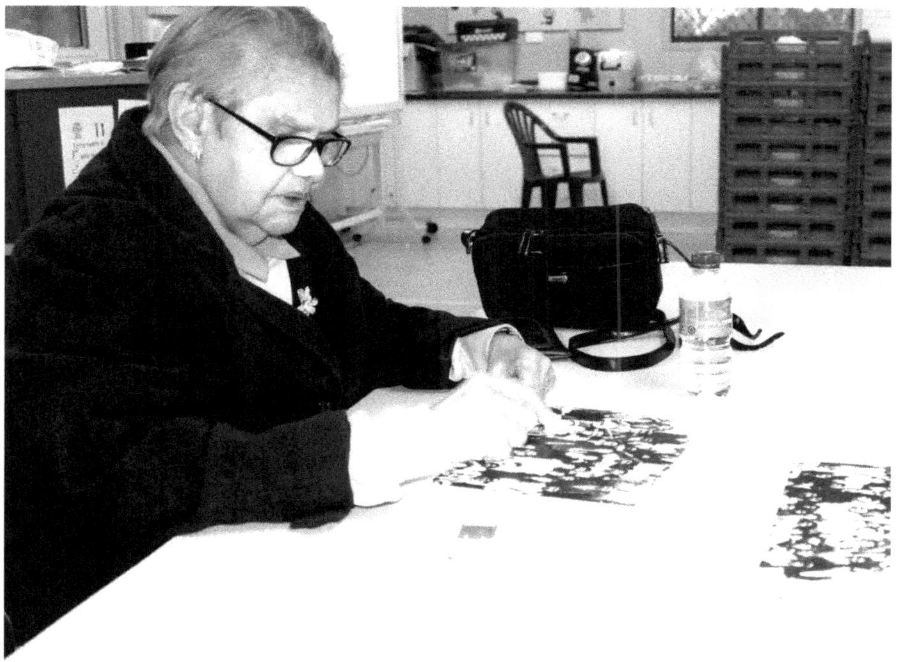

FIGURE 2: Margaret Murray incorporating photographs into her storytelling.

thousands? Perhaps because photographs did become more accessible — Margaret mentions the availability of Box Brownie cameras as one of the reasons collections grew. As collections became established, they started to be used to further individual, family and group interests. My observations and interviews confirm Macdonald's assertion that snapshots became a source of capital in social relationships for Wiradjuri women. Among other uses, photographs help construct portraits of families, add truth to lineage and provide access to people who are no longer there.[4] They also add to the identity of the collector by making connections to people and places. Margaret is respectfully referred to by her peers as a walking encyclopaedia due to her large collection of photographs and her knowledge of community history. My interest here is with the aspect of social relationships that deal with representations of identity — I am interested in the ways that photographs of people from Erambie are read and interpreted in the construction of Wiradjuri identities.

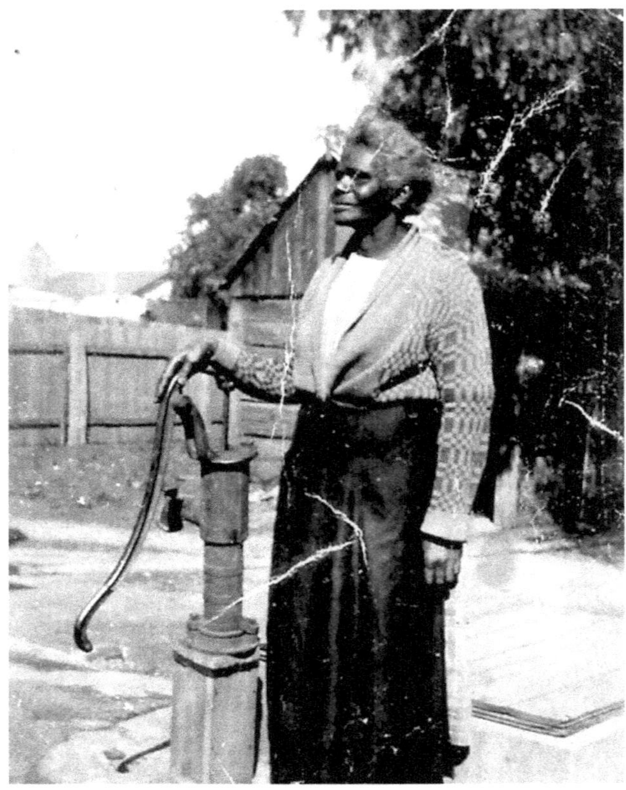

FIGURE 3: Erambie matriarch Jane Murray.

MEANING AND IDENTITY

There is an important photograph of Jane Murray that was probably taken during the 1920s, at the beginning of the 'mission era' at Erambie (Figure 3). It was taken in the yard of the doctor's office where she worked. It is the best quality of the few remaining photos of the community matriarch. Erambie storytellers make use of this photograph — which they say is an excellent likeness of the dignified and much-loved leader — to tell stories about a lot of topics. Dozens of narratives are read from it, but they draw mainly upon her likeness whenever they engage with a wider discourse about race.

In 1999 I witnessed a discussion of this photograph that left me determined to prove that Jane Murray was Koori. A group of Erambie elders was seated around a table talking and shuffling through a photograph collection. The most senior woman in the group held up a copy of this photograph and said that 'she was a wonderful woman', and 'she brought me into the world under a tree on the mission'. The next thing she said remains in my mind as clear today as when I heard it. She said, 'You know, she was a "negress"'. Another woman asked 'What makes you say that?' The reply was that it was the way she dressed, her tightly-curled hair and her singing voice that proved she was a 'negro'. The discussion moved on when no genealogical evidence could be recalled to settle the matter. The idea that one of the women held up by many to be representative of a group of cherished Wiradjuri women was not in fact Koori did not sit right with me, and I have been searching this photograph, and others, attempting to read genetic features for the truth about Jane Murray's lineage ever since.

Two primary readings of this Jane Murray photograph have emerged since that day. First, Murray's granddaughters June and Margaret read the photograph in ways that reinforce their family's special position of leadership within the Erambie Wiradjuri community. June says that the photograph accurately depicts the 'dignified' and 'proud' woman that she knew: 'She used to tell me, "stand straight and hold your head in the air". That woman has always been the same, head in the air, and that's the sort of person she was.' Using this photograph, June tells a story of a universally respected leader. Margaret reiterates June's (and other community members') assessment and adds that a doctor in Cowra held their grandmother in great esteem, and even boasted about her ability to treat ailments and birth children. The doctor, Margaret says, told people, 'If Janey don't know, then you come to me'.

The second common way I have seen this photograph read is in response to representations of Koori identity. The women who briefly debated Murray's background in 1999 also mentioned a 1934 *Cowra Free Press* article that reported remarks made about Kooris by the white mission manager. The manager reportedly told the Cowra Teachers Association that 'We people of today know little of the better class of black, and judge the race upon the class we do know.' He went on to describe 'Aborigines' as a 'child race', which was rapidly heading towards extinction, before concluding that they should be treated as children. Some of the group recommended caution at labelling Jane Murray anything but Koori. They said that claiming that this capable senior woman was not Koori might be seen by some to support the ideas expressed by the manager.

No one still living can say for certain whether Jane Murray was Koori. That is not to say that there are not strong opinions either way. June says that her older cousins claimed her grandmother was a 'negro'. However, when another relative made the same claim to one of her peers (and used this photograph as evidence), it was dismissed as 'nonsense'. After reading a 1939 inspector's report to the Aborigines Welfare Board that claimed strong 'negro blood' in the community, even outweighing the Koori blood in many cases, Margaret wondered whether the claim was an attempt to discredit and undermine the authority of the community leaders.

It is frustrating that I have not found a record of Murray speaking directly about her racial background. However, there are two newspaper articles that tell us how she was described (and she would have been aware of these descriptions) in the public discourse on race. During a 1920 appearance as a witness in a court case she was described as 'an aboriginal' while a young man from Erambie was described as a half caste.[5] Cowra newspapers at the time reported the detail court officials went to in order to establish an Aborigine's exact caste. In 1926 a magistrate is quoted in the *Cowra Free Press* defining the term 'Aborigine': 'The word "Aborigine" under the Act means any full-blooded or half-caste aboriginal native of NSW.'[6] This indicates that in 1926, at least, Jane Murray was legally considered to be Aboriginal (she would have to be at least a half-caste to be called Aboriginal in a courtroom). A second *Cowra Free Press* article in 1926 reported on a controversial move to expel the Murray family from Erambie.[7] This second article offers further clues to Murray's background. At a public meeting held to challenge the expulsions, an inspector from the Aborigines Welfare Board read out the mission manager's duties. They included a clause to 'discourage the presence of further half-castes on the mission'. The inspector also announced that Jane Murray did not accept rations even though she was entitled to receive them. Jane Murray is quoted as excitedly reacting to the threat to expel her family from Erambie by saying, 'Why don't you put off the half-castes and quarter-castes? We are the original owners.' Murray appears to be saying that she is more Koori than a 'half or lesser caste' person. That her response about caste was not questioned during this heated confrontation by the government officials who recorded the 'caste' of a person as a matter of course, along with her eligibility to receive rations, suggests to me that she defined herself as Aboriginal.

Further evidence that Jane Murray identified as Aboriginal can be found in another newspaper report about her family. Her well-known boxing son Doolan was described in the *Cowra Free Press* as 'a true son of Australia'.[8] When Jane Murray passed away in 1937, the *Lachlan Leader* obituary classified her as 'one of the oldest aboriginal residents of Erambie'.[9] Also, her maiden name was Morey and her mother's maiden name was Lane — there are Moreys and Lanes buried in the Koori cemetery at Brungle Aboriginal Station, where her family had lived. Historian Peter Read has published oral history testimonies from Erambie residents who knew Jane Murray, which give still further clues. Read found that Murray was one of a group of strict senior women who refused to speak Wiradjuri outside their own peer group. Her oldest son, Frank Broughton, is also quoted in Read: 'My mother could speak it [Wiradjuri].'[10]

All of the above evidence does not dismiss June's or Margaret's long-held belief that their grandmother was a 'negro' who found a home within the Wiradjuri community.[11] After discussing evidence to the contrary, June remained adamant in her belief: 'I still think she was not an Aboriginal. That's what I think. Her features, everything was different. You know by looking at her and the way she was dressed.' Looking at the photograph, June compares Jane to her maternal grandmother:

> She was quite different to Granny Dolly [who] to me was the full-blood Aboriginal woman. Granny Dolly looked more Aboriginal and tribal. Between the two grannies, one was different to the other in that way. And, one looked real Aboriginal and of course she spoke the language. I've never seen Granny Murray speak any [Wiradjuri] language. It was him [Harry Murray] and Granny Dolly.

After further reflection June illustrates the uncertainty associated with her grandmother's background when she adds:

> But I wonder you know, I'm still chasing to find out who she was. Whether her father was African or something. We've got her features, see it in Dad [Doolan Murray]. Some said she was and some said she wasn't. So, it might have been just talk. But, we looked at the way she was. It's still the big question. I've just got to know more about her.

Given the attention to detail about caste and race in government documents and even Cowra's newspapers at that time, it is unlikely that Jane Murray would repeatedly be mistakenly described as Aboriginal. It makes sense, then, to say that Jane Murray was at least part Koori. However, the search raised an important question about why people are concerned with this woman's racial background. British cultural theorist Stuart Hall describes why classification of this type is important to people:

> Classification is a very generative thing...It is not just that you have blacks and whites, but of course one group of those people have a much more positive value than the other group...[anthropologist] Mary Douglas describes this in terms of what she calls 'matter out of place'...You know exactly where you are, you know who are the inferiors and who the superiors are and how each has a rank.[12]

Some of the narratives of this photograph classify and re-classify Jane Murray's identity in relation to ideas about race. These narratives undoubtedly responded to other representations. So, one reason June and Margaret talked about the way that their grandmother carried herself was to respond to a discourse of deficit where the racial identity of Kooris is assumed to be inferior. The readings of photographs came after decades of stories told to counter negative representations of Kooris.

BANKING IDENTITIES

Wiradjuri storytellers paint pictures of wonderful community crafted through impressive leadership. One example of this is a photograph Margaret owns of her parents inside their humpy in the Frog's Hollow Wiradjuri community (Figure 4). It was taken in 1960 by a white newspaper photographer who Margaret says wanted to write a story about Koori people. She chose the photograph from the thousands in her collection to use as she told me a seemingly well-worn story (although it is the first time I have seen this photograph and heard of this particular event) about how her father represented the Wiradjuri community. The photograph, and the story Margaret tells about how it came to be, communicate a range of ideas about Aboriginal people.[13] The reading of this photograph is an excellent example of a positive everyday story, told and retold within the Koori community and strategically shared with outsiders.

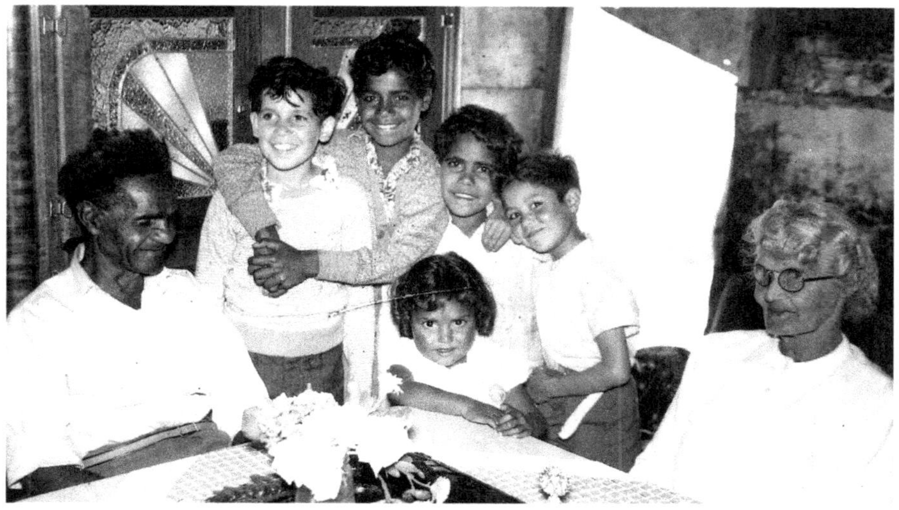

FIGURE 4: Herbert 'Doolan' and Ethel Murray with grandchildren at their Frog's Hollow home.

Wiradjuri storytellers bank positive images of individual and group identities partly to balance the steady flow of negative representations. African-American teacher bell hooks defines 'banking' as a method of education where the students are 'memorising information and regurgitating it' as 'knowledge that could be deposited, stored and used at a later date'.[14] hooks sees little value in this method. In contrast, Wiradjuri storytellers place great value on banking knowledge as a culturally responsible way to teach. Again, this is probably in part a reaction to representations that assume Kooris have 'lost their traditions and "failed" to become the citizens expected of them'.[15]

Both Margaret and June told a story about a community, and a leader, who understood that a photograph can produce an important representation. Participating in the making of this photograph indicated 'a sophisticated awareness of white discourse' within the community.[16] Margaret reads the photograph in this way:

> He said, 'It's for a good cause', that's when they were fighting for the Three Way [a yet-to-be-built Wiradjuri community in Griffith, New South Wales] homes. 'They can come into my home,' he said. 'It's clean, they can take photos and just show the white man how we're living,' but they were humpies, built out of tin, kerosene tins packed together.

This is Margaret's photograph. She was present when it was taken. Therefore, it was her story to tell. June supports Margaret's story and adds her own reflections:

> You wouldn't think they're coming from a humpy. To me, when I look at that picture I feel saddened that my mother never had the privilege to live in a house. Dad said, 'You can come and look in here if you're doing something good for the community.' Invited him [a local newspaper photographer] into the house and they were surprised to walk in to see how nice and clean the little humpy was. There were flowers and a tablecloth on the table. So they showed they were clean-living people, even though they lived in humpies.

Both ladies add further to their carefully crafted family portrait with personal observations of their father. Margaret (accurately, I am told) credits her father with social and material improvements at Frog's Hollow: 'This old man must have had a good education. He used to do all the writing [letters to government agencies] when people asked for help.' To Margaret, her father represented a typical Murray man, because they were 'always doing things to help their people'. June points to parts of the photograph as she adds:

> Again he's fighting for his people. They built the houses for them then. Looks as though he was starting to age there. But he was still helping his people. They leaned on him. He looked proud to me. That's how I remembered him there.

My reading of the photograph, and its accompanying narratives, was primarily concerned with finding a truth of lineage. I had optimistically hoped that a close reading of this photograph of Doolan would prove the Koori identity of his mother. For me, the image of one of my heroes as an older man was confronting, as well as comforting.[17] As a young athlete Doolan looked like the other Wiradjuri men from Erambie. Here, he did not look as Koori as he had then. Seeing him as an older man, living away from Erambie, was also an unwelcome reminder of what our community lost due to his absence. On the other hand, it was comforting to see the humble family man from the stories I had memorised. This photograph was made to tell something about Wiradjuri people. It neither proves nor disproves racial identities. It does, however, make finding proof that the Murray family exemplify Wiradjuri excellence even more important, because it shows that our elders recognised the importance of representations of race.

WIRADJURI EXCELLENCE

While I found some comfort in the ideas revealed about Kooris in the image of Doolan Murray in his humpy, the 'mythical sense of knowing' the man in the photograph was equally important.[18] The next photograph Margaret shared with me (Figure 5) caused some anxiety because it challenged a basic assumption — something I thought I knew about him. Margaret tells me that this man was her father, and I see an elderly man who I do not recognise. Doolan had left Erambie when my mother was a young girl, and he passed away when I was a baby. I knew him through storytelling — a few photographs of him as a young athlete, and my own newspaper and document-based research. The image of a man whose sporting prowess, leadership abilities and collectivist view of life (which he focused on community building) represented a prominent and powerful image of what it means to be a good Wiradjuri does not match the man in this photograph. This man looked like an African-American sharecropper from an Ernest Gaines novel. June sometimes jokingly likens her younger brother (Doolan's son) to the 'Chicken George' character from the television series based on Alex Haley's novel *Roots*. The man in this photograph would not look out of place sitting proudly and defiantly on the porch of a plantation shack in Gaines' *A gathering of old men*. Looking at this man, I wondered what my relationship with him would be if he did not physically represent a Wiradjuri hero. The value of this photograph, as Macdonald suggests below, is uncertain because it can be read as not clearly connecting a community hero to a Wiradjuri identity.

> Through the photos, one gains access to the person who is no longer here. Photos have taken on the role of linking the living and the dead in ways that were once mediated through myth...Photos are the material evidence of connectedness to what is now 'past'. The more photos connect, the more they are valued.[19]

Other Kooris say Doolan looks Aboriginal. Immediately this photograph becomes more valued. Is it the emotion added through narrative that changes what I see? The answer seems to be that it does. It is certain that the narrative of Jane Murray's image affects the ways this photograph of her son Doolan is read. Equally important to the way emotion affects a reading is the fact that we at Erambie are brought up to believe Doolan Murray was one exceptional example of the value of Wiradjuri traditions and values. His image may be our most important representation because he was Cowra's first sporting idol. Other men from Erambie are remembered as examples of what is good about the community, but none has the broader local profile of the feted boxer. We are connected to him, and he to our Wiradjuri forebears, through the continuity of the traditions and values we are told he represents. This is consistent with Lear's assessment of Crow child-rearing practices:

> Children were brought up in ways meant to instill the excellences of character as understood by the Crow. These traditions may have differed on particular virtues — or excellences — but they agreed that the virtuous person is one who has the capacity of character and body that enable him or her to lead an excellent and happy life.[20]

Our community is connected to the past through images and representations of men like Doolan Murray. Therefore, any questioning of Doolan's Wiradjuri identity may weaken the community's connectedness to past Wiradjuri identities.

The clothing that Doolan Murray wears in this picture contributes to how I see him. He looks African-American to me partly because of the way he is dressed. Another photograph of his younger brother seated beneath a gum-leaf shelter, his body painted as a tribal man and a boomerang in hand for a 1950 parade float, can be used to demonstrate this point. Doolan's younger brother does not look remotely African in appearance. Countless times storytellers have produced photographs of Erambie men dressed smartly as evidence of their character. They use these photographs, and the dress sense of the men, as an example of Wiradjuri excellence. Here, the same focus on clothing raises questions about Doolan's identity. I know him totally based on what I am told.

Photographs draw us into relationships with the Erambie elders who we idolise.[21] They draw me into a relationship with the subject and the narrator.[22] Photographs link generations, as Margaret has noted, and they are used to teach values. Storytellers teach about values using biography. Values are taught to younger people by telling stories about how cherished elders responded to events and issues. For example, when Margaret explains why she was 'very proud' to nominate this photograph of her father to be enlarged and displayed in his honour at a new Griffith Koori medical centre building, she adds a reading of the image:

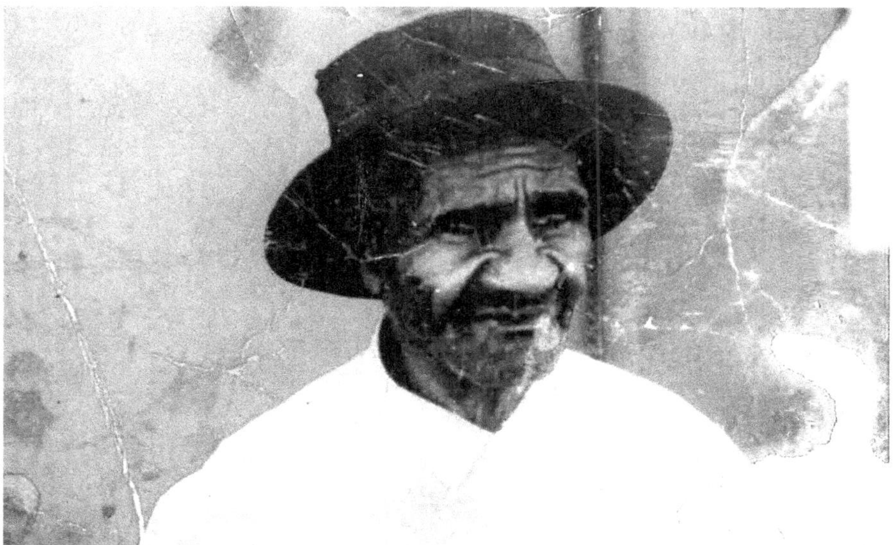

FIGURE 5: Herbert 'Doolan' Murray.

> [T]he kind of man he was, his handshake was his word. He always had a suit on, hat on, he'd tip his hat to the ladies, talk to the babies. Down in Griffith, they all used to know him. Mister Murray, there he goes. That's from this old feller [pointing to her father's picture].

June uses the photograph to explain why her father was being recognised close to four decades after his death:

> They should recognise him. He did a lot for the people down there. Even in his old age he was still helping them out. He deserves to have something there...When he died there was no money for his funeral, to bury him. When he [Doolan] paid for his own funeral, it was by the shake of a hand you know, they trusted one another. Him and the undertaker, no receipts or anything were given out and when he [the undertaker] died they couldn't find receipts. They said Doolan had come down all the time and anyone passed away in the Three Ways or anyone [Kooris] down here, he'd come and help them and made arrangements to get them buried. The money went. So, that's how good he was and he never had nothing to bury himself in the finish.

This family snapshot of Doolan will be used to make a public representation of the achievements and character of a Wiradjuri leader. It will add the context of time and history to contemporary advancements by recognising the efforts of past leaders. Could another way of reading this photograph involve the attribution of 'negro' blood, which would for some people amount to evidence denying the existence of such excellence within the Koori community? Historically, advancements and positive achievements within the Erambie community were often explained by some as the result of efforts by white authorities. Later, the alleged presence of 'negro' blood was also used for this same purpose. Advancements and achievements at Erambie were not viewed by authorities as evidence of Wiradjuri excellence.

A *BIDJA*

In contrast, there is another oral history told where Wiradjuri elders developed a strong community in spite of outsiders. This 1920s photograph of Erambie patriarch Harry Murray (Figure 6) is as important to the community as the one taken of his wife, Jane, around the same time.[23] It is distributed among community members as a treasured reminder of Murray's achievements on behalf of Wiradjuri people. By reflecting on the ways that this photograph has been used by Murray, and drawing upon analysis of parallel stories of cultural transition, we can gain a greater understanding of what he was hoping to achieve by sitting for this portrait. This admittedly speculative analysis, focused as it is on narration of the image, considers what the portrait of a Wiradjuri *bidja* (leader) means to the Erambie community close to a century after it was taken.

At the time this photograph was taken, the fifty-year-old Harry Murray had been an unchallenged leader at Erambie for more than twenty years. Read quoted Erambie residents' summaries of Harry Murray's position as leader. One resident told Read, 'Everyone seemed to look to the Murrays...they were the first people to go to.'[24] Another resident said, 'The people would go and tell Mr Murray, and he'd tell Mr Constable [the first manager of Erambie Station]. He'd tell him, he wouldn't hesitate. He never swore, you know. He said, "You can't stand over my people".' Murray's leadership was seriously challenged in 1924 when a government manager was appointed and the reserve became a station. Life on a managed station threw up challenges for the leader of the relatively free community. Erambie had been an unmanaged reserve gazetted in 1890 until a government ultimatum to either

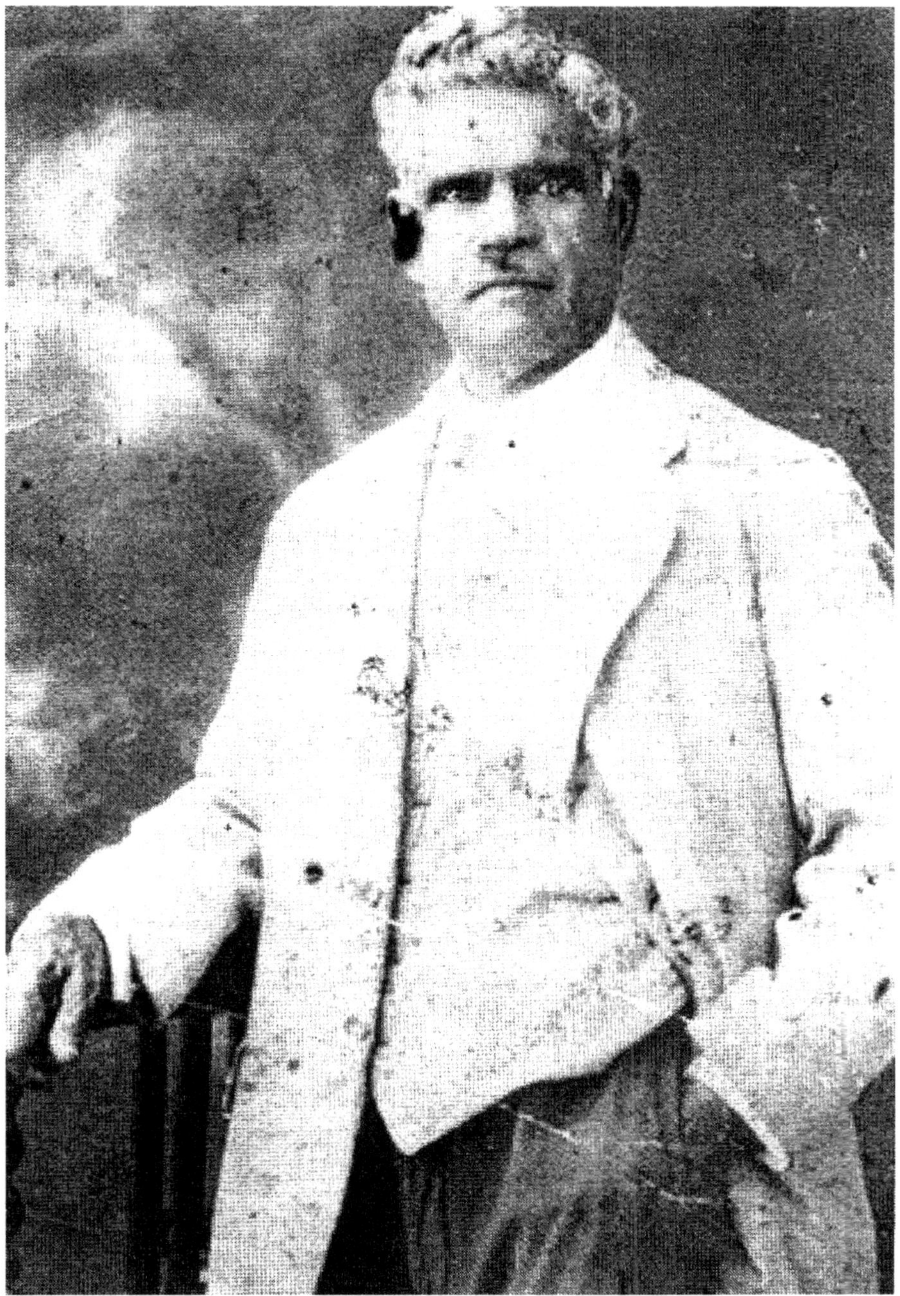

FIGURE 6: Harry Murray Senior.

accept the appointment of a manager or have the reserve relocated further away from the town. Melissa Lucashenko asks her readers to imagine life with the kind of restrictions and intrusions on life that people faced on the managed stations:

> To gain some very slight understanding of mission life, think about your present boss. Now let's say that this person will be boss, not just of your working hours, but of your entire life, for an indefinite period. It could be one year; it could be the next 20, until he or she is replaced, through a distant government decision, by another manager from an alien culture. Imagine that you need this person's permission to leave your suburb, to visit another town, to be out after dark, to operate an electrical device, to chop down or plant a tree in your garden, to change jobs, to marry, to move house. Imagine that this person can fire you or provide you with a cushy job, remove your kids if he or she wishes, banish you from your home, cut your hair, order you flogged, fine you or imprison you without trial if you try to abscond. This person also controls your bankbook, which you probably have never seen. An important underlying assumption is that this person automatically considers you his or her physical, intellectual and social inferior. There is no system of appeal should you disagree with his or her decisions; there is no requirement on him or her to do anything other than keep you alive. Such was mission life for Aborigines throughout most of the 20th century.[25]

On top of the type of intrusions Lucashenko describes, Murray faced the additional challenge of a government attempt to usurp his leadership. Imagine being a fifty-year-old grandfather, a respected and accomplished leader within a community, and having this type of control forced upon you.

Comparing the ways that other leaders dealt with the new way of life on managed reserves offers a way to understand how Murray responded to change. Within a few decades of each other, Comanche Chief Quanah Parker and Wiradjuri *bidja* Harry Murray posed for strikingly similar photographs. Both images are typical of portraits of prominent citizens made at that time. They pose against sparse backdrops in suits and hats (Murray's suit jacket and hat are white, his trousers dark; Parker's entire outfit is dark in colour). Murray and Parker wear the formal dress of white people in these photographs. However, Parker made a public commitment to 'taking the white man's road'.[26] Murray did not make this statement verbally. However, he and Parker both made visual statements towards a commitment to the white man's road by dressing in a way that the white man might understand as gentlemanly. This suggests that Murray understood the need to adjust the way he led. Moreover, the photographs suggest that both Murray and Parker constructed an image of their leadership using the new language of the photograph as a way of communicating and reinforcing their place to people outside the community. The two established leaders needed to show another group of people, using those people's language, that they were leaders.

Murray and Parker's paths to the white man's road were similar. Respective governments wanted to deny their core identities as warriors.[27] Both moved their people into government-controlled reserves in attempts to ensure survival. Harry Murray played a key role in having a school built at Erambie. He oversaw the running of the school, including making recommendations about the teachers who were employed at the school. He requested a Koori teacher and an evangelist from Cummeragunga be appointed at the Erambie school. He was buried in the Catholic cemetery at Cowra. Murray was also 'keen to effect' changes discussed with Cowra Council staff.[28]

Both men tried to manage how their identities were represented. Gwynne has described how Parker refused to recount his deeds as a warrior, who killed many, in an attempt to control how white people viewed him.[29] Murray once threatened to sue a mission manager for a libellous attack on his identity as a friendly, respectable and upstanding member of the community. Parker entered into the cattle industry, while Murray operated a sheep-droving business. Both saw their people line up to receive meagre rations as a replacement for discontinued ways of living. Parker joined the ration line, while Murray refused. Both leaders were confronted by white men who were greatly respected by their government employers and tasked to subdue them. On the reserves, both men were living in close proximity to other leaders. Whereas Parker was condemned as a sell out by his own people (rival leaders mainly, who were unable to match Parker's political skill, having positioned himself as a leader above others), Murray managed to retain support among Wiradjuri people living at Erambie.[30]

For all his commitment to engaging with European ways and accessing their services, Murray continued to speak the Wiradjuri language, despite it being banned on the station. He worked to build Erambie as a separate community, which accessed the mainstream on its own terms. As Margaret and June have noted, he stressed that Wiradjuri people and culture were equal to what the white man had to offer. June recalled that racial pride was a key lesson he passed on. Both leaders were at times enthusiastically cooperative or fiercely oppositional to change. This put them both at odds with government intentions to assimilate their people into white society.

Government imposition of station/reservation regimes on Wiradjuri and Comanche people was prefaced by a discourse of inferiority. Gwynne's account of how the United States government moved to end Comanche ways of living and confine them to a reservation demonstrates how government responded to representations of Comanche as savage and uncivilised.[31] Cowra newspapers had long represented Kooris as inferior to white people. The *Cowra Free Press* described a 'dying' and 'childlike race', and regularly headlined articles about 'coons', 'nigger trouble', 'darktown', 'abos and liquor' and a 'beastly Queenslander'. On 12 February 1924, the *Cowra Free Press* published a joke about the Koori caricature 'Jacky'.[32] The joke said that Jacky had been denied work by a white boss because there was not enough work for the white men already employed. The punch line was, 'Jacky said, "The little bit I'll do will not make a difference".' Just months prior to the 'Jacky' joke, the 10 July 1923 *Cowra Free Press* reported that Harry Murray had 'expressed great indignation that [a Koori man labelled by the newspaper as a 'filthy nigger'] had been described as a resident of Erambie Mission! He was a "stranger to all residents there" and had been "recently warned off the Goollagong camp".'[33] Harry Murray challenged the idea that Aboriginal people were inferior when he confronted newspaper representations that painted Kooris in a bad light.

Black feminist writer Audre Lorde writes that for people located 'outside the structures', the 'master's tools will never dismantle the master's house'; Lorde concedes that, while engaging with the master's tools will not bring about 'genuine change', it can 'allow us to temporarily beat him at his own game'.[34] I am suggesting here that Harry Murray posed for his portrait as part of a broad understanding of the importance of representation of his identity as a leader. He understood that Wiradjuri excellence paralleled what was considered excellence on the white man's road. The man that excelled among his own people also excelled, and was seen to excel, in white man's terms. He presented an individual image of himself as a man worthy of respect in ways that white people understood. This may have been at odds with Wiradjuri ways, where leadership was demonstrated according to collectivist values rather than individual promotion.

When the inevitable conflict occurred between Murray and the government manager, Murray used the individual image of a leader he had created to counter a generalised image of the uncivilised black man. He then appealed to the people of Cowra to support him as a man who deserved to be treated fairly. When the government officials and the mission manager tried to discredit Murray with accusations of bad character, they did not fit with the image people had of him, and were therefore not accepted.

The *Cowra Free Press* published three articles about the attempt by the manager to expel Harry Murray from Erambie. A Friday 28 May 1926 account of 'The Murray case' outlines how local white people supported Murray against the manager and the Board. The article, much of it a transcript of the public inquiry, suggests that Murray drew on his reputation within the wider Cowra community to out-manoeuver the manager and the Board by pitting his representation of his own identity against theirs. Murray, and his family, had been the subject of many complimentary stories in the *Cowra Free Press* over many years. This, coupled with business and personal relationships he had developed, meant the Board and the manager (who had lived in the town for only a couple of years) would be pitted against the prominent local citizen depicted in this photograph.

The article begins by restating that Murray had 'for many years enjoyed the reputation of being the "uncrowned king" of the local Aborigines'. An incident between Murray and the manager is then described, where Murray 'took strong exception' to the manager's treatment of two Koori men at Erambie. An argument followed. At this point, the article reports that a local health inspector, two local merchants and two business associates of Murray provided glowing accounts of him as 'honest', 'straightforward', 'trustworthy in every way' and 'clean living', a man of 'good character'. The Board representative countered that the manager was worthy of praise and that Erambie was the 'worst' reserve in New South Wales until he took control. Any positives that could be attributed to Erambie were 'as a result of the efforts of the Aborigines Protection Board officer'. He added that the Board was not seeking to have Murray 'humble his manhood in any way' but merely to 'behave' and 'conform to the rules'. At this point, it is reported that Murray's white supporters challenged the attack on Murray's character and the Board's decision to expel him. This drew accusations from the inspector that people would be surprised at 'what sort of man Hy. Murray is', and that the 'Murray you see in town, with his glib tongue, is vastly different to the Hy. Murray that comes back to the camp'.

Other insulting accusations were made against Murray. However, they were disregarded, as people trusted the Murray they saw in town — some had stated that they had known him for more than thirty years — and accused the manager of threatening to shoot Murray. Neither the Board representative nor the manager denied the threat had been made but suggested Murray had been 'treated leniently'. Murray won a compromise and the expulsion was not enforced. Ultimately, however, Murray's victory proved to be as temporary as Lorde suggests.[35] Even though he saw off a number of managers, the constant intrusions led Murray's sons to leave the mission. Margaret describes how her father finally left the managed station after his father's death to live on unmanaged reserves in Victoria and southern New South Wales.

> Well the manager, I remember, [we] was over working on the cherries, Dad had us over there, we were only kids. Old Fuller, he was the manager here then. We came home in the middle of the night and Dad went over to tell him we were home the next morning. Fuller said that Dad should have come over last night and reported. In the middle of the night! He was putting us kids down and making a fire. Well that was it. Dad said 'No. I'm leaving'. Just packed up and left.

This photograph of Harry Murray represents him accurately as a leader and prominent citizen of Cowra. I have suggested here that Murray used a portrait of himself to challenge representations of his Koori identity as inferior or 'childlike' and in need of control by government authorities. In addition, he used the photograph to continue individual, family and group narratives about his place within the Erambie community, as well as more generally in the wider community.

Margaret and June use this photograph of their grandfather to continue building their family portrait (Figure 7). Margaret suggests that the manager and the Board wanted her grandfather expelled because of the respect people had for him as a leader. She says that the photograph is a good representation of the type of man he was:

> He was always like that, he was always dressed. He was never a shabby old man. Dad was the same, he was always dressed, hat on, tip it to the ladies. He was one of the real old gentlemen because all his photos are the same. I've never seen him untidy or anything.

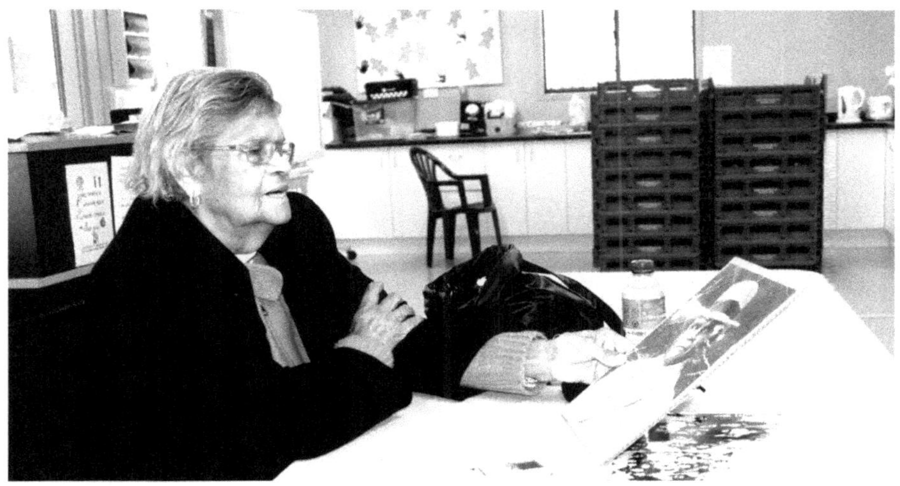

FIGURE 7: June Murray reading a photograph of her grandfather, Harry Murray, at Erambie, 2011.

Margaret reads this photograph as further proof of her family's place within the Erambie community:

> Grandfather was the boss of the mission, he never swore. I think he was very well respected because even the police would go straight into other houses. But him, No! That's the kind of man he was, they had respect for him. Today, everyone is at a distance. Everyone started moving away. You know, kids growing up somewhere else. But the mission there, like I said, very close.

June also built on her family portrait when she delivered the following welcome to country at a Friday 8 July 2011 National Aboriginal and Islander Day Observance Committee (NAIDOC) event:

> It is customary to acknowledge traditional custodians at an event like this one. My family, the Murrays, have always been connected to this country. We are the recognised custodians. Today, I would like to acknowledge all of our Wiradjuri ancestors with special mention of the contribution of my grandparents Harry and Jane Murray, who built the community we today call Erambie. They managed our people's transition into a modern world with pride and dignity. They represented all that is good about being

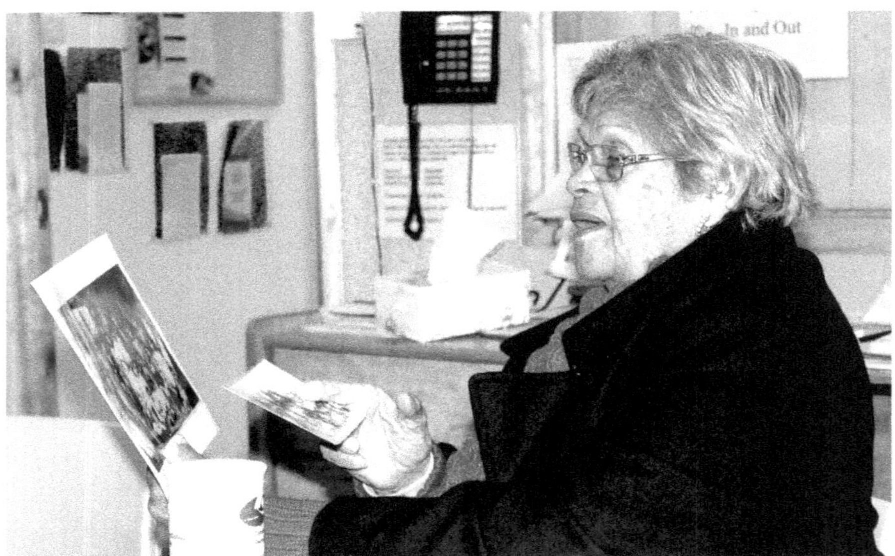

FIGURE 8: June Murray reading a 1937 Erambie community portrait, 2011.

> Wiradjuri people. They passed down Wiradjuri values and connection to this place through generations. They were open and welcoming leaders who demanded respect for tradition and place. In the spirit of my grandparents, I want to welcome you today to Wiradjuri country. We acknowledge today the contribution and values of our people of the past as we look toward the future.

Later that same day, June tells me that her grandfather showed strength and courage to lead the community through great changes:

> Tribal part, they were coming away from the tribal, so his father [Samuel Murray] must have been a great man too...Well he stopped them [the police] taking Mum back to the station she was working at. He told them when they came there to take her, she went there [to Harry Murray's house at Erambie] for shelter, and they wouldn't dare enter his house, so she stayed there.

June and Margaret have lived away from Erambie for decades. They left the mission with their father, Doolan, when they were still children. Still, Erambie remains home to them — they visit often — and they are considered community elders and storytellers. A measure of the respect still held for them and their family within the Erambie community is that June was invited to perform a welcome to country without drawing criticism from within the community. Anyone familiar with the internal politics of a Koori community will understand the significance of no one challenging June's right to deliver a welcome to country. This is in part due to the family portrait constructed through storytelling using photographs. As they both often say, photographs are proof not only of their connection to Erambie, but also of the special place their grandparents hold as leaders and representatives of Wiradjuri people.

CONCLUSION

What do photographs mean to Wiradjuri people today? Wiradjuri culture was not ended by colonisation. Of course, drastic changes occurred to everyday life and ways of living. But change does not equal ending. In some instances new technologies and ways of doing things were compatible with existing practices, and so were incorporated into a dynamic and continuing culture. Photographs are valued based on how well they link people to places and the past. The real value of photographs is that they connect people in the present. They tell us something about Wiradjuri people, even those that are not in the frame. Wiradjuri storytellers have appropriated photographs into what they do because they fit in to the joyful scene of people sharing stories. Relationships are built across generations and over piles of worn photographs. The storytelling scene acted out at the kitchen table covered in photographs repeats and continues the meaning and process of an ancient Wiradjuri oral history tradition. Within this tradition the uses of photographs are many and varied. This reflects the oral history tradition they have been incorporated into. Photographs trigger a number of narratives about representations of identity and place. These narratives are further complicated as they occur within a wider discourse about race. If the use of photographs by Wiradjuri storytellers can be summarised, it would be that they matter because representations matter. They fit in.

NOTES

1. Interview with Margaret Murray at Erambie, Friday 8 July 2011. There has been some very minor tidying up done to interview transcripts (quotes) to assist with clarity. Care has been taken not to alter meaning and both ladies interviewed have read and approved all changes that were made.
2. Two knowledgeable and gifted storytelling sisters, June and Margaret Murray, graciously agreed to share their photographs and participate in interviews. Together we chose four 'mission era' photographs of prominent Wiradjuri elders from one family (the Murrays) and they read them to me and reflected on their

value to the community. It is normal and proper for me to refer to Margaret and June as aunties because they are my mother's first cousins. However, it seemed to get in the way of the story to add 'Aunt' to each of the many references I make to them, so I decided to refer to them by their Christian names throughout the text.

3. G Macdonald, 'Photos in Wiradjuri biscuit tins: negotiating relatedness and validating colonial histories', *Oceania*, 73(4):225–42, 2003.
4. R Barthes (trans. by R Howard), *Camera lucida: reflections on photography*, Vintage Books, London, 1981.
5. 'Alleged stealing in company: youth charged', *Cowra Free Press,* 19 May 1920.
6. 'Aboriginal couple on holidays', *Cowra Free Press,* 21 May 1926.
7. 'The Murray case', *Cowra Free Press,* 28 May 1926.
8. 'From the Cootamundra Liberal', *Cowra Free Press*, 10 August 1921.
9. 'Obituary: Mrs Harry Murray', *Lachlan Leader*, 23 August 1937.
10. P Read, *Down there with me on the Cowra mission: an oral history of Erambie Aboriginal Reserve, New South Wales*, Pergamon Press, Sydney, 1984, p. 13.
11. P Rimas-Kabaila & Ed Radclyffe, *Survival legacies: stories from Aboriginal settlements of southeastern Australia*, Canprint, Canberra, 2011. Jane Murray's marriage certificate lists her birthplace as Cootamundra, New South Wales (within Wiradjuri country).
12. S Hall, *Race, the floating signifier*, Media Education Foundation, Northampton, 1997, p. 3.
13. J Lydon, *Eye contact: photographing Indigenous Australians*, Duke University Press, Durham, 2005.
14. b hooks, *Teaching to transgress: education as the practice of freedom*, Routledge, London, 1994, p. 5.
15. Macdonald, above n 3, p. 239.
16. Lydon, above n 13, p. 23.
17. Doolan Murray's sports career was a topic in my honours and doctoral theses. I have idolised him and other elders from Erambie since childhood. See L Bamblett, *Our stories are our survival*, Aboriginal Studies Press, Canberra, 2013.
18. D Porat, *The boy: a Holocaust story*, Melbourne University Press, Carlton, 2010, p. 218.
19. Macdonald, above n 3, p. 236.
20. J Lear, *Radical hope: ethics in the face of cultural devastation*, Harvard University Press, Cambridge, 2008, p. 63.
21. 'Elder' is used at Erambie as a term to define leadership and age. It is also used to describe people who have passed away.
22. Macdonald, above n 3.
23. The photograph of Harry Murray is undated, so the 1920s date I have used is based on estimating Murray's age by his appearance at the time it was taken. He looks as if he is in his fifties in the photograph, which would date the picture in the 1920s. This would date the photographs of Jane and Harry Murray I use in this chapter at the start of the 'mission era' at Cowra. Erambie regressed from a reserve to a government-run station in 1924. Margaret and June agreed with my estimates.
24. Read, above n 10, p. 14.
25. M Lucashenko, 'Who let the dogs out?', *Griffith Review*, 8(winter):133–46, 2005.
26. SC Gwynne, *Empire of the summer moon*, Scribner, New York, 2011, p. 285.
27. ibid., p. 259.
28. 'The Murray case', *Cowra Free Press*, 28 May 1926.
29. Gwynne, above n 26.
30. ibid.
31. ibid.
32. 'Jacky to boss', *Cowra Free Press*, 12 February 1924.
33. 'A serious offence', *Cowra Free Press,* 10 July 1923.
34. A Lorde, *Sister outsider: essays and speeches by Audre Lorde*, Crossing Press, Berkeley, CA, 2007, p. 112.
35. ibid.

VICTORIA

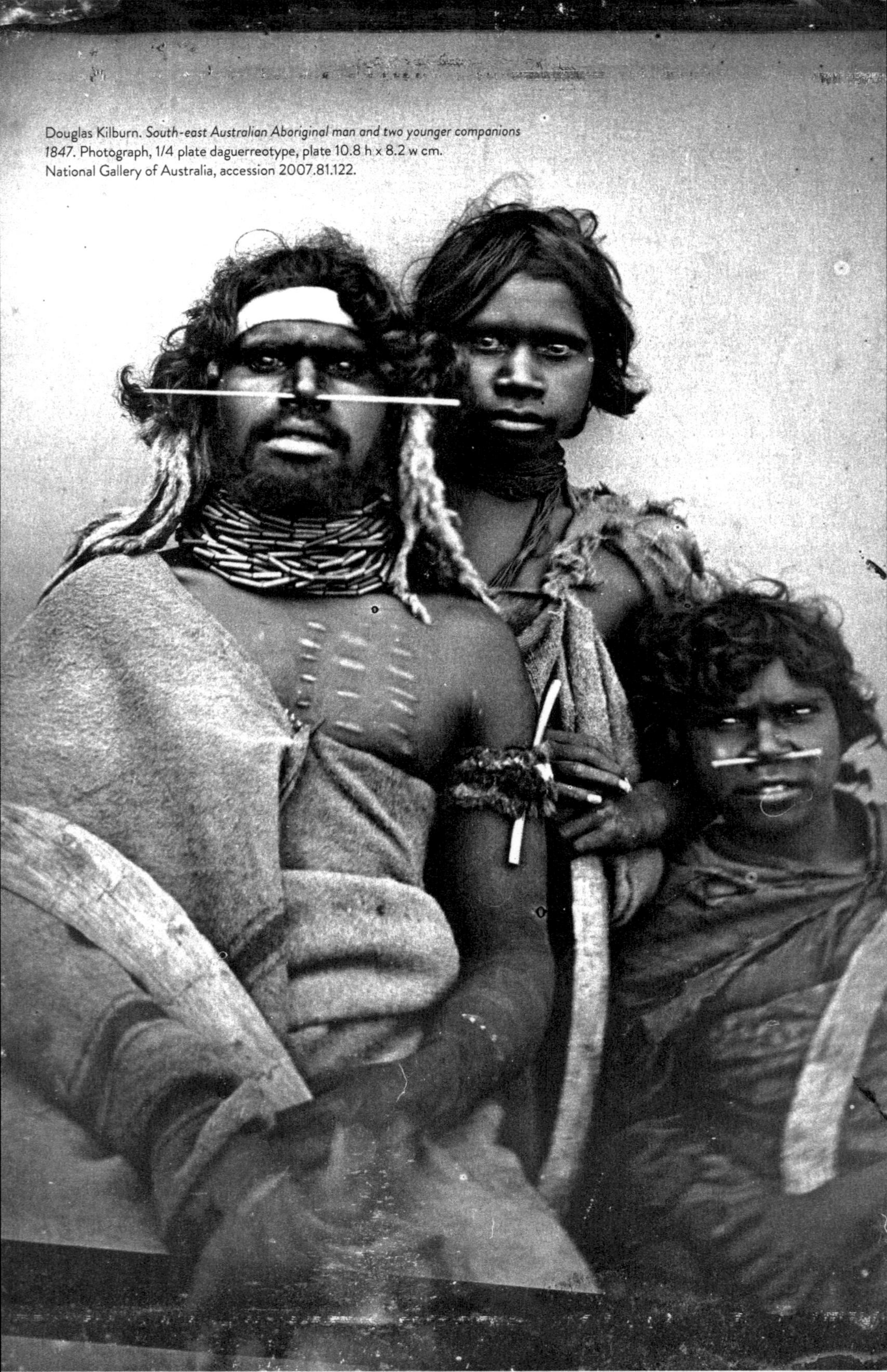

Douglas Kilburn. *South-east Australian Aboriginal man and two younger companions 1847*. Photograph, 1/4 plate daguerreotype, plate 10.8 h x 8.2 w cm. National Gallery of Australia, accession 2007.81.122.

Chapter 5

PHOTOGRAPHING KOORIS: PHOTOGRAPHY AND EXCHANGE IN VICTORIA

Jane Lydon

From their first encounters with photography, Kooris — the Indigenous people of Victoria — showed an active interest in the medium. They saw and engaged with photographs in the form of daguerreotypes within a decade of white settlement of the colony of Port Phillip — even before the first portraits of Aboriginal people were produced. In this chapter I examine historical interactions between photography and Indigenous people in the Port Phillip district — known from 1851 as Victoria — and the rich and vital meanings photographs have today. My guiding question has been 'How does photography express the process of cross-cultural exchange?'

Following sporadic attempts to establish settlements along the coast of Victoria, in 1835 Melbourne was founded by an entrepreneurial association of wealthy squatters led by John Batman. Over the following decade, an influx of pastoralists saw the astonishingly rapid invasion of the traditional country of the people of the Kulin Nations (Figure 1) — leading to violence, murder and rape. Over this decade, British humanitarians sought to soften this brutal struggle for the land, and the British Colonial Office appointed five 'Aboriginal Protectors'; by 1848, however, Governor Charles Joseph La Trobe concluded that the experiment had 'totally failed'. During the violent decades of the 1840s and 1850s, various local attempts were made to settle the Indigenous people in 'black villages', small farming communities where they would learn 'the arts of civilised life' and become Christians.[1]

In 1843 pastoralist and naturalist John Cotton took up the station Doogallook in the Goulburn River valley, on the traditional country of the Taungurong people.

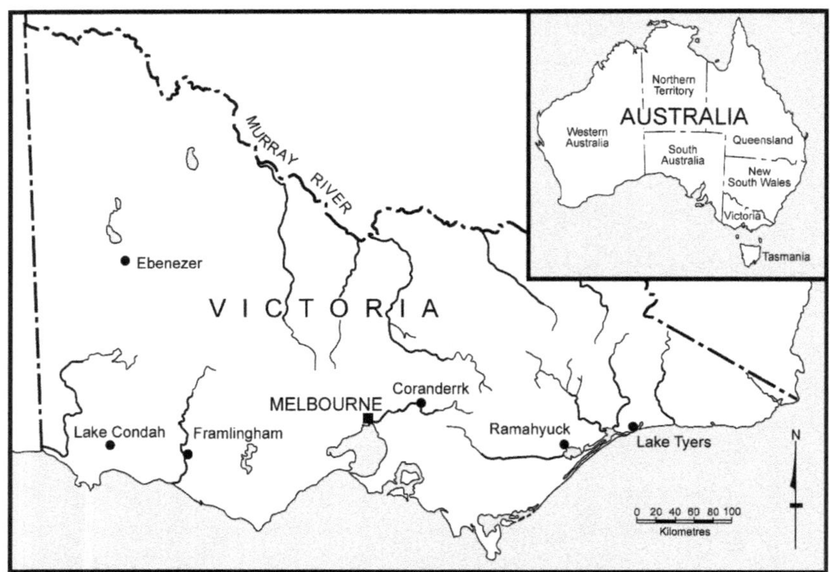

FIGURE 1: Map of Victoria, showing missions established around 1860.

Cotton wrote to his brother in England about his encounters with 'Mr William Hamilton', who visited his home and admired his family portraits in the form of daguerreotypes.[2] This was no doubt the leader of the Neenbullock clan, also known as Billy Hamilton, who had been jailed in 1843 after a confrontation with the local Assistant Protector, William Le Souef.[3] Cotton wrote to his sister-in-law:

> Your portrait and William's [his brother] ornament one side of our sitting-room, and they never fail to attract the attention of a half-civilised black known by the name of Mr Hamilton, who usually pays me a visit when he is anywhere in the neighbourhood, and, pointing to the pictures, says: 'That one your brother', then, turning to the other, 'Lubra belonging to your brother'. Mr Hamilton has some notion of drawing himself, and when he was here last, a few days back, he asked for paper and pencil, and drew several figures of blacks fighting, dancing, etc. Mr Hamilton speaks English remarkably well, and assumes the manner of a gentleman.[4]

Hamilton was interested in the images' ability to stand in for kin, to root the viewer in a world of family connections that demonstrated identity and relatedness — a use of the medium that continues to be important for Kooris into the present.

In 2010 Hamilton's great-great-granddaughter and Taungurong Elder Maxine Briggs wrote that 'Victorian Aboriginal people continue to search out the pieces of their shattered communities like some kind of emotionally charged jigsaw puzzle'; she explained that

> These revered ancestors who were captured in the collections of 19th century photographs are blood relatives, they are not distant relatives because they lived a hundred years or so ago, they live on in the photos and we are responsible for them just as we are for our living kin.[5]

For white settlers the medium was a way of recording new sights and peoples, and some were quick to grasp its commercial possibilities as a means of satisfying the curiosity of distant audiences. Cotton, himself, had ambitions — never realised — to photograph the Taungurong, and in August 1848 he commented, 'When the new plates arrive from England I hope to be able to take portraits of the blacks; they would be very interesting, I think, to you at home and might be a source of profit to myself.'[6] He was well aware of the work of Melbourne-based photographers such as George Goodman, who had arrived in Sydney to set up a studio in 1842 and visited Melbourne in 1845, in that year reporting a remarkable profit of £870. In December 1848 Cotton noted:

> Mr Kilburn is doing them well, I understand, at Melbourne. We have been taking some of the blacks this morning, but there is some defect or other in every plate. It is a very delicate operation, and requires much practice and nicety. If I can procure a guinea or two for each portrait I take of the blacks, it will add grist to the mill.[7]

In July 1849 he mused:

> I wish some of our eminent painters would take a voyage to Australia — they would learn many a beautiful effect not attainable in Europe, and the natives would be a source of great profit to them. Their figures have such a noble, picturesque effect when clothed in the possum rug. I think Eastlake might give a hint of this sort to some of our men of colour at home. They would make much by their studies on their return to England.[8]

However, his brother William did not agree with this assessment, and advised against sending any photographs, on 'the probability of the photographs not

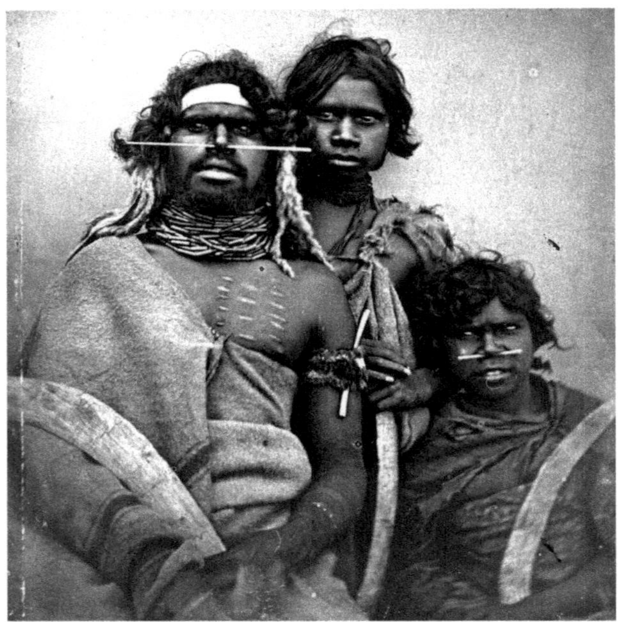

FIGURE 2: Douglas Kilburn. *South-east Australian Aboriginal man and two younger companions 1847*. Photograph, 1/4 plate daguerreotype, plate 10.8 h x 8.2 w cm. National Gallery of Australia, accession 2007.81.122.

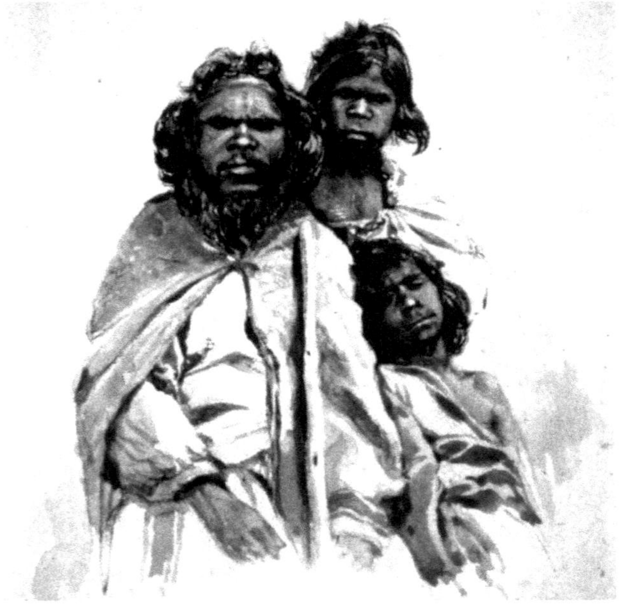

FIGURE 3: John Skinner Prout. *Family group, Australia Felix* [Victoria]. Drawing on paper. British Museum, accession AN76102001.

selling at all, for I really do not think a purchaser will be found, if we may judge of the Australian beauties by the photograph portraits published in [William] Westgarth's *Australia Felix*'.[9]

Westgarth's popular guide for prospective settlers was one of the first to include photographs of Indigenous Australians, in the form of engravings based on Douglas Kilburn's remarkable 1846–47 daguerreotype portraits of Kulin people in cloaks and traditional adornments, as well as blankets and other appropriated items.[10] Westgarth, however, did not offer a favourable view of Indigenous Australians: as historian Jessie Mitchell notes, his account was typical of such accounts during the 1840s in emphasising the colony's potential for settlers, but characterising Aboriginal people as lazy, savage and doomed to extinction.[11] One reviewer noted of Westgarth's discussion of Australian Indigenous people that it was 'a disagreeable subject, because so soon as our curiosity is gratified, every philanthropic hope is destroyed by the conviction, forced upon us by the failure of repeated attempts, that the race is incapable of elevation'.[12]

Despite this disparaging contemporary framework, Kilburn's four extant daguerreotypes (two more are known to be held in private collections) remain remarkable testaments to the Indigenous people around Melbourne a decade after invasion. They bear traditional scars, ornaments and dress, despite their studio poses and signs of change. As the first photographic record of Australian Aboriginal people, Kilburn's photographs were quickly copied by artists such as John Skinner Prout, who produced a beautiful watercolour sketch in late 1846, seemingly based on a Kilburn daguerreotype now held in the National Gallery of Australia.

Seven years later, one of Eugene von Guérard's first projects, upon settling in Melbourne, was to produce a watercolour sketch, based on a daguerreotype now held by the National Gallery of Victoria.[13] Together with Westgarth's illustrations, these interpretations of the photographs were widely circulated among a curious European audience.[14]

Kooris, as the Indigenous people of Victoria are known, were highly visible in the landscape during the 1850s, despite the destructive effect of the gold rushes, with their influx of miners. Although officials sought to keep them away from white settlement, they continued to travel across traditional country, and visited towns and the diggings to satisfy *their* curiosity about European culture and people — as evident in visual records such as the paintings and drawings of

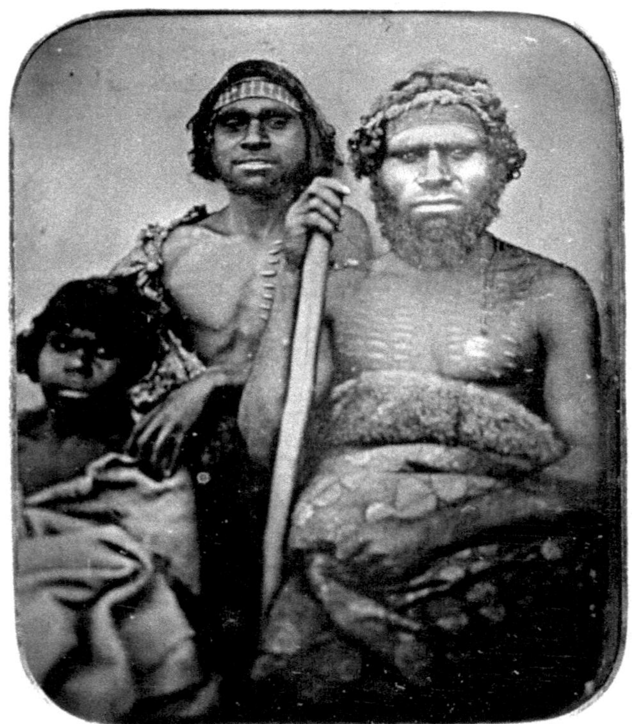

FIGURE 4: Douglas Kilburn. *No title (Group of Koorie men).* Daguerreotype, leather, wood, velvet, brass, c. 1847. National Gallery of Victoria, purchased from Admission Funds, 1983.

Eugene von Guérard and William Strutt. As photographer and digger Antoine Fauchery commented:

> They always wander from place to place without ever staying anywhere for more than three or four days. Divided into nomadic tribes made up of 15 or 20 individuals, they are seen now in the bush, now in the towns, and still more frequently on the diggings, which they visit by preference.[15]

From 1851 photographers were able to imitate this mobility following the invention of the wet-plate collodion process, which allowed photography in the field and its subsequent mass reproduction; this phase saw the proliferation of professional photographers, many recording distant landscapes and peoples.

During this decade Indigenous people were often well known to settlers by sight, a fame facilitated by the display of their portraits in photographers' windows:

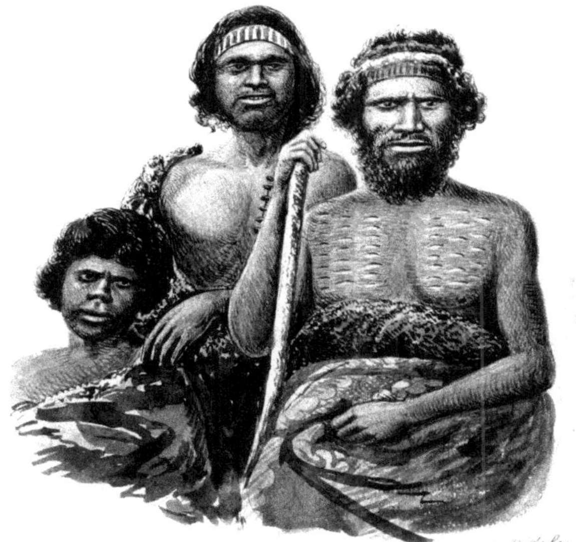

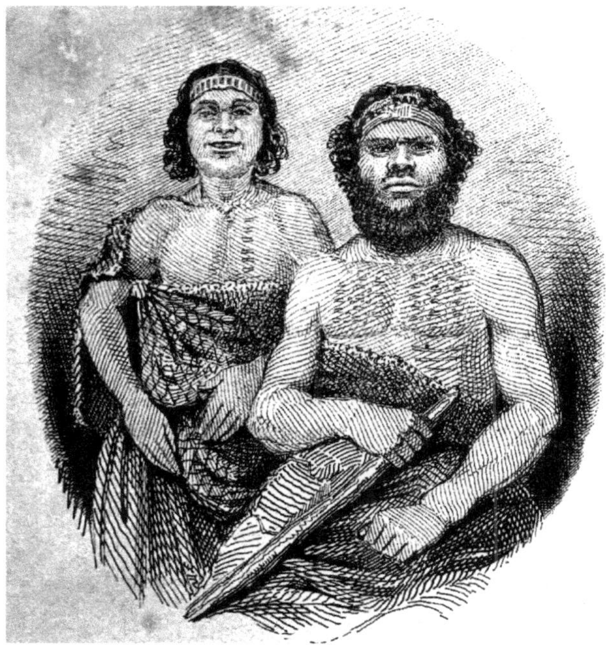

TOP: FIGURE 5: Eugene von Guérard. *Series 01: Australien Reminiszenzen: a collection of illustrations of Australian Aborigines and their weapons, together with geographical profiles in N.S.W., Tasmania and Victoria, and miscellaneous prints*, c. 1846–58, 1858. Watercolour sketch. Mitchell Library, PXA 54, 16b.

BOTTOM: FIGURE 6: William Westgarth. *The colony of Victoria: its history, commerce and gold mining*, 1864, engraving, frontispiece.

in 1857 the botanist and linguist Daniel Bunce noted that he had recently observed the 'two most faithful likenesses' of Boonwurrung couple Sally Sally and Jemmy displayed 'in a window in Elizabeth-street, by Mr Haseldon [sic]'.[16] Like Kilburn a decade earlier, Hubert Haselden used a series of portraits of Kulin people to advertise his 'Daguerrean & Photographic Artists' Melbourne establishment. As is often the case where daguerreotypes have disappeared, the only surviving portrait from this series comprises an engraving, based on a drawing by Nicholas Chevalier, based on a Haselden daguerreotype, of Wurundjeri man Simon Wonga, son of Wurundjeri *ngurungaeta* (leader) Billibellary and his wife Maria.

In 1862 the *Illustrated Melbourne Post* explained that Wonga had 'considerable claims on our notice', being 'the son of Jagga Jagga, the celebrated Port Phillip chief, and friend of Batman. The interesting couple will be readily recognised, not only by Melbournites, but by many through the surrounding districts, where Simon and his lubra pay their periodical visits.'[17]

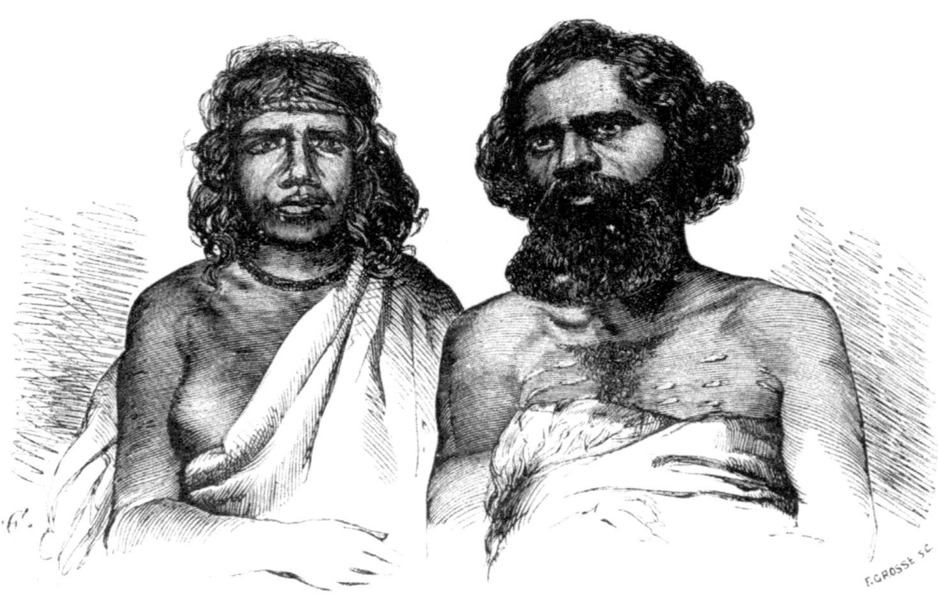

FIGURE 7: Engraved by Frederick Grosse, drawn by Nicholas Chevalier, based on a photograph by Hubert Haselden. *Portraits of an Aboriginal woman, an average type of the native woman of Victoria, and Simon, the son of Jagga Jagga, the celebrated Port Phillip chief and friend of Batman.* Wood engraving, sheet 9.7 x 14 cm. National Library of Australia.

The Indigenous subjects were considered local celebrities, well known to the residents of the settlement and beyond. Wonga, in particular, played a key role in the fortunes of his people during these decades and was of considerable interest to European viewers. There is evidence that Wonga was equally interested in the results of photography: in 1857 he exchanged the nest and egg of a superb lyrebird, known by the Wurundjeri as the *Bullan-Bullan*, for two photographs — possibly even Haselden's daguerreotypes. The German artist, explorer and naturalist Ludwig Becker told how:

> I put myself in direct communication with him [Wonga] in order to obtain as much information as he could give from his own experience, concerning the native animals, etc. By presenting him and one of his relations with their respective photographic portraits, I succeeded at last in making them fulfill a long given promise, and accordingly they brought a nest and egg of the *Menura Superba* to Melbourne.[18]

The photographic record reveals how Indigenous lives were changing in response to invasion. This was the decade in which James Hunter Kerr was producing his series of the Dja Dja Wurrung/Djadjawrung people near Boort. Kerr had settled there in 1849 and was on friendly terms with them.[19] His images show them participating in the life of his station, working as domestic servants or stockmen, and using guns, as well as maintaining aspects of tradition including dress and camping. All Kerr's images are posed, and some must have required considerable co-operation from his subjects — for example, shown 'asleep' in their shelters, giving a performance or 'quarrelling'. He noted that he later showed his photographs to the Taungurong when they visited his station.[20] By contrast with this record of everyday life, several of these images were eventually reproduced in travellers' accounts that emphasised the value and necessity of colonisation, and the unworthiness of the Indigenous inhabitants' rights to the land; these narratives framed images that aimed to depict an idealised and untouched 'primitive'.[21] Figure 10 was published as an engraving, titled *Prince Jamie and his friend*, as the frontispiece of Kerr's 1872 book, *Glimpses of life in Victoria by 'a resident'*. For these public accounts, which shared a narrative structured by exploration, possession and progress, images of 'Prince Jamie and his friend' in traditional garb were selected, following a long tradition of representing 'primitive' people as a counterpart to settler triumph.

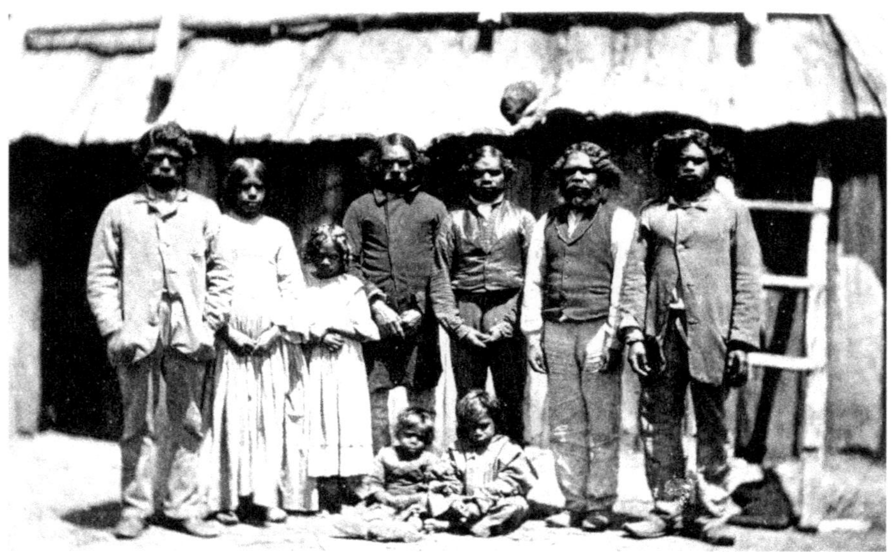

FIGURE 8: Richard Daintree and Antoine Fauchery. *Beembarmin (Tommy Farmer) and his wife Norah, Yerrebulluk (Dicky) and his daughter Ellen* [Group of Aboriginal men, women and children, standing in front of slab hut, wearing European clothing, all whole-length, full face]. Albumen silver. State Library of Victoria, accession H84.167/42. Cultural permission Dja Dja Wurrung Clans Aboriginal Corporation.

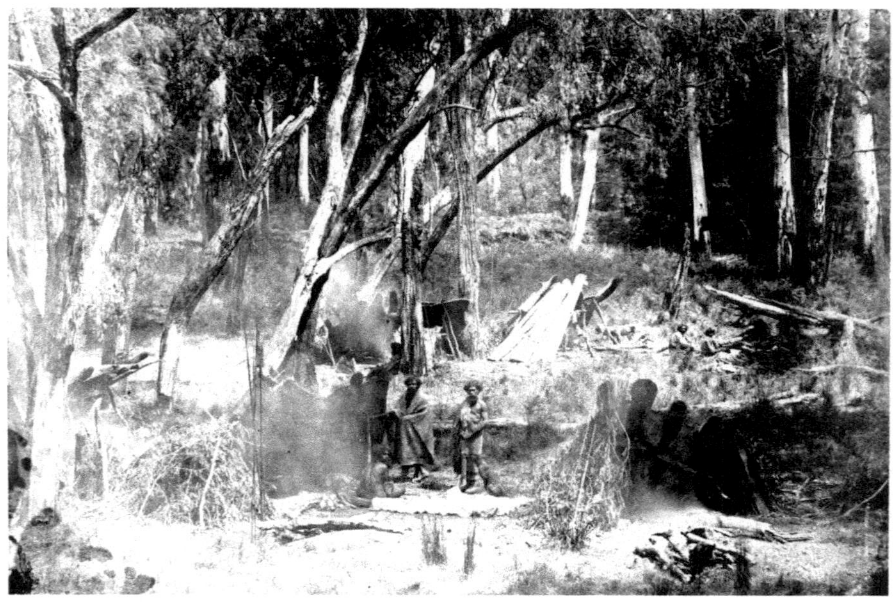

FIGURE 9: Richard Daintree and Antoine Fauchery. [Aboriginal camp], c. 1858. Albumen silver. State Library of Victoria, accession H84.167/44. Cultural permission Dja Dja Wurrung Clans Aboriginal Corporation.

In 1858 geologist Richard Daintree and writer Antoine Fauchery opened a photography business and announced their collodion wet-plate series, *Sun pictures of Victoria* (1857–59), a project comprising fifty photographs produced in ten monthly instalments. As the *Argus* noted, it was intended to illustrate 'our colonial celebrities, our landscape and marine scenery, and our public and private architecture' and was the first such photographic assemblage produced in Australia.[22] Fauchery described an album he sent to France as a sampling of the colony's most typical sights: 'There are some of great men, some of towns, some of the mines, some of savages. There is a little of everything.'[23] There were several photos of Dja Dja Wurrung people who had established a farm at Mount Franklin Aboriginal Reserve, including Beembarmin (Tommy Farmer) and his wife Norah, and Yerrebulluk (Dicky) and his daughter Ellen.

Another series of nine images shows a more traditional lifestyle, with signs of change, such as clothing.[24] A comparison between the stockman and campers of Kerr's series with the farmers at Mount Franklin shows how some Kulin were able to participate in the settler economy and maintain their ties to country.

MISSIONARIES AND PHOTOGRAPHY: 'TELL JANE I WANT HER LIKENESS'

However, by 1859 an inquiry heard that most Aboriginal people, dispossessed by pastoralism and goldmining, were in a 'most disastrous' position; the inquiry recommended the establishment of a series of reserves across the state, and in 1860 the Central Board for the Protection of the Aborigines was established.[25] Ebenezer Mission had already been created on the traditional country of the Wotjoballuk in 1859, and over the following years Coranderrk was settled by Taungurong and Wurundjeri people near present-day Healesville. Ramahyuck, Lake Tyers, Framlingham and Lake Condah were also established. These settlements were intended as Christian farming villages, isolated from the bad influence of mainstream white society, yet also to be places of learning and transformation. Although the missionaries and managers of these settlements came from diverse religious backgrounds, they all shared a belief in the essential unity and teachability of their charges, and the camera provided a useful means to argue for this perspective — providing visual proof of their 'success'. Coranderrk, in particular, as the Aboriginal village closest to Melbourne, became

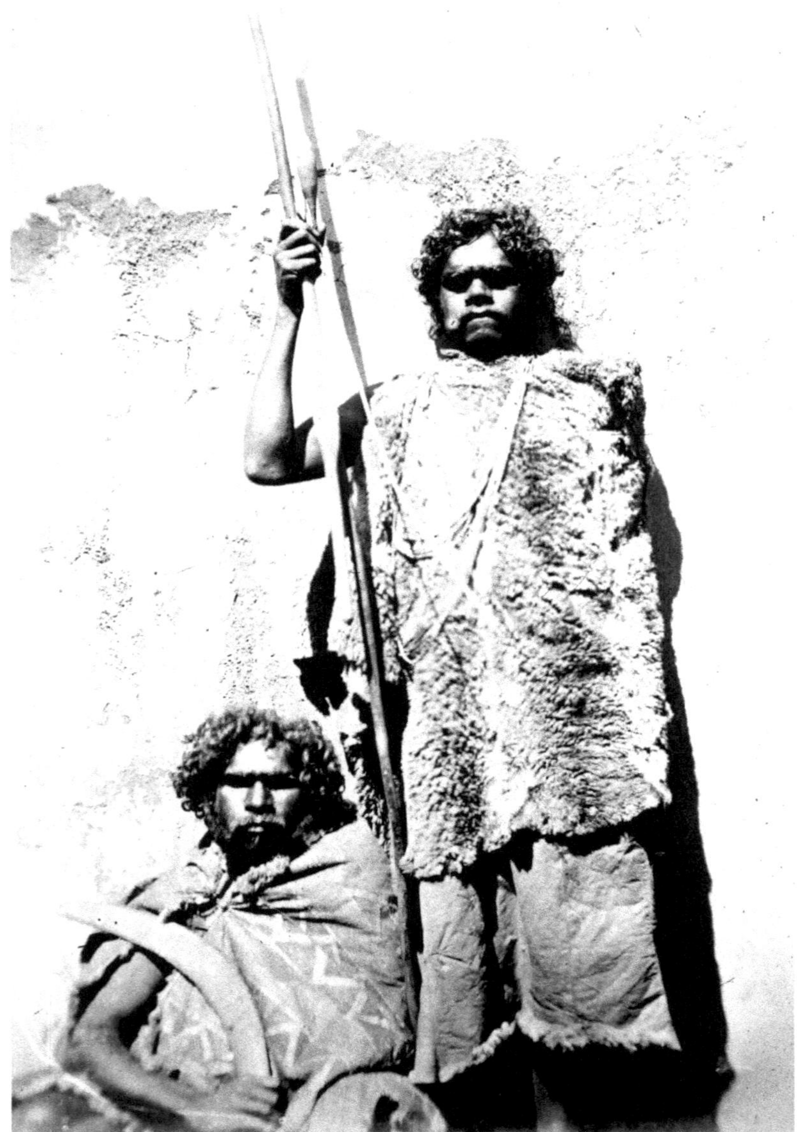

FIGURE 10: John Hunter Kerr, printed by George W Priston. *Prince Jamie and his friend* [Two Aboriginal men, wearing cloaks, one holding a spear, the other a boomerang]. Albumen silver. State Library of Victoria, accession H30158/33. Cultural permission Gary Murray for the Yung Balug Clan of the Dja Dja Wurrung.

OPPOSITE PAGE: FIGURE 11: John Hunter Kerr, printed by George W Priston. *Young stockman* [Full-length portrait of Aboriginal man, standing, holding stockwhip and wearing European clothes]. Albumen silver. State Library of Victoria, accession H30158/28. Cultural permission Gary Murray for the Yung Balug Clan of the Dja Dja Wurrung.

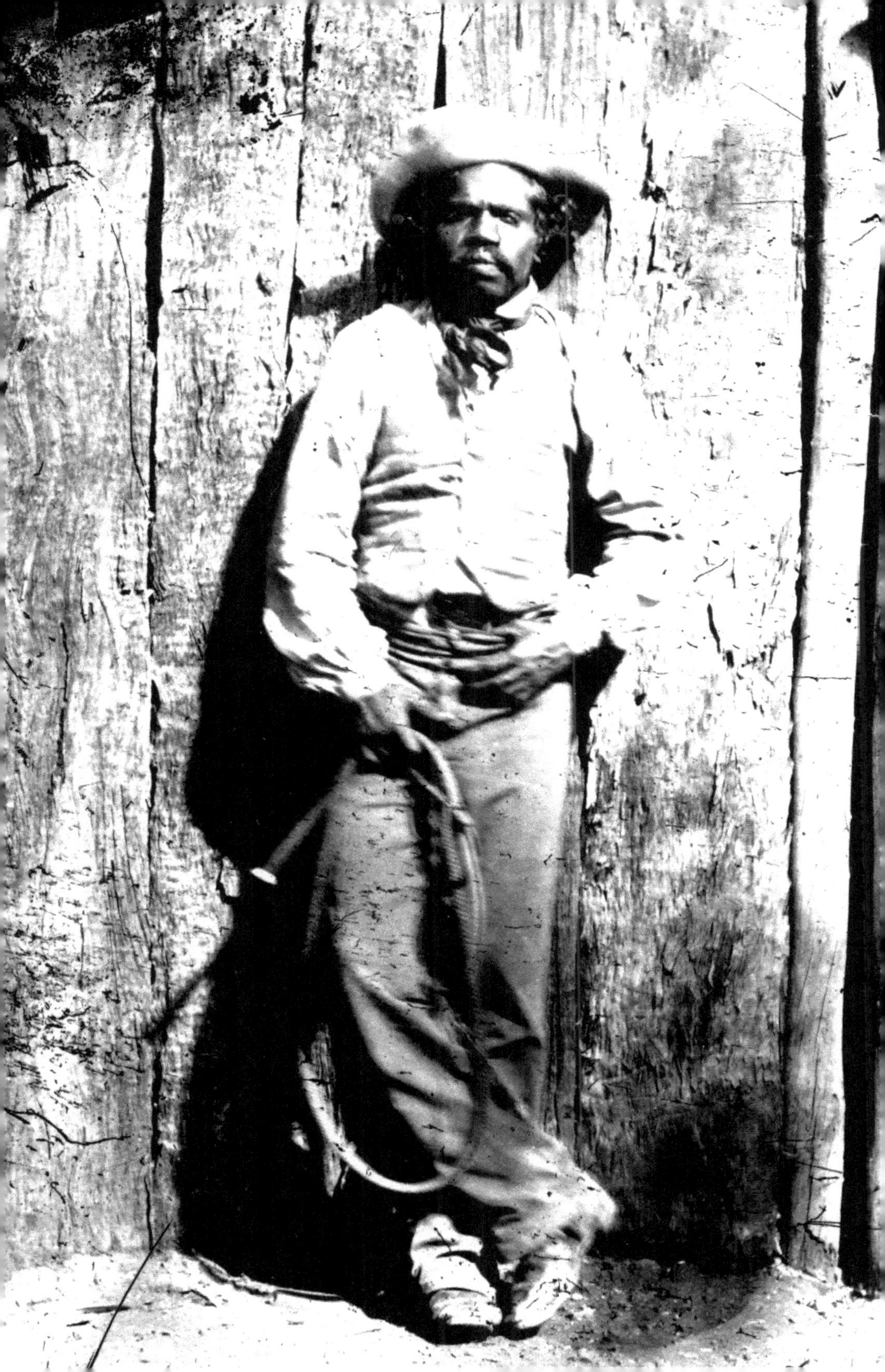

the destination of scientists, administrators and tourists from around the colony and, indeed, the globe.

The Indigenous residents quickly became aware of how they were being represented, and it was frequently noted of Coranderrk that they collected and treasured such portraits. Photographs, visitors reported, were 'highly prized', and in 1876 one visitor stated that 'some of the chief objects of desire' were 'photographic representations of their own and their children's countenances'.[26] Young Italian scientist Enrico Giglioli described how 'the inside walls of [their homes] were in most cases papered with cuttings from English and Australian illustrated journals, and photographs, greatly prized by these people'.[27]

Photographic portraits were also used to create relationships between widely separated Indigenous people whom the missionaries wished to bring together, as well as a means of expressing the often warm relationships between Aboriginal people and missionaries (see Chapters 1 and 7 in this volume). Missionaries were humanitarians who worked hard to help Aboriginal people within the terms of their own culture and time. In 1867, for example, five young Noongar women travelled from Anne and Henry Camfield's Institution for Native and Half-Caste Children in King George's Sound, near the present-day town of Albany, Western Australia (see Chapter 9), as prospective wives to Kurnai men at Ramahyuck, in Gippsland, as a result of the 'happy expedient of exchanging portraits with the Christian natives of King George's Sound'.[28] The girls' portraits had been sent by Anne Camfield, a keen amateur photographer, and, on this basis, the men were reported to be 'already greatly in love'.[29] Coranderrk's respected first manager, John Green, was also interested in photography — but in 1881 he was criticised for trying to attract young women to Coranderrk from other stations by showing them pictures of the young men.[30]

In 1863 Rachel Warndekan had set the precedent for this cross-mission mobility, travelling from King George's Sound to Ebenezer, in north-western Victoria, to marry Wotjoballuk man Nathaniel Pepper. Surveyor, linguist and artist Philip Chauncy, who had worked in the Swan River Colony between 1841 and 1853, visited Ebenezer and described how Rachel treasured a daguerreotype of Henry Camfield as a memento of her ties to home, recalling:

> After church, Mr Spieseke took me to Pepper's cottage, where we found his wife still in bed after a recent confinement. From the comfortable little

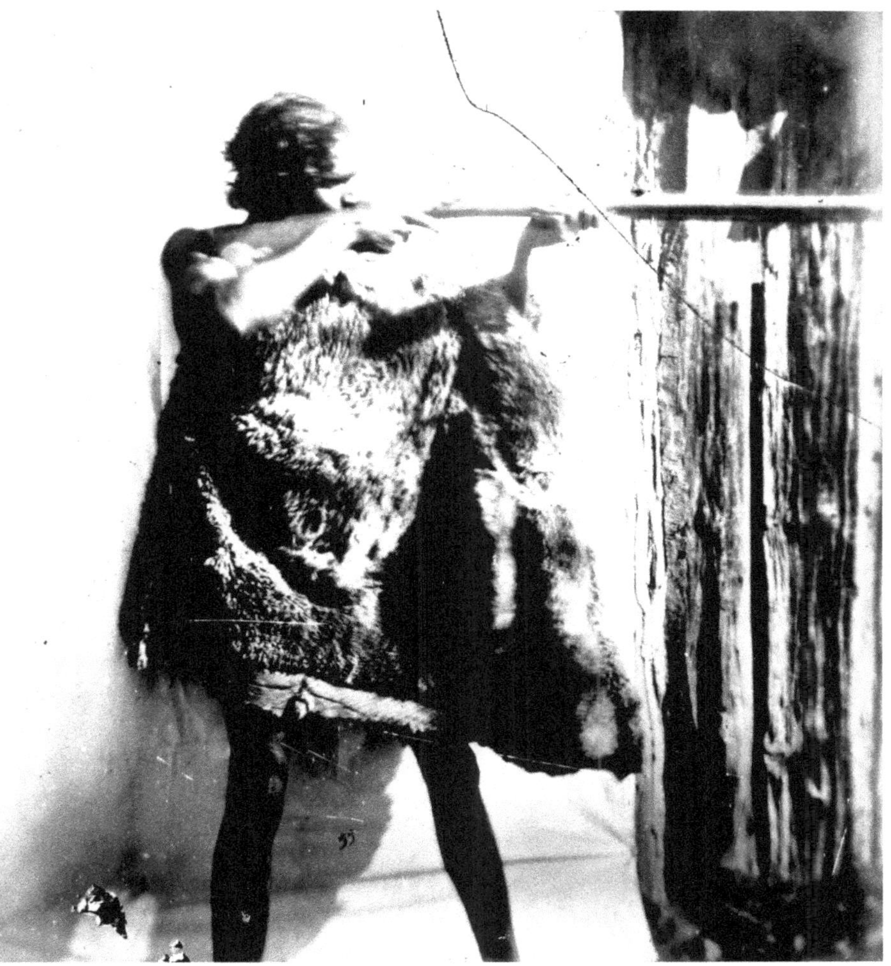

FIGURE 12: John Hunter Kerr, printed by George W Priston. [*Three-quarter-length portrait of Aboriginal man standing, with rifle, in firing pose*]. Albumen silver. State Library of Victoria, accession H30158/25. Cultural permission Gary Murray for the Yung Balug Clan of the Dja Dja Wurrung.

parlor we were introduced to her bedroom by her husband. She was lying with her face towards the wall, but turned her large, lustrous black eyes on us with a look of surprise at seeing strangers enter her room. I spoke to her in her own language of Mr and Mrs Camfield, of King George's Sound, and of the native establishment there; as I did so, large tears stood in her eyes. She then asked her husband to hand down from a bookshelf a daguerreotype case, which she opened, and I at once exclaimed, 'Ki!

> Neeja, Mr Camfield', at which she seemed much delighted, as I was doubtless the first person she had seen since she left the Sound who had been acquainted with her native place and early friends.[31]

In 1873 a seventeen-year-old Wurundjeri woman, Jemima Wandin, who was living at Coranderrk, wrote to her 'dear Old Friend' Daniel Matthews at Maloga to request a photograph of his wife ('Tell Jane I want her likeness') and signed herself 'your loving friend'.[32] Photographic portraits were a kind of currency for both black and white, and communicated across racial boundaries. As Jemima's affectionate letter shows, a photograph was a token of friendship, a 'likeness' that would represent Jane's actual presence, uniting viewer and viewed.[33]

Then, as now, Kooris were also sensitive to being portrayed in ways that they considered negative or invasive — as their refusal to pose unclothed or their demand for exorbitant payment indicates. The famous Darwinist Thomas Huxley was politely thwarted in his attempt to obtain such images from Victoria, and, in a general sense, Coranderrk residents determined how they were recorded, as their self-awareness and pride shaped the way they presented themselves to the camera.[34] However, the tension between the local uses of these images and their wider, often global circulation could produce widely differing meanings.

In 1865 one visitor to the homes of Coranderrk residents noted that 'on most of the side mantelpieces were photographs of the ladies and gentlemen of the establishment'.[35] These were probably the first portraits made by Charles Walter, whose records of the station were published in the Melbourne illustrated newspapers. The following year, Walter was commissioned to make a series of 106 portraits for the Melbourne Intercolonial Exhibition, in turn intended as a practice run for the *Exposition Universelle* in Paris in 1867. His remarkable portraits were held in a family album owned by manager John Green, where they were annotated with captions that told stories about many of the subjects. They remain dignified portraits of the Kulin community.

Colonists were eager to satisfy the demand for Indigenous 'data', which intensified during the 1860s as scientists debated Darwin's theory of natural selection as advanced in *The origin of species* (1859). In the context of exhibitions, splendid material displays of colonial progress and wealth, Aboriginal photographs and material culture were presented to introduce a narrative of the civilisation and achievements of the fledgling Victoria: they were considered the 'primitive' childhood of humankind's glorious march into the future, measuring the distance travelled on the road to modernity. As Darwinism became scientific orthodoxy over the following decades, Darwin's theories were applied to humankind in what is often called 'social evolutionism', leading to a hardening of ideas about biological race. This was the larger cultural context for a political battle waged by Coranderrk residents against closure and dispersal — a battle in which they were narrowly defeated with the passing of the *Aborigines' Protection Act 1886* (Vic.). In this context, photographs of Kooris were usually framed by narratives of extinction and inferiority.

By contrast, missionaries and humanitarians often argued that Aboriginal people were as capable of acquiring modern skills as any white person. In this context, photographic evidence became an important demonstration of the abilities of Kooris to live, dress and worship like Christians and was circulated internationally and across Australia well into the twentieth century. Many missionaries made enthusiastic use of photography, such as Daniel Matthews at Maloga Mission on the Murray River, on the border with New South Wales, who used illuminated lantern slides in his fundraising talks.

Visiting scientists bemoaned their difficulties in finding 'authentic' people to photograph, and so, for example, young Italian naturalist Enrico Giglioli bought commercial portraits of seemingly untouched Dhudhuroa-Waywurru people from Thomas Washbourne, who had travelled to more distant regions such as Echuca and Moama. Giglioli and others used these images in Darwinist debates about origins and biology to 'prove' the difference of Indigenous Australians.[36]

However, these portraits sometimes express personal encounters that did not conform to abstract expectations. Giglioli's meeting at Coranderrk with Bunurong man Tommy Hobson resulted in a remarkably intimate portrait that helps to triangulate our evidence for his life story and give it body. Giglioli wrote of his encounter:

> One of these aborigines with whom I spoke, Tommy Hobson by name, had in the past been a great drunkard, but since he settled at Coranderrk, he had not only succeeded in dressing decently himself, his wife and three sons, but had been able to acquire with his own money a horse and harness. I found him in his shack with his wife Maggie and his younger son Thomas Harris. I was moved by the happy and prosperous appearance of this little family. Tommy is no more; and two years after my visit 10 other

> aborigines whom I had found there had died, apart from poor Hobson. Among the Australian aborigines I saw he was one of the most typical, and his wife could be called the local beauty.[37]

Giglioli's portrait of Tommy Hobson clearly shows the same man photographed by Walter one year earlier.

Giglioli's portrait is less formal, as though taken in the course of meeting. Hobson appears more relaxed — his face is open rather than tense, as in Walter's. Notable are the riding crop he holds and the medal around his neck — what did this commemorate? Another group photograph of Tommy, another man and a woman shows his hand placed affectionately on her shoulder.

Hobson was a widely travelled and worldly man. As was common practice for an Indigenous man who formed a close association with a colonist, he became known as Mr Tommy, or Hobson's black, after the squatter Edward William Hobson, who took up a run at Kangerong, on the slopes of Arthur's Seat, on the south-eastern shores of Port Phillip Bay, in 1837. Remaining on his traditional country, Tommy worked for him (looking after his stock, for example)[38] but continued to maintain traditional affiliations and relations, and he participated in a raid by the Bunurong on their enemies in Gippsland in February 1840.[39] He accompanied Edward Hobson when he took a mob of cattle from Port Phillip to Port Albert in 1844, and historian Marie Fels suggests that he played an active part in the search for the supposedly lost white woman of Gippsland in April 1847, and was one of two young Bunurong men who sailed as crew to California in 1849–50 with squatter George Smith on the *Sea Gull*.[40]

By the 1860s Hobson, in his forties, was living at Coranderrk with his family, and in 1866 it was reported that:

> Tommy Hobson has bought a good mare, and a saddle and bridle. A few years ago I could not prevent him from spending all his money in drink; but now he has always money on hand, and he keeps himself, his wife, and three children, always well clothed.[41]

This explains why he chose to be photographed by Giglioli carrying a riding crop!

Walter's portraits of Tommy Hobson's wife Maggie show a remarkably well-dressed and poised woman, dressed crisply in white. In an album of photographs from Coranderrk they pose outside their home, and while the captions emphasise

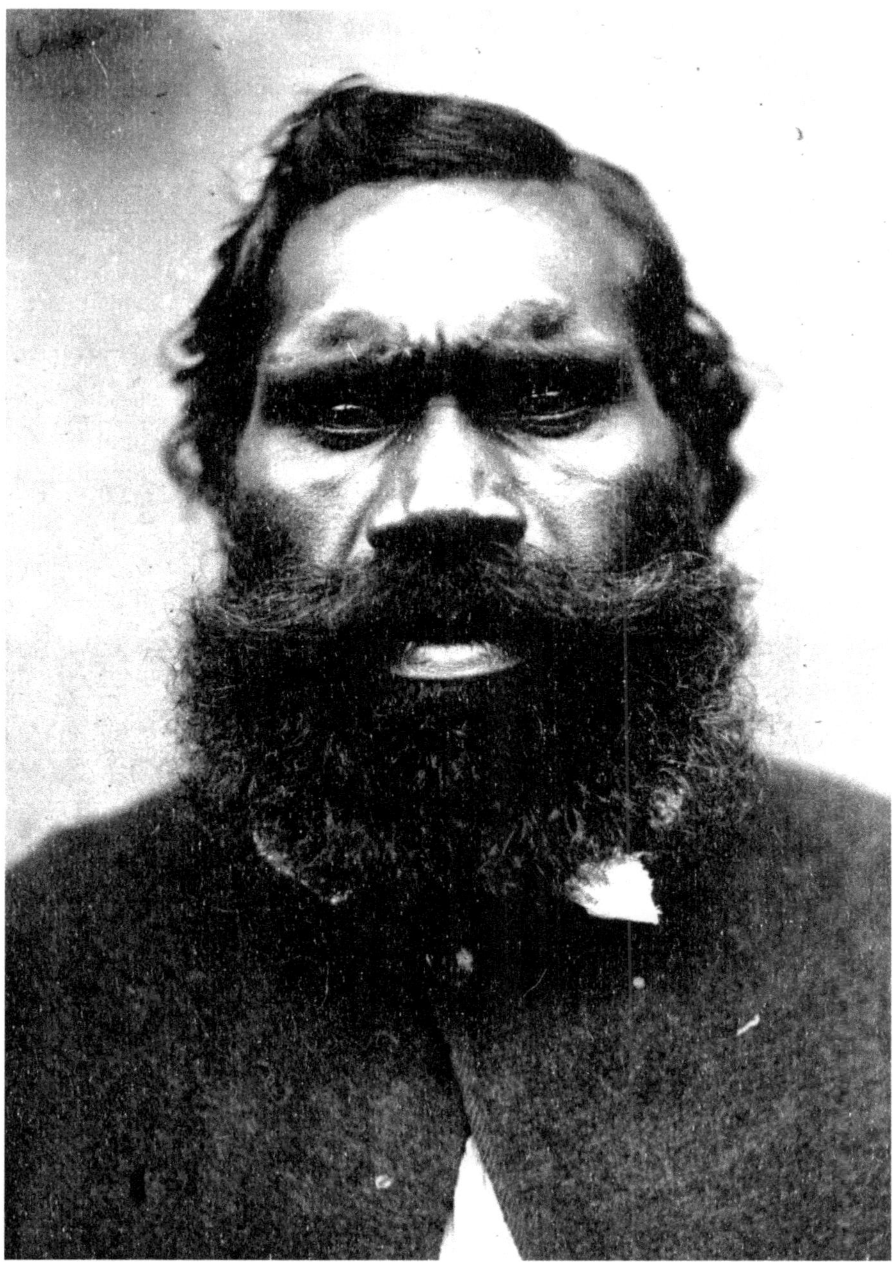

FIGURE 13: Charles Walter. *Tommy Hobson – age 32 – 'Merrin Merrin' when born, 'Drilloury' when father died Yarra Yarra Tribe*. Albumen silver print, 1866. State Library of Victoria, accession H91.1/7.

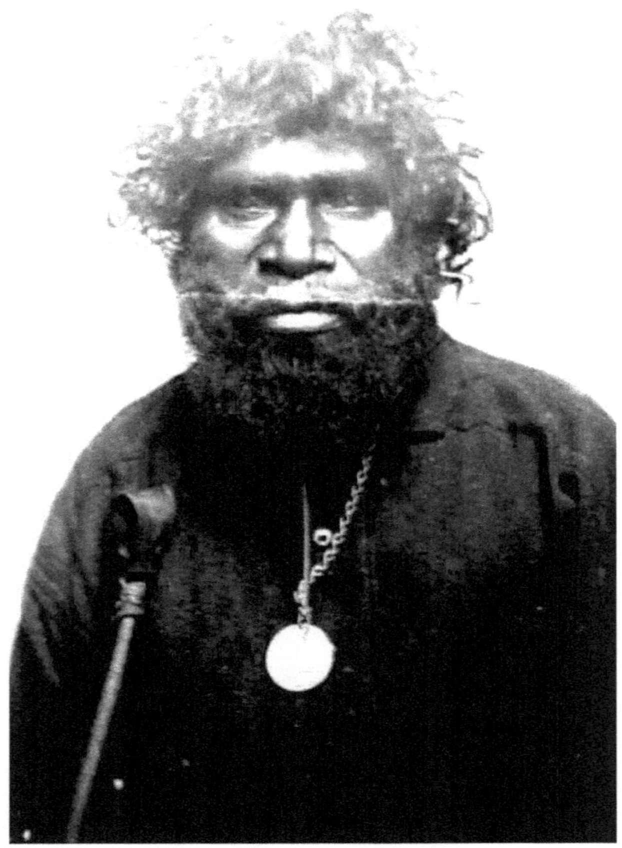

FIGURE 14: Enrico Giglioli. *Tommy Hobson, Coranderrk, May 1867. Carte de visite,* Treloar collection, Adelaide.

the nuclear family, and Tommy as the male head of the household, it is interesting to see that they were accompanied by the manager John Green and his wife and children. Such clues hint at the friendship between these two families, as well as the Hobsons' success in making a home for themselves in Coranderrk village. Sadly, in 1875 Maggie was reported to be dying of 'phthisis' (pulmonary tuberculosis), but was being 'well cared for and attended' by her husband.[42]

Giglioli found Hobson and the other residents of Coranderrk too civilised for his purposes, and travelled further afield (or bought photographs from

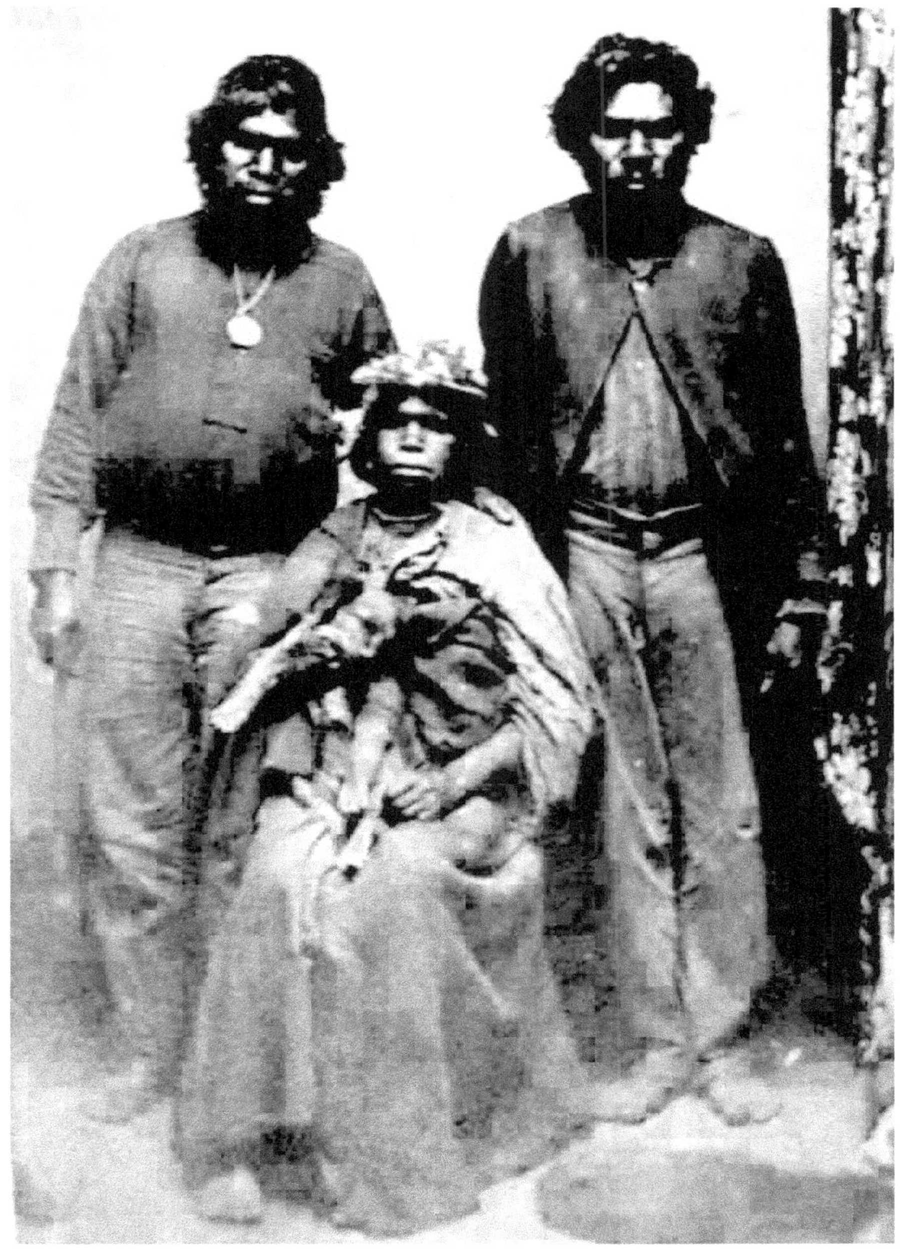

FIGURE 15: Enrico Giglioli. *Group portrait of Tommy Hobson, his wife (?) and another man. Carte de visite*, May 1867. Treloar collection, Adelaide. Bill Nicholson and the Wurundjeri Tribe Land Cultural Heritage Council Inc.

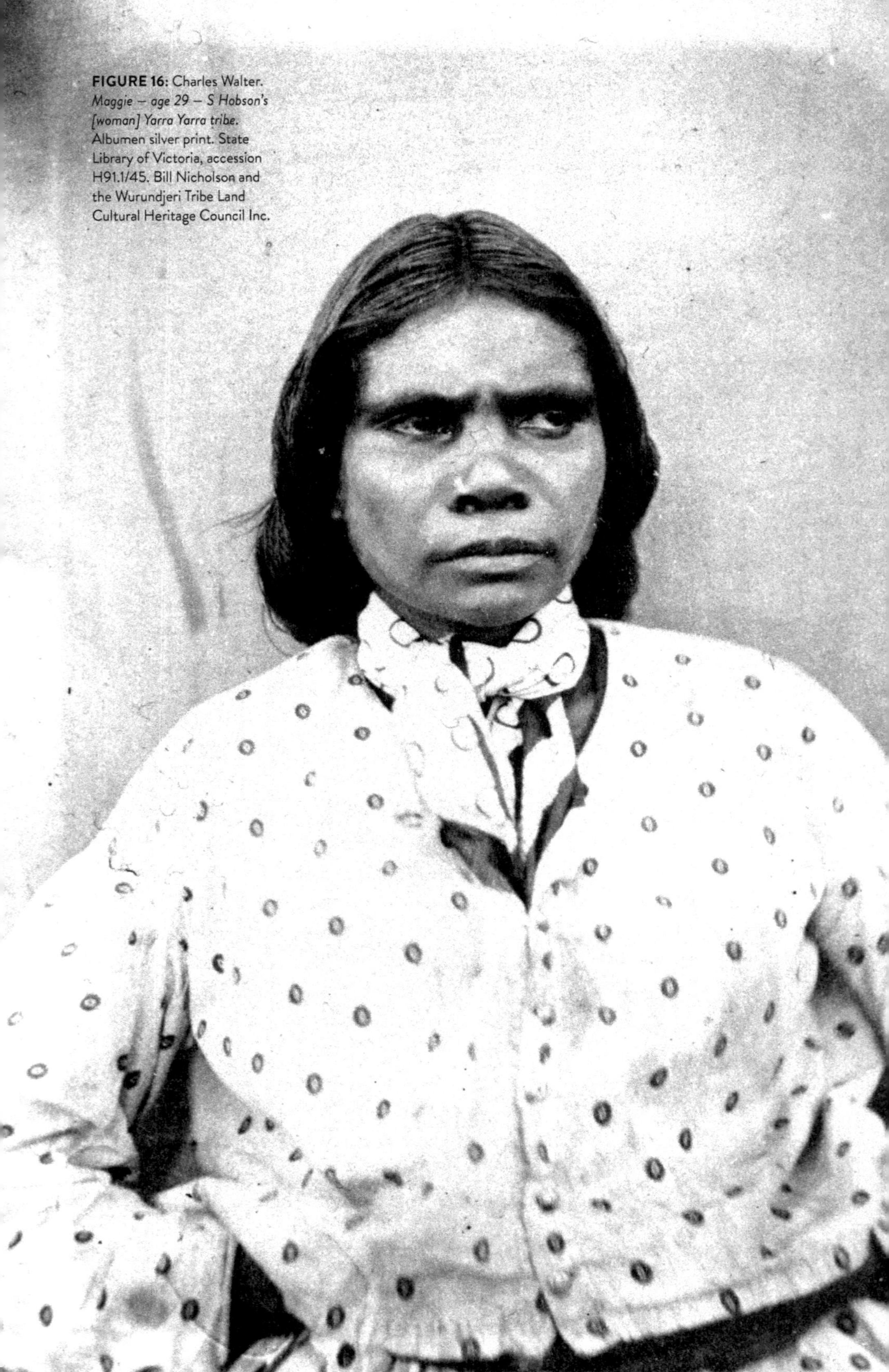

FIGURE 16: Charles Walter. *Maggie – age 29 – S Hobson's [woman] Yarra Yarra tribe.* Albumen silver print. State Library of Victoria, accession H91.1/45. Bill Nicholson and the Wurundjeri Tribe Land Cultural Heritage Council Inc.

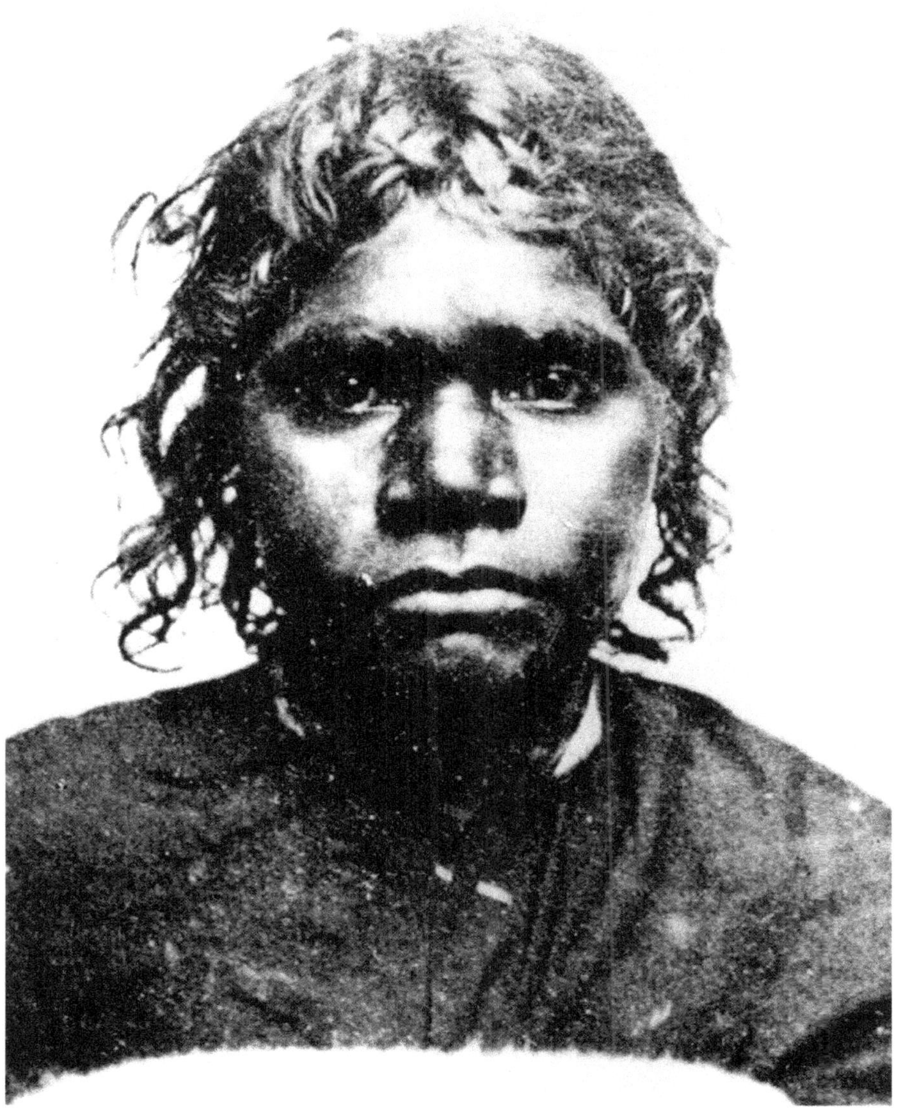

FIGURE 17: Enrico Giglioli. Portrait of Maggie in A Massola, *Coranderrk: a history of the Aboriginal station,* Lowden Publishing Co., Kilmore, 1975, facing p. 41. Bill Nicholson and the Wurundjeri Tribe Land Cultural Heritage Council Inc.

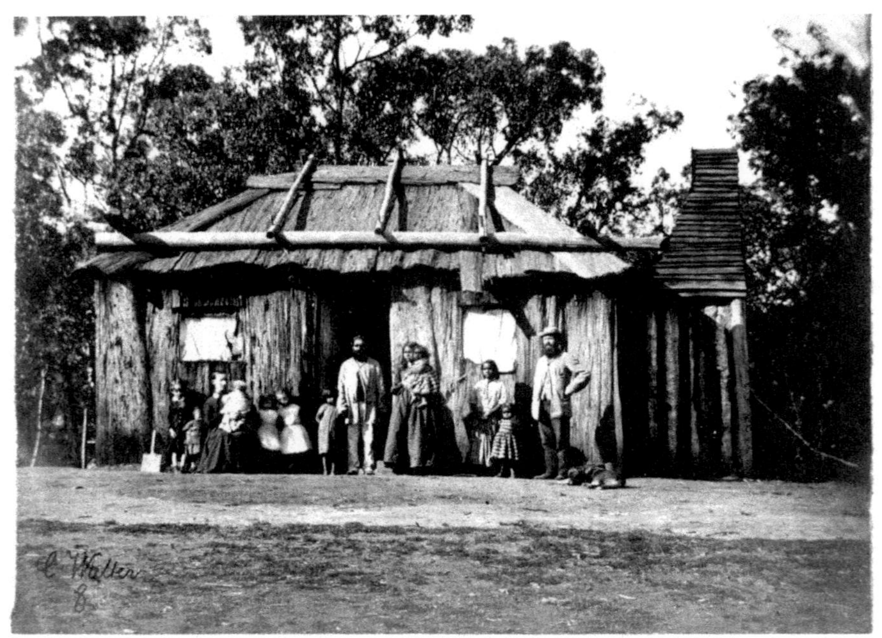

FIGURE 18: Charles Walter, *Tommy Hobson's residence*. Albumen silver print, 1866. State Library of Victoria, accession H13881/9. Bill Nicholson and the Wurundjeri Tribe Land Cultural Heritage Council Inc.

those who did, such as Thomas Jetson Washbourne) for images of Indigenous Victorians. In his book *Voyage around the globe*, he argued in true Darwinian fashion that Aboriginal people were a distinct population that had adapted to their environment over a long period. He reproduced Washbourne's portraits to demonstrate similarities with other Indigenous Australians from around the continent, as well as their difference from other 'races of men' elsewhere.[43]

Today, these images are finding new uses within descendants' own historical narratives to manifest their ancestors and personalise stories from the past. Some are used to flesh out relatives in genealogies generated in pursuit of native title claims. For example, Washbourne's portraits are now enfolded into the history of Dhudhuroa-Waywurru kinship links and ties to country. Gary Murray of the Yung Balug clan of the Dja Dja Wurrung language group notes that some of these 1860s photographs show people of the country of his grandfather, Pastor Sir Douglas

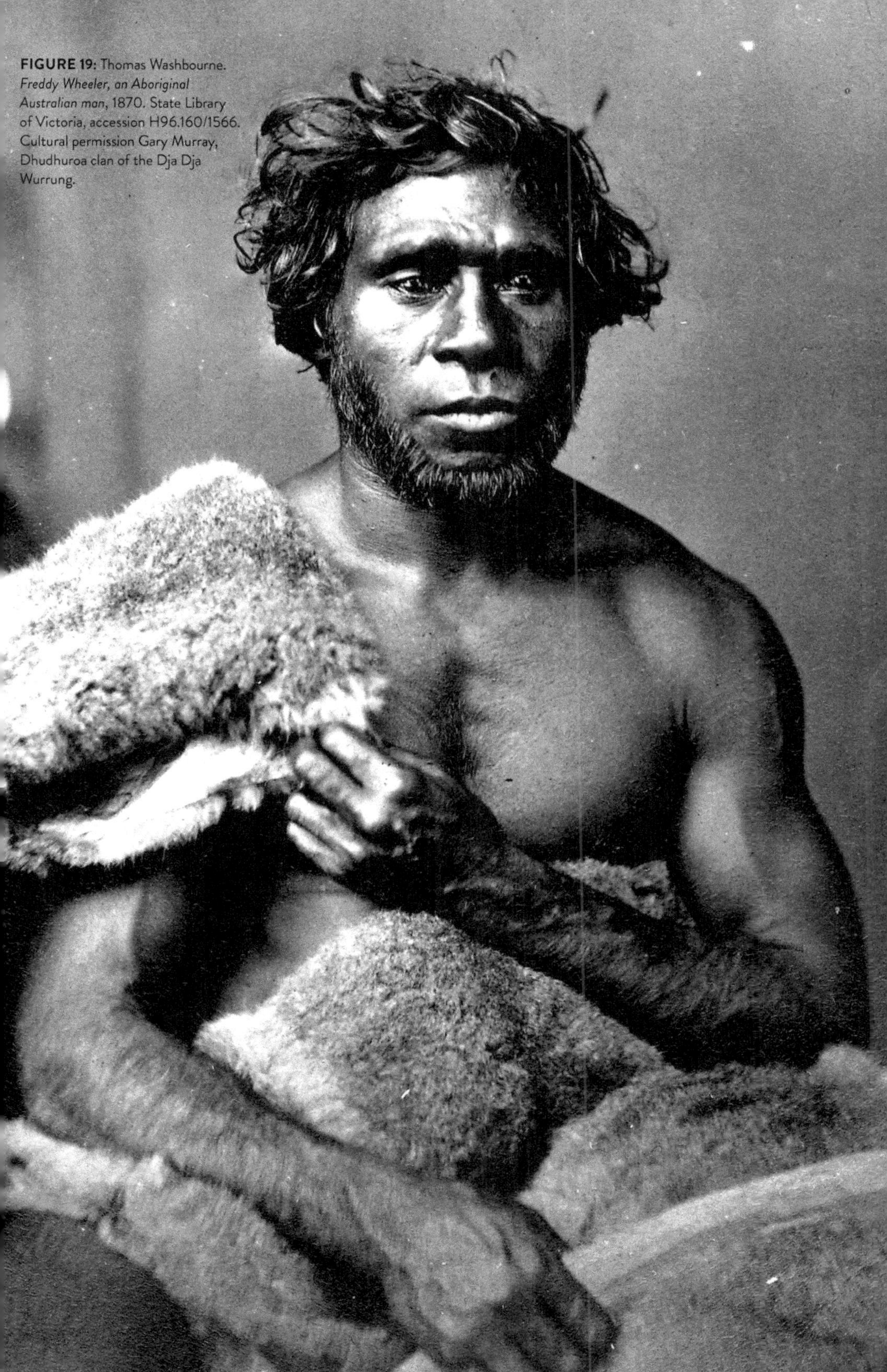

FIGURE 19: Thomas Washbourne. *Freddy Wheeler, an Aboriginal Australian man*, 1870. State Library of Victoria, accession H96.160/1566. Cultural permission Gary Murray, Dhudhuroa clan of the Dja Dja Wurrung.

Nicholls (1906–1988), and great-grandfather, Lerimburneen (also known as King Billy Logan, c. 1820s–1865) (Gary Murray, pers. comm., 10 February 2012). These images show people living on their traditional lands according to a traditional way of life, making oral history and family knowledge concrete, and revealing formerly unknown individuals and their lives. In these ways they counter colonial amnesia and reveal to us the living Indigenous people behind the archives.

ACKNOWLEDGMENTS

I wish to thank the many Koori people who have shown an interest in this research, especially Bill Nicholson of the Wurundjeri Tribe Land & Compensation Cultural Heritage Council Incorporated, and Gary Murray of the Yung Balug and Dhudhuroa clans of the Dja Dja Wurrung people. Research was funded by the Australian Research Council and has benefited from the environment offered by the Monash Indigenous Centre. I also thank Marie Fels, David Clarke and Elizabeth Willis for their comments.

NOTES

1. La Trobe to Colonial Secretary, 18 November 1848, cited in Henry Reynolds, *Dispossession: black Australians and white invaders*, Allen & Unwin, Sydney, 1989, p. 192.
2. Letter from John Cotton, November 1845, in G Mackaness (ed.), *The correspondence of John Cotton, Victorian pioneer 1842–1849 in three parts*, Australian Historical Monographs, Sydney, 1953, p. 28.
3. Hamilton's son, also known as William Hamilton, later settled at Coranderrk during the 1860s. For an account of early Taungurong encounters, see A Massola, 'Notes on the natives formerly inhabiting the Goulburn Valley', *The Victorian Historical Magazine*, 28(2):45–58, 1958.
4. Mackaness above n 2, p. 28.
5. M Briggs, J Lydon & M Say, 'Collaborating: photographs of Koories in the State Library of Victoria', *La Trobe Journal*, 85:106–24, 2010, pp. 119, 121.
6. He had received a daguerreotype camera and supplies from London by October 1846. In June 1848 he wrote, 'We have been progressing well with our experiments in taking sun portraits, and I hope shortly to have several portraits which may be interesting'; Mackaness, above n 2, p. 28.
7. WM Cotton to John Cotton, n.d. [1849] in Mackaness, above n 2, p. 59.
8. ibid.
9. WM Cotton to Robert Hudson, 4 December 1849, in Mackaness, above n 2, p. 64.
10. W Westgarth, *The colony of Victoria: its history, commerce and gold mining,* S Low, Son and Marston, London, 1864.
11. J Mitchell, '"The galling yoke of slavery": race and separation in colonial Port Phillip', *Journal of Australian Studies*, 33(2):125–37.
12. 'Review', *Sydney Morning Herald*, 15 June 1848, p. 2 (review of W Westgarth, *Australia Felix. Historical and descriptive account of Port Phillip*, Oliver and Boyd, Edinburgh, 1848).
13. E von Guérard, *Series 01: Australien Reminiszenzen: a collection of illustrations of Australian Aborigines and their weapons, together with geographical profiles in N.S.W., Tasmania and Victoria, and miscellaneous prints,*

c. 1846–58, 1858, Mitchell Library, PXA 54. See M Tipping, *An artist on the goldfields: the diary of Eugene von Guérard*, Currey O'Neil, Melbourne, 1972; and J Boddington, 'Daguerreotype portraits of Aborigines', *Photofile*, 2(4):5.

14. Westgarth, above n 10.

15. A Fauchery, *Letters from a miner in Australia; translated from the French by A.R. Chisholm; with drawings by Ron Edwards*, Georgian House, Melbourne, 1965, p. 96.

16. D Bunce, *Australasiatic reminiscences of twenty-three years' wanderings in Tasmania and the Australias*, Hendy, Melbourne, 1857, p. 74.

17. *Illustrated Melbourne Post*, 5 July 1862, p. 2.

18. L Becker, 'The nest, egg and young of the lyrebird (menura superba)', *Transactions of the Philosophical Institute of Victoria*, vol. 1, 1857, pp. 153–4. I thank John Kean for his re-telling of this story: J Kean, *Empirical eye: scientific illustration in colonial Australia* (in preparation) to be published by Museum Victoria.

19. JH Kerr, *Glimpses of life in Victoria by 'a resident'*, M Hancock (ed.), Miegunyah Press, Melbourne, 1996[1872]; for an exploration of his photographic work, see E Willis, 'People undergoing great change: John Hunter Kerr's photographs of Indigenous people at Fernyhurst, Victoria, 1850s', *La Trobe Journal*, 76:49–71, 2005; E Willis, 'Re-working a photographic archive: John Hunter Kerr's portraits of Kulin people, 1850s–2004', *Journal of Australian Studies*, 35(2):235–49, 2010.

20. Kerr, above n 19, p. 149.

21. These appeared in an 1860 popular travellers' account, *Le tour du monde*, and an 1862 English version, as well as the frontispiece of Kerr's 1872 memoir: Willis, 'People undergoing great change', above n 19.

22. D Reilly & J Carew, 'Introduction' in *Sun pictures of Victoria*, Currey O'Neil Ross on behalf of the Library Council of Victoria, Melbourne, 1983, p. 10.

23. ibid., p. 25.

24. C Cooper, 'Early photographs of Aborigines in the picture collection', *La Trobe Journal*, 43:32–5, 1989.

25. *Report of the Select Committee of the Legislative Council on the Aborigines*, Legislative Council, Victoria, Votes and Proceedings, Session 1858–1859, D8, 1859. See also R Broome, 'Victoria' in A McGrath (ed.), *Contested ground: Australian Aborigines under the British Crown*, Allen & Unwin, St Leonards, 1995.

26. *Argus* (Melbourne), 1 September 1876, p. 7.

27. EH Giglioli, *Viaggio intorno al globo della r. pirocorvetta italiana Magenta negli anni 1865-66-67-68 (Voyage around the globe on the Magenta)*, V Maisner e Compagnia, Milan, 1875, p. 773.

28. P Chauncy, 'Notes and anecdotes of the Aborigines of Australia, by Philip Chauncy, J.P., District Surveyor at Ballarat' in R Brough Smyth (ed.), *The Aborigines of Victoria: with notes relating to the habits of the natives of other parts of Australia and Tasmania, compiled from various sources for the Government of Victoria*, Cambridge University Press, Melbourne, 2010, pp. 221–84.

29. Hagenauer to Chase, 23 February 1866, MS 3343, National Library of Australia (NLA), Canberra, pp. 24–5. A later consignment of wives was sent in May 1866: Hagenauer to Chase, 19 May 1866, NLA MS 3343, p. 56.

30. J Ferres, *Coranderrk Aboriginal Station, report of the Board appointed to enquire into and report upon the condition and management of the Aboriginal station at Coranderrk*, Government Printer, Melbourne, 1882, p. 136.

31. Chauncy, above n 28, p. 261.

32. D Matthews, *An appeal on behalf of the Australian Aboriginals*, Echuca, 1873, transcribed by D Barwick in 'Notes on Mrs Jemima Burns Wandin Dunolly (c.1857–1944)' for the Nevin family, typewritten manuscript, date unknown, Hunter family private collection, Melbourne.

33. J Lydon, *Eye contact: photographing Indigenous Australians*, Duke University Press, Durham & London, 2005, p. 31.

34. ibid., pp. 1–2, 170–2.

35. *Fifth report of the Board for the Protection of the Aborigines*, John Ferres, Government Printer, Melbourne, 'Report of Board Inspection on 22 July 1865', p. 4; 'Country sketches: the

blackfellows' home', *Australasian* (Melbourne), 5 May 1865, p. 135.

36. J Lydon, '"Veritable Apollos": aesthetics, evolution, and Enrico Giglioli's photographs of Indigenous Australians 1867–78', *Interventions*, March 2013, DOI:10.1080/1369801X.2013.776237.

37. Giglioli, above n 27, p. 774.

38. CA McCallum, 'Hobson, Edward William (1816–1890)', *Australian Dictionary of Biography*, National Centre of Biography, Australian National University, viewed 6 November 2013, <http://adb.anu.edu.au/biography/hobson-edward-william-2251>.

39. LH Bennett, 'Account of a journey to Gippsland', 7 May 1844, p. 182, and 26 May 1844, pp. 188–9, cited in MH Fels, *'I succeeded once': the Aboriginal Protectorate on the Mornington Peninsula, 1839–1840*, ANU E Press, Canberra, 2011.

40. Fels, above n 39.

41. 'The Aborigines', *Argus* (Melbourne), 14 June 1866, p. 6.

42. *Eleventh report of the Board for the Protection of the Aborigines*, John Ferres Government Printer, Melbourne, 1875, Appendix II, p. 8.

43. Giglioli, above n 27.

QUEENSLAND

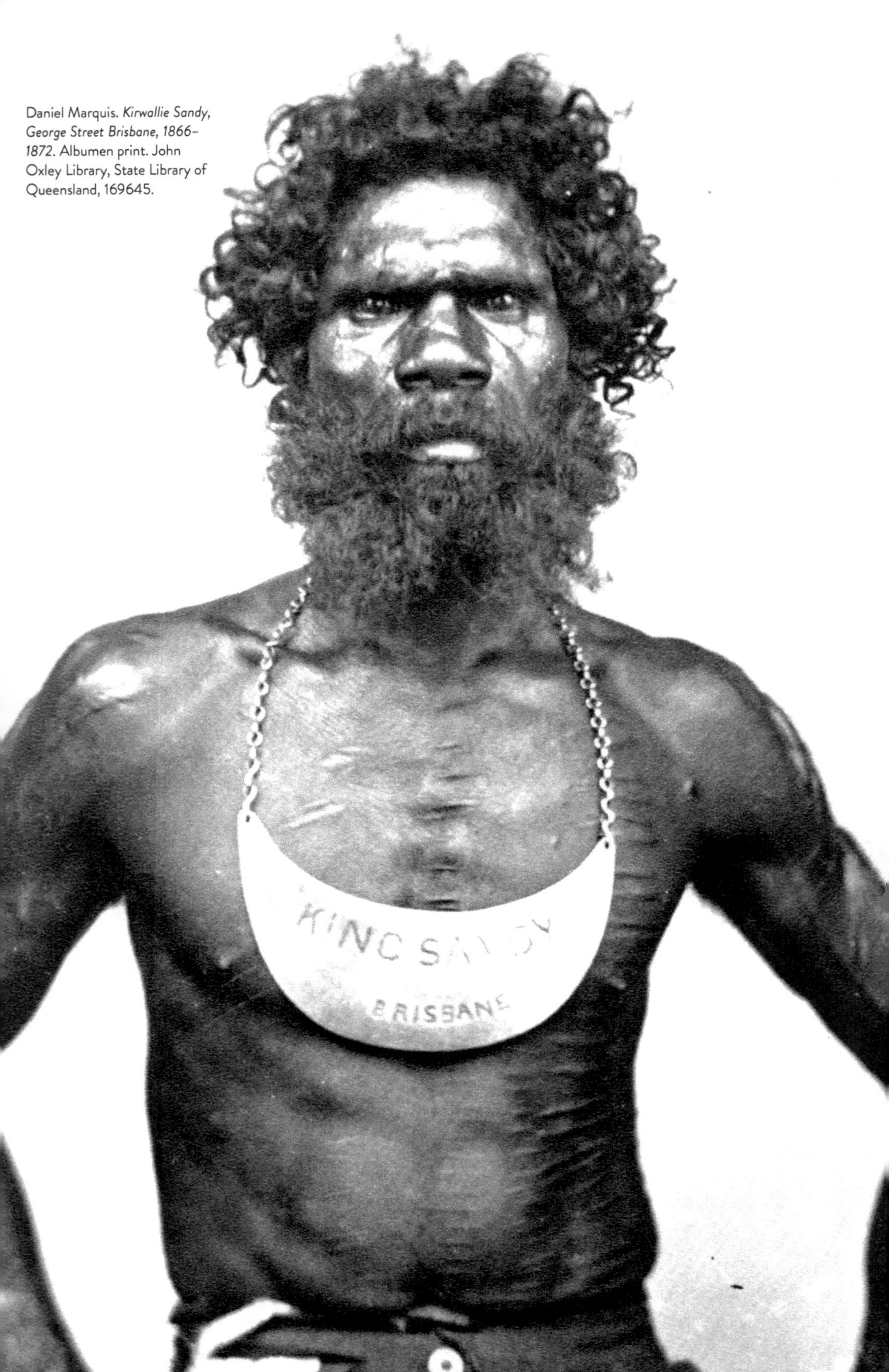

Daniel Marquis. *Kirwallie Sandy, George Street Brisbane, 1866–1872*. Albumen print. John Oxley Library, State Library of Queensland, 169645.

Chapter 6

ABORIGINAL PEOPLE AND FOUR EARLY BRISBANE PHOTOGRAPHERS

Michael Aird

PORTRAITS OF OUR ELDERS

In 1991 I curated an exhibition titled *Portraits of our elders*, which documented studio photographs of Aboriginal people dating from the 1860s to the 1920s. The early photographs were from a time when Aboriginal people had little control over the way in which they were portrayed; in the later photographs, they had a degree of control over how they were seen. These photographs were part of the political process that Aboriginal people were going through, and photographs of well-dressed, confident Aboriginal men and women walking into studios as paying customers documented this. In particular, a photograph of Katie, Lilly and Clara Williams (Figure 1), which appears on the cover of the exhibition book, was the image that first gave me the idea to initiate the exhibition.[1] I was struck by the photograph; the beauty of my grandfather's aunties, and the confidence they demonstrated, inspired me to put together the exhibition and book.

On the day the exhibition was launched at the Queensland Museum, one of my mother's elderly cousins questioned why I had not included a photograph of her grandmother, who was also my great-grandmother. I explained that the main aim of the exhibition was to put together a selection of quality studio portraits that addressed issues of both photographic history and Aboriginal history, and that I could not find a photograph of her grandmother that was suitable. Regardless of my explanation, she made it clear that she wanted her grandmother to be included in the exhibition.

Her request reflected something that I have seen many times — that older Aboriginal people often have a genuine determination to see the story told of how wonderful their parents or grandparents were, people who achieved so much through difficult and changing times — people who struggled to stay in their traditional country and keep their families together, while also living with the ever-present threat of government intervention. Regardless of the changes that have occurred in Aboriginal society, historical photographs have played an important role in documenting how Aboriginal people have asserted their connection to family and country. In this chapter I explore the history of producing such photographs, and their subsequent uses by Indigenous relatives.

EARLY BRISBANE PHOTOGRAPHERS

During the 1850s several professional photographers visited Brisbane and advertised their services in local newspapers.[2] Some of them worked in Brisbane for short periods then moved on to other districts, but Sylvester Diggles can be credited as the first resident photographer to settle in Brisbane in 1855.[3] By the early 1860s several more photographers had established studios in Brisbane, as they could see the benefits of locating their businesses in the central business district in order to be commercially viable. Over the following decades many more photographers joined them.

Much of my research has been devoted to determining specific details that may help with identifying which photographers took particular images, the names of the people featured, and the dates and places of the photographs. Identifying the work of particular photographers is complicated because they were often very transient. The issue is further confused by the fact that specific photographers may have worked for other photographers prior to establishing their own businesses. In turn, many photographs and negatives may have come under the control of other photographers following their deaths or for other reasons, such as the sale of a business or the merging of photographers under the one studio name.

During the 1860s it was possible to take photographs outdoors during daylight hours, but the technology of the time was much better suited to working within studios. For this reason the majority of photographs from the 1860s and 1870s were taken in studios. Even itinerant photographers of the time would take charge of spaces, such as vacant shops or within rooms of other established businesses, and set up temporary studio-type settings.

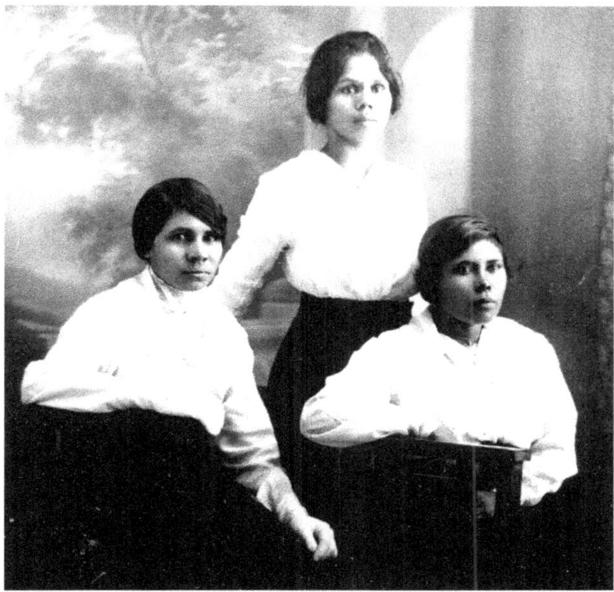

FIGURE 1: Peter Hyllested. *Katie, Lilly and Clara Williams*. Photo-print, Beaudesert, c. 1924. Courtesy Doris Yuke Collection, Queensland.

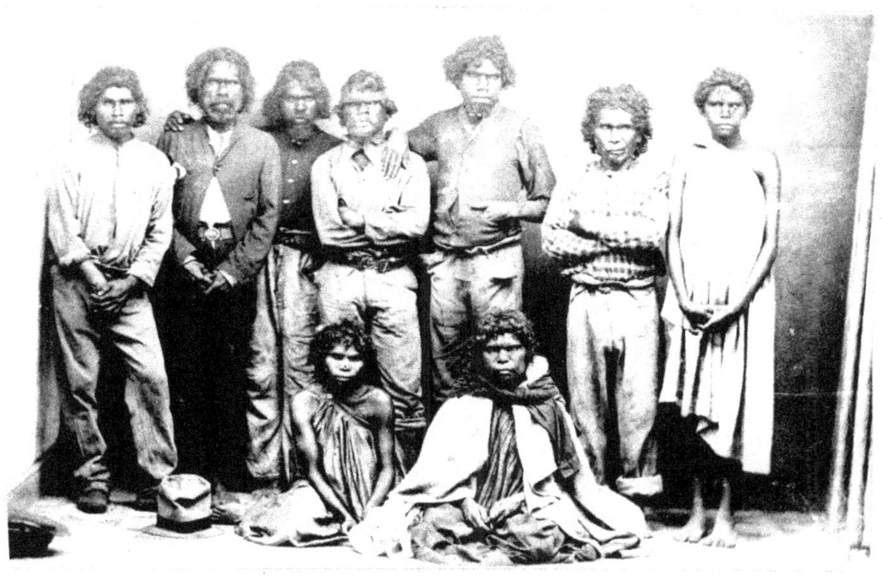

FIGURE 2: John Watson (standing: Nudla, Nikki, Mickey, Tundarum, Weerum, Buckner, Lucy; seated: Nancy, Maria). Group from Durundur in John Watson's Queen Street studio, Brisbane, 1867. Albumen print. National Library of Australia, Rex Nan Kivell Collection, NK10389.

When looking at these photographs, such as one by John Watson of a group from Durundur (Figure 2), I first asked the question, 'did Watson travel the seventy or more kilometres to Durundur to take this photo, or did these people travel to Brisbane?' There is nothing elaborate about the setting in which the photograph was taken, so I considered that it could have been taken within a room of the homestead at Durundur Station.[4] But after careful examination of several features, such as the pattern in the carpet, the curtains, the skirting board and the direction of the light in other photographs credited to Watson, I determined that this photograph was taken in Watson's Queen Street studio. This raises the question of how he got this group to enter his studio and comply with his demands to stand still for extended periods of time.

Early Brisbane photographers would have no doubt formed some sort of relationship with the Aboriginal people living in the local area, and it has been demonstrated that some interaction happened between photographers and Aboriginal people from other regions who occasionally visited Brisbane. What needs to be considered is that the commercial precinct of Brisbane in the mid-1800s would have proved quite an attraction for Aboriginal people from throughout the broader region as a place where European commodities could be obtained.

To some degree, Aboriginal people were valued by early settlers as a source of manual labour, and also for their knowledge of what was considered a strange landscape for Europeans. The Aboriginal people had the skills to easily secure natural food resources, such as fish, crabs, oysters and kangaroos, which could be traded for European commodities such as sugar, flour and tea. Photographers also valued Aboriginal people — they saw them as something exotic to be photographed, and in turn they could profit from selling these images. I have no doubt that the Aboriginal people were well aware that the photographers intended to profit from them, and at times they would have negotiated some form of payment prior to posing.

An example of a subject demanding payment prior to being photographed can be found in an article titled 'A king of shreds and patches', which was published in 1904 with a photograph of Alexander Sandy (Figure 3).

> King Sandy was photographed at Boonah in the Fassifern district. The native modesty of the Aboriginal monarch is such that many vain attempts

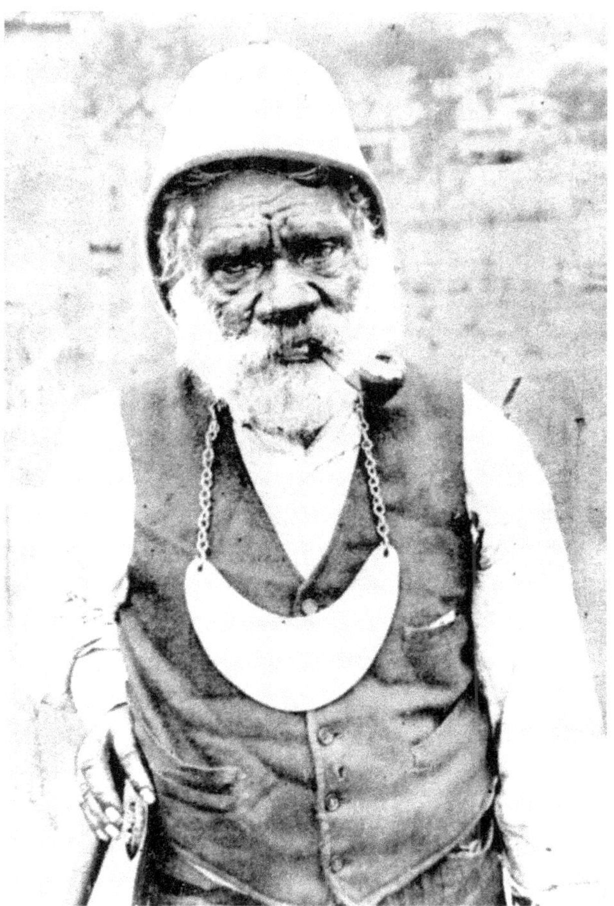

FIGURE 3: H Burbank. *Alexander Sandy, Boonah, 1903–1904.* Albumen print. State Library of Queensland, JOL9609.

> have been made to get him to 'sit', but at last he has been persuaded to lay aside his barrier of diffidence and stand before the camera, the useful shilling being the deciding factor in the transaction.[5]

In many cases I have found that much of the published information available about photographers can prove to be confusing and sometimes inaccurate, as a lot of previous research has relied upon post office listings and newspaper advertisements. This sort of research often does not properly describe the extent of the work that some photographers actually did and does not explain the complex relationships between many of the Aboriginal people in these photographs.

By the late 1800s there was an ever-increasing number of photographers working with Aboriginal subjects, and too many photographers operating for me to document them all, but I have focused on a few that are known to have photographed Aboriginal people from the broader Brisbane region. The following are just some of those photographers, with an indication of the main years of their careers that I focused on: Thomas Ham (1861–70), William Knight (1861–98), John Watson (1855–75), Thomas Bevan (1860s), Daniel Marquis (1866–78), Albert Lomer (1862–1905), Thomas Mathewson (1861–1900s), Oscar Fristrom (1883–1918), John Hogg (1886–1921), Poul Poulson (1882–1925), Ada Driver (1890s–1920s), James Bain (1879–1918), Robert Pumfrey (1893–95), Harry Alder (1890s) and Roland Ruddle (1905–19).

I also extended my research into other regions, such as north and central Queensland, as well as Noosa and Gympie to the north of Brisbane, the Darling Downs and northern New South Wales. This research has included photographers such as Heinrich Muller (1866–74), Chris Roggenkamp (1862–1918) and his brother Martin Roggenkamp (1868–1907), Joseph Wilder (1861–82), John Preston (1886–98), Will Stark (1888–1920s), Henry Lightoller (1890s–1900s) and Peter Hyllested (1891–1933). Identifying the work of particular photographers in other regions has assisted in eliminating some photographs of Aboriginal people that have been previously misidentified as being taken in Brisbane — in particular, I have included a section on Richard Daintree (1863–70) for this reason.

The following is a summary of four early Brisbane photographers I have researched — John Watson, William Knight, Thomas Bevan and Daniel Marquis — as the majority of photographs taken of Aboriginal people in Brisbane during the 1860s can be attributed to them.

JOHN WATSON

By 1854 John Wheeler had established a photographic business in Sydney and was trading under the name Wheeler & Co. He was soon joined by the English photographer James Freeman, and by November 1854 the business name was changed to Freeman Brothers & Wheeler. James Freeman had brought from

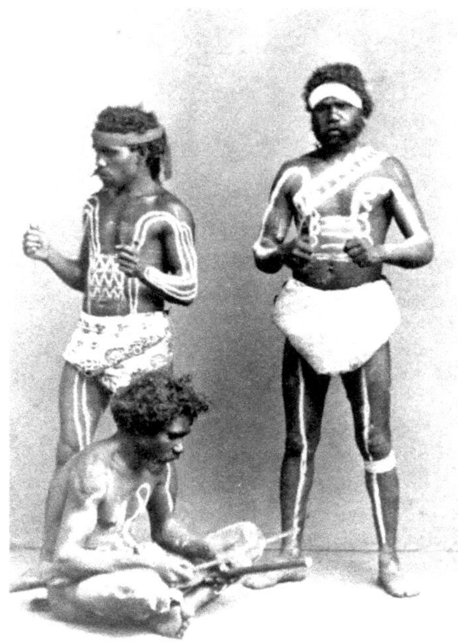

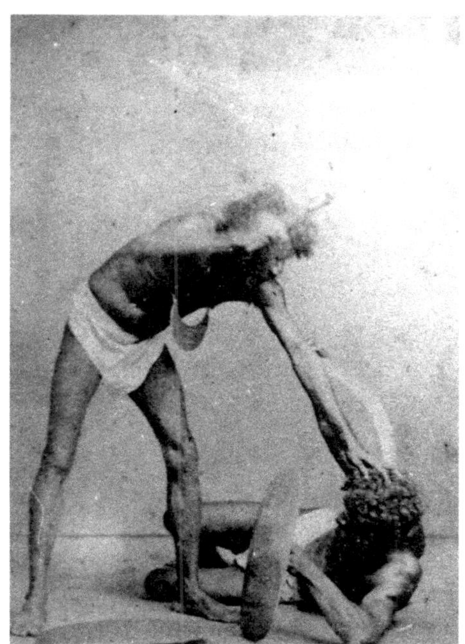

LEFT: FIGURE 4: John Watson. *Kirwallie Sandy and others in John Watson's Queen Street studio, Brisbane, 1862–67*. Albumen print. National Gallery of Australia, Paul Costigan Collection, Canberra.

RIGHT: FIGURE 5: John Watson. *Kirwallie Sandy in fight scene. Queen Street, Brisbane, 1860s*. Albumen print. State Library of Queensland, JOL15111.

England a technique for producing collodiotype (wet-plate) photographs, along with 'a first rate Artist from England to colour all kinds of Photographic Pictures with the highest finish'.[6] By early 1855 the company had become simply Freeman Brothers. Wheeler then moved to Brisbane, and by late 1855 he had established a studio with John Watson. Their business was known as the Brisbane Photographic Rooms. Wheeler returned to Sydney in 1862 and Watson opened his own studio in Brisbane between 1862 and 1875.

One photograph, owned by a private collector shows three decorated men, and on the back the photograph is stamped 'Watson Publishers — Queen Street' (Figure 4). It can be assumed that this photograph was printed sometime after Wheeler left the studio in 1862. I have identified six photographs of Aboriginal people that can be credited to Watson. The State Library of Queensland has copies of three photographs of men in fight scenes. No information is attached to these images. It appears that they were taken by Watson, as there are numerous similarities with the Watson photograph held by the private collector. A stand-out feature in one photograph is a man wearing a breastplate. Even though the copy prints that I have access to are not very clear, I am sure that it is Kirwallie Sandy wearing the plate, as he appears in the National Gallery of Australia photograph and one State Library of Queensland photograph (Figure 5).

Another photograph that I have concluded was taken by Watson is of a group from Durundur Station (Figure 2). My assumption is based on the pattern in the carpet on which they are standing. The same carpet can be seen in a photograph of Gilbert Elliot taken on 4 April 1870 and held by the State Library of Queensland. This photograph is clearly identified as being taken in Watson's Queen Street studio. Another photograph in the State Library of Queensland, dated circa 1870 and identified as Watson's work, also features the same carpet. This indicates that the group was in Watson's Brisbane studio, and he did not take the photograph at Durundur.

I have located two copies of the Durundur group photograph — one is held by the Queensland Museum, with details of the names of each person attached, along with the caption 'Queensland natives — 1867'. The other copy is held by the National Library of Australia, and again no photographer is identified, but attached is the caption 'Aboriginals, Brisbane'.

WILLIAM KNIGHT

William Knight had been working in Victoria since 1851, and in 1861 he moved to Queensland to work as an engraver and photographer for Thomas Ham, who had established his first studio in Brisbane the same year. Ham was also involved in the cotton and sugar industries on the Pimpama and Albert rivers from 1862 to 1869, and he died in 1870.

Most of the photographs credited to Ham were more likely to have been taken by Knight, who was his studio manager. Only a few studio portraits are specifically identified as being taken by Knight, and he is better known for taking several high-quality Brisbane streetscapes. He married Thomas Ham's sister-in-law, Bertha Sara, and they had eight children. He retired in 1898 and died five years later. He was not impressed with Brisbane when he first arrived, but he settled and remained there for the rest of his life.

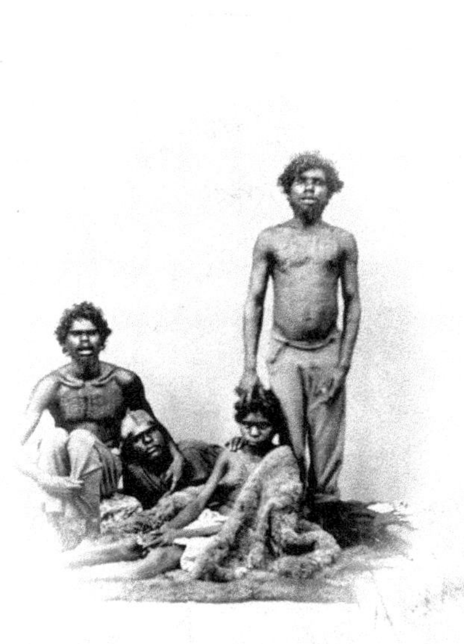

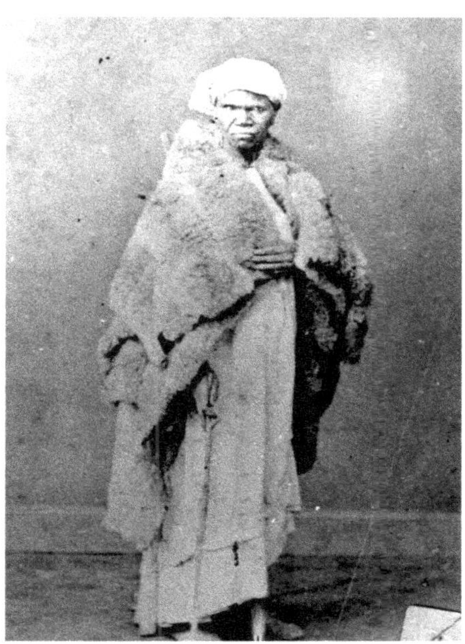

LEFT: FIGURE 6: William Knight. *Group in Thomas Ham's George Street studio, Brisbane, c. 1862*. Albumen print British Museum, Oc,B80.17.

RIGHT: FIGURE 7: Edward Forster. *Woman with possum skin cloak*, Maryborough, c. 1872. Albumen print. State Library of Queensland, JOL33800.

Three photographs of Aboriginal people taken by Knight are held in the collection of the British Museum. They are stamped on the back with the inscription 'Thos Ham & Co Engravers Lithographers Photographic Artists George Street Brisbane'. One of the series has written on it in pencil 'WK'. This note supports my assumption that most photographs identified as being produced by Thomas Ham's studio were actually taken by Knight. The British Museum identifies the date of these photographs as around 1862. It seems reasonable to assume that these photographs were taken in the initial years of his time working in Brisbane.

After viewing the William Knight photographs from the British Museum, I have been able to link them with another three photographs that I now believe were also taken by him. One of these is held by the John Oxley Library and features three females sitting on what appears to be a possum skin cloak or rug. Two of the British Museum photographs also feature a fur cloak or blanket. At least one person in each of the British Museum photographs is sitting on a box or low footstool that has been covered, so it is not possible to identify what it is. The same can be seen in one of the State Library of Queensland photographs, where a young woman is sitting on an object of a similar height. There seem to be enough similarities in the style of these photographs, and the material features of the studio, for me to assume that they were taken by Knight.

Another unidentified photograph held in the State Library of Queensland features a woman wearing a possum skin cloak. For many years I was under the impression that it may have been taken in Victoria. Then for some time I thought that this photo may have been taken in Brisbane by Knight. But I am now confident that it was taken by Edward Forster in his Maryborough studio in Queensland. Recent research has identified that this image is one of a series of photographs of Aboriginal women taken by Edward Forster.[7] This is the only other known photograph of a possum skin cloak taken in Queensland, apart from the series of photographs by William Knight that feature a similar cloak. Even though several historical documents indicate that possum skin rugs were traditionally made in south-east Queensland, only two photographers documented them.

THOMAS BEVAN

Thomas Bevan was operating a studio in Victoria in 1860, and some time after that he moved to Queensland. In November 1864 he has been recorded as working as a travelling photographer in Toowoomba. He later established a studio in Gympie from 1870. He died in 1893 and his son Agrippa Bevan carried on the business until 1912. He obviously worked in Brisbane at some point, but I am not sure of the dates.

The British Museum has a collection of thirteen *carte de visite* photographs that have been identified as being taken by Thomas Bevan. They are clearly identified as coming from Queensland, as it is written on the front of the photographs. All of these photographs were taken inside a studio, with the exception of one of a young woman and child lying beside a fire in a camp scene. The British Museum has catalogued these images as being taken in Brisbane in the 1870s. The fact that Bevan was working in Gympie in the 1870s means that the photographs were either taken in Brisbane in the 1860s or Gympie in

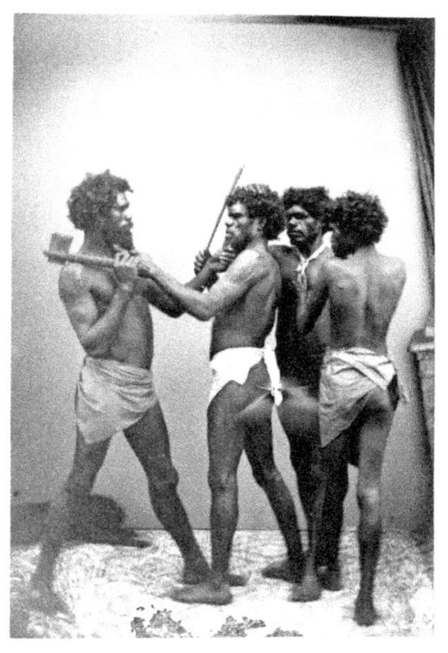

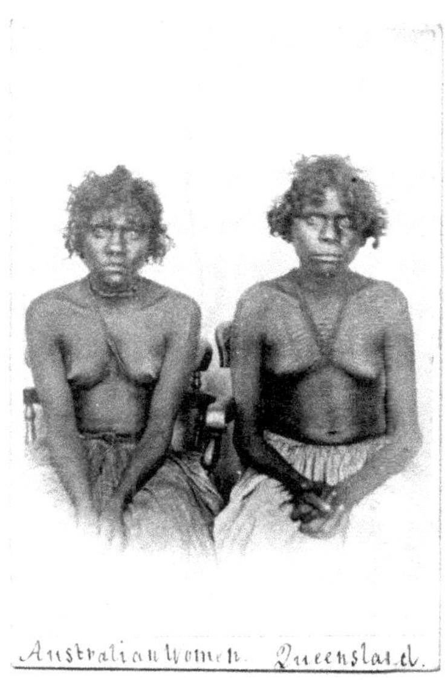

LEFT: FIGURE 8: Thomas Bevan. *Kirwallie Sandy and others in fight scene, Brisbane, c. 1860s.* Albumen print. British Museum, Oc,B70.5.

RIGHT: FIGURE 9: Thomas Bevan. *Women photographed in Brisbane*, c.1860s. Albumen print. British Museum, Oc,B70.10.

the 1870s. My assumption is that it is far more likely that they were taken in Brisbane in the 1860s.

Two of these photographs feature Kirwallie Sandy, a well-known identity in the Brisbane region in the 1860s. This in itself helps confirm that the photographs were taken in Brisbane. Copies of these same two photographs are held in The University of Queensland Anthropology Museum, but no relevant information is attached to them. In the Anthropology Museum photographs, a patterned carpet can clearly be seen, while somebody has attempted to disguise the carpet in the British Museum photographs. This may have been done by manipulating the original glass negative, or possibly an original photograph was manipulated and then a copy negative was made. One woman who appears in the family scene with Sandy also appears in the photograph of a fight scene, so possibly this is a staged situation where Sandy is 'preventing his wife' from being stolen by the other men.

The Canberra-based anthropologist Nicolas Peterson purchased a set of six images at an auction. These photographs had no information attached. Peterson was confident that they were of Queensland people, and it appears that his assumption is correct. One of the photographs is the same as one of the Bevan images held by the British Museum, and the others were all obviously taken around the same time and in the same studio.

Copies of two images from this series, one held by Nicolas Peterson and one held by the British Museum, are also held in the State Library of Victoria. But in the library's collection, they are identified as being taken by Alfred Wren in his Elizabeth Street studio in Melbourne between 1867 and 1870.[8] Unless more information is found, I will remain confident that these images were actually taken by Thomas Bevan in Brisbane.

DANIEL MARQUIS

From the available photographic record it appears that Daniel Marquis was the most active Brisbane-based photographer of Aboriginal people in the 1860s. He operated a photographic studio at 82 George Street, Brisbane, from 1866 until his death in 1879. I have managed to identify more than seventy photographs of Aboriginal people taken by Marquis during his time working in Brisbane. After his death, Daniel Metcalfe took over his studio under the name Imperial Photo Company. Metcalfe later worked with William True Bennett.

The State Library of Queensland holds a photograph album that belonged to the Archer family and which contains a series of artworks and photographs from the Brisbane region — in particular, a series of photographs of Aborigines that were taken by Marquis. Even though he is not credited in the album, there is no doubt he was the photographer, as several of these same images are held in other collections and are clearly identified as being taken by Marquis.

One clue that connects these photographs to Marquis' George Street studio is the painted backdrop that features a re-creation of a panoramic view of Brisbane, with landmarks such as the Brisbane River, the original Victoria Street Bridge, and the Springhill windmill, all clearly identifiable (Figure 10). Whoever put the album together obviously did not want to include any nudity, so several photographs have been cropped to avoid the display of women's bare breasts. Fortunately, examples of these same photographs exist in other collections,

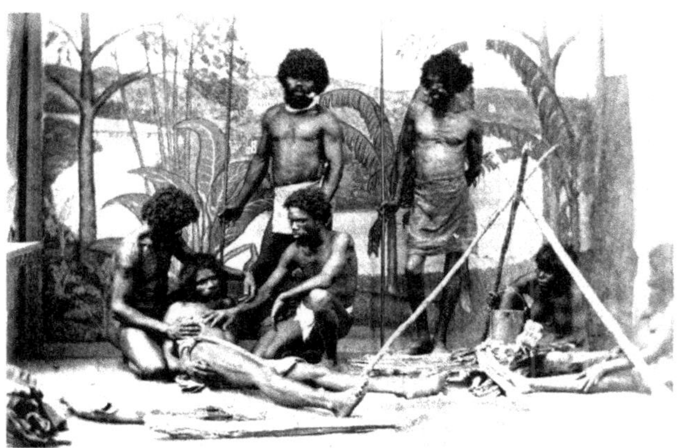

FIGURE 10: Daniel Marquis. *Group with painted backdrop of the Brisbane River in Daniel Marquis's George Street studio, Brisbane, 1866–70*. Albumen print. Queensland Art Gallery, 994.056.

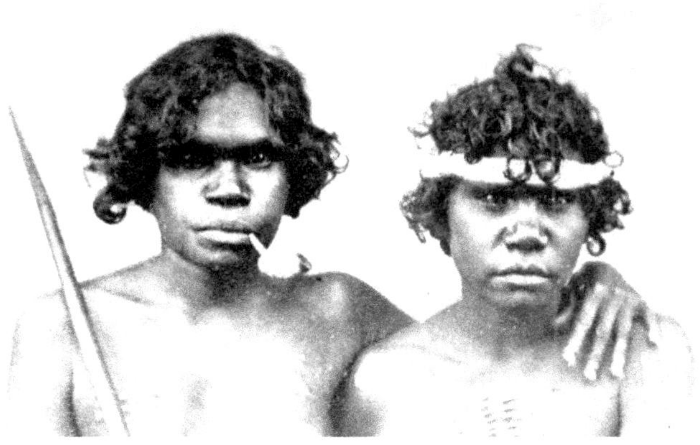

FIGURE 11: Daniel Marquis. *Half-length frontal portrait of two young women, George Street studio, Brisbane, c. 1866–1870*. Albumen print. Museum Godeffroy collection.

so we can see the entire images. A photograph of a bare-breasted woman and baby demonstrates the extent of the cropping; the woman has been cut out and completely removed, and only the baby appears in the Archer family album. In another photograph, only the heads and shoulders of two young women can be seen, as the rest of their bodies have been cut from the image (Figure 11). This led historian John Steele, in his book *Aboriginal pathways*, to make the mistake of referring to them as 'two boys'[9]; the copy of the complete photograph held by the Pitt Rivers Museum shows that they are not boys at all.

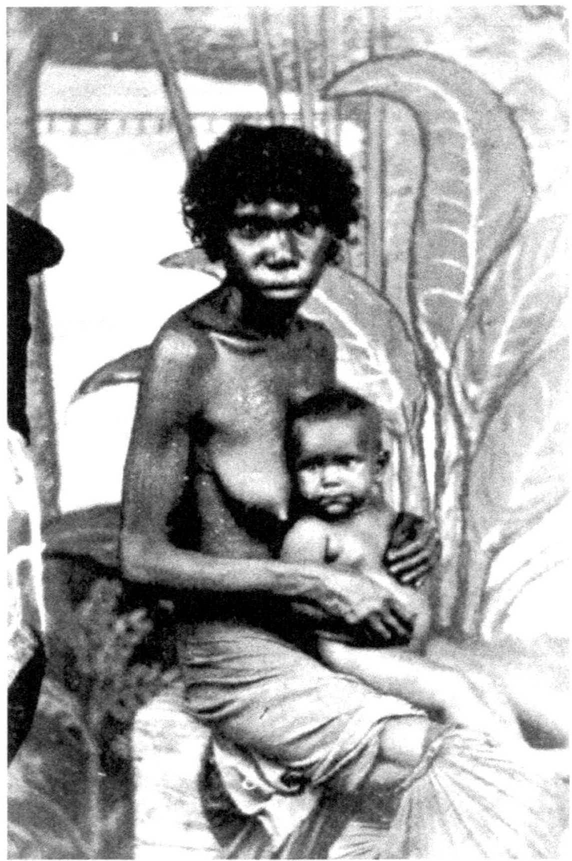

FIGURE 12: Daniel Marquis. *Woman and child, George Street, Brisbane 1866–70*. The University of Queensland Anthropology Museum, 31326.

The German naturalist Amelie Dietrich worked in Queensland from 1863 to 1872 as part of a scientific collecting expedition for the Museum Godeffroy in Hamburg. She returned to Germany with nineteen photographs of Aboriginal people from Queensland. Ten of these photographs later became part of the founding collection of the Pitt Rivers Museum and were transferred to Oxford in 1884.[10] Six of these photographs were catalogued as coming from Brisbane and the other four were identified as being from Rockhampton. I am confident that the four from Rockhampton were taken by Joseph Wilder, and the six photographs from Brisbane were taken in Daniel Marquis' George Street studio (Figures 12 and 13).

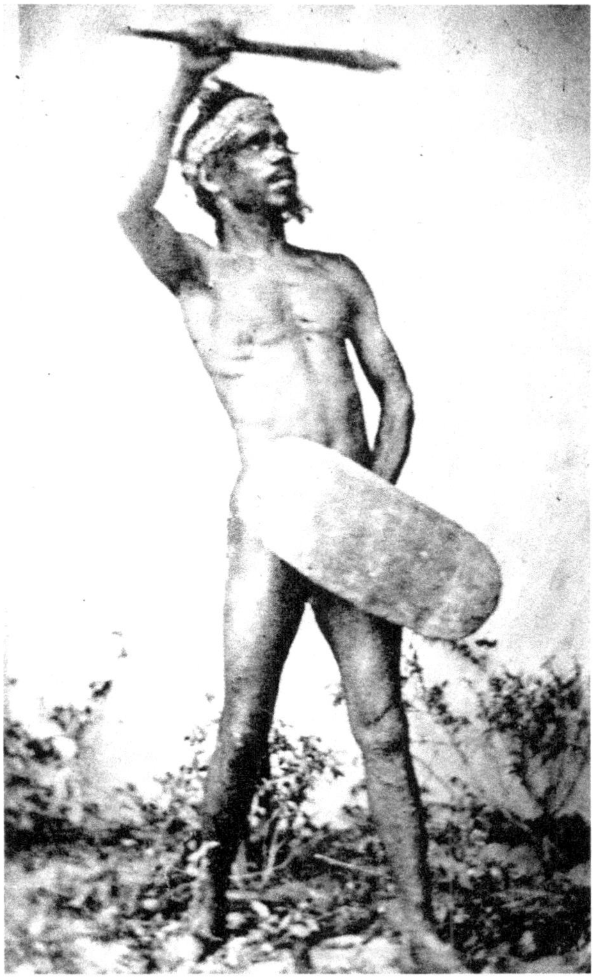

FIGURE 13: Daniel Marquis. *Man posing with club and shield, George Street, Brisbane, c. 1866–1870*. Albumen print. Pitt Rivers Museum, University of Oxford, 1998.249.5.4.

There is some confusion with the dates of these photographs. They are generally described as being taken between 1863 and 1865, as that is when Dietrich spent time in Brisbane. The dates may be correct in regards to the Rockhampton photographs, as Wilder was operating at that time. However, the same cannot be said regarding the dates of the Brisbane photographs, as Marquis did not open his studio until 1866. I trust that Dietrich most likely purchased these photographs on a return trip to Brisbane on her way back to Europe in 1872.

RICHARD DAINTREE

Another photographer worth discussing is Richard Daintree, as he has often been credited as taking photographs of Aboriginal people in Brisbane. In particular, he has been credited as taking the photograph of Kirwallie Sandy wearing the breastplate, inscribed 'King Sandy — Brisbane' (Figure 14).[11] However,

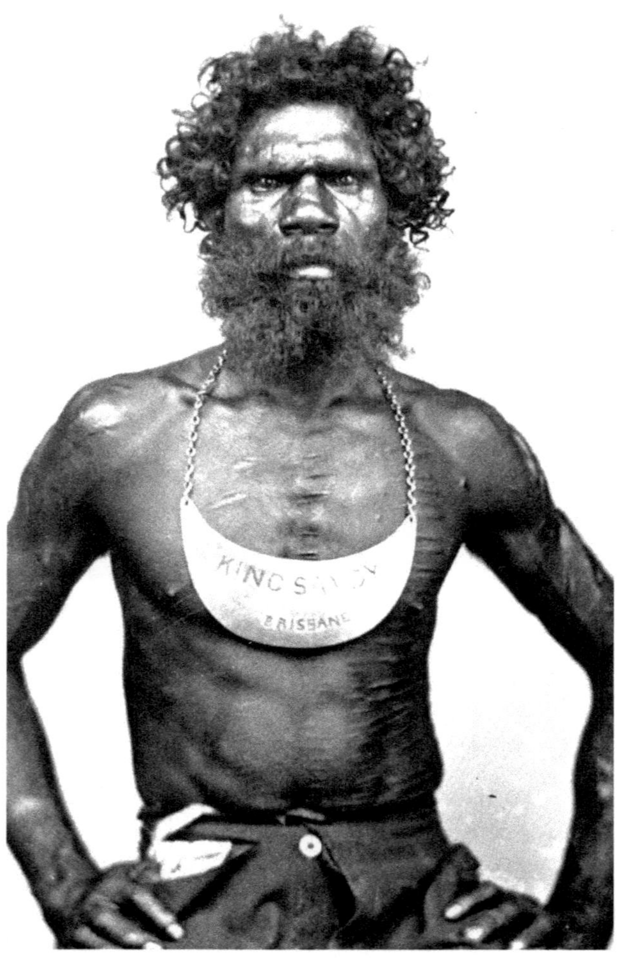

FIGURE 14: Daniel Marquis. *Kirwallie Sandy, George Street Brisbane, 1866–1872.* Albumen print. John Oxley Library, State Library of Queensland, JOL169645.

my more recent research confirms that this photograph was in fact taken by Daniel Marquis, and I am convinced that Daintree most likely did not take any photographs of Aboriginal people during his occasional visits to Brisbane.

Richard Daintree visited Queensland in 1863 to begin his partnership in the pastoral industry with William Hann in the Burdekin district of north Queensland. In 1864 he left Victoria to live in north Queensland, first living at Bluff Downs, before building a house and settling on Maryvale Station with his wife.[12]

In 1869 Daintree was appointed Government Geologist for North Queensland and is noted as pioneering the use of photography to document geographic survey work.[13] In this role he travelled to London as commissioner in charge of Queensland's contribution to the 1871 Exhibition of Art and Industry.[14] This exhibition was a showcase of geological specimens, maps, photographs and other items that demonstrated the wealth and prosperity of Queensland and was aimed at encouraging migration to the state. The following year Daintree was appointed Agent-General in London and he continued producing promotional exhibitions.

Each year until his early retirement (due to ill health) in January 1876, Daintree obtained negatives from Queensland to make a more comprehensive photographic record of its industries and major towns. These negatives were enlarged by the autotype process and hand-coloured in oils in London — and at Daintree's instigation were later circulated around exhibitions and museums in multiple series.[15]

Looking at photographs of Daintree's 1872 and 1873 exhibitions, it is obvious that he was displaying photographs taken by Marquis (Figures 15 and 16). There is no doubt that at least four of these photographs were taken in Marquis' Brisbane studio, as other copies of the same or similar images have been firmly identified. One photograph exhibited in 1872 was of well-known Brisbane identity Kirwallie Sandy. Two copies of the exhibition prints in exact format are held in the Queensland Museum, which demonstrates that many of the photographs were returned to Australia. The Queensland Museum claims to hold around 175 copies of the hand-coloured photographs attributed to Daintree.[16] It does need to be questioned, however, exactly how many of these were actually taken by Daintree.

Even though it is known that Daintree did take photographs of street scenes in Brisbane, there is no indication that he actually took photographs of

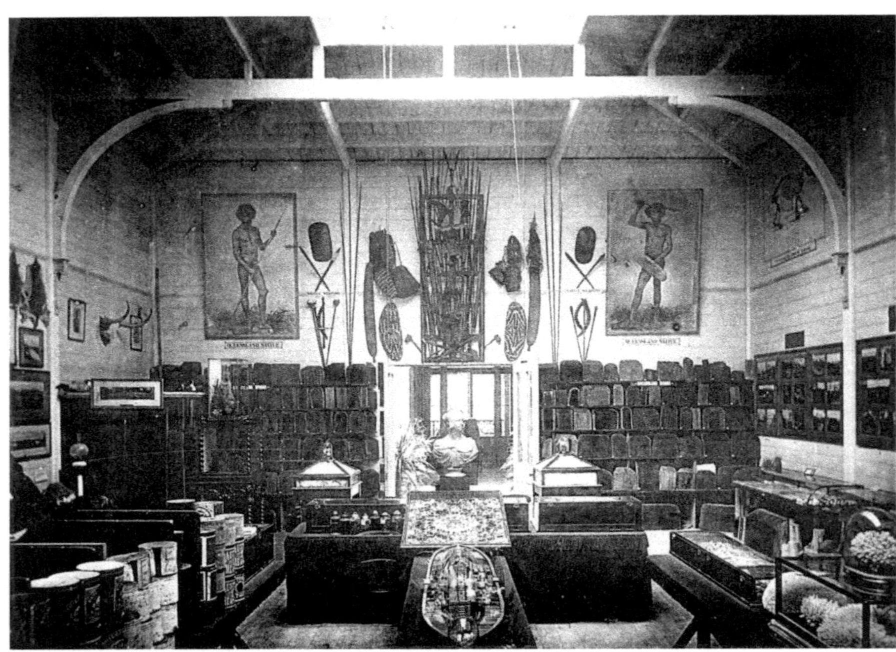

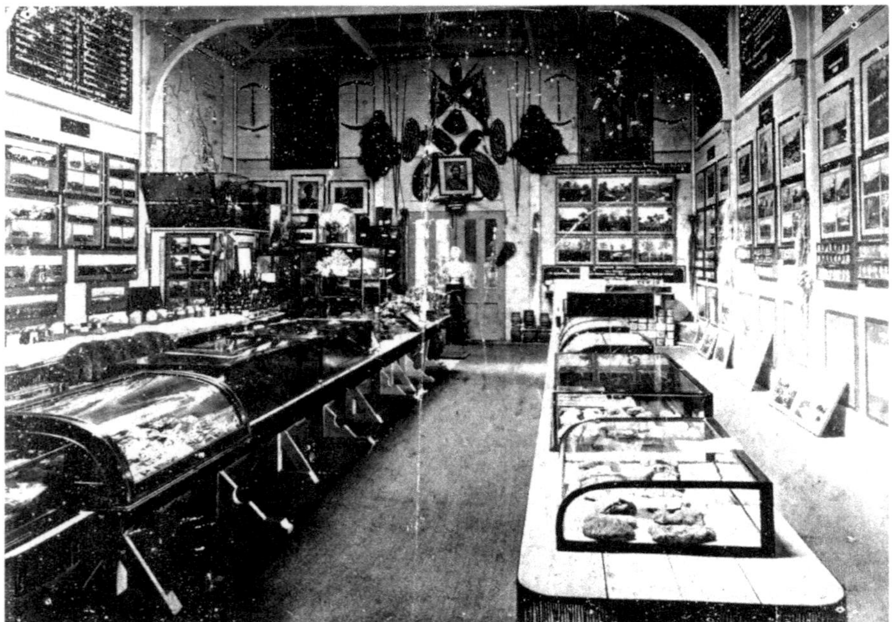

TOP: FIGURE 15: Heliotype Company. *Queensland Exhibition, London, 1872.* Albumen print. John Oxley Library, State Library of Queensland, JOL54131.

BOTTOM: FIGURE 16: *Queensland Exhibition, London, 1873.* Albumen print. Queensland Museum, JE250.

any Aboriginal people while he was in Brisbane. Marquis can be credited for supplying many of the photographs of Aboriginal people that Daintree exhibited in London, which in turn has created a degree of confusion, as many of Marquis' photographs have since been incorrectly credited to Daintree. I have managed to sort out much of this confusion by identifying which photographs were taken by Daintree, and which were taken by Marquis. In some of Daintree's studio photographs we see elaborately painted studio backdrops, and in other photographs he made use of a plain canvas background and a few branches and leaves on the floor — very similar to techniques used by Marquis (Figure 17).

In one Daintree photograph of a group of men and boys, an artefact — a spear-thrower that is unique to the broader Townsville region — gives some idea of the location (Figure 18). By itself it does not firmly tie the photograph to an exact location, but to some degree it supports the possibility that many of his studio photographs were taken at Maryvale Station, his permanent home, and he would have had close contact with the Aboriginal people who worked on his property, as well as those that lived in the nearby camp mentioned in William Hann's diaries.

Quite a bit is known about where Daintree travelled, and the locations of several of his landscape, pastoral and mining scene photographs can be identified, proving that he did travel extensively with his camera equipment.[17] But the question that needs to be asked is whether he travelled with painted studio backdrops and heavy metal stands, which were used to keep sitters still during the long exposure times. Considering the fact that he was not a commercial portrait photographer, I do not think he would have been motivated to travel with a full studio setup. Instead, I assume that his studio photographs were taken at his home in north Queensland, or at nearby locations where it was feasible to transport his equipment. I am confident that he did not take any studio photographs of Aboriginal people in the Brisbane region.

THE IMPORTANCE OF PHOTOGRAPHS

When looking at photographs of Aboriginal people taken more than a hundred years ago, the viewer often considers the huge changes to Aboriginal culture and the landscape, especially when looking at photographs that were taken in areas that are now highly urbanised, such as Brisbane and the surrounding regions of

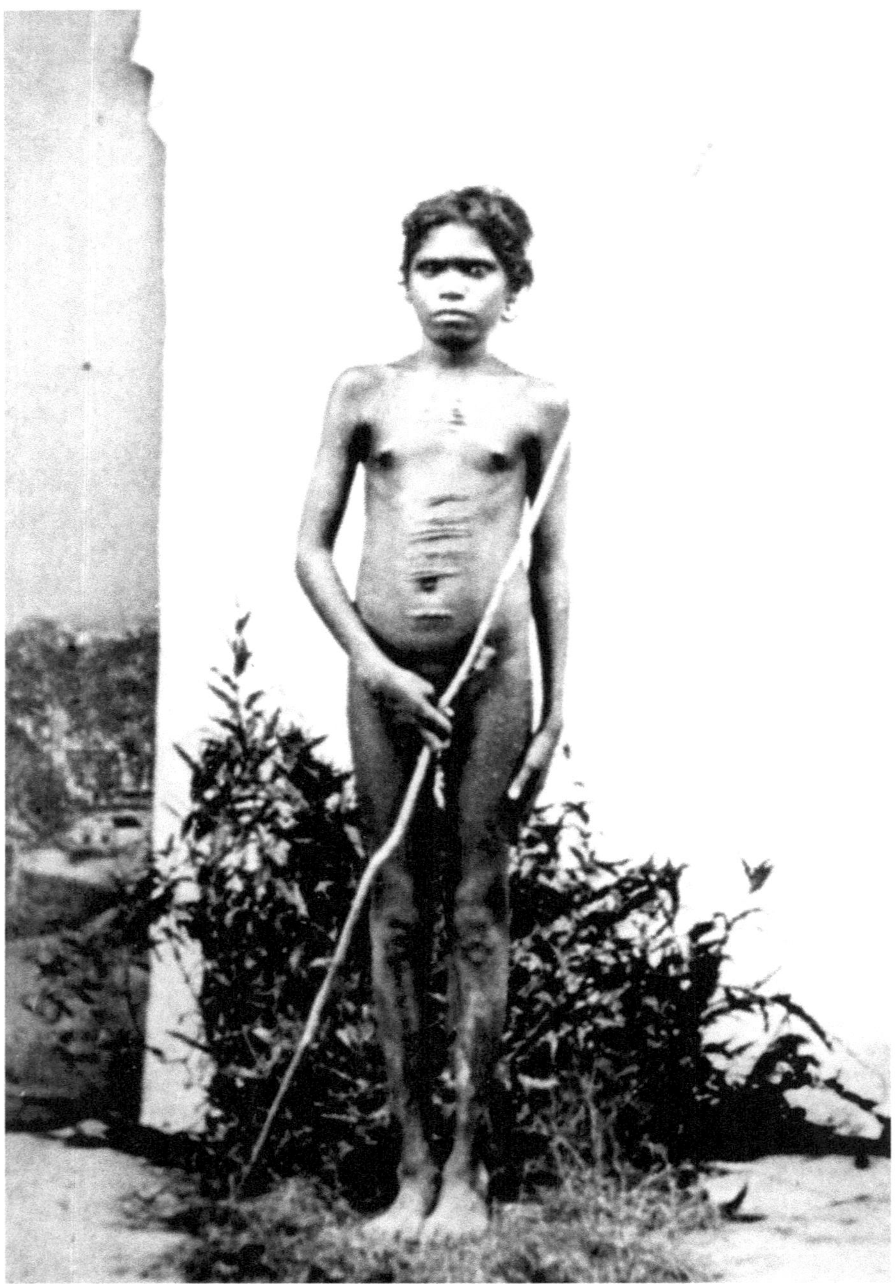

TOP: FIGURE 17: Richard Daintree. *Studio portrait of girl holding fishing rod*. Burdekin River region, north Queensland, c. 1864–69. Albumen print. State Library of Queensland JOL24572.

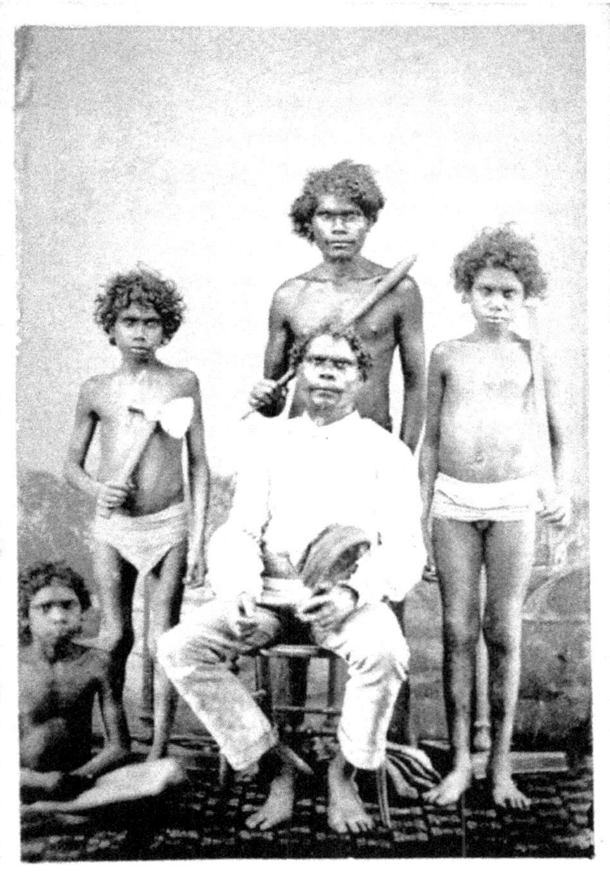

FIGURE 18: Richard Daintree. *Men and boys, Burdekin River region, north Queensland, 1864–69.* Albumen print. The University of Queensland Anthropology Museum, 31616.

south-east Queensland. Only a limited number of photographs were taken in the 1800s of Aboriginal people from my traditional country of the Gold Coast. I am very familiar with these photographs and have done extensive research on most of the individuals featured, and have documented how these photographs have been claimed by relatives as an important part of our history.

Sadly, some photographs have been used to exclude Aboriginal people from their history and identity. Captions such as 'The last of the tribe' are examples of how this has happened. Some photographs have at times been used to further the causes of modern Aboriginal factional politics, but in general early photographs play an important role in how Aboriginal families publicly state their genuine connection to country.

There is no doubt that identifying when and where particular photographers worked provides important clues to the identity of some of the people in the photographs. Just as importantly, identifying the ages of individual Aboriginal people, or finding out when they were born or when they died, is an important way of determining who exactly features in the photographs. With the ever-increasing involvement of Aboriginal people in documenting our own histories, we will gain a much more accurate understanding of the people featured in these old photographs and their exact connections to country and the future generations of their descendants. It is important for everybody working in the education, arts and cultural industries to take every effort to portray Aboriginal history and culture in a fair and accurate way.

NOTES

1. M Aird, *Portraits of our elders*, Queensland Art Gallery, Brisbane, 1993, p. 65.
2. R Fisher, '"Through a glass darkly": photographers and their role in the Moreton Bay region before 1860', *Journal of the Royal Historical Society of Queensland*, 12(3):297–316, 1985, p. 298.
3. ibid., p. 300.
4. I Wild, *Lengthening shadows on Durundur country*, Woodford Bicentennial Committee, Woodford, Qld, 1988, p. 2.
5. 'A king of shreds and patches', *The Queenslander*, 23 January 1904, p. 22.
6. 'Advertising', *Empire*, 4 November 1854, p. 3.
7. Thanks to Marcel Safier, who in 2012 provided with me with a copy of a photograph of a different woman in the same studio as the woman with the possum skin cloak. On the back of this photograph it is identified as being taken by Edward Forster at his Maryborough studio.
8. S Braithwaite, The foundation of Aboriginal photography in Victoria, unpublished manuscript, Aboriginal Visual Histories Project, Monash University, 2009, p. 38.
9. J Steele, *Aboriginal pathways in southeast Queensland and the Richmond River*, University of Queensland Press, St Lucia, 1983.
10. C Morton, 'Ten Queensland photographs', *Rethinking Pitt-Rivers: analyzing the activities of a nineteenth-century collector*, 2010, viewed 15 November 2013, <http://web.prm.ox.ac.uk/rpr/>.
11. Aird, above n 1, p. 7.
12. IG Sanker, *Queensland in the 1860s: the photography of Richard Daintree*, Queensland Museum, Brisbane, 1977, p. 2.
13. ibid., p. 73.
14. J McKay, 'A good show: colonial Queensland at international exhibitions', in *Memoirs of the Queensland Museum, Cultural Heritage series*, vol. 1, no. 2, 1998, p. 247.
15. ibid., p. 248.
16. Sanker, above n 12, p. 5.
17. ibid., p. 120.

SOUTH AUSTRALIA

Dedicated to Thomas Edwin Trevorrow, 1 May 1954 – 18 April 2013

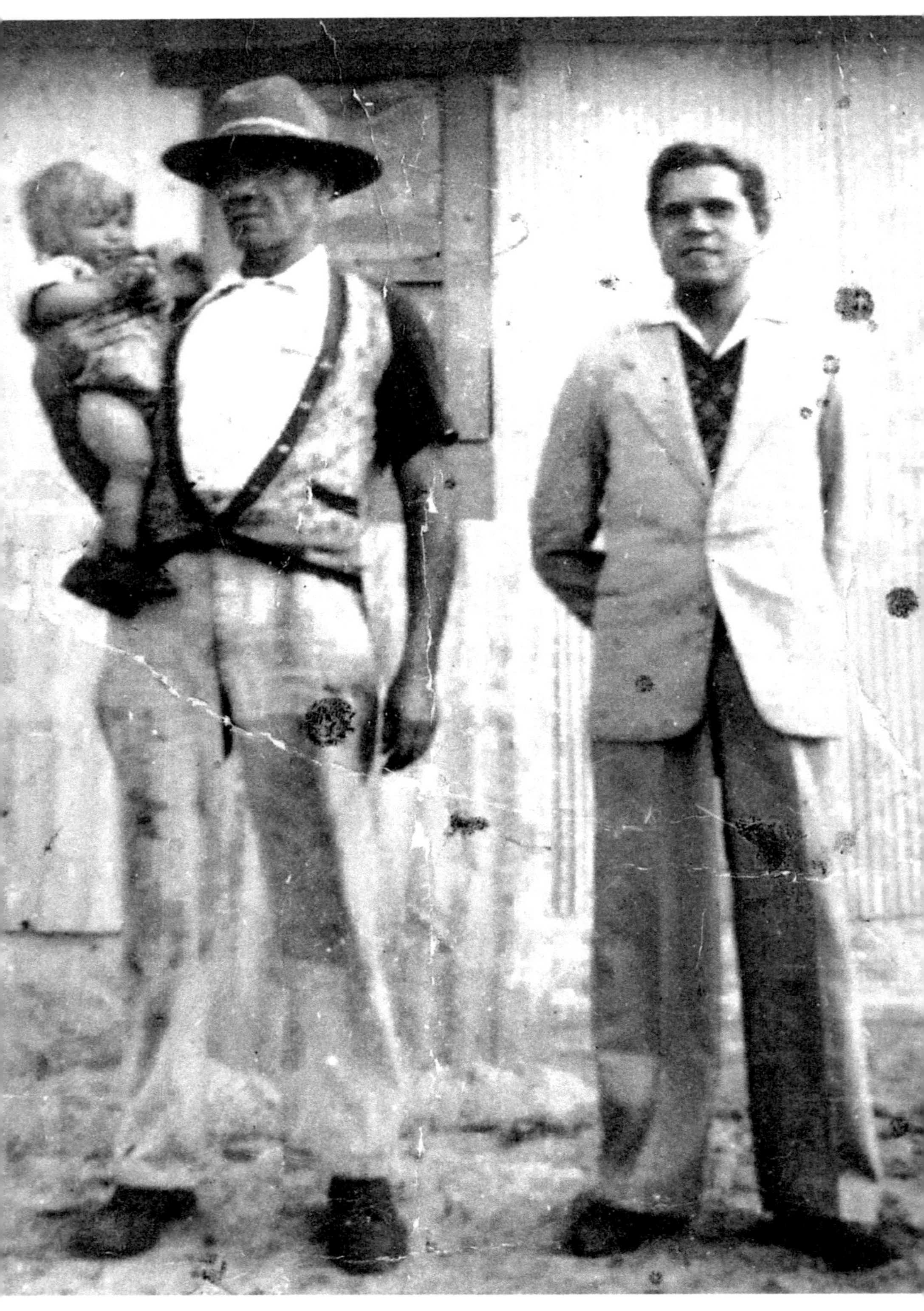

Little fella in his father's arms; Uncle Joe Trevorrow holding baby Tom, and Choom (Joe Trevorrow Junior), c. 1955. Courtesy Ellen and Tom Trevorrow.

Chapter 7

PHOTOGRAPHING SOUTH AUSTRALIAN INDIGENOUS PEOPLE: 'FAR MORE GENTLEMANLY THAN MANY'

Jane Lydon and Sari Braithwaite

Tenberry (c. 1798–1855) was a senior Ngaiwong man from the Murray River who lived through his people's first violent encounters with white settlers during the 1830s. In 1841 he was appointed native constable at Moorundie, the first European settlement on the Murray, after explorer and colonial administrator Edward John Eyre (1815–1901) became its Resident Magistrate and Protector of Aborigines. With Tenberry's help, Eyre was successful in preventing further clashes between the local Indigenous people and overlanders travelling through the region. Settlers recognised Tenberry's key role as a cultural mediator, and in February 1846 one newspaper account noted that:

> Tenberry has always been on the most friendly terms with Europeans, and it is to his influence and co-operation that they, in a large measure, owe the peaceful occupation of the Murray River, and the happy establishment of amicable relations with the once hostile, and much-dreaded tribes of the Murray, Rufus, and Darling Rivers.[1]

Tenberry's remarkable early portrait survives in England, collected by a missionary who saw him as 'King' Tenberry, a 'noble savage' and guardian of tradition who was doomed to disappear (Figure 1).[2] Although contemporaries may have seen Tenberry as a relic of the past, his photographic portrait brings him to life again, remaining a powerful testament to his strength and experience. The camera focuses squarely and intensely on Tenberry's face, and especially his eyes, rendering his troubled expression with remarkable clarity. He is shown not as a 'type' but as an important individual in his own right, expressing his respected status within cross-cultural colonial society. His descendants value this portrait today as a record of a famous ancestor and his extraordinary life.

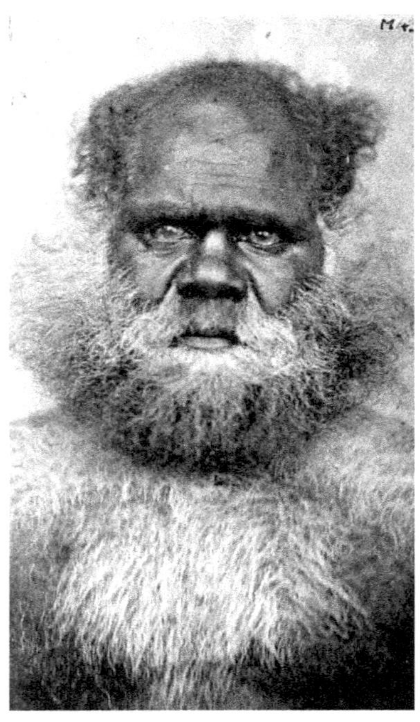

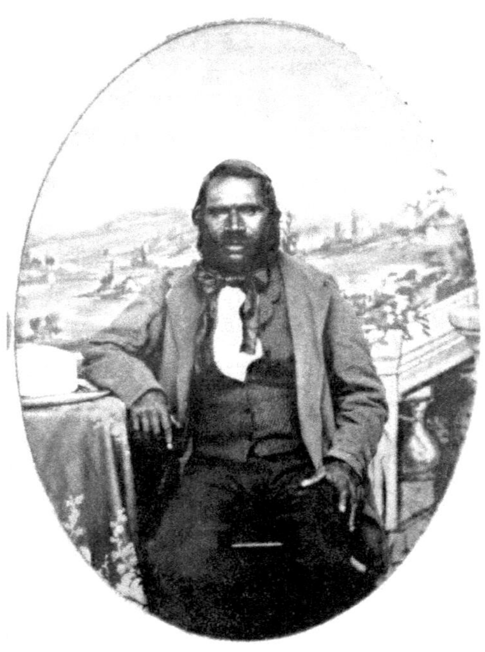

LEFT: FIGURE 1: *Tenbury (aet c.60) Chief of the MURRAY BEND tribes. 1847. S. AUSTRALIA.* Albumen print. Courtesy of the Pitt Rivers Museum, PRM1998.249.33.1. Moral/cultural permission Cynthia Hutchison and the Ngaut Ngaut Mannum Aboriginal Community Association.

RIGHT: FIGURE 2: *Jacky – now known as Master Mortlock.* Ambrotype, c. 1855. Ayers House Collection, Adelaide, catalogue 4a, accession 0787.

Tenberry had seen profound changes to his world. The colony of South Australia was established in 1836, after the British Parliament passed the *South Australia Act 1834*, and rapid settlement soon saw the decimation of the Kaurna, upon whose traditional country the town of Adelaide was established. South Australia was the only Australian state to be settled entirely by free settlers under Edward Gibbon Wakefield's scheme of small to medium agricultural landholdings. Although the Letters of Patent attached to the *Act* acknowledged Aboriginal ownership and guaranteed land rights for the Indigenous inhabitants, these provisions were generally ignored by the Colonisation Commissioners in London and white settlers, who followed the usual pattern of relations with the Indigenous inhabitants ranging from violence to accommodation.[3] These complex relations were mapped through photography.[4]

JACKEY AND JEMIMA GUNLARNMAN

Other early photographs reveal stories of adaptation, such as the portraits, made around 1860, of Tatiara couple Jackey Gunlarnman and his wife Jemima. They were servants of prominent pastoralist William Ranson Mortlock (1821–1884), and in a well-known portrait of *Jemima, wife of Jacky and William Tennant Mortlock*, Jemima holds the Mortlocks' toddler son on her lap. Evocatively, the young William has wriggled during the long exposure required by the daguerreotype process and is a little blurred, but Jemima's somewhat stern expression is clear and well defined.[5] Jemima is neatly dressed and has her hair in long ringlets. Jackey's ambrotype portrait (Figure 2) shows him dressed neatly in waistcoat, cravat and suit, seated before an elaborate painted backdrop representing a picturesque landscape that has been hand-coloured in green. Jackey is dignified and serious.[6]

These exceptional portraits testify to the couple's unusual position in the new colony's frontier society. Mortlock had settled in South Australia in 1844 and purchased the Yalluna run, twenty-five miles north of Port Lincoln, on the Eyre Peninsula, traditional country of the Pangkala and Nauo along the coast, and the Kokatha in the interior. Mortlock had supposedly 'rescued' Jackey from the Tatiara district in 1845, and persuaded him to work on Yalluna. Nine years later, Jackey and Jemima lived in a house that 'contained three rooms, and was worth 5s to 8s per week as rent. He had lived there since last March twelvemonth. He could read a little and write after a fashion', and was 'said to possess a very fair degree of general intelligence'.[7] The story was told that:

> On one occasion, when Bishop Short was visiting the station, the prelate asked Jacky why he did not take a wife, and the native expressed his objection to marrying a woman belonging to another tribe. Next time that the Bishop journeyed to Eyre Peninsula he took with him a lubra whom he had secured in the Tatiara district, and introduced her to Jacky, who soon afterwards married her. The couple led a very happy and useful life on Yalluna.[8]

The harmonious picture this conjures up is undermined by other evidence for bitter conflict. The history of contact in the Port Lincoln district throughout the 1840s and 1850s was particularly violent and bloody, perhaps because of an earlier phase of contact with white whalers and sealers along the coast who had abducted Indigenous women. In 1859 one such incident involving Mortlock and his brother-in-law Andrew Tennant was reported in unusual detail, revealing the often fraught and brutal relations between settlers and the Indigenous people: the Government Resident at Port Lincoln described how a man named Colotoney had died of injuries allegedly inflicted by Tennant. Colotoney claimed that Tennant had 'beaten him with waddies, had tied him up and whipped him with a stock whip and had kicked him — that blood ran down his legs — that he was beaten for allowing his sheep to mix with others'.[9] Several statements by Indigenous residents of nearby Poonindie Mission and those living in camps around it endorsed Colotoney's account. Yet the inquest was derailed by Mortlock, who initially tried to halt the inquiry on the grounds that 'it might probably seriously affect the character of Mr Andrew Tennant, a young man just entering the world'; then he endeavoured to show that it was a frivolous proceeding by remarking that 'everybody knew that it was general practice in the bush to thrash the natives when they deserved it, it being the only way of managing them'.[10]

Tennant was reported to have tortured and assaulted several other local Aboriginal men in various horrible ways.[11] Colotoney had fled to Poonindie as a refuge, and the missionary Octavius Hammond clearly viewed Tennant's behaviour as criminal, although his attitude contrasted strongly with those of Mortlock and his circle. Such evidence indicates that the Ayers House portraits were not an expression of Indigenous people as equals; rather, they emerge from a strictly hierarchical worldview in which Jackey and Jemima were valued in the subordinate role of servants.

'THE NUCLEUS OF THE NATIVE CHURCH': POONINDIE MISSION

By contrast, the remarkable series of portraits commissioned by Anglican clergymen at Poonindie Mission during the 1850s and 1860s express a conception of the essential unity of humankind and the equal capacity of their subjects in a distinctively inclusive vision of Indigenous people.[12] These daguerreotypes and ambrotypes, held in British and Australian archives, were rediscovered during 2012 and mark a radical departure from contemporary — and later — photographs of Indigenous Australian people. They point to a rare visual theme that flourished in South Australia during these years under the impetus of Anglican Church leaders commemorating the achievements of Christianised Aboriginal farmers.

In 1848 the new Anglican Bishop of Adelaide, Augustus Short (1802–1883), arrived in the colony with his Archdeacon Matthew Hale (1811–1895). With Protector Moorhouse's support, Short and Hale proposed the establishment of Poonindie, a 'training institution' on the southern Eyre Peninsula where children and young adults could be further educated and Christianised, away from the 'corrupting' influence of their parents.[13] By early 1853 the clergymen were delighted with their small flock, and Short later described how:

> After hearing them, and asking them questions, I agreed with the Archdeacon that there was good ground for admitting them by baptism into the ark of Christ's Church, believing them to be subjects of God's grace and favour. We held regular evening service at sundown; and after the second lesson, I baptized Thomas Nytchie, James Narrung, Samuel Conwillan, Joseph Mudlong, David Tobbonko, John Wangaru, Daniel Toodko, Matthew Kewrie, Timothy Tartan, Isaac Pitpowie, and Martha Tanda, wife of Conwillan.[14]

Short's and Hale's vision was distinctive in defining the Aboriginal subjects as gentlemen, the 'nucleus of a native church'. Short's ideas about 'civilising' Indigenous people were shaped by his own upper-class worldview — including his experience of public school, the belief in personal demeanour as a sign of status, and the importance of cricket. Crucially, missionaries argued for the transformative potential of Indigenous people — often against those who argued for their essential difference on racial grounds. In the intensely politicised context of mid-century Victorian science, great weight was given to debates about human history and difference. In attempting to counter ideas of the essential difference of Indigenous Australians, visible evidence for achievements at Poonindie took on particular significance. Immediately after the group baptism, Short wrote of the young men:

> I was agreeably surprised to see them nicely dressed in the usual clothing worn by settlers; cheque shirts, light summer coats, plaid trowsers, with shoes and felt hats—articles mostly purchased with their own earnings.

> They were better dressed than the labouring class in general at home... Not far off was a small native camp, and the contrast between these two groups would have convinced any candid observer of the truth for which the Archdeacon has always steadily contended, viz. that the Aborigines are not only entitled to our Christian regard, but are capable, under God's blessing, of being brought out of darkness into light, and from the power of Satan unto God.[15]

In this way, Short conflated the appearance of the people of Poonindie, measured by their clothing and personal grooming, with their spiritual transformation. Portraits of the residents of Poonindie assumed value as missionary propaganda, incorporated into longer textual narratives for distant, British audiences.[16] The 'cheque shirts' and 'plaid trowsers' revealed progress made on the road to civilisation. Short concluded that 'There is now a small body of trained Christian natives, the nucleus of the native Church.'[17]

This first group of Aboriginal converts was frequently compared with aristocratic young upper-class Englishmen — especially on the sporting field. Six months after the group baptism, in February 1854, Sam (Conwillan), 'Sam junior' and Charlie were in Adelaide, and were invited to play cricket with the pupils of St Peters College, also founded by Short.[18] The Adelaide *Register* reported that 'The Port Lincoln natives from Archdeacon Hale's establishment are very fine fellows. They speak pure English, without the slightest dash of vulgarism and are in truth far more gentlemanly than many.'[19] Short often praised their refined behaviour and principles of Christian fellowship expressed through the noble game of cricket.[20] During this visit, Hale sent two star pupils, Samuel Conwillan (also Kandwillan) and Nannultera to have their portraits painted in Adelaide by John Crossland.[21] These well-known works are statements of the achievements and standing of their sitters. The young Nannultera holds his cricket bat aloft, poised and graceful. Samuel Conwillan calmly poses with a book, a sign of his important role within the mission community as catechist, responsible (in the absence of the missionary) for the congregation's spiritual welfare (Figure 3).

Short and Hale also commissioned photographic evidence of their success, which has survived in the form of their recently rediscovered collections in England. Several of these portraits were treasured by Hale until the end of his life, including five early photographs that are very similar to Crossland's

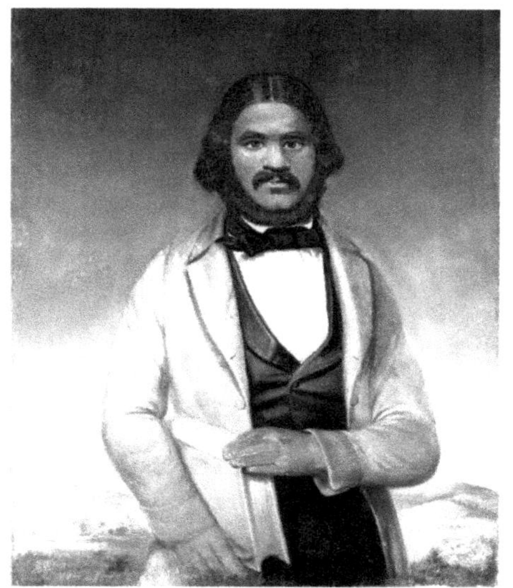

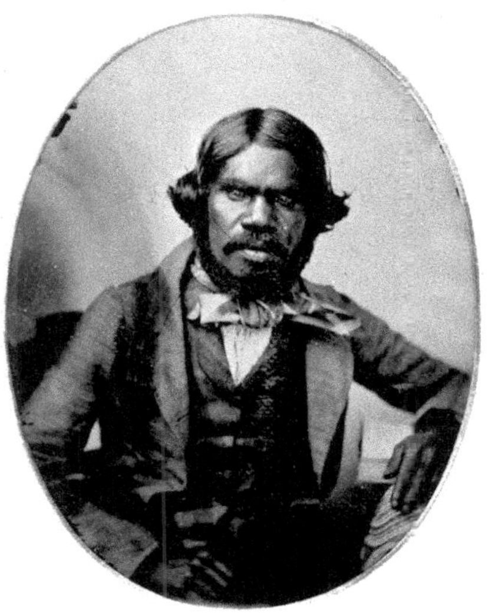

LEFT: FIGURE 3: JM Crossland. *Portrait of Samuel Kandwillan, a pupil of the natives' training institution, Poonindie, South Australia [picture].* Oil on canvas, 1854. Rex Nan Kivell Collection NK6294, National Library of Australia, Canberra.

RIGHT: FIGURE 4: *Aboriginal man of Poonindie.* Ambrotype. With the permission of Special Collections, University of Bristol Library, Papers of Mathew Blagden Hale, DM130/239.

painting. They express the significance assigned to this group from 1853 by the Anglican leaders Short and Hale as evidence for the mission's success and a more generalised capacity for Indigenous civilisation and Christianisation.

These two remarkable portraits (Figures 4 and 5) are ambrotypes, a technique invented in 1851 that produced a positive image on glass and was very quickly taken up in Australia after 1854.[22] If these portraits were made before 1860, when Samuel Conwillan died, one is likely to portray him, as he was one of the most highly regarded Aborigines at Poonindie in the early years.[23] He was often mentioned as a committed Christian and leader of his community, and the story was often told how:

> The natives were moral in their conduct, and able to resist temptation when sent with drayloads into Port Lincoln. It is remembered how 'Conwillan' on one occasion having loaded his own dray with goods from a coasting vessel according to orders, was found by the Archdeacon rendering the like service to a settler, whose teamster was lying intoxicated on the beach.[24]

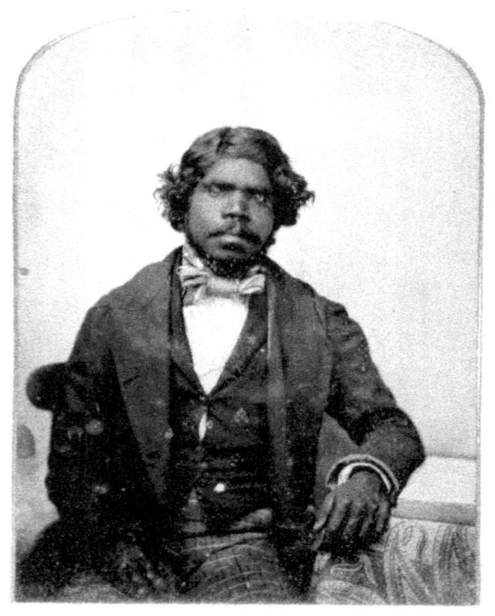

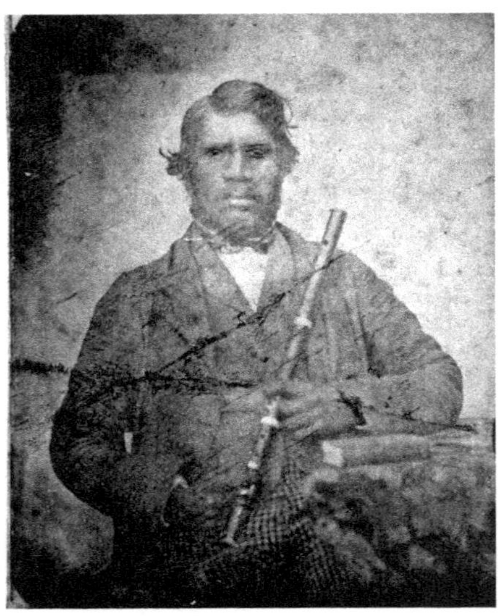

LEFT: FIGURE 5: *Aboriginal man of Poonindie*. Ambrotype. With the permission of Special Collections, University of Bristol Library, Papers of Mathew Blagden Hale, DM130/238.

RIGHT: FIGURE 6: *Aboriginal man of Poonindie holding a flute*. Copy of ?daguerreotype. With the permission of Special Collections, University of Bristol Library, Papers of Mathew Blagden Hale, DM130/241.

A further Bristol portrait shows a man holding a flute (Figure 6 and see figure 7).[25] This might portray either Conwillan or Tolbonco (also Tolbonko), of whom in 1858 one of the mission trustees, Rev Hawkes, noted:

> My old friends Konwillan [Conwillan] and Tolbonco (of St. John's Sunday school) knew me at once, and appeared glad to see me. They always lead the hymns with their flutes: both of these young men read and conduct the services of our church by turns on Sunday morning, when Mr. Hammond is absent celebrating divine service at St Thomas's, Port Lincoln.[26]

We now know that other Poonindie portraits were collected by Poonindie's missionaries. Octavius Hammond, superintendent at Poonindie between 1856 and 1868, left behind photographic portraits of well-dressed, carefully posed subjects that emphasise their dignity and successful adoption of European civilisation (for example, Figure 8).[27] Octavius Hammond must have known almost all the residents of Poonindie throughout the mission's life. Like Hale's collection, the portraits suggest a personal relationship with the subjects, and were kept in a personal, domestic context as mementoes of known individuals rather than circulated among a public audience.

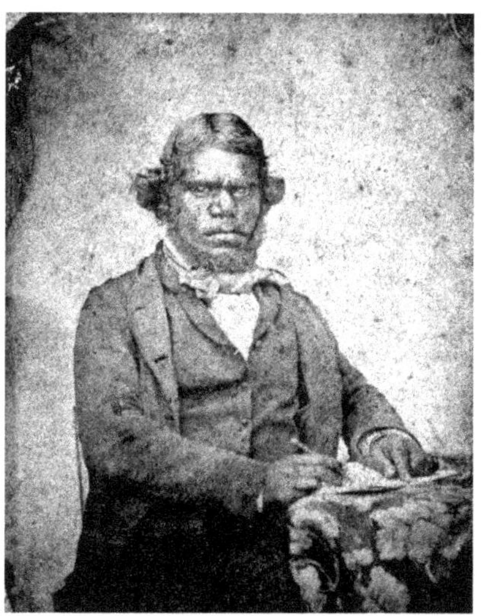

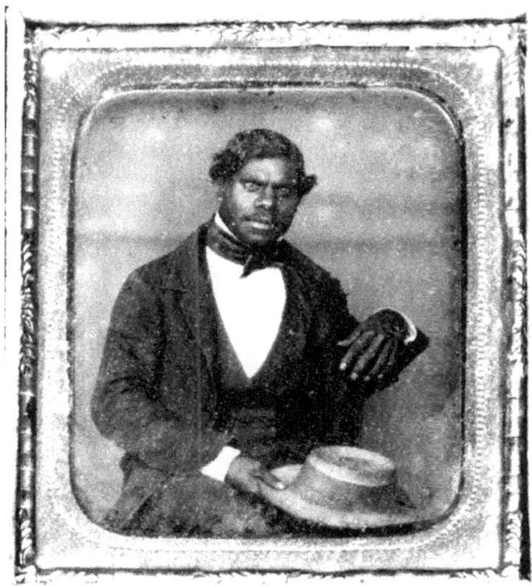

LEFT: FIGURE 7: *Aboriginal man of Poonindie*. Copy of ?daguerreotype. With the permission of Special Collections, University of Bristol Library, Papers of Mathew Blagden Hale, DM130/240.

RIGHT: FIGURE 8: *Aboriginal man*. Daguerreotype. Mill Cottage Museum Collection, Port Lincoln.

Another eleven South Australian photographs are held by the Pitt Rivers Museum in Oxford, apparently collected by Bishop Short. While having some elements in common with Hale's Bristol collection, as an entity this series constitutes a classic visual conversion narrative, generated by juxtaposing images of Indigenous people leading a traditional way of life with those who have adopted a Western lifestyle. Seven images show Indigenous people wearing kangaroo skins and bearing elaborate cicatrises. They form a powerful contrast with four studio portraits, including a portrait of Poonindie man James Wanganeen, and three that were commissioned to demonstrate the work of lay missionary Christina Smith, who established an Aborigines' Home and school at Mount Gambier between 1865 and 1867, under Short's sponsorship. For Short, photographs were a tool that served to shape understandings of the people the missions aimed to reform, and to document his achievements in the field.

It is significant that all three of the missionaries collected portraits of James Wanganeen, both alone and with his third wife, Mary Jane, which expressed his status within the community. Wanganeen was a Maraura man from the Upper Murray who had attended the Native School in Adelaide in the late 1840s and

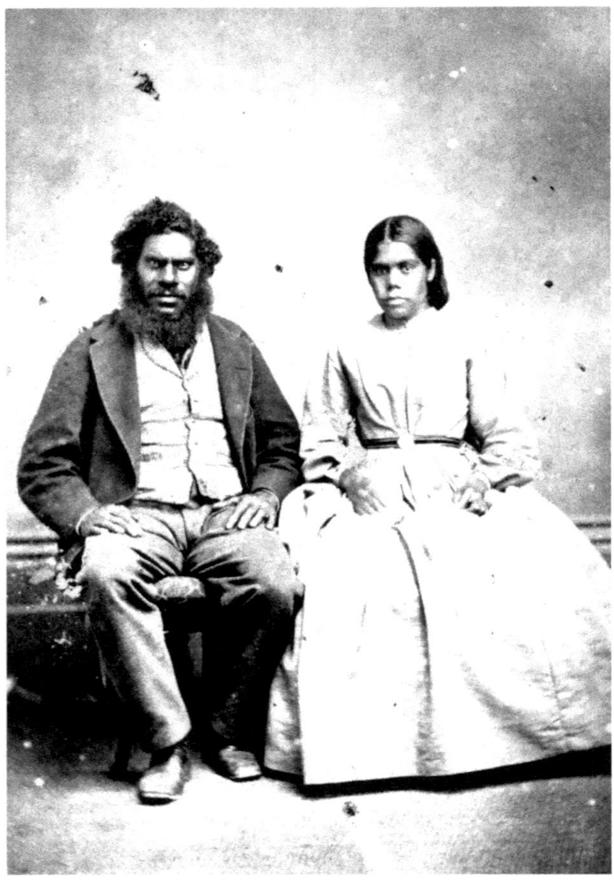

FIGURE 9: Townsend Duryea. *James and Mary Jane Wanganeen. Carte de visite*, c. 1867–70/1. With the permission of Special Collections, University of Bristol Library, Papers of Mathew Blagden Hale, DM130/231.

was then transferred to Poonindie in 1850. He was baptised in 1861, after Hale's departure, and during the 1860s rose to prominence as an evangelist among his own people.[28] The Reverend F Slaney Poole later recalled that 'One of the members of the choir, named Wanganeen, was a handsome and intelligent aborigine, and he used to read the service on occasions when the superintendent or myself was not present'.[29]

Today, descendants such as Lynnette Wanganeen, James' granddaughter, have long studied the family history, trying to imagine what he looked like.

Lynnette was thrilled to be able to see him through his photographs. With Elva Wanganeen, they have circulated copies around the family, along with the information uncovered by research.

When Short visited Poonindie in 1872, he reaffirmed his belief that 'the like feelings [of]...Etonians and Harrovians at the cricket matches at Lord's prov[e] incontestably that the Anglican aristocracy of England and the "noble savage" who ran wild in the Australian woods are linked together in *one brotherhood of blood*'.[30] Ultimately, however, the Indigenous people of Poonindie experienced the contradiction between idealising missionary rhetoric and actual colonial practice: by the 1880s a more authoritarian regime led to increasing disputes between the residents and mission staff, and some longstanding residents were expelled from the mission as a result.[31] Under increasing pressure from nearby white settlers who coveted the large area of fertile land leased by the Poonindie trustees, the Anglican Church surrendered their leases in 1894 and the area was opened up for subdivision.[32] Only one Poonindie man, Emanuel Solomon, was successful in gaining one of the blocks.[33] Most of the other residents, some who had been at Poonindie for more than forty years, were transferred to Point McLeay or Point Pearce missions. A few others remained on Eyre Peninsula, some working for white farmers, while others, particularly local Pangkala and Nauo people, drifted into fringe camps at Port Lincoln or other nearby settlements. Sadly, the missionaries' imagined future for the Indigenous residents of Poonindie was never realised.

1860S: GROWING CIRCULATION

By the 1860s photographs of Aboriginal people began to assume significant commercial value, due to their growing scientific and popular interest and technological developments such as the invention of the *carte de visite* around 1860. In the wake of social evolutionism, an interest emerged in recording the supposedly disappearing race. The established Adelaide photographers — 'Professor' Robert Hall, Townsend Duryea, Bernard Goode and Henry Davis' Adelaide Photographic Company — began to compete for the popular market locally and abroad.

One entrepreneur was Noah Shreeve, in 1864 a 'Commission salesman, storekeeper and importer of fancy goods' in Weymouth Street, who published a guide for emigrants titled *A short history of South Australia*, because, as he explained, 'many are coming; and with the experience I have shown, I might be a little guide to them'.[34] Shreeve described the 'native blacks', focusing on those he knew personally who lived in Adelaide, whose 'chief work is horse-breaking, in which they are very good, excellent riders, and very active.'[35] He commented, 'In the month of April, many of them come down from different parts of the north country'[36] and this yearly visit seems to have been a good opportunity for Adelaide's rival photographers to record the interesting visitors. Over the following month several notices of images available were advertised: for example, on 3 May the *South Australian Register* announced that

> We have had an opportunity of seeing a number of well-executed photographs of several aborigines, male and female, whose faces are not unfamiliar to the people of Adelaide. The artist is Mr. B. Goode, of Rundle-street who, we think, has been very successful in his efforts to catch the features, expression, and general appearance of the blackfellows, their lubras, and piccaninnies. It is interesting to have correct representations of a race which seems to be fast disappearing from this land.[37]

Clearly, these images were seen to have commercial value, and later in 1864 Shreeve registered twelve portraits with the Copyright Office in London (where he had also entered his book), including some of Bernard Goode's portraits.[38] By 1865 the Adelaide Photographic Institution claimed in its advertisements to have 4000 *cartes de visite* portraits for '18s per dozen', and an album of 'city views and Aboriginal portraits, 10s per dozen, assorted'.[39] Portrait commissions were also carried out by official request for international exhibitions, such as London in 1861, William Barlow's series at Point McLeay for Paris in 1866,[40] and London again in 1873.[41] Such representations often stressed the difference of their subjects by showing them naked or partially undressed, despite their altered lifestyle.

NGARRINDJERI AND POINT MCLEAY MISSION

The Ngarrindjeri form an Aboriginal nation of eighteen language groups who inhabit the Lower Murray, Coorong and Lakes area of South Australia. Their lands and waters extended thirty kilometres up the Murray from Lake Alexandrina,

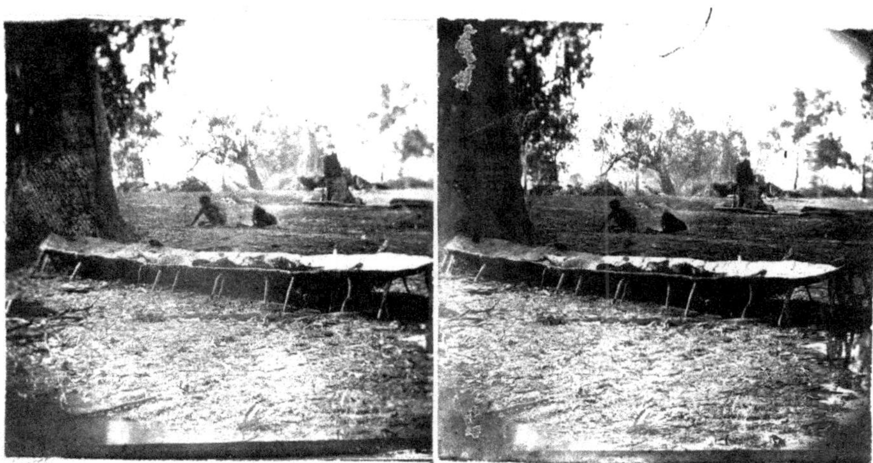

FIGURE 10: George Burnell. *Aboriginal canoe building.* Stereograph, 1862. State Library of South Australia, B12659.

the length of the Coorong and along the coastal area to Encounter Bay. They were much photographed from the early 1860s, providing a rich resource for descendants — as Karen Hughes and Ellen Trevorrow explore in the following chapter.[42] Many resided at Point McLeay Mission (renamed Raukkan in 1982) after its establishment on their traditional country in 1859 by the Aborigines' Friends Association and missionary George Taplin.[43]

In 1862 George Burnell and EW Cole travelled from Echuca down the Murray River in a small boat, taking stereoscopic portraits of settlers and Aboriginal people en route, as well as views of landscapes and the flora and fauna. Burnell took some photographs at the Yelta Mission in Victoria and at least three photographs of Aboriginal people along the Murray River in South Australia.[44] As Philip Jones points out, these show Indigenous people in context, unlike later 'isolating' views.[45] One remarkable image shows Aboriginal people making a bark canoe on the lower Murray (Figure 10).

Burnell and Cole arrived in Point McLeay in May and stayed several days (Burnell was Taplin's brother-in-law). They took a number of photographs of the people and the mission during that time.[46] Burnell subsequently offered for sale in Adelaide boxed sets of fifty-six *Stereoscopic views of the River Murray*.[47] In January 1868 Barlow returned to Point McLeay and put on a show of 'dissolving views', a technique in which two lanterns projected on to the same spot dissolved seamlessly from one image to the next.[48] It is easy to imagine the Ngarrindjeri enjoying such a display of Burnell's river journey series, which, as Ken Orchard notes, 'succinctly recapitulates the narrative flow of a river journey', ending with their own home.[49]

Point McLeay has remained home to many Ngarrindjeri into the present. In December 1874, 161 people were living at the mission, including those working on neighbouring stations.[50] Around 350 other Ngarrindjeri people worked on distant farms and stations, while some continued to lead a nomadic life, moving between the ration depots on the lower Murray and the fringe camps that developed at Goolwa, Victor Harbor, Murray Bridge, Strathalbyn and other towns in the region.[51] Although Taplin had strongly opposed many traditional customs in his early days, by the 1870s he was carefully recording cultural information, which he published in an ethnographic study, *The Narrinyeri* (1874), and in *The folklore, manners, customs and languages of the South Australian Aborigines* (1879).[52] Duryea's composite photograph of five oval portraits (four Ngarrindjeri men and one woman) was used as the frontispiece for *The Narrinyeri*.[53] Such accounts circulated in the context of social evolutionism, in which images and information about Aboriginal culture had become scientific evidence for their biological difference. Popular notions of biological difference only strengthened over the last decades of the nineteenth century, distancing these photographic subjects from their own lives and experiences.

In 1911 the South Australian Parliament passed the *Aborigines Act 1911*, which established the Aborigines Department with the Chief Protector as its head. The new Act gave the Chief Protector wide powers over most aspects of the lives of Aboriginal (i.e. 'full-blood') and 'half-caste' people throughout the state. In 1913 an inquiry into the reserves and missions recommended their transfer to the control of the Aborigines Department, under state control.[54] When the *Aboriginal Lands Trust Act 1966* (SA) was proclaimed, all reserves in South Australia were vested in the Aboriginal Lands Trust.

Doreen Kartinyeri's mother, Thelma Rigney, who grew up on Raukkan, had 'a lot of photos of the family stuck on the wall. There was a lovely one of her grandmother, Mutyuli, and old James Rankine, who used to work together at Poltalloch in the late 1800s.'[55] She remembers that tourists were a constant presence:

> The Protector let white people come in and see the way Aboriginal people lived. Buses would go from Adelaide to Goolwa for the ferry tours regularly through the summer, and forty or fifty people would come into Raukkan on the boat. The visitors took a lot of photographs, and sometimes they would send a copy back to Raukkan school. The steamer had been coming into Raukkan from back in the late 1800s, and I've got photographs showing all the little girls wearing white aprons over their school clothes. I remember my Aunty Rosie saying she got sick of having to dress up in a little white pinnie every time the steamer came in. I don't know whether those people thought that's what people on the mission wore all the time.[56]

As the following chapter explores, Ngarrindjeri and other Aboriginal people took their own photographs or acquired images of themselves that they continue to value as an important heritage resource into the present.

ACKNOWLEDGMENTS

We thank Cynthia Hunter and the Ngaut Ngaut Mannum Aboriginal Community Association. We also acknowledge Tom Gara, whose research report has been of great value in preparing this overview.

NOTES

1. 'Aborigines of South Australia', *Illustrated London News*, 14 February 1846, p. 108.
2. Now held by the Pitt Rivers Museum, University of Oxford. This print was almost certainly made from a glass negative, and was perhaps copied from an even earlier daguerreotype. Already a well-known figure to colonists, his portrait was painted by Hermann Schrauder in 1851, and subsequent engraved versions continued to circulate over following decades. For extended discussion, see S Braithwaite, T Gara & J Lydon, 'From Moorundie to Buckingham Palace: images of "King" Tenberry and his son Warrulan, 1845–55', *Journal of Australian Studies*, 35(2):165–84, 2011.
3. P Brock & D Kartinyeri, *Poonindie: the rise and destruction of an Aboriginal agricultural community*, Aboriginal Heritage Branch and SA Government Printer, Adelaide, 1989, p. 2.
4. T Gara, 'Survey of nineteenth century photographs of Aboriginal people in South Australia', unpublished report for Aboriginal Visual Histories project, Monash University, 2010; P Jones, 'Ethnographic photography in South Australia' in J Robinson assisted by M Zagala (eds), *A century in focus: South Australian photography 1840s–1940s*, Art Gallery of South Australia, Adelaide, 2007, pp. 102–7.
5. The photograph was probably taken either at Port Lincoln or at one of the Mortlock pastoral properties on Eyre Peninsula by an unknown photographer. J Messenger, 'Daguerreotype portraits, 1840s – c.1860' in Robinson assisted by Zagala (eds), above n 4, pp. 28–9.

6. These portraits are held in the Ayers House Collection in Adelaide, donated in September 1979, all catalogue 4a: accession 0787, *Jacky — now known as Master Mortlock*, and 0784, *Jemima and W.T. Mortlock. Taken about 1859. Same person.* A missing portrait, 0783, *Wife of Jacky — Known as Master Mortlock — 1855*, presumably formed a pair with Jackey's portrait, and was perhaps made in 1855.
7. His name had been placed on the West Torrens electoral roll by a Mr Paxson, seemingly as a joke, but following testimony from Mortlock, the Court of Revision retained his name; 'Court of Revision — West Torrens', *South Australian Register*, 15 July 1854, p. 2; 'The native "Jackey"', *Sydney Morning Herald*, 'Extracts from the South Australian Register: something new', 5 August 1854, p. 3.
8. *Pastoral pioneers of South Australia*, vol. 1, Publishers Limited Printers, Adelaide, 1925, p. 93.
9. Chief Secretary's Office no. 819 61/59, from AJ Murray, Government Resident, Port Lincoln 26/1859, cited in Brock & Kartinyeri, above n 3, p. 7.
10. Chief Secretary's Office no. 819 61/59, from AJ Murray, Government Resident, Port Lincoln 26/1859, cited in Brock & Kartinyeri, above n 3, p. 8.
11. The Resident noted that the evidence showed that Colotoney was already very ill with a lung complaint and was not in a fit state to be shepherding sheep in the first place, let alone to be beaten and kicked for failing to do so; Chief Secretary's Office no. 819 61/59, from AJ Murray, Government Resident, Port Lincoln 26/1859, cited in Brock & Kartinyeri, above n 3, p. 8.
12. For an extended discussion focusing on Hale's series held in Bristol, see J Lydon & S Braithwaite, '"Cheque shirts" and "plaid trowsers": photographing Poonindie Mission, South Australia', *Journal of Anthropological Society of South Australia*, Special Issue: Aboriginal Missions 37: 1–30 Dec 2013; also J Lydon and S Braithwaite 'Photographing "the nucleus of the native church" at Poonindie Mission, South Australia', *Photography and Culture*, forthcoming 2014.
13. Brock & Kartinyeri, above n 3, pp. 3–4; P Brock, *Outback ghettos: a history of Aboriginal institutionalisation and survival*, Cambridge University Press, Melbourne, 1993, p. 24.
14. Augustus Short, 'The Poonindie Mission, described in a letter from the Lord Bishop of Adelaide to the Society for the Propagation of the Gospel', *Missions to the Heathen*, no. xxv, Diocese of Adelaide, South Australia, printed for the Society for the Propagation of the Gospel, London, 1853, pp. 17–18; also, 'The native mission at Port Lincoln', *South Australian Register* (Adelaide), 14 March 1853, p. 3; at that time there were fifty-four residents, including eleven married couples, the rest children (including thirteen from the Port Lincoln district). Most of these names were also listed by George Wollaston (son of Archdeacon Wollaston), who spent part of 1852 managing Poonindie Mission Station; when he departed in February 1852 he was presented with a book and a letter signed by fifteen Aboriginal elders (original residents): Nytchie, Nwrouny, Mannere, Kandwillan, Popjoy, Bidpowie, Kewerie (or Keurrie), Mudlong, Tootko, Pathera, Kadlingare, Yarrioke, Tartwin, Coordinga and Friday. This momentous event took place a decade before the feted conversion of Wotjoballuk man Nathaniel Pepper at the Moravian-run Ebenezer Mission in north-western Victoria.
15. Short, above n 14, pp. 17–18.
16. The literature on this genre is now wide ranging, and addresses examples and processes usually in regional terms. See, for example, P Jenkins, 'The earliest generation of missionary photographers in West Africa', *Visual Anthropology*, 7:115–45, 1994; V Webb, 'Three missionary photographers in the Pacific: divine light', *History of Photography*, 21(1):12–22, 1997; KT Long, '"Cameras never lie": the role of photography in telling the story of American Evangelical missions', *Church History*, 72(4):820–51, 2003. Short and Hale were diligent in reporting progress to their financial supporters in the form of popular accounts written for a wide audience — especially for the senior missionary societies of the Church of England, The Society for the Propagation of the Gospel in Foreign Parts and the Society for the Propagation of Christian Knowledge, which had sponsored Poonindie.
17. Short, 'The Poonindie Mission', above n 14, pp. 17–18. In his book *The Aborigines of*

Australia, Hale later noted that 'We held regular evening service at sundown; and after the second lesson I baptized Thomas Nytchie, James Nurrung, Samuel Conwillan, Joseph Mudlong and Martha Tanda, wife of Conwillan', MB Hale, *The Aborigines of Australia: being an account of the institution for their education at Poonindie, in South Australia: founded in 1850 by the Ven. Archdeacon Hale*, Society for Promoting Christian Knowledge, London, 1889. Both Short and Hale claim to have baptised the converts.

18. This boarding school for colonial youth was not dissimilar from the mission in its aims and approach, which Short described in 1853 as 'educating their minds, shaping their characters, and making their souls Christian'. Named after Short's own former school, The Royal College of St Peter in Westminster, it was seemingly established along similar lines as Poonindie in 1847; K Thornton, *The messages of its walls & fields, a history of St Peter's College, 1847 to 2009*, Wakefield Press, Adelaide, 2010, viewed 8 August 2012, <www.stpeters.sa.edu.au/#history>.

19. *The Register*, 7 February 1854; see discussion in J Daly, '"Civilising" the Aborigines: cricket at Poonindie, 1850–1890', *Sporting Traditions: The Journal of the Australian Society for Sports History*, 10(2):59–68, 1994.

20. Short, above n 14, pp. 19–20.

21. J Tregenza, 'Two notable portraits of South Australian Aborigines', *Journal of the Historical Society of South Australia*, 12: 22–31, 1984.

22. J Cato, *The story of the camera in Australia*, Institute of Australian Photography, Hong Kong, 1979; A Davies & P Stanbury, *The mechanical eye in Australia*, Oxford University Press, Melbourne, 1985.

23. Brock & Kartinyeri, above n 3, p. 16.

24. A Short, *A visit to Poonindie, and some accounts of that mission to the Aborigines of South Australia*, Adelaide, 1872, p. 8.

25. These are seemingly copies of daguerreotypes or ambrotypes and were taken during the same studio session, as indicated by their identical setting, pose and clothing.

26. GW Hawkes, 'Poonindie Mission', *South Australian Register*, 28 September 1858, p. 3.

27. Six daguerreotypes and ambrotypes were rediscovered in November 2011 by Pauline Cockrill, Community History Officer with History SA, at Mill Cottage, a house museum at Port Lincoln, built for storekeeper Joseph Kemp Bishop, son of John Bishop, one of the district's first settlers and a trustee of Poonindie. Joseph married Elizabeth Hammond, Octavius' daughter, in 1868.

28. Brock & Kartinyeri, above n 3. In 1864 he travelled to the Ngarrindjeri with Rev. BT Craig, Missionary Chaplain for the Bishop of Adelaide, and in 1865 with James Unaipon, William Kropinyeri and Harry Tripp; George Taplin, South Australian Museum, carbon copy diary kept by Rev. George Taplin, AA 319/11/4, 1 January 1963 – 2 August 1865.

29. 'An interesting career', *The Register*, 1 September 1921, p. 7; PA Howell, 'Poole, Frederic Slaney (1845–1936)', *Australian dictionary of biography*, National Centre of Biography, Australian National University, viewed 7 November 2013, <http://adb.anu.edu.au/biography/poole-frederic-slaney-8075>.

30. Augustus Short, 1871, quoted in Hale, above n 17, p. 100.

31. Brock, above n 13, pp. 50–1.

32. C Raynes, *A little flour and a few blankets: an administrative history of Aboriginal affairs in South Australia 1834–2000*, State Records SA, 2002, p. 28; see also J Raftery, *Not part of the public: non-Indigenous policies and practices and the health of Indigenous South Australians 1836–1973*, Wakefield Press, Adelaide, 2006, pp. 108–9.

33. Brock, above n 13, pp. 55–6.

34. Noah Shreeve, *A short history of South Australia*, printed for the author, London, 1864, p. 40, viewed 7 November 2013, <http://nla.gov.au/nla.aus-vn4695455>.

35. ibid.

36. ibid.

37. 'Photography', *South Australian Register*, 3 May 1864, p. 2.

38. Photographs of Aboriginal people registered at the Copyright Office in November 1864 held in the Public Record Office, London, National Archives, copy 1/7.

39. 'Adelaide Photographic Institution', *South Australian Advertiser*, 12 September 1865, p. 1.
40. RJ Noye, *Dictionary of South Australian photography, 1845–1915*, Art Gallery of South Australia, 2007 (CD attached to Robinson assisted by Zagala (eds), above n 4), p. 35.
41. A list of items to be sent to the Great Exhibition in London in 1861 included some 'photographs of natives'; *Advertiser*, 26 October 1861, p. 2; *Advertiser*, 28 February 1873, p. 7, cited in Gara, above n 4, p. 6.
42. See Philip Jones' excellent overview in Robinson assisted by Zagala (eds), above n 4.
43. G Jenkin, *Conquest of the Ngarrindjeri: the story of the Lower Murray lakes tribes*, Rigby, Adelaide, 1985, pp. 78–9.
44. One of Burnell's photographs taken at Yelta Mission is in the State Library of South Australia (PRG 1258/2/2365).
45. Jones, above n 4, p. 105.
46. Noye, above n 40, p. 59.
47. K Orchard, 'George Burnell 1830–1894' in Robinson assisted by Zagala (eds), above n 4, p. 68.
48. Jones, above n 4, p. 104.
49. Orchard, above n 47, p. 68; see also K Orchard, 'Regional botany in mid-nineteenth century Australia: Mueller's Murray River collecting network', *Historical Records of Australian Science*, 11(3): 389–405, 1997.
50. Report of the Sub-Protector of Aborigines for half-year ending 31 December 1874, Aborigines' Office, Adelaide, 1874, viewed 15 November 2013, <http://archive.aiatsis.gov.au/removeprotect/59891.pdf>.
51. R Foster, 'Tommy Walker walk up here...' in J Simpson & L Hercus (eds), *History in portraits*, Aboriginal History Monograph no. 6, 1998, pp. 195–7; Report of the Sub-Protector of Aborigines for half-year ending 31 December 1875.
52. G Taplin, *The Narrinyeri: an account of the tribes of South Australian Aborigines inhabiting the country around the Lakes Alexandrina, Albert, and Coorong, and the lower part of the River Murray: their manners and customs, also, an account of the mission at Port Macleay*, JT Shawyer, Adelaide, 1874; G Taplin (ed.), *The folklore, manners, customs, and languages of the South Australian Aborigines/gathered from inquiries made by authority of South Australian Government*, E Spiller, Acting Government Printer, Adelaide, 1879.
53. Noye, above n 40, p. 105, fn 399; see also Jones, above n 4, p. 105.
54. Raynes, above n 32, pp. 36–9.
55. D Kartinyeri & S Anderson, *Doreen Kartinyeri: my Ngarrindjeri calling*, Aboriginal Studies Press, Canberra, 2008, p. 5.
56. ibid., pp. 16–17.

Chapter 8

'IT'S THAT REFLECTION': PHOTOGRAPHY AS RECUPERATIVE PRACTICE, A NGARRINDJERI PERSPECTIVE

Karen Hughes and Aunty Ellen Trevorrow

A thick winter mist floats above the Coorong waters at the end of the road, spreading through the mallee scrub to Camp Coorong, the Ngarrindjeri Culture and Education Centre, near Meningie, South Australia.[1] The Ngarrindjeri are a South Australian Aboriginal nation, comprising several peoples with a common language, whose land and waters (*ruwe*) take in the River Murray, lakes Alexandrina and Albert, the vast Coorong wetlands and the Southern Ocean coast, all part of Ngarrindjeri traditional land and sea country (*yarluwar-ruwe*). While Ngarrindjeri bore the harsh brunt of first-wave invasion in the South Australian colony (and in the unruly decades that preceded formal colonisation), as a nation they have managed to survive, and today flourish and nurture strong cultural connections to their land and waters, and to one another.

Ngarrindjeri elder and young grandmother Aunty Ellen Trevorrow has been up early helping her grannies (grandchildren) head off to school. She deposits a generous armful of freshly prepared rushes (*Cyperus gymnocaulos*) on the table, beside a stack of photo albums and snapshots selected from a collection she has passionately assembled over many decades. Soon the rushes, photos and stories will become entwined. We are equipped for a day of weaving and *yunnan* (talking) about the importance of photography and the overlapping and multilayered meanings her collection holds. This chapter comes from this day-long conversation, begun in July 2012 — but, like a piece of Ngarrindjeri weaving, it has been richly expanded through conversations between ourselves and others over the ensuing months, illuminating the central role that photos play in continually reconnecting the living and the dead, the past and the present; replenishing the knowledge that underpins the personal and cultural wellbeing at the heart of Ngarrindjeri futures.

We write this chapter out of our longstanding mutual interest in Ngarrindjeri history and the stories of the Old People, and the way that photographs can expand on what is currently known. We met in 1997, when I (Hughes) was working with Ellen's paternal grandmother, the respected elder Aunty Hilda Wilson, on my doctoral research — and we now share a friendship that has family-like dimensions. As a historian, I have a deep interest in the way Ngarrindjeri and non-Indigenous cultures have become entangled — my maternal family has lived in Ngarrindjeri country since the 1850s, and much of my research has stemmed from the tensions, as well as the productivity, of some of these relationships. Ellen was tutored by knowledgeable elders during her formative years and is deeply committed to nurturing, researching and transmitting Ngarrindjeri history and living knowledge, both within her community and across cultural divides, through the educational work of Camp Coorong.

The first part of this chapter focuses on Ellen's family album (which includes photos on display in the Camp Coorong Cultural Heritage Museum), and explores the way photos, whether from family albums or archival collections, elicit important stories that can have a healing ability, connecting generations and helping to piece together fractured histories and lives torn asunder by the state. The second part focuses on a set of extraordinary photographs, mostly taken by Ngarrindjeri photographers, from the album of Uncle Tom Trevorrow, Ellen's husband, which documents the social life of Meningie–Coorong fringe camps. These images point to the ways that photographs can become key entry points into rich and different kinds of histories, beyond the institutional radar — histories that might otherwise be unavailable from other sources.

'THE WEAVING OF OUR STORIES AND OUR MOVEMENT IN FAMILY': AUNTY ELLEN'S ALBUM

Ellen collects photos for her family; others also share in helping to establish albums for her children. The photos have immense, immeasurable value because of the way they show family and connection.

Karen: What kinds of photos do you have in your personal collection?

Ellen: I have a personal collection of the family, photos of my children growing up and also my nieces and nephews. Over the years I've worked on an album for each of my children, so they've all got their personal album and are able to keep strong family stories connected, and pass these on to the next generation. That's the weaving of our stories. Each time I get given a new photo I think about where it should go, where it will have a home and a future value, so that further stories will be told. But when the right time comes to pass on certain photographs usually my *miwi* (spiritual connection) lets me know who the photo should be given to, so that powerful stories can be cared for and carried in the future.

I have a small collection of old photos, but that's where you miss out because the camera wasn't around in our time. Like Mum had her collection, but we haven't got those now because someone else liked the photos that Mum had in her collection: it got taken. A lot of people are giving back photos, which is really very important. I have some precious and important photos that have been given to me to take care of. I'm not a camera person. I don't have my own camera, but there's family who take photos and always pass on photos to me and that's how I get my collection.

Karen: Because they know that you'll keep them all, too.

Ellen: Yes, I'm one of those. It's really important to have that collection, like Alice and Bill Abdulla (my sister-in-law and brother-in-law) always had their collection.[2] They've got photos of our young ones and when it's time to give them out, Alice would do that. When Debbie, my niece, has been given a special photo, she'll give us a copy and so would Sherrie, her sister — it's really important to pass on what is so special. Someone always passes on an old photo and that's really good for the collection. Tamara and Luke (Ellen's daughter-in-law and son) have their special collection. When our young ones do photography at school, that's when their collection of photos [will] start. There's a strong movement in the family then, and it is so special and has strong values. Photographs can open a doorway to richer stories.

Karen: So when you get new photos, how do you display them, or what do you do with them?

Ellen: My recent ones I show for a while, and then they get put into storage. I've got one of those plastic containers on wheels and we have seven children, so I've started seven containers belonging to each of our children. I don't know what they're going to do with them, but that's what I have done for them.

QUEEN ETHEL

Photographs of two distinguished and knowledgeable *miminar* (women), given the title of 'Queen' in colonial times — Queen Louisa Kontinyeri (c. 1821–1921) and Queen Ethel Whympie Watson (c. 1887–1964) — are displayed in the Camp Coorong museum.[3] Aunty Ellen and her husband Uncle Tom Trevorrow, along with many other Ngarrindjeri families, trace their lineage from these remarkable female elders.

Ellen: Two very important and special photos that I like seeing in the museum are of Queen Ethel [Figure 1] and Queen Louisa [Figure 2]. Queen Ethel is in Tom's family line. We've got one of her from down the south-east. And she was a strong weaver, also, so I always look at the weaving tradition on both sides of the family line: we've got Queen Ethel there from down the south-east, and on my side Queen Louisa around Wellington, the river and the lakes — so they're pretty significant photos that we have that reflection back to.

These photographs are of individuals who are still with us — in their descendants and their traditions. When Aunty Ellen speaks about 'that reflection', she is referring to the explicit cultural, emotional, intellectual and spiritual knowledges that particular photos hold. These affective properties are opened up through the connectivity of viewer and subject. A particularly important aspect of this reflection also comes from the knowledge gained through one's *miwi* during this process. *Miwi* for Ngarrindjeri is 'the inner spirit', which is one's sixth sense and through which important knowledge is gained.[4]

Ellen: Queen Ethel is Tom's great-grandmother, the grandmother of his mother, Aunty Thora Lampard. She grew up down in the south-east, near

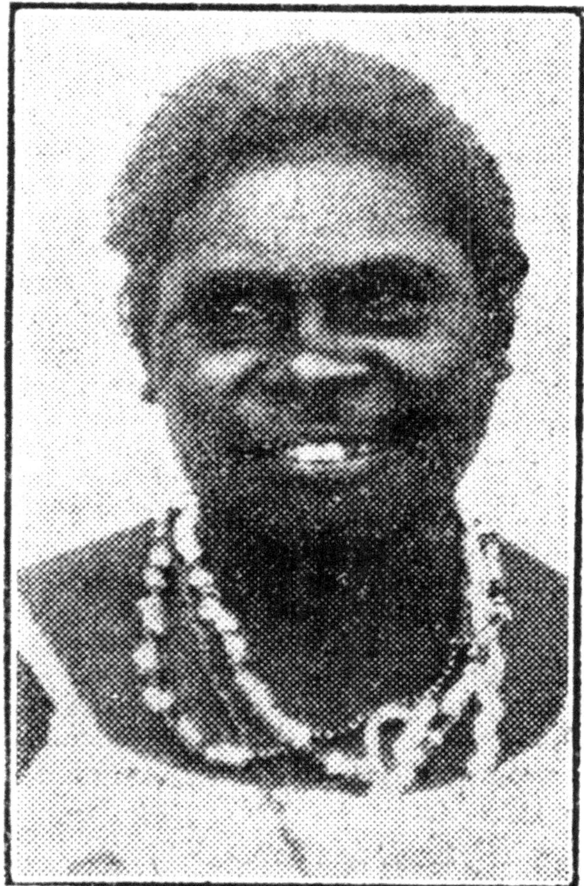

FIGURE 1: *Queen Ethel Wympie Watson.* Photograph in 'A dusky ruler', by ESA, *The Register*, 11 May 1927, p. 10.

> Kingston, around that area. They've got a monument of her at Kingston. She had to be a strong survivor, one of the leaders of her people, like my great-great-grandmother, Louisa Karpany. They were strong elders in their family groups.

A copy of an article from *The Register*, 11 May 1927, containing this photograph of Granny Ethel, as her family know her, is mounted at the entrance to the museum at Camp Coorong. The article recalls Granny Ethel speaking about her early life in the south-east of South Australia, and the ritual that distinguished her as a leader of her people:

> My aunt Catherine [Gibson] told me that when she was made Queen, there was big Doings. Days of dancing, hunting, and making feast, and all our wurlies full of people. Then she wore some native beads, and the chief one of the tribe made long talk, and there was much corroboree. So she became the head of us all. But when I was made Queen it was not so big a time. We went away back into the bush, and there were night fires and corroborees, and I wore the beads, too.[5]

In the first decade of the twentieth century, Granny Ethel was nursemaid to the young Norman Tindale in Kingston. Her influence is credited for possibly igniting his future passion for better understanding the complexity of Aboriginal cultures.[6] As a fledgling anthropologist in an emergent field, Tindale later relied on Granny Ethel's expertise in language and genealogies to help set the direction of his fieldwork and to lay the groundwork for his monumental collaboration with the Ngarrindjeri elder Milerum.

QUEEN LOUISA

In the 1915 photograph of Queen Louisa Karpany (née Kontinyeri; Figure 2), which is exhibited in the Camp Coorong museum alongside a vibrant collection of traditional weaving, she carries a swathe of baskets woven from rushes. The designs are remarkably similar to those practiced by Aunty Ellen, her third-generation granddaughter, and Ellen's daughter Tanya Trevorrow (Figure 4). Living knowledges and the embodiment of strong female leadership are visible in these images of close women kinfolk, and inspire younger generations of Ngarrindjeri women. Today, elders such as Aunty Ellen continue to hand down their cultural practices through family lineages at times deemed appropriate by *miwi*.

> Ellen: Grandmother Louisa Karpany was a strong leader, a very strong leader in movement. What can I say? She had a daughter Pinkie Mack [Figure 3], my great-grandmother, who was George Ezekiel Mason's daughter.

When Ellen raises the important cross-cultural relationship between her Indigenous and non-Indigenous forebears, it is evocative of the uncovering of the relationship between Sally Hemings and Thomas Jefferson as a foundational American couple, which unsettled assumed social norms.[7] Born before South Australian colonisation, Grandmother Louisa lived to be at least a hundred and

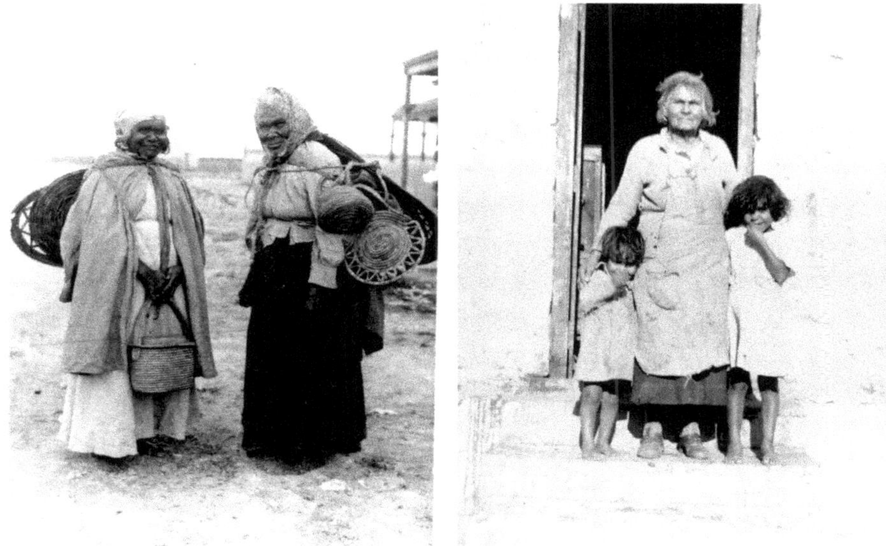

LEFT: FIGURE 2: *Queen Louisa Karpany (nee Kontinyeri)* (right) *and companion*, c. 1915. M Angas collection, South Australian Museum, Anthropology Archives.

RIGHT: FIGURE 3: Pinkie Mack (centre), with granddaughters Daisy Brown (left) and Emily Brown, at Brinkley, East Wellington, 1943.

capably negotiated the titanic changes the new arrivals brought. As a young girl, a *yartuki*, she witnessed the British explorer Charles Sturt sailing into the waters of her country in 1831, as she hid trembling in the rushes. This story was passed down from her daughter Pinkie Mack (1854–1956) to Ellen's mother Aunty Daisy Rankine (1936–2009) (Figure 3). George Ezekiel Mason (Ellen's great-great-great-grandfather) was a Scottish-born policeman, appointed the first Sub-Protector of Aborigines at Wellington between 1842 and 1862 as the new colony took hold.[8] The land and waters around Wellington are highly significant for Ngarrindjeri, where the River Murray as a living body flows into Lake Alexandrina before emptying into the Great Southern Ocean through the Murray Mouth.

Empathetic with the Ngarrindjeri, Mason formed a substantial relationship with the respected and accomplished Louisa Karpany, while both remained married to others. Karpany and Mason had two children, George Karpany and Margaret Mack (better known as Pinkie because of her fair skin), whose descendants include Ellen and her family, as well as many other Ngarrindjeri families living today. Indeed, Wellington's history, from its inception, was one of cultural crossings and double vision.[9]

As few public photographs exist of Mason, he remains an intriguing figure on the early South Australian frontier. Far more photographs, however, survive of Granny Louisa; several of these were taken by Edward Stirling (1848–1919), a founding director of the South Australian Museum and contributor to the emergent discipline of anthropology. Stirling drew on Karpany's immense body of historical and scientific knowledge for some of his publications, much like Tindale with Granny Ethel.[10] Mason and Karpany's daughter, Pinkie Mack, also left a substantial historical imprint, both within her family's heritage and through her rich accounts of song and ceremonial cycles, women's cultural practices, Ngarrindjeri language and more, which were partially recorded by Ronald and Catherine Berndt in the 1940s.[11] Skilled, knowledgeable and pragmatic, these Ngarrindjeri women were anthropologists, scientists and historians in their own right. Aunty Ellen and Uncle Tom's embrace of cross-cultural relations continues this tradition initiated by these fore-mothers, placing value on educating the wider non-Indigenous community about Ngarrindjeri knowledges, history, ethics and cultural practices through the work of Camp Coorong.[12]

A decade ago, when reflecting on the 1915 photograph of Louisa Karpany, taken when she was in her nineties, Ellen's mother, the late Aunty Daisy Rankine (née Brown) (Figure 3), noted, 'We're getting the past back of my ancestors. I'm the fourth generation. We've got the sixth generation now who can still feel the spirit of her around us.'[13]

> Ellen: In the old photos, like the one that's in our museum here, there is Queen Louisa with her weaving. I think that's really important for the future weavers. And we have the photos to show that this was around years and years ago. The tradition continues down and we're here still today. I really like the photo because it's important for the families and their continued stories. There's a beautiful big 'sister basket' there on her shoulder. The loops and patterns and things like that we've been taught by our elder Aunty Dorrie Kartinyeri, and we still continue to weave. From the photo you have that reflection: to be able to look back on those things.

Soon Ellen's niece Deborah Rankine joins in with our discussion. Debbie is also an accomplished weaver who lives in Ngarrindjeri country between Raukkan and Meningie, overlooking Lake Albert. She represents the sixth generation referred to above by her grandmother Aunty Daisy, carrying the spirit of Granny

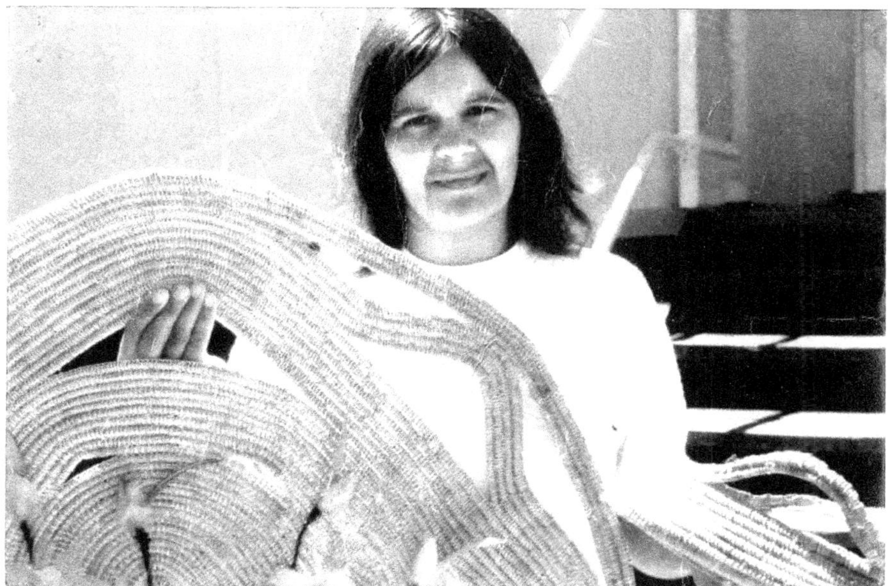

FIGURE 4: Ellen Trevorrow with one of her first weavings: 'With the weaving, I thoroughly enjoyed it and I reminisced on my grandmother quite a bit. It all started with a Year Nine art class, that's how I got into schools, I always weaved. I played sports, I always mixed, but when I weaved it opened things up, and I made a lot of friends through weaving. It brought people together.'

Louisa Karpany and the inherited cultural and storied places of her world — and yet another generation has been born since.

> Debbie: I reckon there's a part of it, just to identify too. Like what Aunty Ellen was saying about the Old Fellas. It gives an idea to the younger generation, the features, the backdrop, the clothing. It gives them an idea of how they were back in the days. When they're looking at it, an elder is talking. With the photographs, when it's a memory, a memory of a place or a person or an event, you can put yourself back in there — back in that time.
>
> Ellen: So that family line has a strong connection. They were a survival people, living off the land. That line comes down to my grandmother Ellen Edith Brown (nee Sumner), Pinkie Mack's daughter, she was a strong survivor. I was about five years old when her husband passed away, Grandfather William Brown. And she was a housemaid to the McFarlane family at Brinkley, I was with grandmother from the age of five. She raised me up to the age of eleven and I moved this way to the Coorong with

Mum. But she was a very strong lady, *very*, Ellen Brown. She had a strong line and of course that would have been bred into her, handed onto her, the strong line of survival. It's been passed on to us, that strong line in the survival stage. Debbie could say that too, a strong line of survivors. Very important, the first things that you put first: you know how to cook, how to manage. They were all passed on to us in our younger years. We were washing dishes at the age of four and five years old.

Debbie: To see my great-grandfather Old Dardle [Manuel Karpany; Figure 5] in the museum photo collection was pretty cool. I don't know really much about that far back. I sort of only know today. So it's pretty cool to see a photo from back there and then still have Aunty Ellen and Uncle Tom and Uncle Darrel Sumner to actually tell stories, to pass on

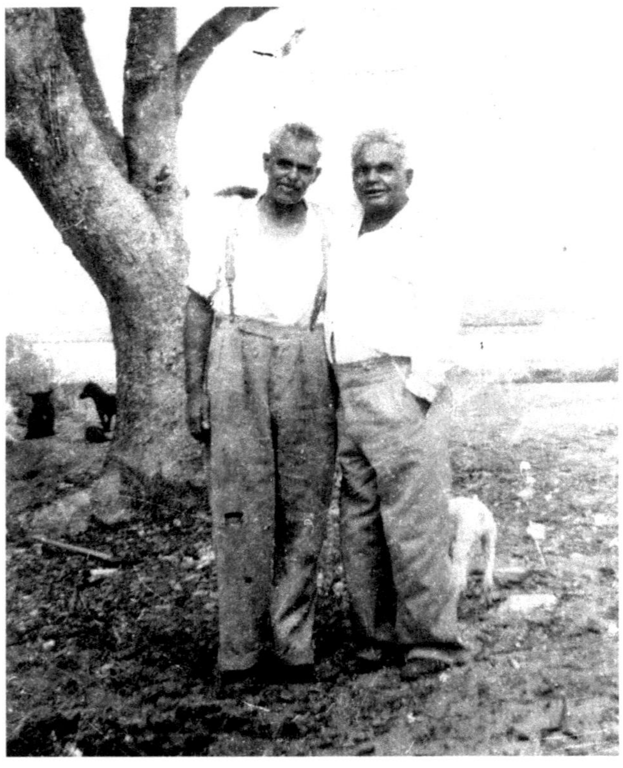

FIGURE 5: Old Dardle (Manuel Karpany; right) and Uncle George Karpany at Marrunggung, East Wellington, c.1960. Courtesy of Ellen Trevorrow.

information. And also with the ones that Aunty Ellen's been talking about, like Queen Louisa, Queen Ethel and Pinkie Mack, what very strong women they were. It's inspirational.

'SEPARATED UNDER FALSE PRETENCES': WILLIAM AND PATRICK BROWN

Treasured among the photographs in Ellen's family collection is a portrait of her maternal grandfather, William Charles Brown, and his younger brother, Patrick (Paddy) Joseph Brown, as children (Figure 6). Taken in 1910, William and Patrick, in formal Edwardian clothes and aged approximately ten and eight, confront the camera with barely muted terror and shock. Their fear is palpable, yet restrained by an overriding sense of dignity and self-presence that defies their circumstances. This image was recorded shortly after the boys had been snatched from their family, near the Riverland town of Renmark, under what was shown contemporaneously to be false pretences.[14] After being held overnight in a jail and placed under the control of the State Children's Council, the children were transferred to the Industrial School in Edwardstown, Adelaide, without their parents' knowledge or consent.[15] The image was designed explicitly as propaganda, and was published in the *Report of the South Australian Chief Protector of Aborigines* that year as an example of colonial ideas of 'uplift' used to promote the project of child removal and 'training'; the accompanying caption read, 'Fine boys doing well under the care of the State Children's Council.'[16] Enfolded back into family, after the photograph was recovered during research for the 1988 book *Survival in our own land*, it is now deeply cherished, and much copied and shared among Grandfather William's descendants — an image of connection, in stark contrast to its original intent.

Ellen's aunt, Emily Webster (born in 1930) (Figure 3), known fondly as Nanna Emmo, William Brown's only surviving child, wakes each day to a poster-sized print of the portrait blu-tacked to her bedroom wall in Adelaide. It is one of few photos taken of her father. For Nanna Emmo the photograph 'refreshes memories' of a beloved parent, who passed away in 1960, and emphasises the strong family bonds of her childhood spent at Raukkan and along the River Murray and lakes. Often the family would jump in a boat and row 'along the four waters, evading the welfare'.[17] The photograph recalls memories of a special

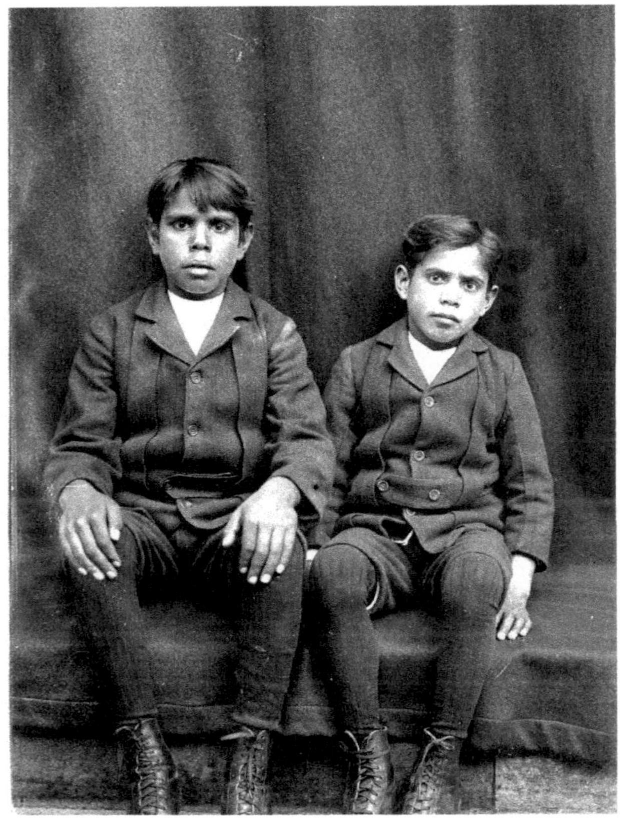

FIGURE 6: William (left) and Patrick Robinson Brown as children at the Industrial School, Edwardstown, 1910. Courtesy of Ellen Trevorrow and the South Australian Archives.

family trip when Emily was about nine, when her father rowed nearly 200 kilometres along the River Murray, with his wife and children, to an island near Nildottie, for a precious last reunion with his mother, Emily Robinson (Rollison), before she died.[18]

For Ellen, recovering this photograph — together with a later discovery of a 1923 newspaper article documenting a petition her paternal great-great-grandfather William Rankine presented to the South Australian Governor in protest against the *Aborigines (Training of Children) Act 1923* (SA), which legalised child removal — inspired her collaboration on a book, *They stole our land and took our children*, published out of Camp Coorong. This drew on further historical photographs and original documents of protest. More recently, Ellen's youngest sister, Margaret Long-Alleyn, has also written vividly about the loss of Grandfather William and Grandfather Paddy:

> One day great grandmother was warned to take the children somewhere else but she did not understand why at the time...The morning of the separation grandfather and his dad was working on the property and the oldest son William, his little brother Paddy was snatched from work by Mr Panton which the boys were shoved into the car under false pretences of being neglected. Great grandfather got on his bike and rode and rode to chase after the car and yelling out for his children to be returned. Mr Panton kept driving and driving, just would not stop for my great grandfather. While the car was still in great grandfather's sight he would not give up peddling his bike for his children and just in front of great grandfather eyes the car had disappeared out of sight, great grandfather just collapsed to the ground, sobbed and sobbed yelling out his sons' names William, Paddy. Great grandfather knew in his heart that was the last time he will ever see his sons again...Once grandfather had grown up and left the Industrial School he had not spoken much of his childhood and the heart ache of being torn from his family always stayed close to his heart.[19]

> Ellen: Looking at the photograph now I think about Mum (one of William Brown's daughters) in her time, like that'd been a hard time. I reckon I was about five when my grandfather, William Brown, passed on, but to get a photo like that and knowing what had happened. I think back on grandmother too, Nanna Ellen Brown, she would have known about this and this is why she was very protective over us. She always kept us out the back, never in the front, we were seen and not heard, and we *had* to go to school. So grandmother would have known.

Ellen hadn't been told the story as a child but now understands the extreme, ever-present watchfulness and care exerted over children in her family.[20]

> Ellen: Nanna Brown had three of us. And it seemed like, when you look back over it, two of her daughters had children out of marriage, that's what it looks like. Mum wasn't married when she had Billy and I, and the other sister, Aunty Margie, she was the second daughter, she had Michelle out of marriage. So I believe that grandmother was pretty protective. But,

> sitting *yunnan* with Uncle Neville, I sort of had, a reflection back, I can remember us, I didn't remember at the time, that we did feather flowers with Nanna May, which I'd forgotten about. You know you forget but you talk about it and the memory lane comes back. Yeah, so you see that photograph, and in my collection I've got another photo of grandfather in his Army uniform with his four daughters. And when you look at those four girls, you're looking at Glenda, Michelle, myself and Sharon, because the four daughters have got four girls that look like their mothers.

Sadly, the ramifications continue more than a hundred years later. Ellen's mother, Aunty Daisy, never stopped searching during her lifetime for Uncle Paddy's family, the legacy of their removal a cause of ongoing pain and dislocation. On leaving the Industrial School in the late 1920s, the brothers became cruelly separated by further outsider policies and the issuing of exemption certificates, which served to define Aboriginality in terms designated by the state for purposes of assimilation. William fell in love with Ellen's grandmother, Ellen Sumner, at Point McLeay and happily relinquished his exemption certificate to marry her. Patrick married a non-Aboriginal woman, Marion, and remained classed as 'exempt' under changes to the *Aborigines Act 1911* (SA), and their children all married partners in the mainstream community. More than a century later, the photograph has incubated vital information to reunite William and Paddy's descendants, who were dislocated through government policy. From this, a startling photo has re-emerged; it is a studio portrait of the brothers as young adults after their release from the Industrial School, and is held in the collection of Grandfather Patrick's daughter-in-law.

Seeing for the first time the brothers pictured together as adults has enabled the segregated families to firmly recognise their shared identity and to begin to know the stories behind the forces that wedged them apart. Emily Webster's presence has been critical to confirming the identity of her father in the photograph, highlighting the urgent nature of photographic return and of sharing photos while first generation descendants are still alive.[21]

> Ellen: If we lose that one generation it's going to still be a puzzle and take a longer journey to heal the connection of family identity. Photos can help bring a circle of closure.

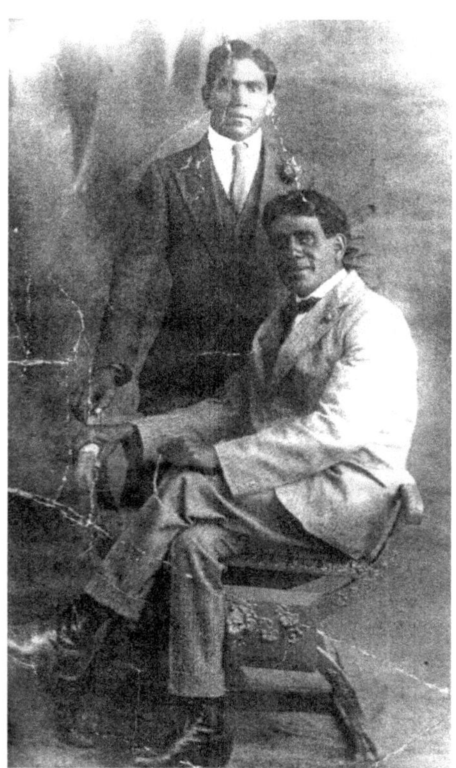

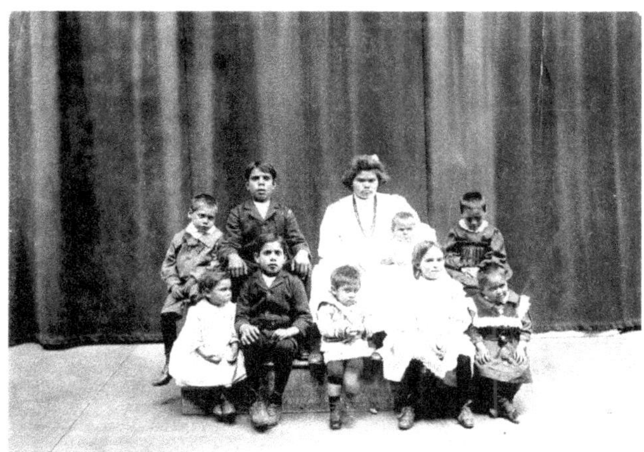

LEFT: FIGURE 7: Patrick Joseph Brown (left) and William Charles Brown, c. 1929. Collection of Mrs Douglas Brown.

RIGHT: FIGURE 8: *State children*, 1911. South Australian Museum.

But the circle of family has yet to be completed; this story is far from over. A companion photograph to Figure 6 — of 'state children' (including William and Patrick) recorded as being taken the following year, in 1911 (Figure 8) — reveals two smaller children to the left of William and Patrick. The boy, who appears about three or four years old, is their younger brother Robert (Uncle Bob) Rollison. He later married Ngarrindjeri woman Hazel Stanley and lived at Meningie.[22] But the infant girl, thought to be their missing sister, Daisy, after whom Ellen's mother was named, has disappeared from available historical records. Fragments of information remembered from Ellen's mother suggest that as an adult she may have lived in Victoria. Ellen and her family continue to search for 'Aunty Daisy' and her descendants, whom they hope to find while they still have one member left of the first generation.

UNCLE TOM'S ALBUM: REMEMBERING A WAY OF LIFE

All of the photos Ellen has collected of her husband Tom Trevorrow's family were taken away from the colonial gaze. They celebrate the Ngarrindjeri generations who grew up in fringe camps, educated by elders, living outside institutional and mission influence.[23] These have been sourced from private collections held by Ngarrindjeri, as well as, occasionally, by non-Indigenous families. They offer a vivid perspective and analysis of a unique period in an era that largely denied Aboriginal people control over their lives and access to the resources to record their own images.[24]

> Tom: [Fringe camp families were] living on the land at a time when you weren't allowed to live in the town, because only white people were allowed to live in Meningie, blackfellas weren't allowed to. Yet we had to be close enough to town for kids to go to school, otherwise Welfare would have stepped in. A lot of Ngarrindjeri people didn't want to live on the Point McLeay Mission, at Raukkan, yet couldn't live traditional along the Coorong because the land had been taken away, so they had to live, we could say a 'semi-traditional lifestyle', in bush camps — the old bag huts, tin huts, tents. Always where there was fresh water and plenty of bush tucker, kangaroo and emu as well as rabbits and fish, birdlife and eggs,

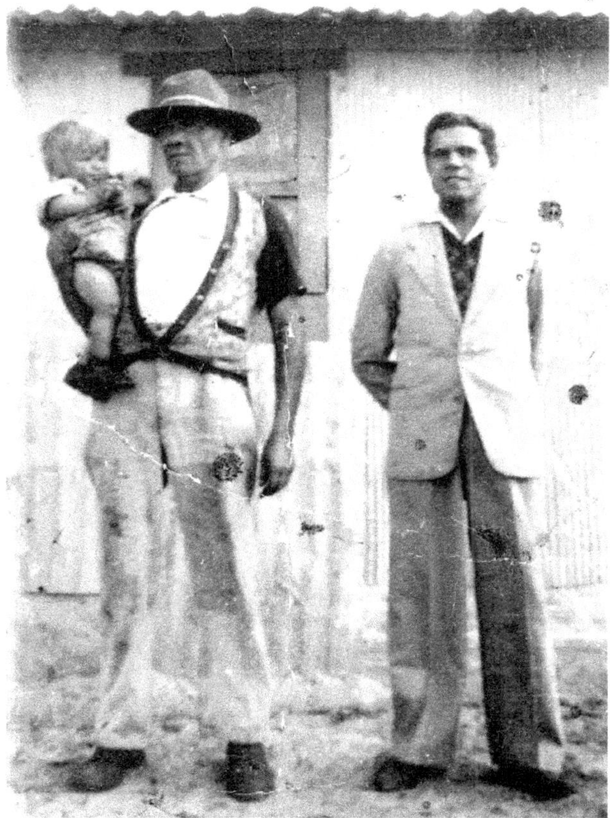

FIGURE 9: *Little fella in his father's arms*; Uncle Joe Trevorrow holding baby Tom, and Choom (Joe Trevorrow Junior), c. 1955. Courtesy Ellen and Tom Trevorrow.

> mallee-fowl, so we lived off the land. That carried on up until my time, before we were allowed to live in the towns with the other people.

Ellen pulls out a photo of Tom taken in 1955 (Figure 9), a chubby, well-nurtured baby, proudly cradled in the strong arms of his father, Joe Trevorrow, at the Old One Mile Camp. Next to them is Tom's brother Choom (Joe Trevorrow Junior), who, in his younger days, assisted Tom Kruse to take the mail across the Oodnadatta–Birdsville track. Behind them stands a hand-built, cobbled-together home made from repurposed metal and wood. This image vividly evokes the camaraderie, resourcefulness and proud independence of Ngarrindjeri family life in the Meningie–Coorong fringe camps in the mid-twentieth century.

The Meningie–Coorong fringe camps are an important cultural and spiritual base of the Trevorrow family and part of their Country. When Ellen and Tom's youngest son Hank (seen in Figure 20) turned thirteen in June 2012, he took his father back to the Old Three Mile Camp to celebrate his coming of age.

Born in 1954, Uncle Tom Trevorrow was raised in a large, loving extended family along the salt-pan, mallee scrub and sand dune country south of Meningie at One Mile, Three Mile and Seven Mile (Bonney Reserve). Today, Camp Coorong is not far from the old Seven Mile Camp at Bonney Reserve. The fringe camps stretched throughout Ngarrindjeri country all along the River Murray, following the Southern Ocean coast from Kingston to Victor Harbour. Fringe camps often provided a sanctuary away from government-administered reserves: 'There was freedom of space, you were not tied up behind walls' (Aunty Rita Lindsay, pers. comm., September 2012). Tom's sisters recall playing knucklebones, as well as hopscotch, with bits of broken china from the rubbish dump, and using the clay-pan (which is now the Meningie aerodrome) for a barefoot skating rink. The camps were near fresh water wells and bush tucker, and were places of fish and game.

> Tom: It was a good life, but we just wanted people to leave us alone. But people wouldn't; police wouldn't; Welfare wouldn't; ignorant racists wouldn't, they'd come out making fun of us, and terrorise the camps. Coming in and turning the car headlights on and skidding around and blowing the horn, and firing guns off. All those type of things we had to live through, all that rubbish. 'Let's go and stir the natives up, go and frighten the shit out of them', that was their attitude, mentality.

This was a time when the Aboriginal Protection Board was trying to forcibly remove Aboriginal children from their homes. A nourishing place of freedom, play, creativity and familial love could rapidly change into a place of fear and tragedy whenever children heard elders shout, 'Black car — move!' (Walter Richards and Connie Love, pers. comm., September 2012). Thus childhood photos, as Ellen points out, can sometimes be a heartbreaking visual journey because of the attention they draw to who is missing from the frame. Most notable is Tom's younger brother Bruce Trevorrow, who in 2007 was awarded a historic victory, after ten years, over the State of South Australia for his wrongful and illegal removal. A seemingly innocent photo (Figure 10) of Tom with his much-

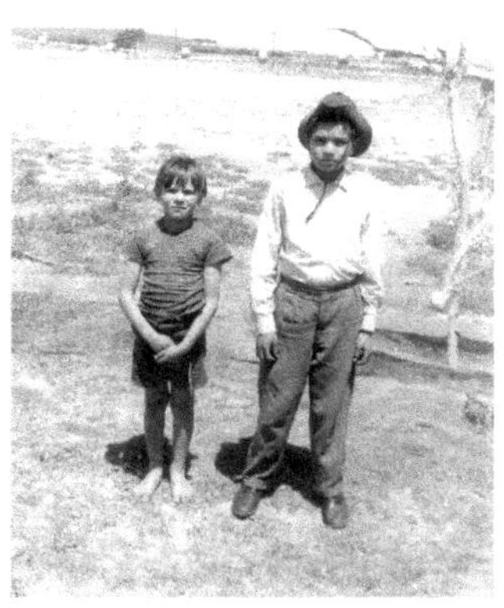

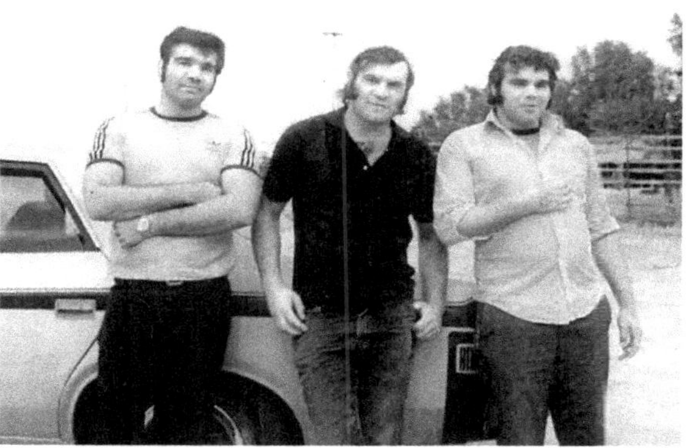

LEFT: FIGURE 10: Tom and George Trevorrow, aged about five and eight, c. 1959. Courtesy of Tom and Ellen Trevorrow.
RIGHT: FIGURE 11: (Left to right) brothers George Trevorrow, Tom Trevorrow, Bruce Trevorrow. Courtesy of Ellen and Tom Trevorrow.

loved older brother George Trevorrow, dressed in cowboy gear, also signifies the sadness and injustice of Bruce's absence in this and other photographs.

When he was thirteen months old, the Aboriginal Protection Board took Bruce, without his parents' knowledge, from a hospital where he was being treated for gastroenteritis and placed him with a white foster family in Adelaide. The Board refused to tell his parents where he was or allow them to see him, despite his mother's ongoing requests. He was eventually returned to his family ten years later, but the damage was irrevocable. Bruce suffered recurrent mental illness as a consequence of the removal. In a landmark legal judgment, which for the first time upheld the right of a Stolen Generations survivor to compensation, Bruce was awarded $775,000. Critical in deciding this was the Court's finding that Bruce's siblings, who stayed with their parents in the fringe camps and later in towns throughout Ngarrindjeri country, 'went on to lead resilient lives, whereas Bruce had an impaired ability to cope with the problems of life'.[25]

A poignant photo from the 1970s (Figure 11) shows brothers George, Tom and Bruce, together again as young men, leaning confidently against a car, looking ready to take on the world. The image almost seems to redress the loss of a child, but, for Bruce, putting back the shattered pieces was impossible; his father, Joe, passed away before Bruce was returned to his family.

> Ellen: When I look at this photo I have my thoughts on their father [Uncle Joe Trevorrow], because he never got to see Bruce again. Tom was about eleven when his Dad died. His Dad was a hard-working battler. They had a big family, a big family but...

Ellen hoped to include Bruce's story alongside that of her grandfather in *They stole our land and then they took our children,* but was advised that it 'wasn't a wise thing' while the court case was in process.

> Ellen: The court case went for ten years. Ten years, Karen, and to win a case in a sad way, and then he passed away.

Bruce died in Bairnsdale, Victoria, in June 2008, aged fifty-one, just five months after he received compensation. The case took as long as Mabo, and exacted a similar personal toll.

Ellen and Tom drove to Canberra in February 2008 to meet Bruce and his family for the long-awaited watershed moment of the National Apology. The following year, Aunty Alice Abdulla, one of Bruce's older sisters who helped care for him as a baby, spent the anniversary of the Apology at the One Mile Camp near her home in Meningie, quietly reflecting on the time before Bruce was stolen.

AUNTY CHARLOTTE RICHARDS: A PIONEERING NGARRINDJERI PHOTOGRAPHER

Many of these evocative photos from Tom's album were taken by Aunty Charlotte Richards, a prolific Ngarrindjeri photographer from the 1940s to the 1980s. Charlotte Richards stands out as a remarkable early Indigenous photographer who deserves wider recognition for her work. Her beautiful and distinctive images of family life subtly portray the warm and intimate sociality, the resilience and creativity of families and individuals in the fringe camp communities during the mid-twentieth century. Aunty Charlotte, born about 1930, was the daughter of Ruby Koolmatrie (Nanna Tingie), a respected Ngarrindjeri woman, and Grandfather Nulla (Walter) Richards, an esteemed Barngarla traditional doctor. She is aunt to the distinguished Ngarrindjeri singer-songwriter Ruby Hunter.[26] With her sister Irene (Figure 13), Aunty Charlotte grew up in camps along the Riverland and Coorong, and lived for a considerable time at One Mile fringe camp, 'doing a little bit of schooling in Meningie' (Aunty Rita Lindsay, pers.

comm., Meningie, September 2012). From an early age she had a passion for photography and was almost never without her Box Brownie camera. A hallmark of many of her early photos is a pet magpie, which was also her *ngatji* (totem) (Figures 12 and 13).

> Tom: Aunty Charlotte had a camera; always had. She loved cameras and music and magpies. She carried her pet magpies with her everywhere she went. She fed them and looked after them and taught them how to talk, and they'd talk. She was Aunty to [the singer] Ruby Hunter. She and her sister, Irene Richards, Ruby Hunter's mum, they've both passed away now.

For people raising large families in the camps, a camera (and the associated costs of processing and prints) was an unaffordable luxury. But Aunty Charlotte didn't have children to support and, according to her nephew, 'never lived in a house

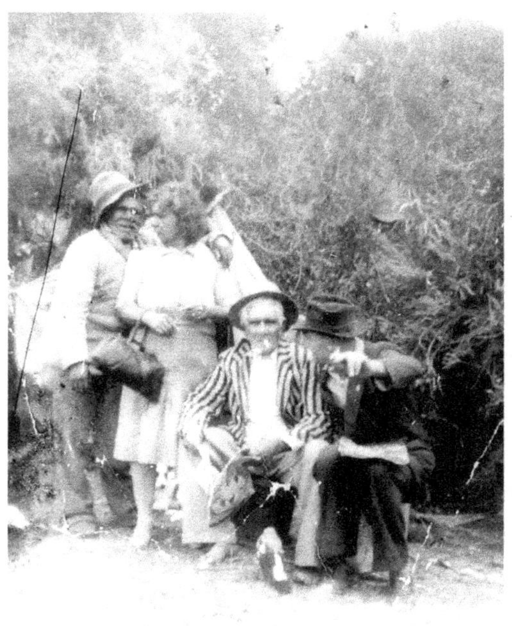

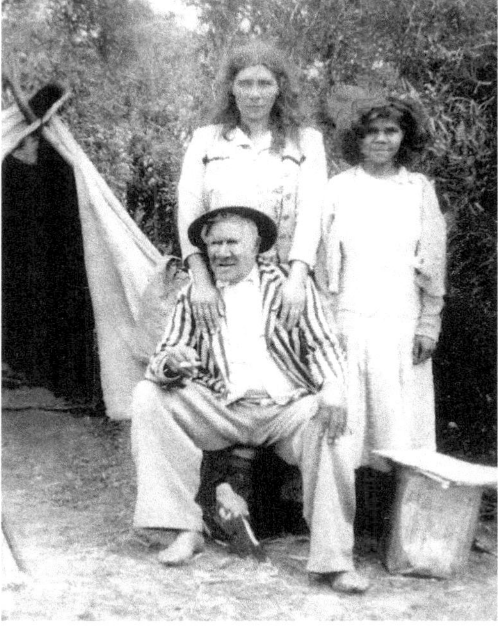

LEFT: FIGURE 12: Uncle Poonthie (Joe Walker), Aunty Belle (Isabel Koolmatrie, Joe Trevorrow's sister), Aunty Irene Richards and an unknown non-Indigenous man at One Mile, c. late 1940s – early 1950s. Aunty Joyce Kerswell collection. Courtesy Tom and Ellen Trevorrow.

RIGHT: FIGURE 13: Aunty Charlotte Richards. Uncle Nulla (Walter) Richards, his daughter Irene Richards (mother of Walter Richards, and Iris, Ruby, Jeffrey and Robert Hunter) and Uncle Poonthie (Joe Walker), One Mile, c. late 1940s – early 1950s. Courtesy Ellen and Tom Trevorrow.

and always lived off the land' (Uncle Walter Richards, pers. comm., September 2012). She helped others with the money she earned from sewing bags and picking fruit, and spent her lifetime documenting other people's families so that they would be remembered through her photos, which she generously shared. 'Can I get a photo of your kids?', she would always ask as she circuited the breadth and depth of Ngarrindjeri country, visiting her network of family and friends with her camera (Uncle Walter Richards, pers. comm., September 2012). Her deep and intimate knowledge of Country and traditional survival skills underpinned her mobility and independence, and ultimately her photography.

> Aunty Alice Abdulla: Aunty Charlotte was the one with the camera, always clicking, taking photos of kids and adults. She was highly spirited and full of life, like one of the film stars. She'd wear high-heeled shoes, stockings and red lipstick when she came to the One Mile. She was very beautiful with dark skin and a bushy head of hair; I used to think she looked like one of those kewpie dolls. When I saw her old box, I thought, 'How can you make a photo out of that?'

'Yeah, but a funny old camera: got to turn the motor car upside down, or sideways, see?', Tom remarks affectionately, looking at a photo featuring a convivial group of men which includes his father and two of his older brothers (Figure 15). 'The motor car's supposed to be *that* way...with the boot open.' The double-exposure has produced a magical signature quality to the image.

By any standards, and certainly for her era (much of her youth was lived before the 1967 referendum), Charlotte Richards (Figure 14) was an outstandingly talented and independent woman who lived life on her own terms. With her sister Irene she toured the country and western shows, playing the button accordion. Aunty Charlotte and Tom's mother, Aunty Thora Lampard (Figure 16), were close, supportive friends, often holidaying together, frequently camping along the far reaches of the Coorong.

> Aunty Rita Lindsay: Aunty Charlotte's camps would always be lit up with a lovely fire and they'd be sitting around yarnin' and doing a bit of cooking on the coals. She'd have her little old wind-up gramophone playing country and western music. She loved the camp life, fishing and rabbiting. But she kept great security over her photographs, they were under guard. She

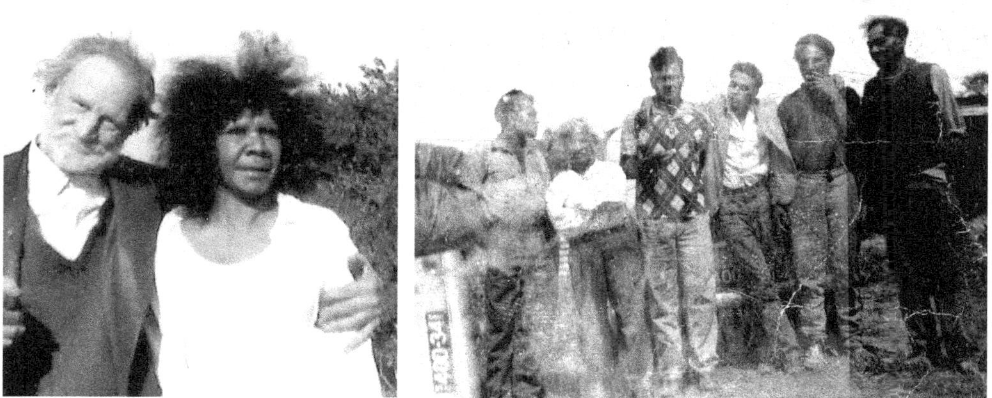

LEFT: FIGURE 14: Aunty Charlotte Richards and her partner Uncle Ron Davis, c. 1960s, Riverland, South Australia. Courtesy Walter Richards and Jeffrey Hunter.

RIGHT: FIGURE 15: Aunty Charlotte Richards. Group of men (including Tom Trevorrow's father and two of his older brothers) and car, One Mile Fringe Camp, Meningie, c. 1950. Double-exposure. Courtesy Ellen and Tom Trevorrow.

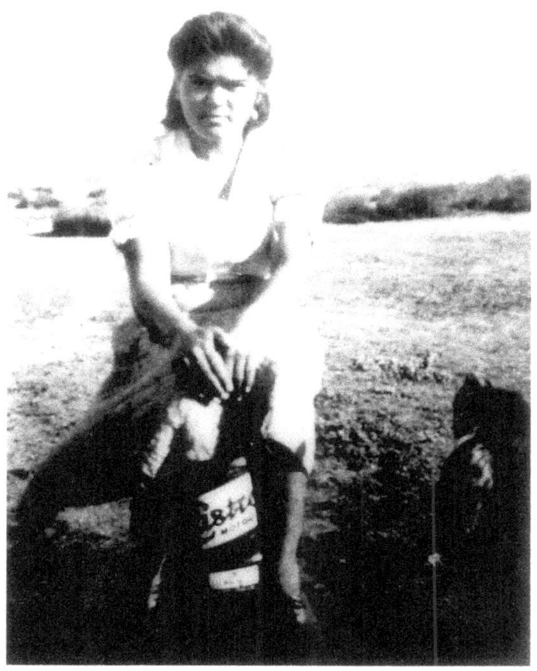

FIGURE 16: Tom's mother, Aunty Thora Lampard, Victor Harbour, c. 1960s. Courtesy Ellen and Tom Trevorrow.

> stored them in big albums inside an old brown suitcase, which must have been waterproof. She wouldn't let anyone mess around with her special stuff, she was very particular. It would all be packed neatly in her car...she always knew even when one photograph was missing.

Aunty Charlotte's photos depict the fringe camps in ways seldom seen outside the Indigenous community. The humour and warm social relations embodied here are missing from most official visual documentations of Ngarrindjeri. You can almost smell the salt air of the Coorong and hear voices of elders sharing stories. Her easy, relaxed portraits, full of exuberance and vitality, provide a unique glimpse into a world in which Ngarrindjeri led productive and resilient lives, resourcefully evaded institutionalisation and cared for one another during a challenging period of intensive state intervention. They celebrate both everyday pleasures and a spirit of survival against the pressures of assimilation. In a sense, Aunty Charlotte's photos anticipate the work of Ngarrindjeri artist Ian Abdulla (who also camped along the River Murray), who documents intimate scenes of lived histories outside the mainstream. Her images express a filmic quality and sometimes an experimental aesthetic that plays with the elements of formal portraiture, such as in Figure 13 where the mallee scrub is used as a studio-like backdrop for photographic subjects posed in a performative tableau.

AUNTY JOYCE KERSWELL: KEEPER OF THE ARCHIVE AND 'A LADY OF HISTORY'

Tom's older cousin Aunty Joyce Kerswell (the daughter of Joe Trevorrow's sister Alice) was a passionate collector of family photos, and it is thanks to her diligent efforts that we have these photos today. Like many other Ngarrindjeri from the fringe camps, she was highly mobile and entrepreneurial, venturing into her own fairground business, starting with a collection of tamed (yet highly venomous) local snakes.

Pictured 'driving her old buck board' on the way to the fairground, Aunty Joyce, dressed in an outsized man's cap, appears the epitome of the young, modern, mobile and independent woman (Figure 17).

> Tom: That's when she had a snake show, and all her snakes are in that old buck board — tigers and brown snakes. That's how she started off, there were a lot of sideshows going on all around, boxing troops and all

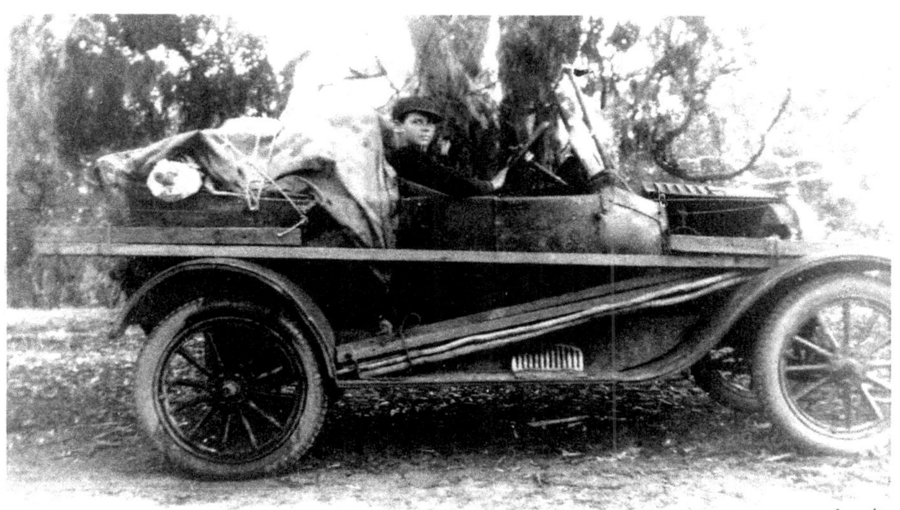

FIGURE 17: Aunty Charlotte Richards. Joyce Kerswell, Coorong, 1950s. Courtesy Ellen and Tom Trevorrow collection.

> that back then. She got addicted to it and then she got her old buck board there and, because she didn't worry about snakes, she had her snakes in there and she used to do her snake show. Then she left to have her own sideshow company, with the big blow-up castles and the fairy floss and the dodgem cars and all of that.

Aunty Annie Mason (Figure 18), the mother of Tom's older sisters, Alice Abdulla and Rita Lindsay, and his brother Choom, would sometimes help Aunty Joyce with her fairground show, travelling across the border to Victoria with her to perform a fire-walking act.

> Ellen: I saw Aunty Joyce's collection of photos, we went down there for an afternoon and she pulled out the old photos and, oh gee, they were beautiful. And they were in good nick. Whatever happened to that? Oh, she was a lady of history you know. And she had a good memory. And when you lose someone like that, it's hard. Aunty Joyce and I created a family reunion at the mulberry tree [the site of the Trevorrow family homestead near Salt Creek] and that's when they brought photos together. The brochure of that reunion would be amongst my collection in the shed, but she brought photos along too on that time. And it was family that came back who didn't know each other.

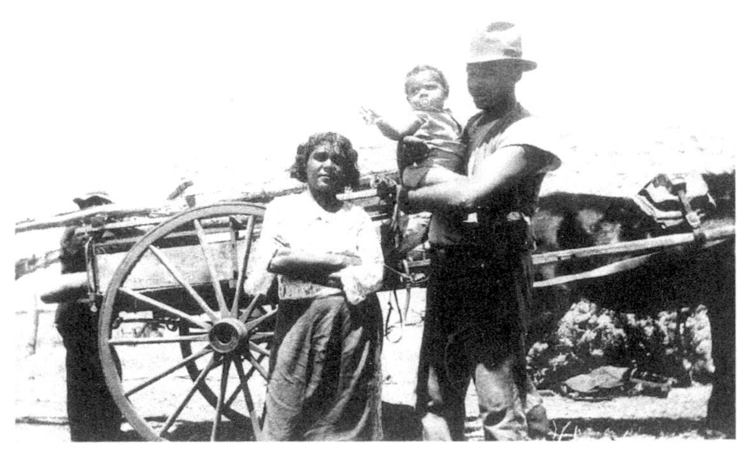

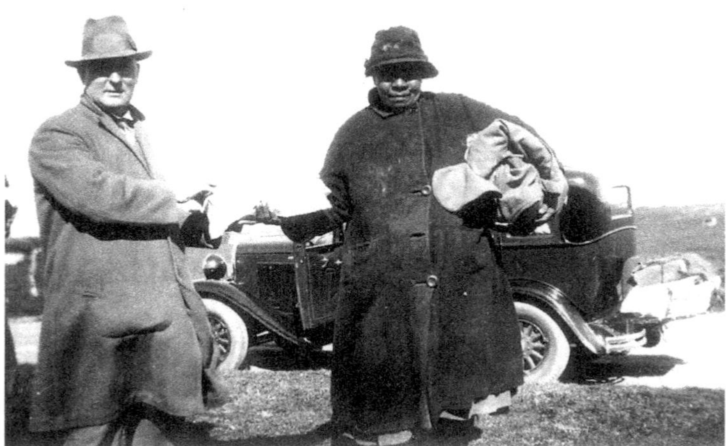

TOP: FIGURE 18: Annie Mason and Joe Trevorrow holding their son Choom (Joe Trevorrow Junior), the Coorong, c. 1940. Courtesy Ellen and Tom Trevorrow.

BOTTOM: FIGURE 19: Alice Walker. Courtesy of Mrs Marion McKechnie**.** Alice Walker and her Cornish-born husband, Jim Trevorrow (not pictured here), were an example of one of the many successful cross-cultural marriages from the colonial era. Alice and Jim raised a large family of thirteen children at their home at Salt Creek. On Alice's death in 1941, a newspaper article titled 'The good Samaritan' (*The Advertiser*, 17 March 1941, p. 17) recalled her many acts of kindness towards travellers who found themselves stranded along the Coorong.

Tom: She gave us some photos. 'I'll go through them, the rest,' she said, 'And I'll get you more.' But then she died and then her daughter or step-daughter sold everything up and took off to America.

MEMORY AND PHOTOGRAPHIC LOSS

Photographs are valuable, and are often copied and shared between Ngarrindjeri families, but rarely loaned — as Ellen says, 'I'm always worried about losing my phone with photos on it'. Too many stories proliferate of photographs never coming back, or collections disappearing when elders pass on. Although collections are held 'under guard' and many of the images we have discussed here hint at loss (particularly the tragic loss of children), sometimes a missing photograph can also carry an acutely heightened presence. Ellen highlights the way a lost photograph, too, can stand in for memories, and how a sense of living place, for instance, is sometimes better remembered through the imprint of a lost photograph: its afterimage standing in for a cultural landscape no longer there.

> Ellen: Others are gone, but when I looked at [where that photograph was taken] in one of the books there's that mapping, the mapping that shows where [George Ezekiel] Mason's house was. So I remember the old remains of that one. But down at Brinkley was a really old house out of tin, a put-together hut. There was Old Dardle's [Manuel (Mintchie) Karpany, one of the grandsons of Queen Louisa Karpany and George Mason] hut just down the hill from Nanna's. That was made of tin, and inside they had the lining of bags, that was their wall lining, hessian bags, a mud floor and an open fireplace. And I remember that, so I'm just not focusing on the image, but on the living area of that place and the people who lived there. Because we used to put a horse and cart and we'd ride around. When Old Dardle [Figure 5] passed away, we ended up living in that house, to us it was warm. We'd come back for holidays and we'd stay there in that old house. But all we've got is here [in our memory], no photographs you know. And it's lovely to look at old photographs.

A combination of water mismanagement, climate change and outsider agricultural practices have irrecoverably changed the Marrunggung shoreline and the cultural landscape of Ellen's childhood south-east of Wellington. Without the recovery of significant photographs, Ellen cautions, the task for elders to pass on stories and all the attendant intangible cultural heritage embedded in them becomes more challenging.

CONCLUSION: RECUPERATION AND THE WEAVING OF OUR STORIES THROUGH PHOTOGRAPHY

The photographs shared from Aunty Ellen and Uncle Tom's collections offer a reflective framework for thinking about the future. They sustain vital connections between ancestors and living generations of younger Ngarrindjeri, opening up what Ellen Trevorrow terms 'a memory lane', a conduit between the living and those who have passed. Several important photographs shared in this chapter show a pattern of powerful, 'pioneering' Indigenous women at the crossroads of cultural negotiations, a testament to the strength of the Old People in keeping culture alive. Later, strong Ngarrindjeri women became photographers themselves: Aunty Charlotte Richards, in particular, saw the value in taking photographs. The keeping of family history via such visual records and the maintaining of ties to Country, evidenced in Aunty Charlotte's rich body of work, has enabled survival and renewal during difficult times, and the depth of her photographic legacy is worthy of further exploration. Photographs possess recuperative powers: inviting conversations about the connectivity of family and Country, strengthening and nurturing identity, and activating *miwi*, the soul substance through which Ngarrindjeri connect to their world and discern something to be true. Certain photographs, such as those of William and Patrick Brown, have played a central role in healing relationships torn asunder by the state, and assist in piecing back

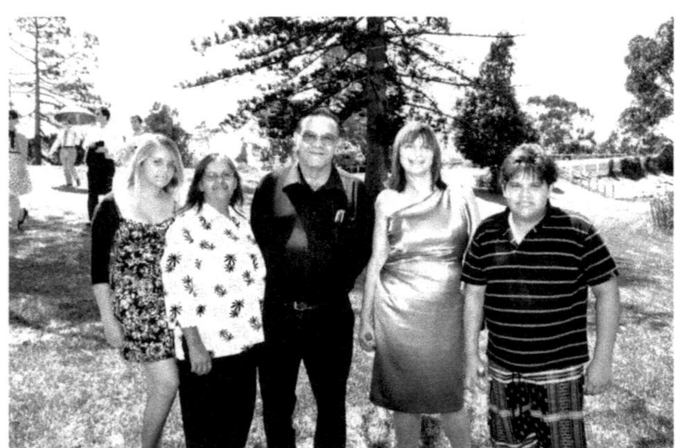

FIGURE 20: Aunty Ellen and Uncle Tom Trevorrow with granddaughter Ellie Wilson and son Hank Trevorrow and Karen Hughes at the wedding of Karen's daughter Elle Blanks, in Ngarrindjeri country, Strathalbyn, 2011.

together shattered families, sometimes in defiance of the original purpose for which they were taken. Once enfolded back into family, these photographs allowed the Brown boys to powerfully bear witness to the injustices of their past. For hundreds of non-Indigenous people who visit Camp Coorong's museum each year, photographs offer a materialised form of storytelling, 'a pedagogy of experience', that fundamentally disrupts the singular settler-colonial view of history, and tells the story of Ngarrindjeri history as one of survival, resilience, resistance, entrepreneurship and powerful agency.[27]

ACKNOWLEDGMENTS

The authors gratefully acknowledge the intellectual contributions of Uncle Tom Trevorrow, Aunty Rita Lindsay, Aunty Alice Abdulla, Uncle Darrel Sumner, Nanna Emily Webster, Deborah Rankine, Margaret Long-Alleyn, Uncle Walter Richards and Jeffrey Hunter and their generosity in sharing their collections. Thank you also to Sari Braithwaite for research support and to Jane Lydon for insightful commentary and editorial advice on an earlier draft.

NOTES

1. Camp Coorong was established through essential access to land through the *Aboriginal Lands Trust Act 1966* (SA). Ellen and her husband Tom Trevorrow jointly founded Camp Coorong with Tom's older brother, the late George Trevorrow, in 1986.
2. Aunty Alice Abdulla, the sister of Ellen's husband Uncle Tom Trevorrow, is an elder and was an Aboriginal Education Worker in schools until her retirement. Now she works as a cultural educator instructing students in feather-flower making.
3. 'Whympie' is the favoured spelling today; old newspaper reports use 'Wympie'. The title 'Queen', while a colonial artefact with no real approximation in Aboriginal cultures, was often bestowed on significant elders to acknowledge their knowledge and leadership and their abilities to negotiate cross-culturally.
4. See D Bell, *Ngarrindjeri Wurruwarrin: a world that was, is, and will be*, Spinifex, Melbourne, 1998, pp. 218–25.
5. ESA, 'A dusky ruler', *The Register*, 11 May 1927, p. 10; for an expanded account of this, see D Bell (ed.), *Kungun Ngarrindjeri Miminar Yunnun: listen to Ngarrindjeri women speaking*, Spinifex Press, Melbourne, 2008, p. 79.
6. See C Mattingley, *Survival in our own land*, Australian Scholarly Publishing, Melbourne, 1998, p. 155.
7. See A Gordon-Reed, *The Hemingses of Monticello: an American family*, WW Norton & Company, New York, 2006.
8. Bell, above n 4, p. 80; K Hughes, 'Same bodies, different skin: Ruth Heathcock' in A Cole, V Haskins & F Paisley (eds), *Uncommon ground; white women in Aboriginal history*, Aboriginal Studies Press, Canberra, 2005, pp. 83–107; K Hughes, 'My grandmother on the other side of the lake', PhD thesis, Department of Australian Studies and Department of History, Flinders University, Adelaide, 2009; K Hughes, 'Microhistories and things that matter', *Australian Feminist Studies*, 27(73):269–78, 2012.
9. See Hughes, 'Microhistories and things that matter', above n 8; K Hughes, 'I'd grown up as a child amongst natives', *Outskirts, Feminisms*

Along The Edge, 28, 2013, p. 1, viewed 29 November 2013, <www.outskirts.arts.uwa.edu.au/volumes/volume-28/karen-hughes>.

10. E Stirling, 'Preliminary report on the discovery of native remains at Swan Port, River Murray with an enquiry into the alleged occurrence of a pandemic among the Australian Aborigines', *Transactions of the Royal Society of South Australia*, 35, 1911, pp. 4–46, 124.
11. See R Berndt & C Berndt, *A world that was: the Yaraldi of the Murray River and the lakes, South Australia*, Melbourne University Press (Miegunyuh Press Series), 1993. *Pukanu*, Pinkie, like her mother Louisa Karpany, provided an exceptionally strong role model of Ngarrindjeri womanhood, which was passed down to Grandmother Ellen Brown, to Ellen's mother Aunty Daisy Rankine, her sisters and their children, and through the family lineage. See Bell, *Ngarrindjeri Wurruwarrin*, above n 4; Hughes, 'My grandmother on the other side of the lake', above n 8, p. 217; and Hughes, 'I'd grown up as a child amongst natives', above n 9, for a more expanded view on these relationships.
12. See S Hemming, 'Camp Coorong — combining race relations and cultural education', *Social Alternatives*, 12(1):37–40, 1993.
13. Hughes, 'My grandmother on the other side of the lake', above n 8, p. 228.
14. See 'Letter from the editor', *Renmark Pioneer*, in T Trevorrow, C Finnimore, S Hemming, G Trevorrow, M Rigney, V Brodie & E Trevorrow, *They took our land and then they stole our children*, Ngarrindjeri Lands and Progress Association, Meningie, SA, 2007.
15. Bell (ed.), above n 5; A Haebich, *Broken circles*, Fremantle Press, Fremantle, WA, 2000; M Long-Alleyn, 'Story regarding my Grandfather William and his brother Grandfather Paddy Robinson-Brown being removed and separated from their family under false pretences', unpublished manuscript, 2011; Mattingley, above n 6, p. 160.
16. Mattingley, above n 6, p. 160.
17. Aunty Daisy Rankine in Hughes, 'My grandmother on the other side of the lake', above n 8, p. 15.
18. Personal communication with Aunty Emily Webster, 2012; Hughes, 'My grandmother on the other side of the lake', above n 8, pp. 216–21.
19. Long-Alleyn, above n 15, p. 1.
20. Aunty Daisy, Ellen's mother, also spoke of her parents travelling 'along the four waters, evading the welfare'; Hughes, 'My grandmother on the other side of the lake', above n 8, p. 15.
21. A surprising lack of resources given to the process of photographic return in Australia has meant that the knowledge of large collections is only partial. Ellen and Tom are keen to see photographic repatriation happen quickly, while the vital knowledge of elders of this generation can provide the necessary connectivity for present and future Ngarrindjeri families.
22. Entry in a Bible, held by Daisy Rankine.
23. See Bell (ed.), above n 5, pp. 118–20.
24. A fascinating, detailed personal account of living along the Coorong in the early to mid-twentieth century from Annie Koolmatrie (nee Mason), the second wife of Tom Trevorrow's father, Joe Trevorrow, can be found in B Ely, *Murray-Murundi*, Experimental Arts Foundation Press, Adelaide, 1981.
25. T Anthony, 'Shaky victory for Stolen Generations', *The Drum*, 10 November 2010, viewed 18 August 2012, <www.abc.net.au/unleashed/40912.html>; Bell (ed.), above n 5, pp. 48–51.
26. *Ruby's Foundation*, viewed 8 November 2013, <www.rubysfoundation.com.au/Rubys_Foundation/About.html>.
27. B MacGill, J Mathews, E Trevorrow, A Abdulla & D Rankine, 'Ecology, ontology, and pedagogy at Camp Coorong', *M/C Journal*, 15(3), 2012, p. 1, viewed 17 September 2012, <http://journal.media-culture.org.au/index.php/mcjournal/article/view/499>.

WESTERN AUSTRALIA

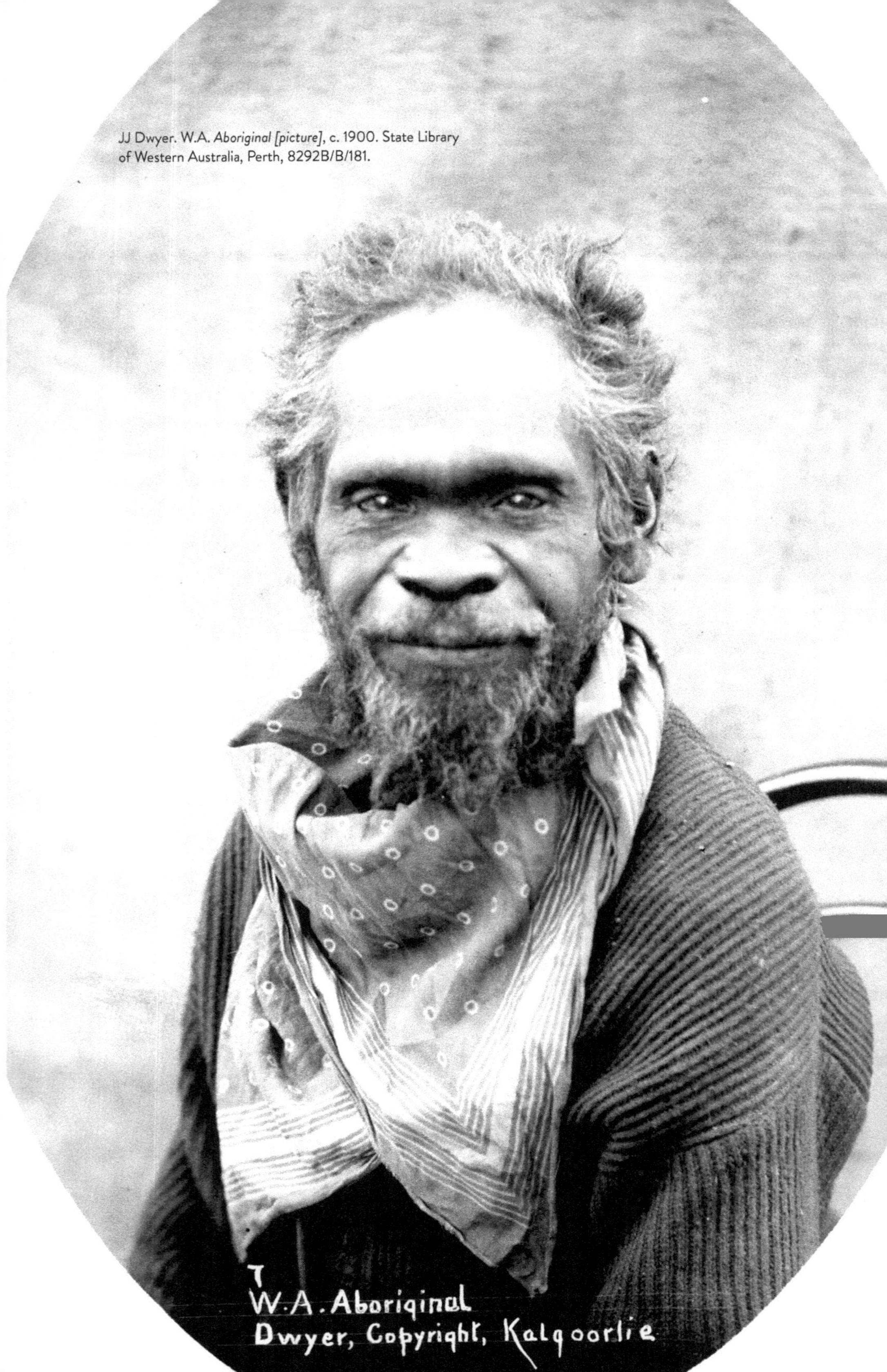

JJ Dwyer. W.A. *Aboriginal [picture]*, c. 1900. State Library of Western Australia, Perth, 8292B/B/181.

Chapter 9

PHOTOGRAPHING ABORIGINAL AUSTRALIANS IN WEST AUSTRALIA

Donna Oxenham

Throughout Western Australia's history — almost from its first days of British settlement to the present day — Aboriginal people's lives have been recorded by photography. The reasons behind collections vary, from an individual's fascination with a race of people who were presumed at the time to be 'dying out' to an attempt by government bodies to prove that their treatment of Aboriginal people was the right one — a quest to indoctrinate and educate, bringing them out of their 'savage' pre-existence into a more civilised lifestyle. Today, however, descendants and relatives of the photographic subjects give the photographs a range of very different meanings, as this chapter explores. But to initially give these photographic collections context I felt it was important to provide a brief history of Western Australia's settler – Aboriginal relations.

British settlers established themselves on the south-western shores of Western Australia in 1829 with the intention of creating a new settlement; the Swan River Colony.[1] Historian Neville Green suggests that:

> the early contact between the European settlers and the Aborigines had been relatively uneventful. The reports and journals of the early settlers suggest that the invasion was initially peaceful because the Aborigines believed the white men were the returning spirits or re-incarnates of their own dead.[2]

As a result, the Noongar people — whose land they found themselves upon — took it upon themselves to care for the colonialists. An excerpt from the *Perth Gazette* in 1833 quotes settler RM Lyon:

> [T]he Aboriginal inhabitants of this Country, are a harmless, liberal kind hearted race; remarkably simple in all their manners. They not only abstained from all acts of hostility, when we took possession; but showed us every kindness in their power. Though we were invaders of their country, and they therefore a right to treat us as enemies, when any of us lost ourselves in the bush, and were thus completely in their power; these noble minded people shared with us their scanty and precarious meal; suffered us to rest for the night in their camp; and, in the morning directed us on our way to head quarters, or to some other part of the settlement.[3]

Thus, the growing colony in Western Australia was composed of several types of people. On the one hand, there were altruistic individuals who believed that Aboriginal people could be saved from the chains of slavery and ultimate demise by 'civilising' them, in a European sense. Conversely, there were others with entrenched Eurocentric, paternalistic views, who maintained that the Aboriginal people were beyond help — the lowest of creatures, who should be treated as such. Because the Western Australian settlement was a free-settler colony, it did not have the luxury of relying upon convict labour to build infrastructure or to add to the settlement's numbers, so from 1829 to 1850 settlers relied quite heavily on the aid of the local Indigenous groups for their survival. As a consequence, a relationship of sorts was formed during the early stages of station homesteads and pastoral leases throughout the latter half of the nineteenth century, as settlers acquired the bush expertise of the Indigenous people.

However, the arrival of convicts to Western Australia as a labour force in 1850 changed what was an already strained relationship and increased the rift in Indigenous–settler relations. Green suggests that:

> the arrival of convicts provided an alternative source of cheap labour and a lessening of interest in training Aborigines for menial tasks. The responsibility for taming and training passed from the priest and the school teacher to the magistrate and the prison warder.[4]

By 1868, 10,000 convicts had arrived in Western Australia. Any chance of Aboriginal people developing a reasonable working relationship and viable economic future with the colony was destroyed with the establishment of a penal workforce.

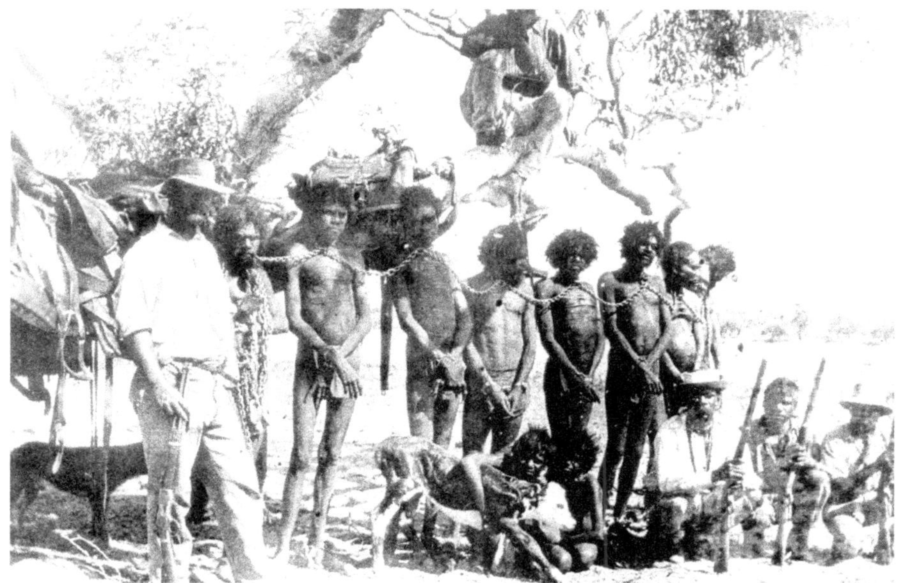

FIGURE 1: *Aboriginal prisoners in chains, posed with a policeman and Aboriginal trackers [picture]*, c. 1890. Photo-print. State Library of Western Australia, Perth, Call number 7816B.

Also, during the early years of the growing colony, white men initially outnumbered the women by four to one,[5] so it was only a matter of time before colonial men began to lure impoverished Aboriginal women into the illegal profession of prostitution. Some Aboriginal tribes offered their women in a ceremonial exchange that signified hospitality or diplomacy.[6] However, more often than not these exchanges were violent transgressions against Aboriginal women. The short-term effects of these 'exchanges' were devastating for both Aboriginal men and women. Not only did the men lose their women, but many lost their lives in retribution against the settlers for the violence often committed or the venereal diseases inflicted upon their people.[7] Also, the absence of contraception meant that a growing population of mixed-descent children was being produced.

As time passed, the Aboriginal population fell increasingly under the control of the white authorities, and the ongoing expansion of the colony resulted in the continued dispossession and cultural desecration of the Indigenous people and forced relocations into settlements that were usually established on the outskirts of towns.

However, a continued Aboriginal resistance hindered development into further so-called 'free-lands'. As a result, the settlers enlisted the aid of the military forces as an additional method of control. The colonial government even recruited a select number of Aboriginal men to fill positions of authority and power as native constables and trackers, in order to 'utilise them in controlling their Aborigines' (Figure 1).[8]

Any retaliation in response to colonial expansion was depicted as criminal behaviour. One particular historical event, which marks an ominous stain in Western Australian history, occurred in 1834. It would become known as the 'Pinjarra Massacre' or the 'Battle of Pinjarra', where more than eighty Pinjarup people were killed as a result of settler requests for military protection.[9] Consequently, the relationship between colonists and Indigenous people in Western Australia during this period not only foreshadowed what was to come later, but also the context in which the Aboriginal peoples' fate would be worked out. Over time, Aboriginal people learned what it meant to be 'Aboriginal' through the eyes of the imperialist settler state. Accordingly, they suffered the immediate and violent impacts of colonisation and bore the full effects of governmental policies of control over Indigenous people.

The law, the church and the missions each developed policies to govern Aboriginal people. In 1904 a Royal Commission conducted by Walter Roth, the Chief Protector of the Aboriginal people in Queensland, into the condition of the Western Australian Aboriginal people led to the passage of the 1905 *Aborigines Act* (WA). Hence, the Aborigines Department became a fully fledged government department under the control of the Chief Protector. Although its stated aim was to 'make provision for the better protection and care of the Aboriginal inhabitants of Western Australia', it soon became apparent that the administrators' intentions were to serve the interests of settler society, and they did more to hinder the Aboriginal people than to assist. The Act allowed for total paternalistic control of every aspect of Aboriginal people's lives.

By powers vested under the Act, the Chief Protector had the power to manage the property of Noongar people, with or without their consent, and his approval was required before an Aboriginal marriage could go ahead.[10] In this way, the law regulated Aboriginal people so that they were segregated from the wider community and placed on reserves and missions, except when their services were required. Indeed, the Act gave Honorary Protectors permission to enter Aboriginal camps at any time, and to remove them from towns arbitrarily.

The *Native Administration Act 1936* (WA) extended the powers of the 1905 *Aborigines Act* and gave the Department of Native Affairs unprecedented power over the daily lives of West Australian Aboriginal people. Section 12 enabled the Minister to cause the removal of Aboriginal people from any place to a reserve, district, institution or hospital. No judicial process was involved and there was no mechanism for appeal. Under Section 8, the Commissioner was given rights over all Aboriginal minors under twenty-one years of age.

Toussaint argues that the 1936 Act's underlying principle was the ultimate absorption — biological, social and cultural — of even those Aboriginal people who had escaped the effect of the 1905 Act.[11] Almost a decade later, the *Native (Citizens Rights) Act 1944* (WA) was found to be just as intrusive in Aboriginal people's lives, and Hodson suggests that in the late 1940s state intervention changed to reflect a new belief that Aboriginality was the result of social environmental influences, rather than heredity influences.[12] This attitude saw the creation of the certificate of citizenship, which allowed Aboriginal people to be recognised as Australian citizens. This, however, did not give Aboriginal people the right to vote as Australian citizens. Among other intrusions, it also demanded of those that obtained a citizenship certificate that they denounce their Aboriginal heritage and culture, to convince the courts that they were 'moral citizens'. They were subjected to medical tests to verify that they did not suffer from venereal disease, and they had to demonstrate that they had had no 'native' or 'tribal' associations for two years prior to their citizenship application. This control led to the eventual degradation of a highly spiritual people.

THE MISSION ERA

Many missions became an important tool in the south-west to implement these legislative policies and to further facilitate the dispossession, both physical and spiritual, of Aboriginal people. With the perceptions of the time depicting Aboriginal people as heathens (possessing no morals in the wider society), the missionaries purported to fill the supposed moral vacuum and were instrumental in the attempted cultural genocide against the majority of Aboriginal people.

The missions imposed an alternative way of life upon the younger generations of Aboriginal communities by breaking down strict customs and traditions of which all of the older generations were knowledgeable. The elderly Aboriginal

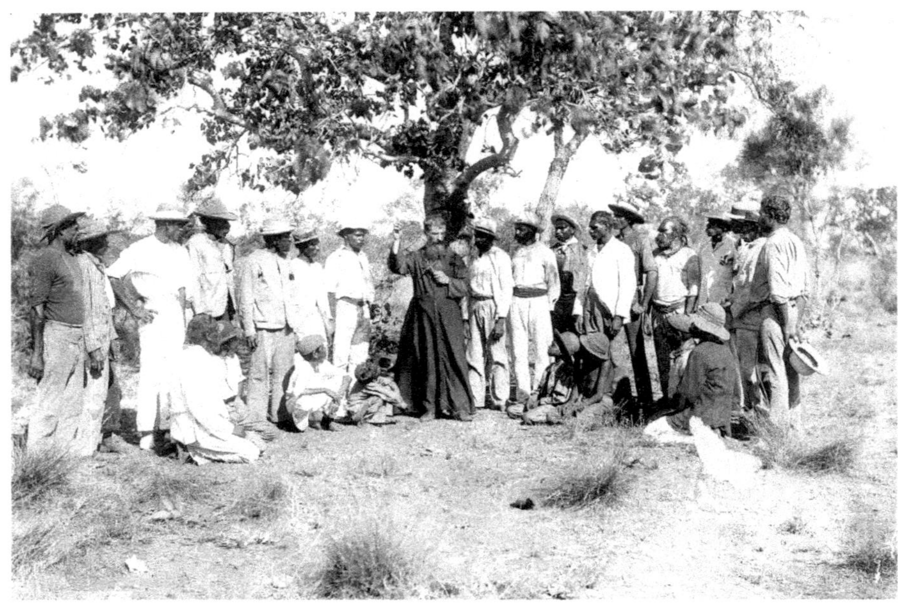

FIGURE 2: *Roebuck Bay natives, Beagle Bay Mission*, c. 1895–1910. State Library of Western Australia, Perth, BA1344/96.

people were separated from the youths of their own clans and were unable to pass on their knowledge and traditions.[13] Missionaries and philanthropists took it as their duty to improve Aboriginal society by teaching them Western ways, and were instrumental in breaking down cultural traditions that had been practised by Aboriginal people for centuries. However, this did not stop Aboriginal elders from continuing their traditions and holding corroborees within the mission system.

Missionaries worked mainly with the children, who were not old enough to fully understand the laws of their people, and re-educated them to the Christian faith and the laws of European society. The institutions set up to receive Aboriginal people under the Western Australian legislative Acts soon became overcrowded holding centres and were ill-managed, cramped and unhealthy. Jack Davis, Aboriginal poet, playwright and activist, who spent time at Moore River Settlement in 1932, recalls that it 'suffered from bad administration and lack of funds...and that the dormitory crawled with bugs and fleas, while the dining room and the cook house were crawling with cockroaches'.[14] Although administrators depicted Moore River and other settlements as places where the inmates settled 'down to a new life of peace, contentment and usefulness', they

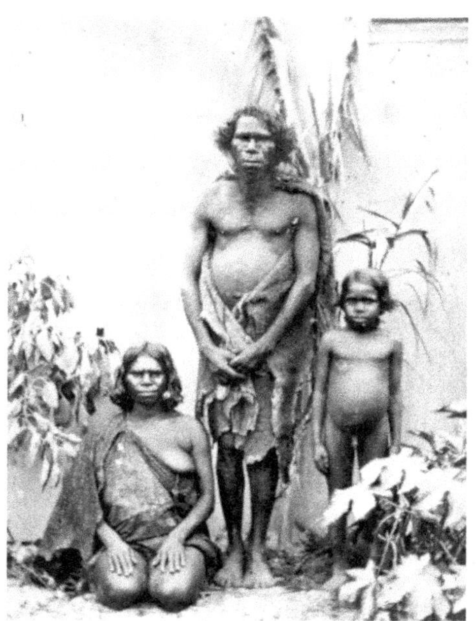

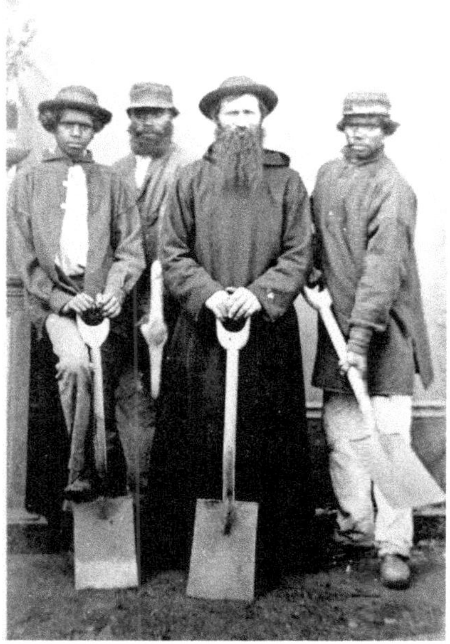

FIGURE 3: *An Aboriginal family [picture]*, 1890–99. State Library of Western Australia, Perth, 2893B/100.
FIGURE 4: *[Three Aboriginal males and a priest holding shovels]*, New Norcia, 1860. Berndt Museum, Crawley, #7506.

were, in fact, horrid, dirty and unhygienic places.[15] The mission life experienced by many Aboriginal peoples varied across the state from one institution to another, but ultimately they were used to irrevocably change a way of life that had been practised for centuries prior to the arrival of settlers.

One photographer, in particular, to photograph changes brought about by missionary interventions was William Pearce Clifton (1816–85). Clifton, a Western Australian amateur photographer, farmer and magistrate, extensively photographed Fremantle during this time period and is considered to be among the best photographers of the town at that time.[16] Along with his parents and fourteen siblings, the Cliftons were the first settlers to establish themselves in the Australind region of the south-west of Western Australia, arriving in 1841. Clifton was appointed the agent for claims to the Western Australian Land Company in 1846, and was a significant landholder and pastoralist in the region, holding office as a Justice of the Peace and Resident Magistrate for Bunbury.[17] Over the years that followed, the Clifton family was actively involved in the establishment and management of the Church of St Nicholas, Australind.

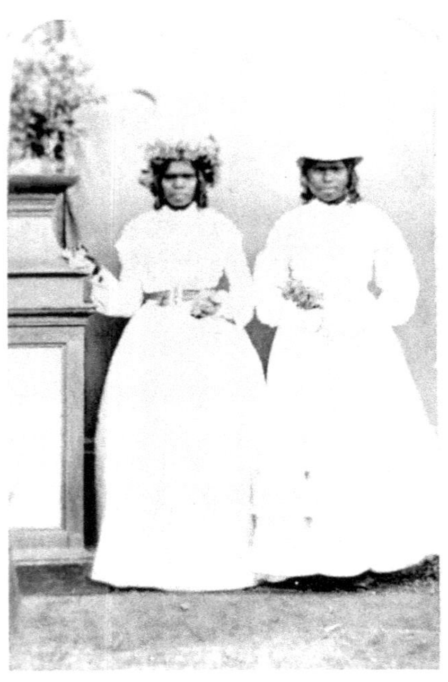

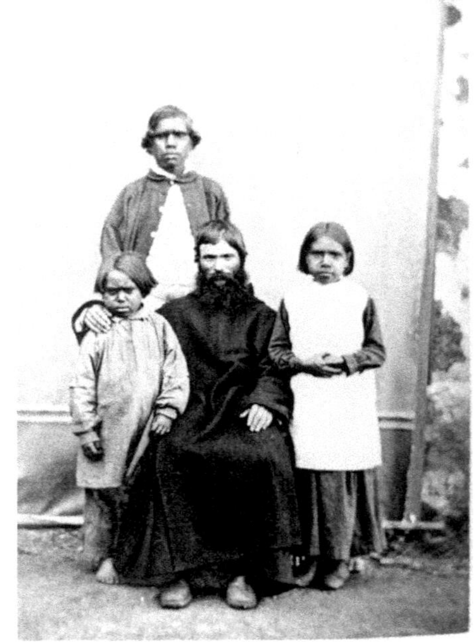

LEFT: FIGURE 5: *[Studio shot of two girls in long white dresses and hats]*, New Norcia, 1860, Berndt Museum, Crawley, #7508.

RIGHT: FIGURE 6: *[A seated priest, two small children standing either side and an aboriginal adult standing behind]*, 1860. Berndt Museum, Crawley, #7500.

It was during this time, however, that Clifton took a particular interest in Aboriginal studio portraits. These striking images were taken around 1860 and concentrated specifically on the Aboriginal people who were placed with, or voluntarily resided at, the New Norcia Monastery, which was established in 1846 by Spanish Benedictine missionaries. Led by Bishop Rosendo Salvado (1814–1900), the mission's aim was to 'civilise and evangelise according to the European ideals of the time, but [Salvado] did so with sympathy for indigenous culture that was rare in his day'.[18]

What is interesting to note is the transition or contrast between Clifton's 'traditional' images, in which the Aboriginal subjects were photographed in their 'native' dress with nature backdrops (Figure 3), as opposed to his images of Aboriginal subjects post their arrival at the mission. The later images emphasise the monastery's influence on the lifestyle of its Aboriginal inhabitants. No longer were they clothed in their traditional garb, but donned Western-style clothing and had seemingly adapted or integrated Western beliefs and customs.

Clifton's intent in recording these images is unknown, as there has been very little information found apart from his public duties. Whether it was from personal curiosity or his belief in the duties of a public officer to record Aboriginal people, the images show the progression and assimilation of the Aboriginal occupants in their attempts to accommodate a lifestyle that was socially acceptable to European sensibilities. Figures 4, 5 and 6 represent this transition.

State government control over all aspects of Aboriginal people's lives continued until 1967, when the Commonwealth was given the power to make laws in respect to Aboriginal people following the 1967 referendum.

A HISTORY OF WEST AUSTRALIAN PHOTOGRAPHY

> Photography draws much of its power from its indexicality, the chemical trace of light reflected off the physical reality in front of the camera. It is this tracing of Indigenous lives that constitutes the enormous potency and political impact of the symbolic sucking of a life force for source communities. Through this process, photographs translate the flow of lived experiences into a series of stilled, muted fragments of space and time, defying diachronic connections and separating the image from its real-life subjects.[19]

Photographers were rare during the early years of settlement in Perth; although there are records of photographers travelling to Perth for short periods of time, many were not primarily focused on recording images of the local Aboriginal people. The colonisation of Western Australia was not a peaceful venture and resulted in many Aboriginal people and nations losing their lives and territories, and the ensuing resistance turned Aboriginal people into society's outcasts. They were labelled 'a dying race', and, as a result, many photographers became interested in capturing 'the natives' in their primal state. Some felt the need to document the changes during the assimilation era, as those who could not adhere to Western ideals were rounded up into missions, prisons and jails, and treated like criminals. Many of these early photographs have been lost over time, but some remain. These collections are now of great significance to Aboriginal people, who see beyond the chains and derogatory captions to the people, places of significance and country that encapsulate who they are as a people today.

The following discussion is a brief look at a few photographers who recorded Aboriginal people throughout the state. Due to the west's small population, photographers were often attracted to the larger populations of the east. As a result, the first photographs in Western Australia were made fifteen years after its European settlement, but by the 1860s there were solid amateur and professional practices in most settled areas. Photo historian Gael Newton suggests that by '1860 some 100 photographers were at work and another 100 or so had practiced for some time since 1841'.[20]

Robert Hall (c. 1821–1866), a publican based in Adelaide, was the first photographer to visit the Swan River Colony at Perth in November 1846, but only a few poor examples of his work have survived.[21] A number of American daguerreotype photographers arrived during the 1850s and set up some of the leading studios of the next few decades. One of the earliest was Samuel Evans, who arrived in Western Australia in 1853 and set up his Daguerrean Gallery, first at Fremantle, then Perth. Not many examples of Evans' daguerreotypes have been identified, although a good scattering of daguerreotype portraits and one view of a Perth street exist in Western Australian collections.[22]

Townsend Duryea (1823–1888) arrived in Melbourne from New York in 1852 as an experienced professional photographer and formed a studio partnership with Alexander McDonald in Bourke Street. He later relocated to Adelaide in 1855 to form 'Duryea Brothers' with his brother Sanford between 1855 and 1859. From this base they toured the regional towns, and paid several visits to Perth, setting up a studio for four to five weeks at a time, and Sanford briefly established a Perth studio from 1857–59.[23] According to Noye, Townsend's career:

> as a photographer was cut short when his studio and entire collection of 50,000 negatives were destroyed by fire on 18 April 1875. This loss was a serious blow to Duryea and historians alike, as the plates were the best record of early South Australian colonial life ever made.[24]

This would also account for the lack of archival photographs to be found in Western Australia.

As a result, photography did not make much of a permanent appearance in Western Australia until Greenham & Evans established the first studio in Perth in the 1870s. Even though the studio's works varied across a broad range of topics and subjects, it did touch upon photographing Western Australian Aboriginal people.

CARTE DE VISITE PHOTOGRAPHY

The *carte de visite* was not used in Australia until Sydney photographer William Hetzer, working between 1850 and 1867, introduced it in 1860. The new style of miniature visiting card portraits was cheaper than daguerreotypes and sets of a dozen were sold for approximately 15 shillings in the mid-1860s, which was half the cost of one daguerreotype. One photographer to make use of *carte de visite* photography was Australian-born John Joseph (JJ) Dwyer.

JJ Dwyer (1869–1928) was born in Gaffney's Creek, a gold mining town in Victoria, where he spent the first fifteen years of his life. After completing an apprenticeship as a blacksmith, Dwyer's interest in photography became his passion and eventually his profession. In 1896 he headed westward to the latest goldfields and eventually landed in Kalgoorlie, where he established himself as a professional photographer:

> Dwyer was a prolific photographer who appeared to delight in his occupation, exploiting every available commercial avenue. His photographs appeared in the *Kalgoorlie Weekly*, and the *Western Argus*, he entered competitions, and he had a selection of his photographs published as postcards.[25]

Although the majority of Dwyer's work concentrated on the growing social life and the expanding infrastructure of the booming mining town, he did make a point of documenting the lives of the Aboriginal inhabitants of the area:

> At the time there was also considerable interest in documenting indigenous people. In Australia, papers read at meetings of the scientific community urged listeners to document 'the passing of the Aborigine' and the expedition of Baldwin Spencer and Gillen to the Northern Territory in 1901 aroused considerable curiosity. As a man of his times Dwyer made his contributions, taking many shots of Aboriginal people, in his studio and in their own setting.[26]

As a result, there are a few examples of Dwyer's work that he had produced as postcards (Figures 7 and 8).

Dwyer's collection, housed within the Library and Information Service of Western Australia, consists of 578 photographs and chiefly chronicles his journeys overseas and in the eastern states. The collection also has a series of

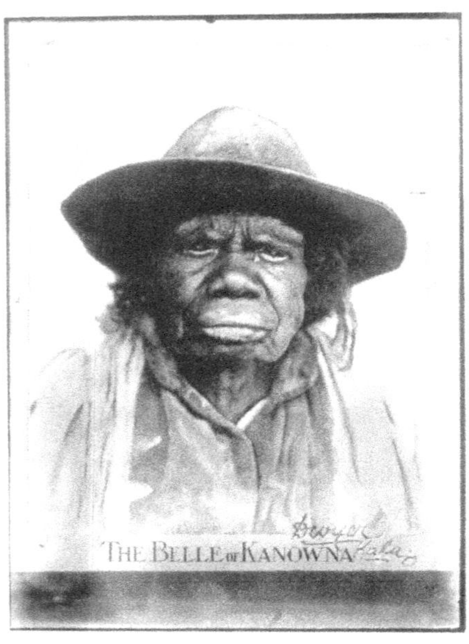

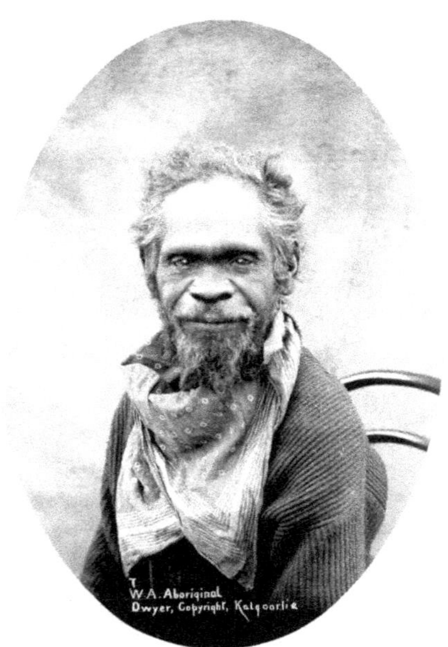

LEFT: FIGURE 7: JJ Dwyer. *The belle of Kanowna [picture]*, c. 189–. State Library of Western Australia, Perth, 8292B/B/180.

RIGHT: FIGURE 8: JJ Dwyer. *W.A. Aboriginal [picture]*, c. 1900. State Library of Western Australia, Perth, 8292B/B/181.

images of mine workings and Aboriginal people in Kalgoorlie, taken between 1900 and 1928. Dwyer varied his photographic themes over the years, from the studio-based portrait shots to Aboriginal people in their natural environment. What is interesting to note is that Dwyer was renowned for his ability to retouch a photograph so as to 'take twenty years off one's age, as he employed retouchers, generally women with a delicate touch, who removed blemishes and wrinkles from the portrait but left "character lines" in'.[27] He did not employ these techniques when photographing Aboriginal people, choosing to capture them in their 'natural state'. We can see this from portrait shots that were taken in his studio (Figures 9 and 10).

Such portraits are symbolic in the sense that they represent a more documentary or scientific approach to capturing the subjects' essence. Dwyer chose to encapsulate them in a way that places them in the category of 'other' — removed from the 'civilized and now' and located as the 'uncultured and ancient'.

FIGURE 9: JJ Dwyer. *An Aboriginal man of the Kalgoorlie region [picture]*, c. 1900. State Library of Western Australia, Perth, 8292B/B/138.

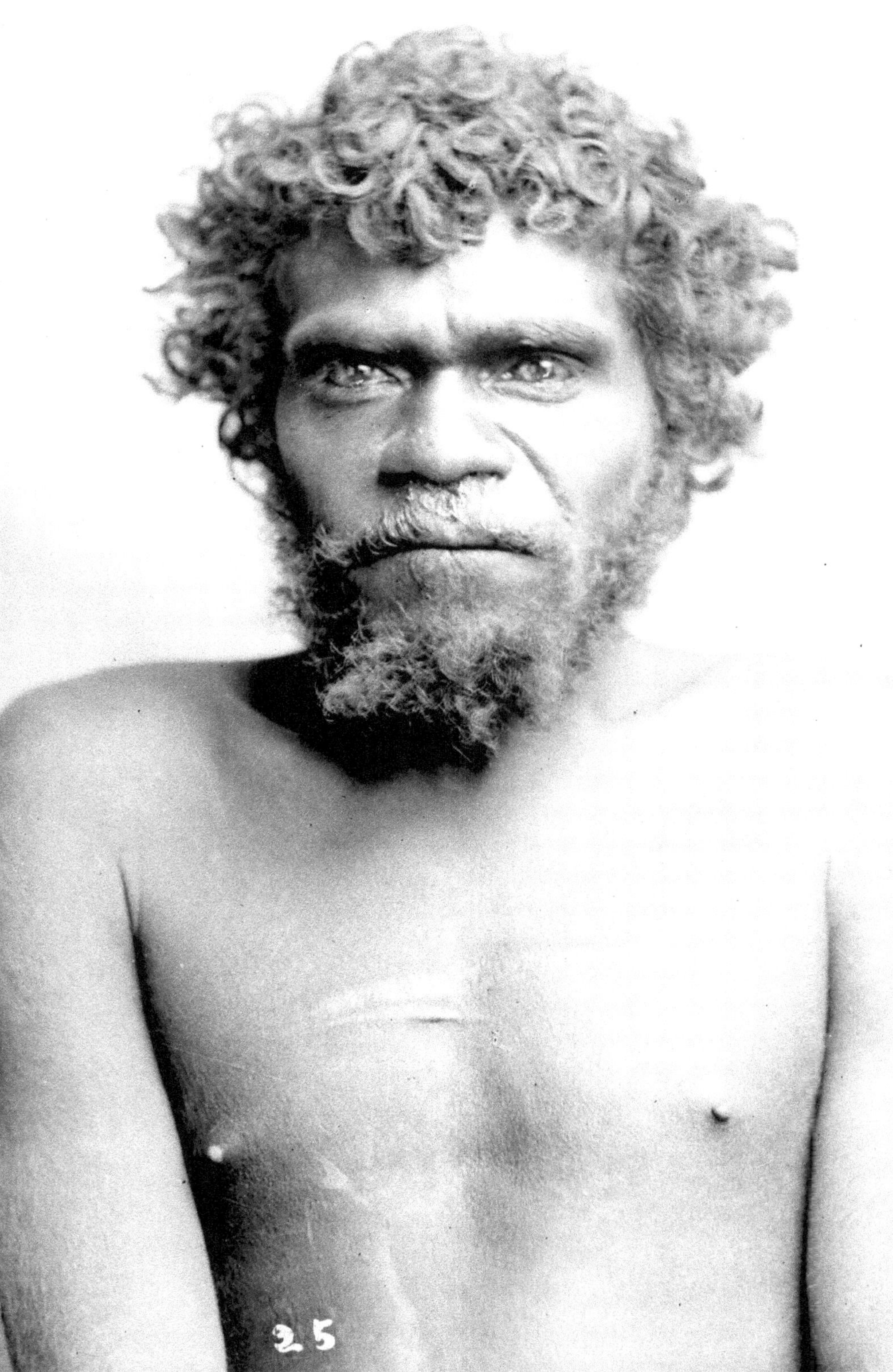

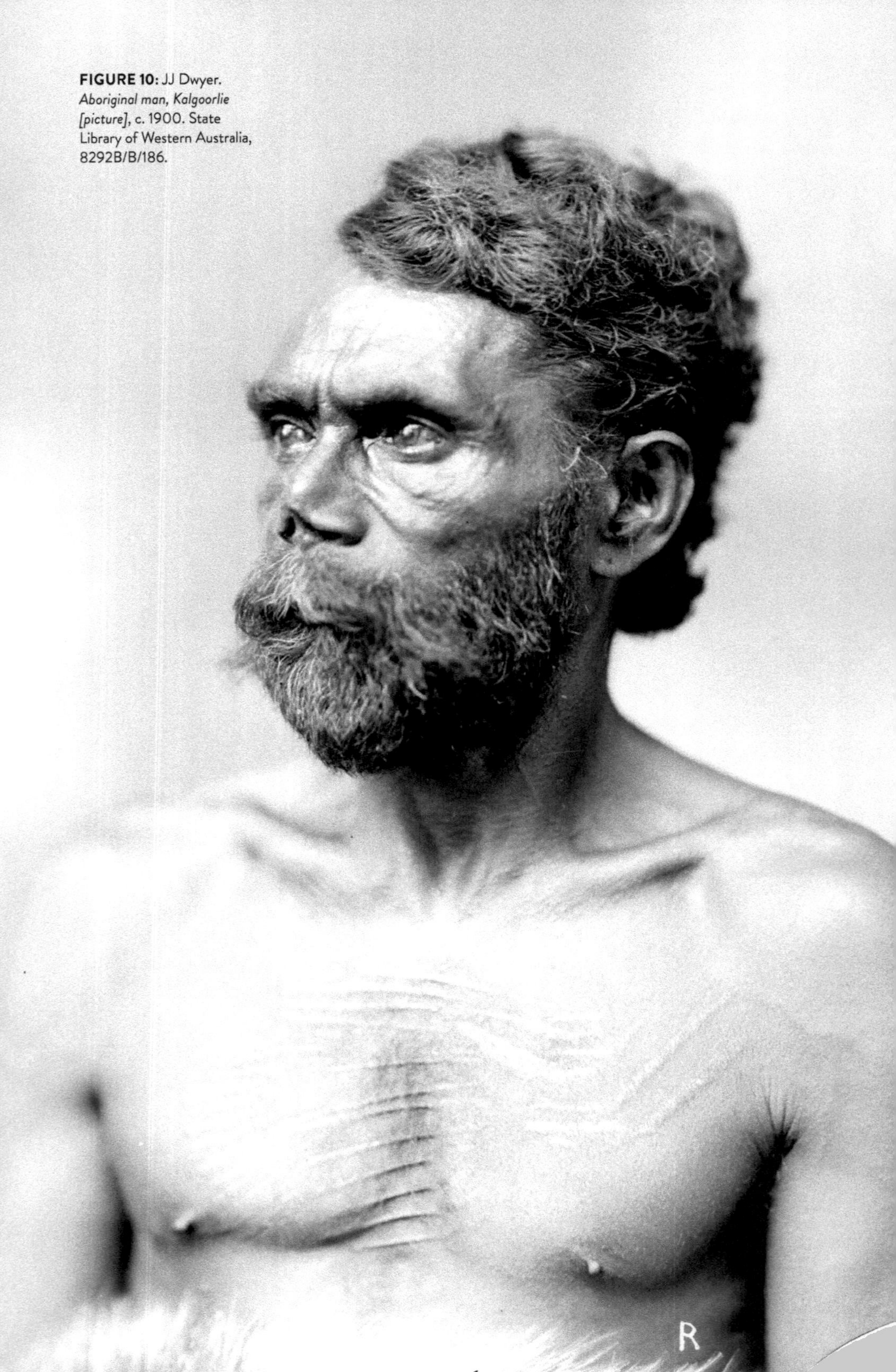

FIGURE 10: JJ Dwyer. *Aboriginal man, Kalgoorlie [picture]*, c. 1900. State Library of Western Australia, 8292B/B/186.

MAJOR COLLECTIONS AND HOLDING PLACES FOR PHOTOGRAPHIC ARCHIVES IN WESTERN AUSTRALIA

BATTYE LIBRARY OF WESTERN AUSTRALIA

The Battye Library's pictorial collection has more than one million images. Its intended aim is to depict all facets of Western Australian social history. However, at present only 10 per cent of the collection is available in a digital format to online users. For those wishing to view the majority of photographic images available, it is necessary to visit the library in person.

It is important to note that categories such as 'Indigenous/Aboriginal Photographic Collections' have been spread out over different categories according to how, when and by whom they were donated. In many situations photographic collections have been donated without information attached to each image, so many photographs have simply been recorded as 'unidentified Aboriginal'. Also, many items in the pictorial and film collections contain images of, or depict, secret/sacred content (the display of which may cause sadness and distress), so they have been removed from the index card catalogue, as well as the photographic volumes.

In saying this, however, the Battye has made tremendous progress with its Aboriginal collections in terms of making the archival collections more accessible to the public. In particular, efforts to return Aboriginal photographs and other materials directly to Aboriginal families, communities and peoples through the new *Storylines* project launched in 2013 will be, in my opinion, the benchmark for other archival institutions across Australia to follow.

BERNDT MUSEUM OF ANTHROPOLOGY

The Berndt Museum of Anthropology is housed within The University of Western Australia. Its primary collections were donated to the museum in 1976 by its founders, Ronald M Berndt and Catherine H Berndt — both successful anthropologists who worked extensively with Aboriginal communities within Western Australia and beyond.

The museum contains one of the largest collections of items from within Australia. Of particular interest are the photographic collections, which house more than 35,000 images — 15,000 of which relate to Western Australia's

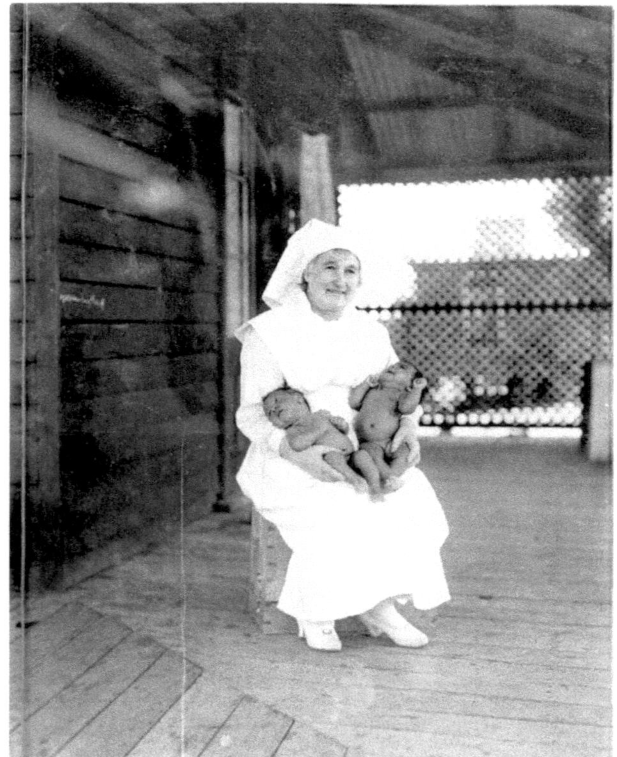

FIGURE 11: *Moore River Native Settlement [Nurse with two infants. Matron with two infants, possibly twins]*, n.d. AO Neville Collection, Berndt Museum, Crawley, #7692.

past. These images have been sourced from government, mission settlements and pastoral stations. Of the vast photographic materials, two collections of particular interest to Indigenous people are the RM and CH Berndt Collection and the AO Neville Collection.

The AO Neville Collection was assembled by this influential official in order to support his arguments for management of Western Australia's Indigenous people and, especially, their assimilation. Henry Prinsep, the first Chief Protector for Western Australia, had aimed for separation, supporting segregation because he was 'convinced that the improvement of the Aborigines' lot (and protection of the wider society) was to be achieved by limiting Aborigines' contact with the white settlement and, where necessary, by removing them from society altogether'.[28] However, the appointment of Auber Octavius Neville (1875–1954) as Chief

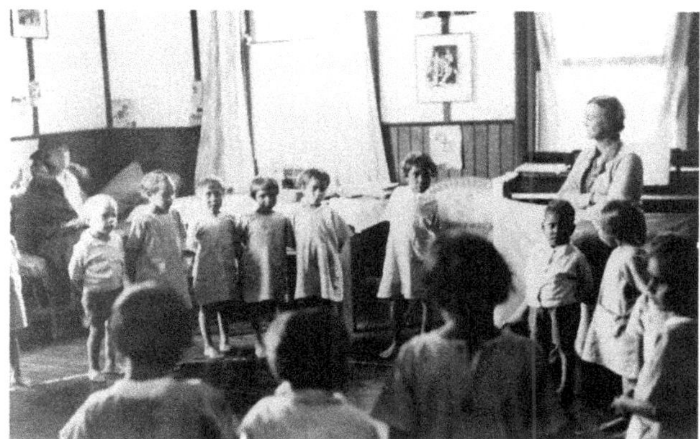

FIGURE 12: *Moore River Native Settlement [Row of children standing in front of the kindergarten teacher]*, 1936. Berndt Museum, Crawley, #697.

Protector in 1915 introduced what would become known as an era of degradation, assimilation and cultural genocide — not only for Noongar people, but for West Australian Aboriginal people in general. Indeed, the consequences of that era are still felt in the Aboriginal community today. It is significant that Neville was an avid believer in documenting all aspects of the assimilation process. As a result, he compiled a vast collection of photographs to help justify the removal of Aboriginal people to missions and pastoral stations throughout the state.

ANTHROPOLOGY DEPARTMENT PHOTOGRAPHIC COLLECTION WESTERN AUSTRALIAN MUSEUM

The Western Australian Museum, established in 1891, has been collecting images of Indigenous people since 1899. Many of the early collections were donated by private sources, but there are also more recent collections.

The museum currently holds around a hundred photographs taken during the early 1900s by Ernest Lund Mitchell (1876–1959) in various regions throughout Western Australia. Mitchell was a successful photographer who dominated the Western Australian commercial and official markets from 1909 until the late 1920s:

> Mitchell's photographs are a rich source of ethnographic information as they show clear details of artefacts such as shields, spears, boomerangs and headdresses. They provide cultural information for those with

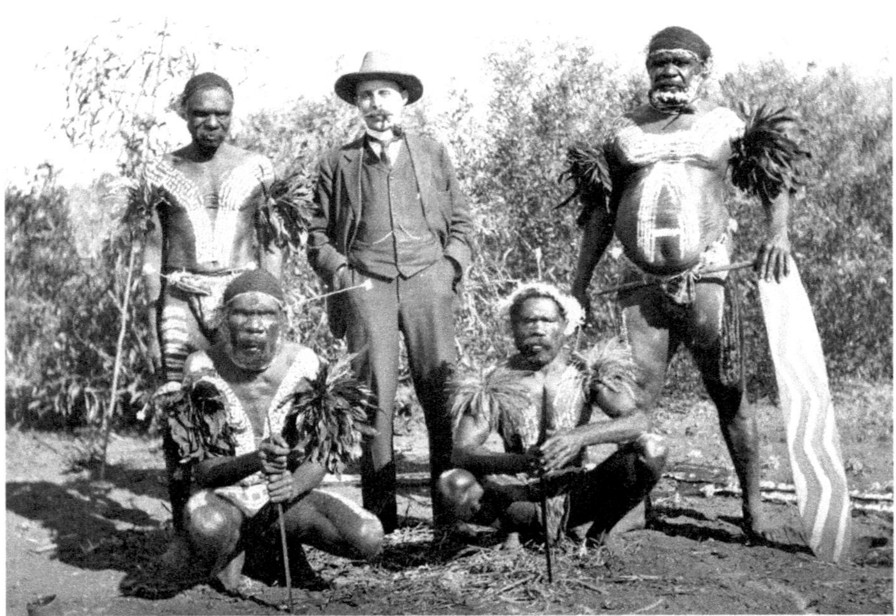

FIGURE 13: EL Mitchell. *Aboriginal men in traditional dress with man in suit [picture]*, c. 1920–30. State Library of Western Australia, Perth, BA1271/162.

> knowledge of its interpretation, though Mitchell himself did not record this information on his negatives or prints. The tone of his captions and their pictorial style suggest that they were not taken with anthropological intent, nor were they created as part of exhibitions, and most circulate outside the strict discourse of anthropology. In spite of not being created specifically to produce anthropological information, the photographs contain features which have made them attractive for anthropological uses almost from the time they were taken.[29]

Although originally commercial in nature, Mitchell's Indigenous photographic collections are an important source for Aboriginal people today.

INDIGENOUS COMMUNITIES AND REPATRIATION PROJECTS

Visual repatriation is, in many ways, about finding a present for historical photographs, realising their potential to seed a number of narratives

> through which to make sense of the past in the present and make it fulfill the needs of the present.[30]

Traditionally, Aboriginal people recorded their history orally and were able to keep alive the memories of loved ones and the knowledge of country without the necessity of the written word or archival record. Since colonisation, however, people's oral histories in many places have become fragmented. Therefore, with access to relevant photographic collections, Indigenous people and communities today are able to amalgamate the archival images with their oral histories. As a result, the concept of time becomes somewhat inconsequential, and the past, present and future co-exist. Not only do they depict images of people's ancestors, their country and places of significance, but they become 'living entities' in their own right — able to remove themselves from the spectrum of time and the Western concept of 'the past' and place themselves within the 'here and now'.

Through access to these images, we, as Indigenous people, are able to come full circle — what was then has become the now. For many, finding and receiving images of one's ancestors may be the only link to the past. It is especially relevant for members of the Stolen Generations, who were forcibly removed from their families and cultural heritage. Thus, they are able to begin a healing process and find — for want of a better term — an 'end in the beginning'.

Historically, Indigenous interaction with institutions like museums and State Government-run libraries and departments has been limited and one-sided. In many cases, Indigenous people became the objects and subject of archival collections — albeit collected and archived through the eyes of the non-Indigenous outsider. When dealing with photographic archives, Edwards suggests that:

> [P]hotographs are amongst the most potent of museum objects. In cross-cultural terms they have an enormous and two-fold potential. They are an evidential source within the communities they depict, inscribing complex layers of cultural information and knowledge, and an important site of negotiation for the development of long-term collaborative relations between museums and communities.[31]

Overall, through allowing Aboriginal communities greater agency and access to these archives, the process of reconciling aspects of the past can begin. With Aboriginal people now looking back at these institutions through the looking glass (so to speak), the relationship between institutions and Aboriginal people can be based upon more equal footing.

In Western Australia a number of avenues are available to Aboriginal communities wishing to obtain copies of photographic collections housed within the archival institutions. The majority of these institutions allow individuals or communities to come in, source relevant materials, and then apply to have copies produced and sent to them. This is usually done at cost price, as most institutions do not have a budget allocation to allow for the repatriation of photographic materials to Aboriginal communities and/or individuals.

However, two institutions in Western Australia that have been instrumental in repatriating copies of visual collections back to Aboriginal communities throughout the state are the Berndt Museum of Anthropology and the State Library of Western Australia. Not only have they begun actively repatriating historical Aboriginal photographic collections, but they have begun the process of digitising and repatriating their extensive sound collections.

The Berndt Museum has, to an extent, been funded to facilitate this process, thus making it easier for Aboriginal communities to receive relevant images and collections of their forebears without the financial costs normally associated with producing copies of images as found in other institutions.

Originally an Aboriginal and Torres Strait Islander Commission-funded endeavour, the Bringing the Photographs Home project — officially launched in 2000 — was designed in response to the *Bringing them home* report, which focused on reconciliation and aided the healing process for the Stolen Generations. As stated on the museum's website:

> The Stolen Generation deserves the opportunity for people to reconnect to their families, even if it is only in photographic form. Sometimes, a photograph is the only record of their forebears. Not only is it important for the older generations to identify their family history, but it is also crucial that this information is passed to younger generations, which is imperative for reclaiming and forming identity.[32]

As a result, a number of repatriation projects have been successfully undertaken by the Berndt Museum throughout Western Australia. For example, in 2000 the museum's archives relating to Goulburn Island were repatriated back to the Warruwi people, and the local Community School acted as a repository. In this instance, the museum was able to hand back a collection of 300 photographic images, as well as sound recordings. Other repatriation projects have since been co-ordinated, with various cultural centres and Aboriginal Land Council representative bodies throughout the state acting as holding centres for the returned materials.

The State Library of Western Australia *Storylines* pilot project, I believe, will change the way institutions deal with their archival collections relating to Aboriginal peoples. This interactive program (which is based upon the Ara Irititja software platform) has the potential to revolutionise the way photographic, audio and other recordings are repatriated back to the Aboriginal families, communities and peoples from which they came. The *Storylines* database currently holds 1500 photographs from the library's heritage collections, 1600 people have been identified within these records, and 168 places such as stations, missions, landmarks and towns have been identified.

RESEARCH PROJECTS

Finally, the Australian Research Council-funded project *Globalisation, Photography and Race: The Circulation and Return of Aboriginal Photographs in Europe*, based at The University of Western Australia, is currently working to return photographs to Aboriginal people. The project has four key European museums as partners — the University of Oxford's Pitt Rivers Museum, the Cambridge University Museum of Archaeology and Anthropology, the Musée du quai Branly in Paris and the Volkenkunde (National Museum for Ethnology) in Leiden. Using digital technology, these collections are being analysed and collated with the aim of returning them to relatives and descendants. The ability to use technology to repatriate archival collections to Aboriginal peoples is not only a sign of the times, but an important tool that Aboriginal people can use to bring their ancestors from the past and place them firmly within the present.

FUTURE DIRECTIONS

Because of the complexities involved with the repatriation of historical photographic collections to Aboriginal communities, it is fundamental that the process of returning photographic materials is handled in a culturally appropriate manner — and it is important to fully understand the significance these compilations represent for Indigenous people. It is often said that a photograph can speak a thousand words, but for Indigenous people these archival images represent so much more:

> [P]hotographs are ultimately uncontainable; they carry an incompleteness and unknowability. There is seldom a 'correct interpretation': one can say what a photograph is not, but not absolutely what it is. Consequently, meanings emerge that are perhaps diametrically opposed to, for instance, colonial intentions of the photographs.[33]

Thus, through Indigenous eyes not only do these photographic collections depict images of people's ancestors, their country and places of significance, they also become 'living entities' in their own right, assuming an independent existence in the present. By recording their histories within an oral tradition, Indigenous people were able to keep alive the memories of loved ones and the knowledge of country. Now, with access to relevant visual archives, Indigenous people and communities today are able to amalgamate the visual image with their oral stories and histories. Western ideas of linear time are undermined, and past, present and future are conflated.

These images are an integral part of an age-old tradition and culture that cannot be supplanted by what outsiders' perceptions of Aboriginal people were at the time of taking a photograph. These collections today are welcomed by the majority of Aboriginal people, who see these records as evidence of their survival and strength, not as depictions of a 'dying race' or the colonised. Consequently, images of Aboriginal people being chained and treated like criminals, for example, are relatively inconsequential to Aboriginal people today. Like the chains that once bound Aboriginal prisoners together, these historical photographic collections bind Aboriginal people to their past.

What is important is the people, places of significance and country that can be found within these images. In my opinion, Aboriginal people are rather forgiving of the past and although some images — and sometimes the captions that go with these images — are distressing, what becomes important is the ability to tangibly hold these photographs of our past, which can reinforce our cultural foundations rather than destabilise them.

The photographic archive is a powerful source of information for Aboriginal people. In each image we see where we've been and in turn what we've become. They are 'living' proof that Aboriginal people are survivors and that our culture has survived through tremendous adversity.

NOTES

1. The King George Sound settlement was established three years earlier and much further south in what was to become known as Albany as a British military outpost intended to forestall any plans by France for settlement in Western Australia.
2. N Green, *Nyungar, the people: Aboriginal customs in the southwest of Australia,* Creative Research in association with Mount Lawley College, Perth, 1979.
3. RM Lyon quoted in Green, above n 2, p. 148.
4. N Green, 'Aborigines and white settlers in the nineteenth century' in CT Stannage (ed.), *A new history of Western Australia,* University of Western Australia Press, Perth, 1981, p. 93.
5. C Mattingly & K Hampton, *Survival in our own land: Aboriginal experience in 'South Australia' since 1836: told by Nungas and others,* Hodder and Stoughton, Sydney, 1988, p. 174.
6. H Reynolds, *The other side of the frontier*, Penguin Books, Ringwood, Vic., 1981, p. 70.
7. AJ Barker & M Laurie, *Excellent connections: a history of Bunbury, Western Australia, 1836–1990*, City of Bunbury, Bunbury, WA, 1992, p. 10.
8. MC Howard, 'Aboriginal Australia in south-western Australia' in RM Berndt & CH Berndt (eds), *Aborigines of the west: their past and their present*, University of Western Australia Press, Perth, 1980, p. 58.
9. D Horton, *The encyclopaedia of Aboriginal Australia,* Aboriginal Studies Press, Canberra, 1994, p. 111.
10. A Haebich, *For their own good: Aborigines and government in the southwest of Western Australia, 1900–1940*, University of Western Australia Press, Nedlands, WA, 1988, p. 85.
11. S Toussaint, 'Nyungars in the city: a study of policy, power and identity', unpublished Masters thesis, University of Western Australia, Perth, 1987, p. 65.
12. S Hodson, 'Nyungars and work: Aboriginal labour in the Great Southern Region, Western Australia 1936–1972', unpublished Masters thesis, University of Western Australia, Perth, 1989, p. 137.
13. AR Radcliffe-Brown in H Reynolds (ed.), *The other side of the frontier*, Penguin Books, Ringwood, Vic., 1981, p. 135.
14. J Davis, *A boy's life*, Magabala Books Aboriginal Corporation, Broome, WA, 1991.
15. GC Bolton, 'Black and white after 1897' in Stannage (ed.), above n 4, p. 144.
16. 'William Pearce Clifton', Design and Art Australia, viewed 11 November 2013, <www.daao.org.au/main/anniversary?date%5Bmonth%5D=5&date%5Bday%5D=1>.
17. In 1840 the Western Australian Land Company was formed in London with the purpose of promoting a large land settlement scheme in the Colony of Western Australia. This was planned by a group of influential men, including William Hutt MP (brother of John Hutt, Governor of Western Australia from 1838 to 1846) and Edward Gibbon Wakefield, upon whose principles of colonisation the company was founded. Marshall Waller Clifton (William Pearce Clifton's father) was appointed Chief Commissioner and his son Robert Williams Clifton (1817–1897) was appointed secretary to Waller; 'Marshall Clifton', Wikipedia, viewed 11 November 2013, <http://en.wikipedia.org/wiki/Marshall_Clifton>.
18. 'The Salvado era: 1846–1900', New Norcia Benedictine Community, viewed 11 November 2013, <www.newnorcia.wa.edu.au/protecting-a-unique-heritage/the-story-of-new-norcia/the-salvado-era.html>.
19. E Edwards, 'Introduction: locked in the archive' in L Peers & AK Brown (eds), *Museums and source*

communities: a Routledge reader, Routledge, London, 2003, p. 84.

20. G Newton, 'Chapter three: extending the franchise' in *Shades of light: online* (based on text from the original book *Shades of light: photography and Australia 1839–1988,* Australian National Gallery, Canberra, 1988), viewed 11 November 2013, <www.photo-web.com.au/ShadesofLight/03-franchise.htm>.
21. ibid.
22. ibid.
23. ibid.
24. RJ Noye, 'Duryea, Townsend (1823–1888)', *Australian dictionary of biography,* National Centre of Biography, Australian National University, viewed 11 November 2013, <http://adb.anu.edu.au/biography/duryea-townsend-3458/text5283>.
25. R Pascoe & F Thompson, *In old Kalgoorlie,* Western Australian Museum, Perth, 1989, p. 11.
26. ibid., p. 7.
27. ibid.
28. Aboriginal Legal Service, *Telling our story: a report by the Aboriginal Legal Service of Western Australia (Inc) on the removal of Aboriginal children from their families in Western Australia,* Aboriginal Legal Service, Perth, 1995, p. 11.
29. J Sassoon, 'Becoming anthropological: a cultural biography of EL Mitchell's photographs of Aboriginal people', *Aboriginal History,* 28:59–86, 2004, p. 65.
30. Edwards, above n 19, p. 84.
31. ibid., p. 83.
32. 'Projects involving the Berndt Museum', Berndt Museum of Anthropology, The University of Western Australia, viewed 12 November 2013, <www.berndt.uwa.edu.au/generic.lasso?token_value=projects&menu=1>.
33. Edwards, above n 19, p. 84.

NORTHERN TERRITORY

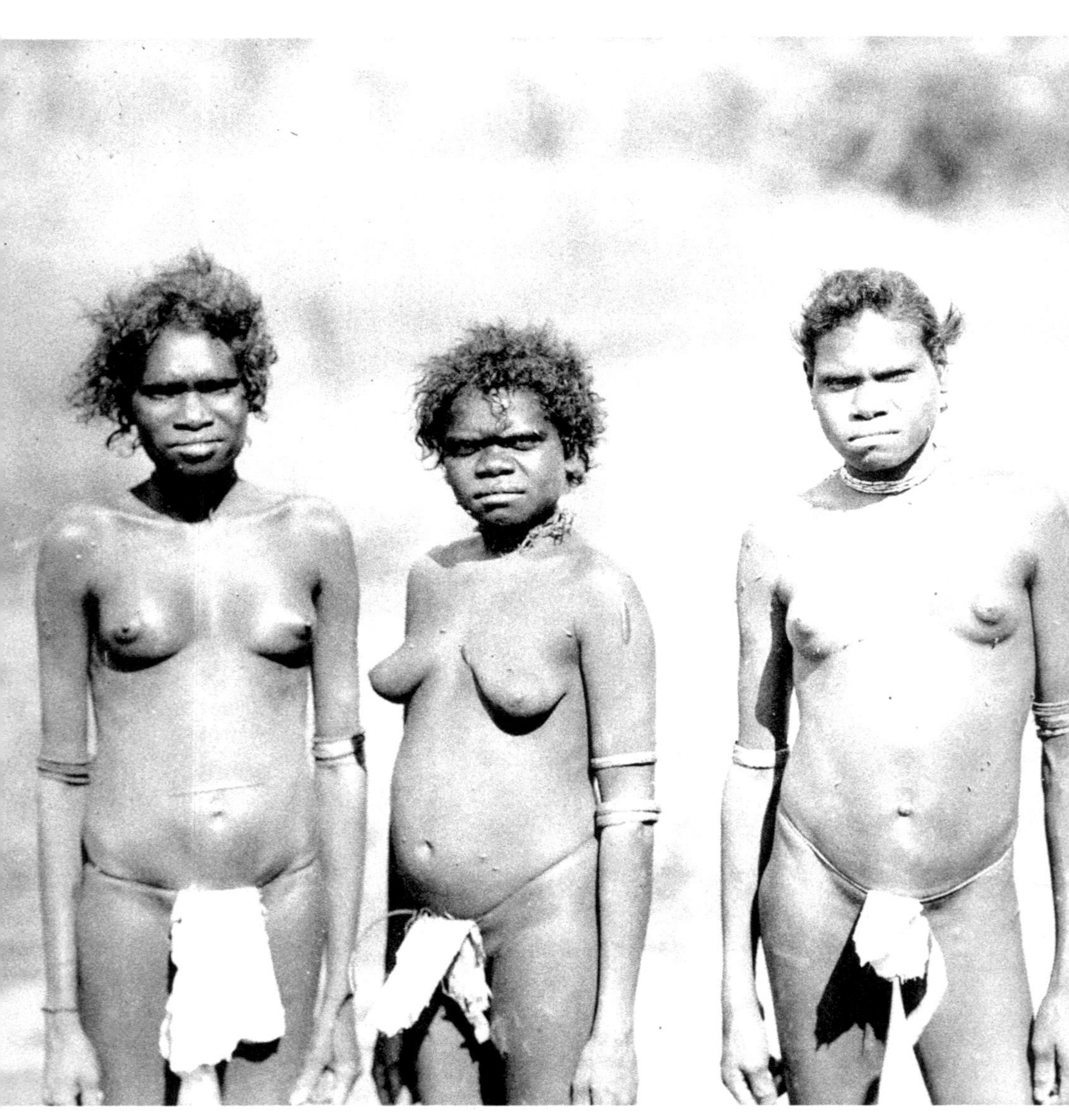

DF Thomson. (Left to right) *Sisters Gularrbanga #1, Gadayurr and Baymarrwangga #1 at Murrungga, central Arnhem Land, Northern Territory, Australia, c. 1935*. Courtesy of the Thomson family and Museum Victoria, TPH1340.

Chapter 10

PHOTOGRAPHING THE OUTBACK: THE LAST FRONTIER?

Jane Lydon and Sari Braithwaite

Of all parts of Australia, the least, although the longest known is that huge expanse now called the Northern Territory. The Australian who visits it is surprised and strangely entranced with this portion of his continent. He is fascinated by the romance of the life and by the varied elements that compose it — the crude beginnings of white man's civilization, the savage state of the Stone Age Aboriginal, and, foreign to both, the peculiar flavour of the East, reminding him that he is now within tropic regions. (Elsie Masson, 1915)[1]

To think such a scene was possible on the coast of Australia! There were four proas anchored close in to the beach, some sixteen large dredging canoes at work, and numerous smaller ones plying between the proas and the beach. On shore were four great smoke-houses, built of bamboo and palm leaves. Of Malays there were about one hundred engaged at various occupations in connection with the preparation of the trepang. Some had only scant clothing, others wore their gay sarongs, and all had gaudy handkerchiefs twisted round their heads...A large number of aborigines,

> men, women and children, most of them in a state of nature, were also present...either assisting the Malays, or lolling about smoking cigarettes made of Malay tobacco, rolled up in pandanus palm leaf...The pity of it was we had no camera. And no man regretted this more than Inspector Foelsche...for he was a most enthusiastic and successful photographer. He had left all his appliances at home, thinking them too cumbersome to carry on a small boat. There were no kodaks about then. (Alfred Searcy describing Adjaka, Bowen Straits, in 1883)[2]

By the 1870s northern and Central Australia were seen as Australia's last frontier, regarded by the city-dwellers of the long-tamed south as torrid, exotic and remote. This vast area encompasses great cultural diversity among Indigenous Australians, and it is important to note that only administrative fiction has defined it as a coherent entity over the past century or so. Colonial visions of its potential productivity and strategic importance were thwarted by a climate considered extreme by British colonists, and attempts to gain a toehold on the northern coast failed over and over again. To the south, Central Australia's semi-arid environment presented similar challenges.[3] In 1863 the British Government ceded control of the region to South Australia, and finally in 1869 the first British settlement was established at Port Darwin. Construction of the overland telegraph line took place between 1870 and 1872.[4] These efforts to explore, settle and exploit the Territory were glimpsed by the camera from the 1860s along the northern coast, and gradually through the 1880s inland, opening the Territory up to distant eyes.[5]

MACASSANS

The history of northern Australia challenges British-centred national myths of a fatal impact upon a pure and primitive race. From at least the eighteenth century, trader fishermen with their crews of Macassan, Bugis, Butonese, Timorese, Malukans and Papuan sailors travelled to Australia each year from Macassar in the province of South Sulawesi (Celebes), leaving with the north-west monsoon in December. The Macassans called the Arnhem Land coast *Marege,* and the Kimberley coast *Kayu Jawa*. Indigenous memory and academic research have revealed the complexity and vitality of these relations, showing that they extended beyond the narrowly economic to encompass marriage and

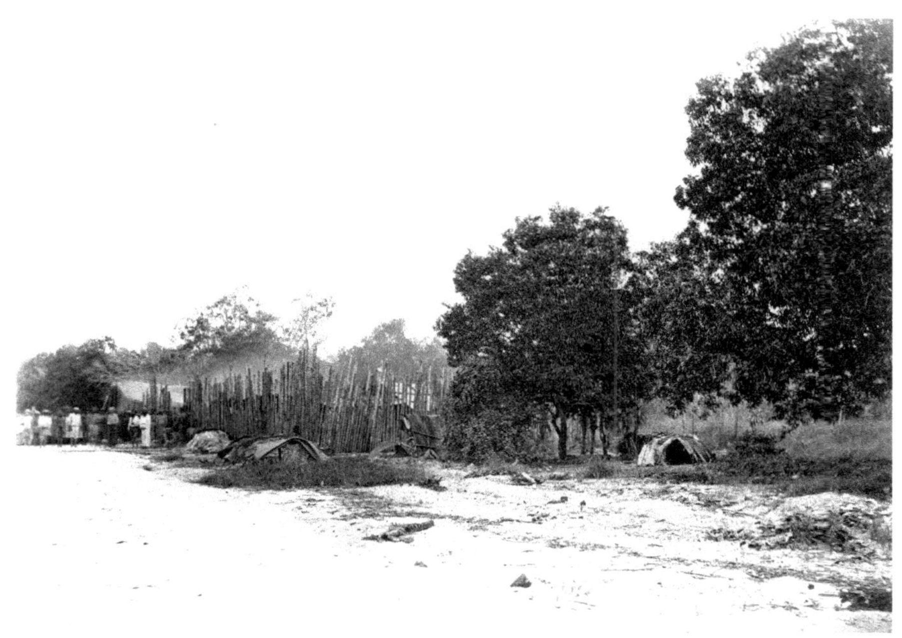

FIGURE 1: Paul Foelsche. *Trepang Fishery Station, Port Essington, 26 March 1875*. State Library of South Australia Adelaide, B10836.

kinship ties.[6] From the earliest exploration of the coastline, an appreciation of hybridity and colour pervades Western representations of the Macassans, and when photographers reached the region they, too, recorded the trade: unlike the visit described by customs collector Alfred Searcy in 1883, police inspector and keen photographer Paul Foelsche (1831–1914) sometimes *did* bother to take his camera when he visited the Cobourg Peninsula between 1875 and 1891.

He produced images of trepangers at work, and a view of a Trepang Fishery Station (Figure 1), which shows a group of Macassans, Aboriginal men and at least one white man standing beside a beach enclosure made of timber posts — presumably the Macassans' station, comprising accommodation and drying sheds for the catch. Small Aboriginal shelters are dotted around it, with spears stuck into the ground, a fishing net spread out to dry, and a rubbish heap to one side. Substantial roofed structures may be seen within the enclosure amid a drift of smoke. The fortified enclosure points to the clashes, as well as amicable exchange, entailed by the long trepang trade (outlawed in 1907). Today Aboriginal people stress that they were equals and participants rather than subordinate victims. Since 1986 Indigenous memories of relationships have been celebrated by reciprocal visits between Arnhem Landers and Macassans, enabling people to conduct ceremonial exchange, meet relatives and remember this significant aspect of their shared past. Marcia Langton, curator of a 2012 exhibition entitled *Trepang,* writes of 'the bravery, excitement, wealth, conflict and friendship experienced by the protagonists for more than a century. What lies at the heart of this story is friendship and alliances forged through trade.'[7]

'STRONG, BEAUTIFUL PEOPLE'

This cosmopolitan history contrasts with the story of relations between European settlers and Aboriginal people during the spread of white settlement into the region from the 1870s. These encounters coincided with the application of the scientific theory of natural selection, encouraging popular notions of biological difference between so-called 'races' of people. Widespread anxiety about racial mixing was especially acute when it came to the polyglot north, as from the early twentieth century officials increasingly attempted to enforce segregationist policies. In 1927 a visitor to Broome's picture theatre described how the Japanese sat on one side of the room, the Chinese sat at the back, Aboriginal families took up a quarter of the theatre and the Europeans sat separately in cane-seated chairs.[8]

Such views were naturalised by scientists seeking to define human difference, in turn reliant upon visual records such as photographic portraits or 'types' of different races. By the late 1860s suggestions for ways of establishing visual comparisons between peoples included methods for standardising such portraits — by including measuring rods or gridded backdrops, for example.[9] It is evident that Australian photographers were aware of this new conventional framework for recording Indigenous people, and produced a range of local imitations. Foremost among these were Foelsche's portrait photographs of the Larrakia, Woolna and Iwaidja peoples, whose traditional lands he policed.[10]

Foelsche had arrived in the newly established Port Darwin in 1870 as Sub-Inspector of the Northern Territory Mounted Police, the most senior police officer in the Territory. It is difficult to overlook his role in the violent conquest of the north during the 1870s and 1880s. There is evidence that during the terrible conflicts of these decades Foelsche co-ordinated punitive expeditions — for example, in August 1875 he sanctioned indiscriminate killing along the Roper River following

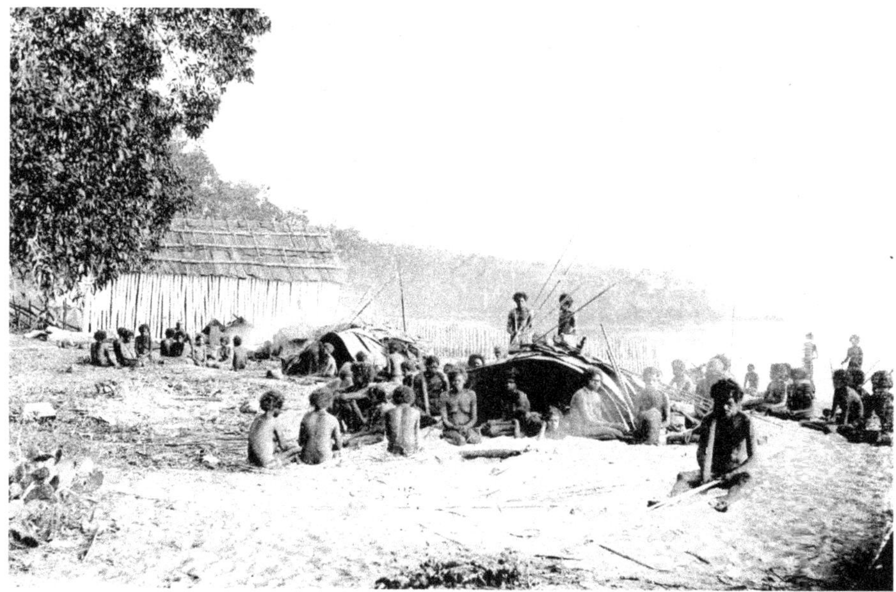

FIGURE 2: Paul Foelsche. *Iwaidja people in camp, Port Essington, November 1877*. National Library of Australia Canberra, PIC P827/27.

the murder of a white telegraph operator at Daly Waters. Foelsche euphemistically described this in a letter to a friend as 'a picnic with the natives'.[11] Nonetheless, the record he produced remains a valuable resource for descendants.

In 1874 he began photographing the Larrakia, on whose traditional country Darwin had been established, using a measuring scale and recording their names and other details. He sent his work to overseas exhibitions, and collected artefacts and information that he submitted to scientific institutions such as the South Australian Museum.[12] The distancing effects of this scientific framework for Foelsche's images have elicited anger and grief from some Indigenous people today, such as Gurindji artist and writer Brenda L Croft, for whom the anonymous subjects remain 'ghosts deprived of rest', their images used to control and oppress their own people. Croft and others emphasise the almost dehumanising effects of such portraits, although note that they remain important family portraits and records of culture.[13]

Foelsche's work was the subject of a major exhibition at the South Australian Museum in 2006 in collaboration with Larrakia, Djerimanga and Iwaidja

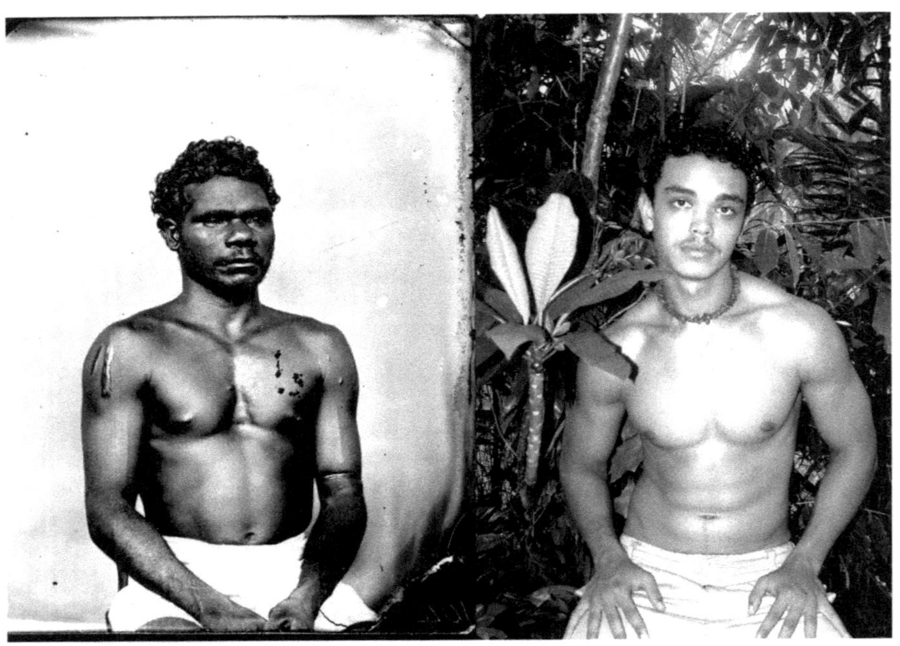

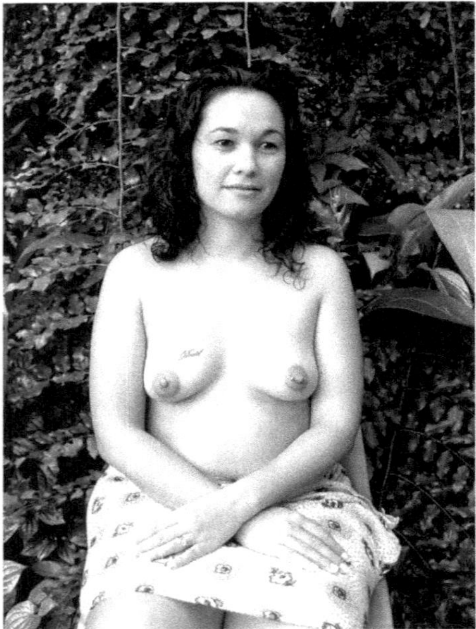

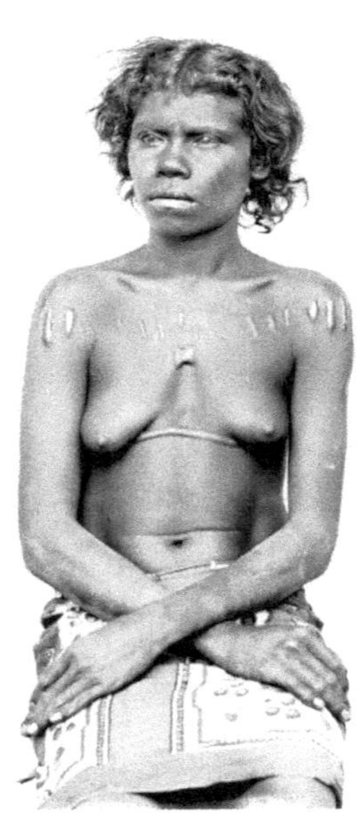

TOP: FIGURE 3: Gary Mura Lee. *Billiamook and Shannon*, 2005. Courtesy of the artist.

BOTTOM: FIGURE 4: Gary Mura Lee. *Mei Kim and Minnie*, 2006. Courtesy of the artist.

communities, and curators Philip Jones and Tim Smith point out that Foelsche's photograph of Iwaidja people in camp at Port Essington (Figure 2) required complete stillness and co-operation from his subjects in making this image, despite its apparently artless informality. They note that '[t]he central figure in this image is the Iwaidja woman known to Foelsche as Flash Poll, a key cultural broker between her people and the South Australians', and argue that '[d]espite his role as a powerful police official, Paul Foelsche prepared these portraits with great care and sympathy. The people they depict all passed away several generations ago, and these images can be regarded safely now, without offending the living or the spirits of the dead.'[14]

Some Indigenous viewers have responded directly to the people within the frame: as the Larrakia artist Gary Mura Lee puts it, 'We see past the measuring stick and all that it represents and we see strong, beautiful people — our people'.[15] In 2005 Lee co-curated with Sylvia Kleinert an exhibition celebrating Larrakia man Billiamook. Following Goyder's establishment of the settlement at Darwin in 1869, Billiamook became a key broker between his Larrakia people and the South Australian colonists. In his engagement with Foelsche, Lee has adopted a tactic of juxtaposition, placing the historical portraits side by side with his own modern studies of relatives. For example, Lee's portrait of his nephew Shannon, alongside one of several portraits of Billiamook produced by Foelsche, forms a diptych (Figure 3). Both Billiamook and Shannon are photographed at around sixteen years of age, their strength and vitality radiating from the image. By emphasising what is shared by these two young men, distant in time but related by family, we see continuity and resilience.[16] Lee created a similar diptych by placing a portrait of his niece, Mei Kim, alongside a Foelsche portrait of Lee's great-great-grandmother, or *alap*, Minnie Duwun, when both were aged twenty-seven (Figure 4).[17] Typical of Foelsche's portraits, his black and white photograph of Minnie has a pale backdrop, focusing our attention on her skin — with ornamental cicatrises — and her strongly modelled face. Mei Kim sits in front of lush greenery, wearing a fuchsia sarong, her colour and warmth contrasting with the stark but exquisite detail of Minnie's portrait in a celebration of Larrakia beauty.

In a sense, Foelsche's personal relations with Aboriginal people, or even his larger role in the machinery of colonialism, become irrelevant to descendants. These portraits are objects that have biographies of their own, changing meaning as they move across culture and time. Once 'data' housed in European museums, or evidence for the frontier's unequal power relations, they are now primarily family portraits and a source of strength.

SEEING THE CENTRE

Up until the construction of the overland telegraph line between 1870 and 1872, inland Australia was mostly a large blank space on European maps. Only gradually did explorers and settlers penetrate the region's diverse terrains. Hopes of finding a vast inland waterway slowly evaporated. In 1860 John McDouall Stuart (1815–1866) led an expedition along the Finke River north-west to the McDonnell Ranges, naming what is now known as Central Mount Stuart. In 1862 he led the first successful European party to cross the continent from south to north, and back again, establishing the route along which transport and communication would later flow. By the mid-nineteenth century, imperial organisations such as the Royal Geographic Society considered photography an excellent tool for map-making. Drawing diverse places and people into a single conceptual field, it would produce a perfect descriptive geography in two-dimensional form.[18] David Livingstone's Zambezi Expedition of 1858–63 was the first expedition to successfully attempt photography, yet Paul Carter points out the absence of photography from Australian exploration until the 1890s, arguing that 'exploration, a process of spatial speculation, was precisely what photography could not visualise', given the unknowability of what they would find.[19] Photography, by contrast, became the tool of scientists and tourists recording sights already known and expected. Carter contrasts the present tense of the explorer's in-the-moment journal accounts with the retrospective photographic view, just as the explorers' Aboriginal guides remembered their path through country by continually looking backwards, performing a double take. In its 'empirical ebullience' the medium recorded sights already known, imaginatively possessing the land.[20]

Many scientific and exploratory expeditions were made possible by the knowledge and skills of Aboriginal people, either as members of the party or through life-saving advice and help en route. Historian Philip Jones suggests that prior to the 'camera-wielding' tourist invasion of the Centre, after the Second World War, Indigenous people were curious to engage with photographers: he

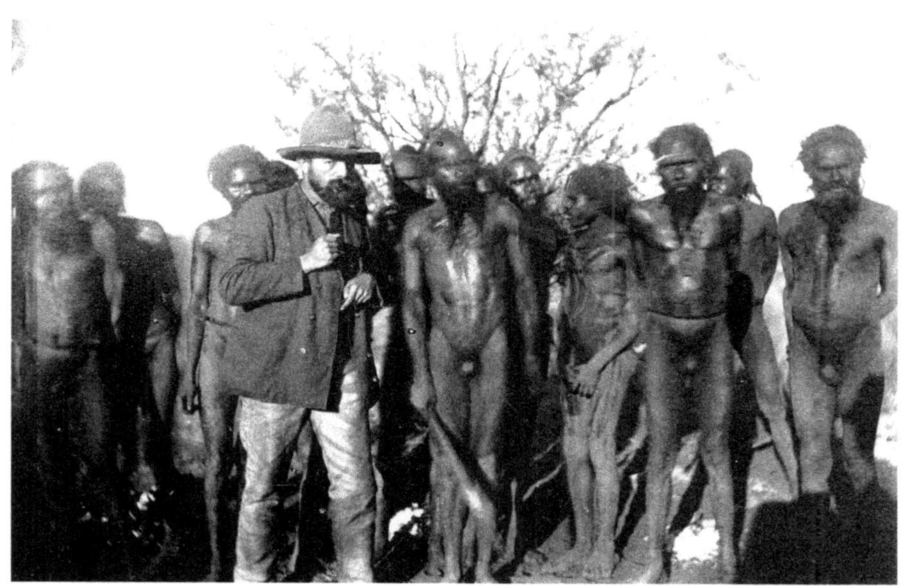

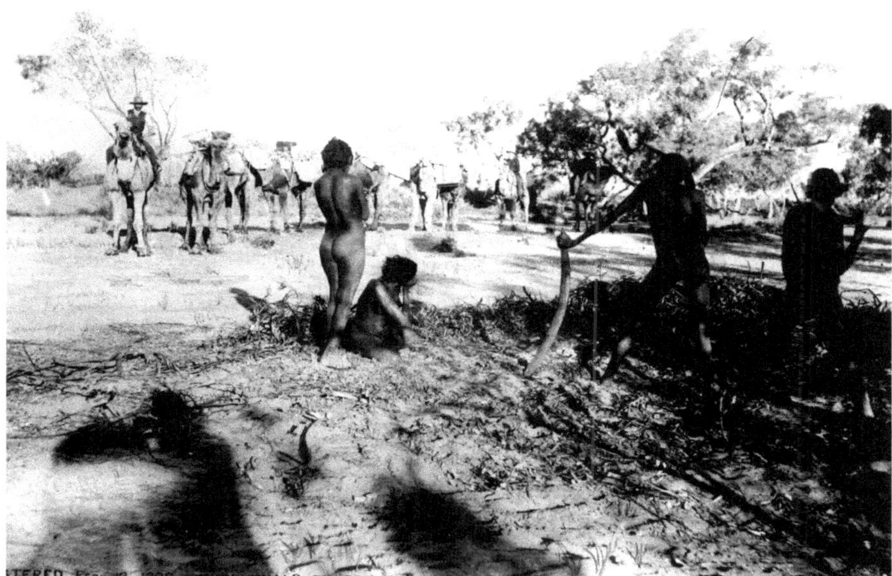

TOP: FIGURE 5: *First natives met with after leaving Birksgate Ranges (closer view, all standing)*. The Elder Scientific Exploration Expedition, 1891–92. State Library of South Australia, Adelaide, B 8442/11. Cultural permission from A͟ra Irititja.

BOTTOM: FIGURE 6: James Taylor. *[Two Aboriginal men, standing, about to hurl their boomerangs at an approaching party of whites on camels] Camel team and Aboriginals*. The Elder Scientific Exploration Expedition, 1891–92. State Library of South Australia, Adelaide, B 8442/11. Cultural permission from A͟ra Irititja.

argues that it was not until the advent of mass tourism that more impersonal relations produced suspicion of the medium.[21] The earliest images from the interior, such as those in Frederick Elliot's (c.1855–97) two photograph albums from the Elder expedition of 1891–92, reveal a mutual curiosity and interest — for example, in an encounter with Pitjantjatjara/Ngaanyatjarra people, the alien white explorer appears incongruous in this Indigenous world, looking sideways, almost furtively at the camera, while the Indigenous men are at full-bodied ease, seemingly amused by the situation (Figure 5).[22]

These people may already have encountered Port Augusta photographer James Taylor, who travelled north along the uncompleted Alice Springs railway line to Warrina on the Oodnadatta Track to photograph people from the Musgrave Ranges on 22 August 1889.[23] These highly staged scenes — including collage effects added in the darkroom in some cases — dramatise first contact and traditional life. One provides a rare attempt to capture an Indigenous perspective, showing a group of Aboriginal men and women, the men about to hurl their boomerangs at an approaching party of whites on camels; the photographer stands behind the Aboriginal people, offering a view from the other side of the frontier (Figure 6). The actors in these performances are described as being from the Musgrave Ranges, clearly Pitjantjatjara people who had travelled south and agreed to participate in these re-enactments. Other images from this series include groups of Aboriginal people 'at William Creek, September 5 1889', another scene of attack by armed Aboriginal warriors against a white man loading his camels, and staged scenes of hunting and climbing trees.

Another remarkable series was produced by Richard Thilwell Maurice, who explored several regions of the inland during the late 1890s and early twentieth century, collecting natural history and ethnographic material for the Royal Geographic Society and private sponsors. Maurice's panoramic camera captured the sweeping landscapes of the interior in dramatic fashion, their linearity punctuated by points of interest, much like the topographical profile drawings of an earlier generation of artists. The low viewpoint of *'Wild Dog' Police Station*, for example, creates a horizon marked by the flimsy hut, flanked by a sapling-built stockyard and wurleys (Figure 7).

In *View in Musgrave Ranges* Maurice's camel train sets out from the left into a country simultaneously mapped by the camera (Figure 8). The viewer's eye pans across the landscape, tracking the party's intended journey. In December 1901,

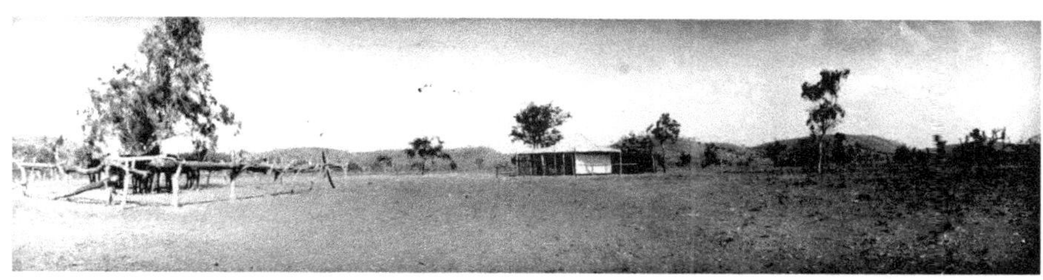

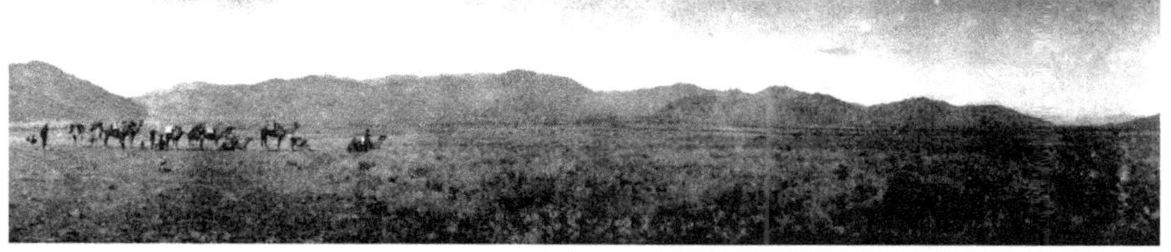

TOP: FIGURE 7: RT Maurice. *'Wild Dog' Police Station*. RT Maurice transcontinental expedition, 1904. Royal Geographical Society of South Australia, Adelaide.

BOTTOM: FIGURE 8: RT Maurice. *View in Musgrave Ranges*. RT Maurice transcontinental expedition, 1904. Royal Geographical Society of South Australia, Adelaide.

after a journey from Ooldea to the Rawlinson Ranges on the edge of Western Australia's Gibson Desert, Maurice returned to Adelaide with three young Aboriginal men named Munjena, Yarrie (Karruninnya) from the Arrindinya, in the Musgrave Ranges, and Peter (Napparinnya Kallatinya) from Tadinya, in the Everard Ranges, who were photographed with 'spears and other weapons' supplied by the South Australian Museum.

> [I]nstead of putting anything on, they took everything off, and there they stood unblushing and unashamed. Although scientists might object to the men in any way being hidden, it was thought advisable to supply them with loin cloths. It was interesting to study the tribal scars and marks on the three men. These are cut with stone, and then ashes are put into the wound, and a scar rises like a cord on the skin...The three boys were all painted with red ochre and whiting [and] stood...ready to be photographed.[24]

While the city studio was concerned to recreate a fantasy of pre-contact authenticity, another photograph of the exploring party shows these three Indigenous men beside the white explorers, all dressed in the same way, standing almost as equals (Figure 10). In 1902 Maurice mounted another expedition starting from Fowler Bay on the Nullarbor Plain in the south, and

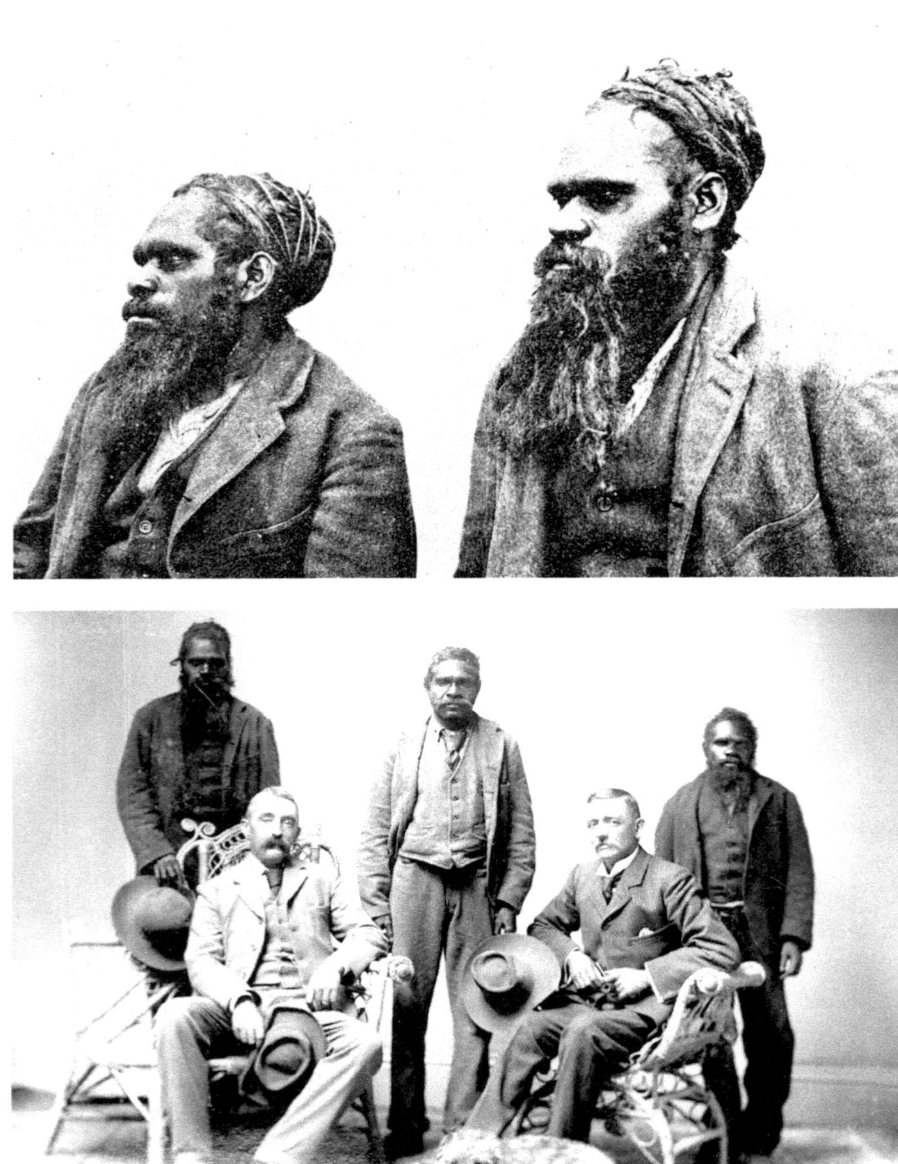

TOP: FIGURE 9: J Gazard. *Aborigines from Central Australia. Town and Country Journal*, 28 December 1901, p. 24. Cultural permission from Ara Irititja.

BOTTOM: FIGURE 10: RT Maurice & Expedition party (*Yarrie, Munjena, Peter, R. Murray, R.T. Maurice, Airedale Terrier Jack*), 1902. State Library of South Australia, Adelaide, B 34142/1. Cultural permission from Ara Irititja.

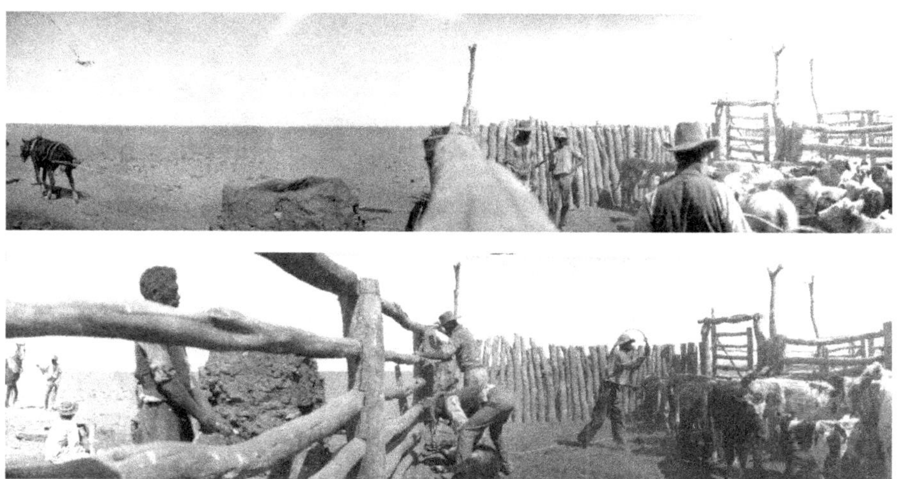

TOP: FIGURE 11: RT Maurice. *Sturt Creek – cattle branding.* RT Maurice transcontinental expedition, 1904. Royal Geographical Society of South Australia, Adelaide. Cultural permission from the Elders of Billiluna Pastoral Company.

BOTTOM: FIGURE 12: RT Maurice. *Sturt Creek – catching and branding calves.* RT Maurice transcontinental expedition, 1904. Royal Geographical Society of South Australia, Adelaide. Cultural permission from the Elders of Billiluna Pastoral Company.

ending at the Cambridge Gulf in the north, again taking Munjena, Yarrie and Peter. They took fourteen camels, travelling through the traditional lands of the A<u>n</u>angu Pitjantjatjara Yankunytjatjara peoples, including the Everard Ranges, the Musgrave Ranges, Ulu<u>r</u>u and Kata Tju<u>t</u>a, and the Cleland Hills. Some of their camels were poisoned in the Tanami Desert, and they reached Sturt Creek Station in the south-east Kimberley four months later. Maurice recorded scenes of life and work across the inland, showing Aboriginal men working in the pastoral industry or imprisoned in chain gangs at Wyndham.[25] His wide-angled landscapes are filled with incident and detail, such as those of the Tjurabalan people (comprising the Walmajarri, Kukaja and Jaru language-speaking groups) now based at Billiluna, south of Halls Creek in the Kimberley region of Western Australia, who lived near the homestead at Sturt Creek, where they worked as stockmen or in the house.[26]

These records of the past are now valuable cultural heritage for descendants, brought together in the ground-breaking and much-loved A<u>r</u>a Irititja project by the A<u>n</u>angu (Pitjantjatjara and Yankunytjatjara people) of Central Australia, as discussed in the introduction to this volume.

POPULARISING RACE

In January 1911, a decade after federation, the Northern Territory was transferred to Commonwealth control, and an administrator was appointed by the Governor-General. There was a particularly close relationship at this time between science, administration and popular views of Indigenous people, embodied by the anthropologist Walter Baldwin Spencer (1860–1929) and his colleague, the Central Australian telegraph operator Francis Gillen (1855–1912). Their work played an important role in disseminating views of Aboriginal people, often through visual media. Spencer arrived in Australia in 1887 to take up the foundation chair of biology at The University of Melbourne. He had already become familiar with the evolutionary typologies of the Pitt Rivers Museum in Oxford. Through his professional and popular publications, Spencer was to profoundly influence contemporary theories on social evolution, including the notion that Aboriginal people represented 'humanity's childhood' — or an early stage in the development of humankind.[27] In this view, the 'authentic' people of remote Australia who continued to lead a traditional way of life were of scientific interest, but those who had changed and adopted aspects of Western lifestyle were not: so in 1892 he visited Ebenezer Mission in north-western Victoria, but, clearly finding its residents of little interest, subsequently went on to research more remote groups. Joining forces with Gillen in 1894, the pair pioneered an anthropological approach founded on extensive ethnographic fieldwork, facilitated by Gillen's familiarity with the Arrernte language and the use of new photographic and film technologies. The rich collections of cultural 'data' Spencer and Gillen amassed were of intense interest to the 'armchair anthropologists' back in the metropolis; their book *The native tribes of Central Australia* (1899) was mined by influential British anthropologist James Frazer (1854–1941), for example, author of the classic study of comparative religion, *The golden bough* (1890).[28]

Spencer and Gillen's visual data played an important role in supporting their scientific arguments. In their popular publications, Spencer and Gillen sought to show Aboriginal people as they would have appeared before contact with whites — without clothes, for example, despite the changed lifestyle of Indigenous people across south-eastern Australia by this time. In 1914, in delivering the Melbourne address to the meeting of the British Association for the Advancement of Science, Spencer showed imagery of traditional Central Australian Aboriginal people and material culture in a standardised 'traditional' format that supported his assertion that 'they represent the most backward race extant'.[29] In the 1890s Gillen gave popular lectures such as 'the Children's lantern entertainment' in aid of the local Benevolent Society.[30]

Despite these public and official effects, Spencer and Gillen have been celebrated by those who point to their deep interest in Indigenous cultures, and the rich heritage they amassed for descendants. Their work is praised for inaugurating a 'fieldwork revolution', transcending the gap between theory and data, and experimenting with new visual technologies in making imagery central to the recording, analysis and publication of their work. The photographs they produced differ from earlier images in that they are action shots, showing ceremonies as they occurred rather than being posed, and creating informal portraits of people.[31] In addition, by the time Gillen met Spencer in 1894, Gillen enjoyed paternalistic yet relatively warm relations with the people they studied, based on long residence in Arrernte country.[32] Gillen negotiated photographing ceremony in exchange for rations such as flour or tobacco in what historian Philip Jones argues was a transparent and straightforward relationship.[33] Gillen's letters to Spencer reveal that the Arrernte and others often enthusiastically collaborated with the pair to record their culture.

Many old men were eager to teach Gillen about their culture, and during his journey 'across Australia' in 1901 with Spencer, they were summoned to record various ceremonies: 'laden with our cameras and the cinematograph we tramped over the hills and up the creek for half a mile where in a secluded spot we found a blackfellow gorgeously decorated awaiting our arrival...we quickly focused the instruments upon him and he performed'.[34] Gillen avidly collected a wide range of objects, including sacred 'Churingas' (*tywerrenge*).[35] However, in July 1897, halfway through a long, chatty letter to Spencer that accompanied a consignment of artefacts, he mentioned ('this between ourselves') his distress at hearing that an old man had been killed for revealing a storehouse of sacred objects (*ertnatulinga*) to another white man. He declared that 'there must be no more ertnatulinga robberies', and noted, 'I bitterly regret ever having countenanced such a thing and can only say that I did so when in ignorance of what they meant to the natives'.[36]

In search of tradition, Gillen and Spencer did not like their ethnographic subjects to wear clothes, Gillen once commenting that 'I have many times visited

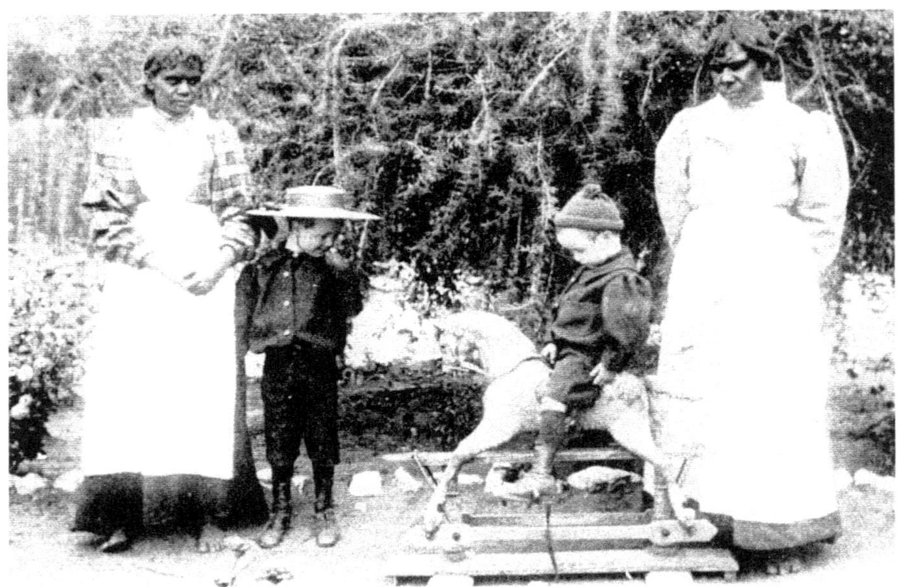

FIGURE 13: Polly Solomon and Dolly standing either side of Gillen children and rocking-horse. Courtesy of Jill Braithwaite. Cultural permission Ian Conway.

ertnatulinga in this locality with the blacks but the rags they wore has always created a certain amount of incongruity and robbed the scene of the solemnity'.[37] However, when he sought to photograph his family's housemaid Polly Solomon 'au naturel', she quickly set him straight: Gillen reported, 'I approached her on the subject with exceeding delicacy, she gave me a look which I shall never forget and scathingly remarked, "You all same Euro, you canta shame! You no big fellow master! You piccaninny master." The emphasis on the picaninny [sic] was something to remember for one's lifetime'; Polly admonished Gillen that 'poto-grafum' (photographing) 'Very good longa bushie lubra, no good longa Station lubra' and finally, 'No good no good potografum lubra cock!'[38] Polly was clearly aware of the loss of dignity that removing her clothes would entail and distinguished her own familiarity with European ways from a more traditional lifestyle. A year or so later, Gillen again wrote of his desire to photograph Polly in a complex passage that reveals jocular, as well as more respectful, attitudes:

> Old Polly Solomon with a bunged eye and lip is at the present a sight never to be forgotten, I tried to persuade the Old fowl to let me photograph her

> this morning (I wish you could have seen her) for your benefit but before I could get the instrument she was scooting away for the hills, swearing like a tom cat in a fit. I have printed a set of the [ceremonial] pictures for Sambo and have had a neat shallow tin case made to hold them and they are to be taken and deposited with the Churinga in the ertnatulinga shortly. Sam was delighted and so was your Okilya, the King.[39]

Here photography could both produce humorous portraits to entertain Gillen's Melbourne-based friend and participate in ceremonial ritual by being absorbed into traditional Arrernte social practices.

Polly was one of numerous Arrernte men and women who adjusted to colonisation by working in the pastoral industry or as domestics at the Telegraph Station. Her husband Solomon was a senior Arrernte man who shared his cultural knowledge with the ethnographers. Polly's concern to maintain her dignity and fend off Gillen's advances expresses her astute grasp of the new medium and its possibilities. Gillen did photograph Polly on several occasions, and these portraits show her as part of the family, in the role of nanny or household worker, dressed in the neat uniform of the times; these betray no interest in her traditional identity or culture (Figure 13).

Another charming portrait held by Museum Victoria shows Polly with a chubby baby asleep in a *pitchi* (wooden cradle) on her lap, and Dolly Aritcheuka, both laughing up at the photographer. This portrait captures the warmth of this moment, as photographer and women share their delight in the precious sleeping child. Here the women are relaxed, dressed comfortably and seated on the ground, their own rich social world to the fore. For others, to whom Gillen was not so well known, there were initial misunderstandings: at Tennant Creek in September 1901, one 'morose old man' suggested that their objective was 'to extract the heart and liver of the blackfellows. His opinion had some weight with a few of the old men and there was much discussion about it'; Gillen arrived in the middle of the debate and there was an awkward pause:

> For an instant I didn't know what to do, the old men were watching me intently and on the spur of the moment I roared with laughter in which they presently joined. To laugh was, as it turned out, the very best thing I could have done, for in five minutes the air of frightened seriousness had left their faces...This, however, is the first occasion upon which I have

> met with the same curious superstition among the central Australian Aborigines and it is not without interest...[40]

Gillen sometimes showed the Arrernte the results of his work — for example, through outdoor lantern-slide lectures at the Alice Springs Telegraph Station. Curator Jason Gibson points out that the Arrernte clearly knew what was contained within *The native tribes of Central Australia*, and told later anthropologists so: in 1929 Hungarian Géza Roheim's request for Dreaming stories was rejected because 'they could all be found' in Spencer and Gillen's book. This suggests that the publication was circulated among the Arrernte.[41] Like other photographs produced by explorers, scientists and tourists in the 'outback', those made by Spencer and Gillen remain a major archive of Indigenous heritage, transcending the immediate circumstances of their making to speak to us directly of their time.

ACKNOWLEDGMENTS

For assistance with copyright and cultural/moral permissions I am grateful to Gary Mura Lee, Sylvia Kleinert, John Dallwitz of the A̲ra Irititja Project, and the Mindibungu Aboriginal Corporation. I also thank Jason Gibson for advice and for sharing his research with me.

NOTES

1. E Masson, *An untamed territory*, Macmillan and Co. Ltd, London, 1915, p. 1.
2. A Searcy, *In Australian tropics*, George Robertson & Co., London, Melbourne, Sydney, Adelaide and Brisbane, 1909, p. 27.
3. The 'Top End', including Darwin and Arnhem Land, is tropical, with wet (November to April) and dry (May to October) seasons and average yearly temperatures ranging from a minimum of 19°C to a maximum of 33°C. Further south lies the semi-arid desert of Central Australia, which ranges in average temperature from 4°C to 36°C; Australian Bureau of Meteorology, Commonwealth of Australia, viewed 18 November 2012, <www.bom.gov.au>.
4. Between 1824 and 1864 four unsuccessful attempts were made to settle coastal areas of the Northern Territory prior to the establishment of Darwin. Finally, in February 1869, George Goyder, the Surveyor-General of South Australia, established a small settlement of 135 men and women at Port Darwin.
5. The historical inclusion of the Territory within different administrative jurisdictions until 1911, when it was transferred to Commonwealth control, caused its story of encounter to overlap considerably with that of neighbouring territories, especially South Australia. For an overview of this history see R D Haynes, *Seeking the Centre: the Australian desert in literature, film and art*, Cambridge University Press, Cambridge, 1999; Philip Jones has discussed the work of photographers in Central Australia in *Images of the interior: seven Central Australian photographers*, Wakefield Press and South Australian Museum, Adelaide, 2011; see also J Robinson assisted by M Zagala (eds), *A century in focus: South Australian*

photography 1840s–1940s, Art Gallery of South Australia, Adelaide, 2007, particularly Philip Jones, 'Ethnographic photography in South Australia', pp. 102–07. Work regarding specific photographers is cited below where appropriate, but see also H Ennis, *Intersections: photography, history and the National Library of Australia*, National Library of Australia, Canberra, 2004; A Sierp, 'Sweet, Samuel White (1825–1886)', *Australian dictionary of biography*, National Centre of Biography, Australian National University, viewed 11 September 2012, <http://adb.anu.edu.au/biography/sweet-samuel-white-4678/text7739>; D Kaus, *A different time: the expedition photographs of Herbert Basedow 1903–1928*, National Museum of Australia Press, Canberra, 2008.

6. For an excellent overview of this history see R Ganter, *Mixed relations: Asian–Aboriginal contact in North Australia*, University of Western Australia Press, Perth, 2006.

7. ibid.

8. BC Ryder, 'A night in Broome', *Sydney Morning Herald*, 14 May 1927, p. 9, viewed 12 November 2013, <http://nla.gov.au/nla.news-article16379136>.

9. The Darwinist Thomas Henry Huxley mounted a project to photograph all races within the British Empire, and sent out a circular to colonial officials requesting images of naked subjects recorded in standard format from several angles. He met with great resistance, yet three series were sent from Australia according to Huxley's specifications. For discussion see P Prodger, *Darwin's camera: art and photography in the theory of evolution*, Oxford University Press, Melbourne, 2009, pp. 68–75; Elizabeth Edwards, *Raw histories: photographs, anthropology and museums*, Berg Publishers, UK, 2001.

10. He photographed more than 260 Aboriginal individuals over a period of fifteen years, from 1877 to 1891. During the 1870s and 1880s his photographs also served to promote the Northern Territory, bringing its mines and other industries to public attention; *The policeman's eye: Foelsche's frontier photography*, South Australian Museum, online exhibition, viewed 9 September 2012, <www.samuseum.sa.gov.au/whatson/exhibitions/policemanseye>.

11. The quotation is from a letter of 14 July 1875 and addendum of fifteenth, John Lewis papers, State Records of South Australia PRG 247, in G Reid, *A picnic with the natives: Aboriginal–European relations in the Northern Territory to 1910*, Melbourne University Press, Melbourne, 1990, p. 67; see also T Roberts, *Frontier justice: a history of the gulf country to 1900*, University of Queensland Press, Brisbane, 2005.

12. RJ Noye, 'Foelsche, Paul Heinrich Matthias (1831–1914)', *Australian dictionary of biography*, National Centre of Biography, Australian National University, viewed 4 September 2012, <http://adb.anu.edu.au/biography/foelsche-paul-heinrich-matthias-3543/text5467>.

13. Carol Cooper and Alana Harris discuss these issues with respect to Foelsche and other photographers working in this mode: 'Dignity of degradation: Aboriginal portraits from nineteenth century Australia', *Portraits of Oceania*, Art Gallery of New South Wales, Sydney, 1997, pp. 15–21.

14. *The policeman's eye: Foelsche's frontier photography*, South Australian Museum, online exhibition, viewed 18 November 2013, <http://archive.is/GoD3>.

15. ibid.

16. G Lee & S Kleinert, *Billiamook: a Larrakia legend*, Charles Darwin University, Casuarina, NT, 2004; G Lee, 'The Larrakia legacy of Billiamook', *Artlink*, 25(2), 2005, viewed 9 September 2012, <www.artlink.com.au/articles/2024/the-larrakia-legacy-of-billiamook/>; 'Interview with Gary Lee', *Peril: Asian-Australian Arts and Culture*, 5 January 2011, viewed 9 September 2012, <www.peril.com.au/2010-2011/edition10/interview-with-gary-lee-2/>.

17. First shown in the inaugural *Togart NT contemporary art* exhibition, Darwin 2006. This work extends Lee's earlier *Nice coloured boys* series, celebrating male beauty and documenting Aboriginal gay and transgender communities. From 2004, however, he began a discrete, ongoing series called *Nymgololo* — a Larrakia word for young man/bachelor — which focused on Aboriginal men in Darwin.

18. M Bell, *Geography and imperialism, 1820–1940*, Manchester University Press, Manchester, 1995,

p. 57. See also discussion in G Newton, *Shades of light: online* (based on text from the original book *Shades of light: photography and Australia 1839–1988*, Australian National Gallery, Canberra, 1988), viewed 12 November 2013, <www.photo-web.com.au/ShadesofLight/default.htm>, and Robert Holden in his commentary on exploration photography, *Photography in colonial Australia*, Hordern House, Sydney, 1988.

19. P Carter, 'Invisible journeys: exploration and photography' in P Foss (ed.), *Island in the stream, a critical history of Australian criticism*, Pluto Press, Sydney, 1988, pp. 47–60.

20. ibid. Of course, the supplies of water needed to develop photographs during much of this period would also have been an insurmountable practical challenge for many expeditions into arid regions.

21. Jones, *Images of the interior*, above n 5, p. 1.

22. The expedition left from Nilpinna Spring, near Cootanoorina in northern South Australia, and explored areas of the Everard Ranges, Birksgate Ranges, Fraser Ranges and Hampton Plains regions in Western Australia; *The Elder Scientific Exploration Expedition, 1891–1892*, photographs [picture]/Frederick Elliott, 107 albumen silver photographs, in National Library of Australia album containing thirty-six albumen plates with printed captions, showing Aboriginal people encountered.

23. RJ Noye, 'Dictionary of South Australian photography, 1845–1915', Art Gallery of South Australia, CD attached to Robinson assisted by Zagala (eds), above n 5, pp. 294–5. T Gara, 'Survey of nineteenth century photographs of Aboriginal people in South Australia, November 2010', report prepared for the Aboriginal Visual Histories Project, Monash University, 2010; J Robinson, 'James Taylor 1846–1917' in Robinson assisted by Zagala (eds), above n 5, pp. 126–7. Robinson notes that Taylor took a series of staged portraits of Mounted Constable Willshire and his Aboriginal officers in 1888 during his prosecution for murder, which may have sparked his interest.

24. 'Photographing Mr Maurice's Aborigines', *The Register*, 5 December 1901, p. 6. They were photographed by J Gazard; *Australian Town and Country Journal*, 28 December 1901, p. 24.

25. *Register News-Pictorial*, Adelaide, 10 April 1929, p. 6.

26. In 1922 this was the site of the Purrkuji Massacre. P Smith, 'Into the Kimberley: the invasion of the Sturt Creek Basin (Kimberley Region, Western Australia) and evidence of Aboriginal resistance', *Aboriginal History* 24:62–74, 2000.

27. A reviewer of their 1904 *The northern tribes of Central Australia* concluded that 'The popular impression that the Australian native is the lowest in the scale of civilisation...will be deepened by this volume'; *Argus*, Melbourne, cited in J Mulvaney, H Morphy & A Petch (eds), *'My dear Spencer': the letters of F.J. Gillen to Baldwin Spencer*, Hyland House, Melbourne, 1997, p. 9. See also WB Spencer & FJ Gillen, *The Arunta*, two volumes, Macmillan, London, 1927, p. vii; for a nuanced discussion of the place of Spencer and Gillen's work in this context, see H Kuklick, '"Humanity in the chrysalis stage": Indigenous Australians in the anthropological imagination, 1899–1926', *British Journal for the History of Science*, 39(4):535–68, 2006.

28. As John Mulvaney concludes, 'He drew upon the assumptions and models of biological evolution and applied them to Aboriginal institutions, beliefs and technology in a mechanistic manner. Although a kindly humanitarian in practice, in theory he saw Aborigines simply as dehumanised "survivals" from an early stage of social development'; DJ Mulvaney, 'Spencer, Sir Walter Baldwin (1860–1929)', *Australian dictionary of biography*, National Centre of Biography, Australian National University, viewed 6 September 2012, <http://adb.anu.edu.au/biography/spencer-sir-walter-baldwin-8606/text15031>. See also H Morphy, 'More than mere facts: repositioning Spencer and Gillen in the history of anthropology' in SR Morton & DJ Mulvaney (eds), *Exploring Central Australia: society, environment and the 1894 expedition*, Surrey Beatty, Chipping Norton, NSW, 1996; N Peterson, 'Visual knowledge: Spencer and Gillen's use of photography in *The native tribes of Central Australia*', *Australian Aboriginal Studies*, 2006/1:12–22.

29. W Baldwin Spencer, 'The Aboriginals of Australia' in GH Knibbs (ed.), *Federal handbook on Australia*, British Association for the Advancement of Science, Australian Meeting, Mullett, Government Printer, Melbourne, 1914, pp. 33–85.

30. 22 August 1899 in Mulvaney, Morphy & Petch (eds), above n 28, p. 158.
31. H Morphy, 'Gillen: man of science' in Mulvaney, Morphy & Petch (eds), above n 28, pp. 44–5. A substantial literature considers the contribution of Spencer and Gillen: see especially Mulvaney, Morphy & Petch (eds), above n 28; P Batty, L Allen & J Morton, *The photographs of Baldwin Spencer*, Miegunyah Press, Melbourne, 2007.
32. In 1875 Gillen was posted to Alice Springs to work as a telegraph operator on the new Overland Telegraph Line from Adelaide to Port Darwin, which was a focus of often violent encounter and exchange between black and white. In 1891, as Justice of the Peace, Gillen arrested mounted police trooper WH Willshire for shooting two Aboriginal men, a 'case most serious and revolting', an act that earned the trust of the Arrernte (as he phrased it in a telegram to the Attorney-General Robert Homburg after an initial inquiry); A Nettelbeck & R Foster, *In the name of the law: William Willshire and the policing of the Australian frontier*, Wakefield Press, Adelaide, 2007, p. 105.
33. Jones, *Images of the interior*, above n 5, p. 7.
34. 1 May 1901, Alice Springs; *Gillen's diary: the camp jottings of F.J. Gillen on the Spencer and Gillen expedition across Australia, 1901–1902*, Libraries Board of South Australia, Adelaide, 1968, p. 332.
35. For example, 8 September 1894, Letter 1 in Mulvaney, Morphy & Petch (eds), above n 28, p. 52.
36. 30 July 1897, Letter 30, in Mulvaney, Morphy & Petch (eds), above n 28, p. 178.
37. ibid.
38. 20 Dec 1895, Letter 16, in Mulvaney, Morphy & Petch (eds), above n 28, 1997, pp. 89–90. Gillen commented, 'Since then I have thought it wise to treat her with the utmost civility'.
39. 23 March 1897, Letter 27, in Mulvaney, Morphy & Petch (eds), above n 28, p. 157.
40. 13 September 1901, Tennant Creek, in Mulvaney, Morphy & Petch (eds), above n 28, pp. 347–8.
41. J Gibson, 'Addressing the Arrernte: F.J. Gillen's 1896 Engwura speech', paper presented at *Conflict and conciliation across empires: objects and performances in historical perspective*, The University of Melbourne, 18 November 2011.

Chapter 11

'THE MYALLS' ULTIMATUM': PHOTOGRAPHY AND YOLŊU IN EASTERN ARNHEM LAND, 1917

Laurie Baymarrwangga, Bentley James and Jane Lydon

In this chapter we explore the uses made of photography by the Yolŋu people of Arnhem Land.[1] We trace the continuities of Yolŋu assertions of law and identity from the early twentieth century to the present, and from visual images to oral histories. As a ninety-six-year-old elder, Baymarrwangga's perspective provides a powerful living link with Ryko's 1917 photograph of men and women from the Crocodile Islands. For Baymarrwangga, this photograph evokes an early story from a longer war of colonialism that continues to threaten her and her people. Ryko's photograph was and remains a means to tell the Yolŋu side of things nearly a century on.

RYKO

Edward Reichenbach, 'the overland cyclist', arrived in Darwin on Thursday 11 June 1914 after an epic journey from Adelaide of 1969 miles in twenty-eight days and seven minutes (Figure 1).[2] A year later, the 'Outdoor Photographer' spruiked his 'splendid selection of photographic postcards of Northern Territory native life and tropical scenery' on sale at his studio 'next to the Darwin Cafe in Cavenagh-street for fourpence each'; he claimed that '"Ryko", the overland cyclist, knows the Territory from south to north, and his pictures are true to life and represent the Territory as it is'.[3]

By December 1915 he had sold his business, but continued to travel around the Territory and contribute a column to the *Northern Territory Times and Gazette*.[4]

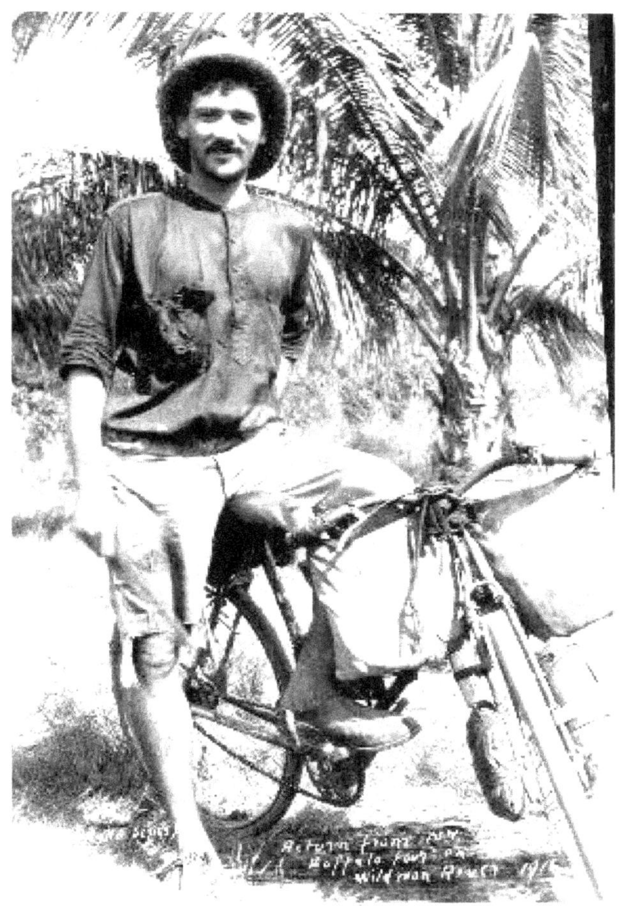

FIGURE 1: Edward Reichenbach. *Cyclist/Ted Ryko*. Karilyn Brown Collection, Northern Territory Library, Darwin, photo no. PH0413/0070.

In 1916, for example, Ryko worked with Melville Islanders to photograph their re-enactment of a clash between British troops and the Tiwi at Fort Dundas between 1824 and 1829 — colonial engagement is an important theme which they commemorated, eighty-seven years later, in the form of a performance.[5]

In November 1916 the murder of two Filipino trepangers and tortoiseshell hunters in the Crocodile Islands group, off the mouth of the Goyder River, was reported by surviving crew (Figure 2).[6]

The following February Ryko visited the scene of the crime on Rabuma (now Rapuma) Island with the Aboriginal Protector, the Reverend James Watson.

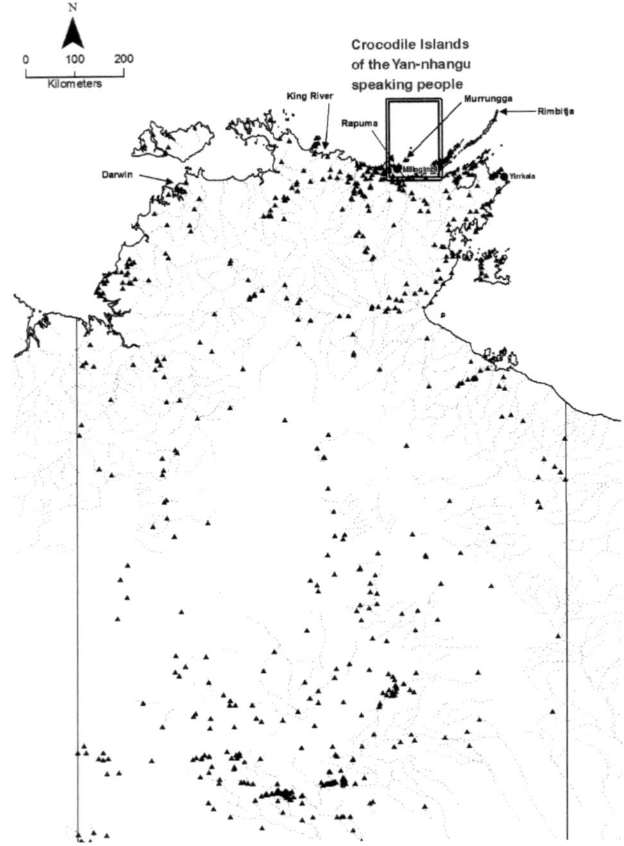

FIGURE 2: Map of Crocodile Islands. Six Seasons Pty Ltd, courtesy of Bentley James.

He wrote about it in his regular newspaper column, giving his account the title 'Crocodile massacre'. He described the place 'exactly as the plunderers had left it that dark tragic September night', and told how '[t]he witnesses who were requisitioned for this trip voluntarily dramatised the whole affair over in detail for us, on the exact ground of the onslaught, among the broken spears and bits of womeras that were still scattered about the sandy beach'.[7]

He attempted to present a direct, little-mediated Indigenous version of events, explaining how the two deceased trepangers, Damian and Francis, had left Darwin in a lugger and sailed to King River, where they picked up 'the usual crew of natives' and proceeded eastward to Limba-jibba Island. This was probably Rimbitja, the Western beach on Martjinba, farthest of the Wessel Islands, in the country of the Nhangu-speaking people, west of the English Co. Islands. They began trepanging operations, but the Malays' 'bouncing style' — that is, threatening workers at gun point — did 'not appeal to the local lads, and after a few days they were obliged to up mud-hook and clear for their lives'.[8] Repulsed by the closely related Nhangu people, their armed coercion would make them no more welcome among the Yan-nhangu, so they took a local interpreter with them and came back as far as Rapuma, in the Crocodile Islands. Here a party of Yan-nhangu-speaking people were employed on the land of the Gurryindi clan, traditional owners of Rapuma, through the linguist. Ryko went on:

> [T]he necessary smoke houses and boilers, etc., were erected. The Malays and their crew slept on the lugger and during the day while the linguist would be translating their orders they simply did nothing but stand over the myalls [so-called 'wild' Aboriginal people] with loaded guns, which they flourished and brandished continually and frequently threatened to shoot them. This slave-driving caper put a nasty taste in the niggers' mouths and they became absolutely scared and were in terror of their lives. Although very few of these niggers had seen weapons before, yet they had heard all about the devastating powers of a rifle in the hands of previous uncompromising visitors. The chiefs and old men held a council. After duly considering their blue outlook, this ultimatum was carried unanimously which was carefully translated and verified by witnesses and murderers and friends to the writer personally, at a subsequent interview.[9]

Ryko presented 'this ultimatum' in the following form:

The Myalls' Ultimatum.

> 'In the interests of our innocence and the indignity that is being showered on us, and the risk we are running of being annihilated any minute.
>
> We will get in first and rid our ancestral shores of such provocating poltroons and take what they have got as indemnity, for why should we run away from this our native land which we inherited from our fore-fathers.
>
> We can't talk or understand English.
>
> Why can't strangers coming to our shores give us a square deal?

> We have enough sense to discriminate between fair play and foul play!
>
> Where can we lodge complaints against such unscrupulous invaders and abolitionists of our race?
>
> Where can we get protection or redress for such conduct towards us?
>
> No response.
>
> So let us go and punish by death according to our own law.[10]

Ryko then described this punishment, as told to him:

> Less than a week after arrival the attack was duly planned and spears buried close handy. It was just dark. During a lull in the trepang boiling operations the two Malays sat down with a pipe for a smoke. At a given signal all fires were 'killed' and two boys sneaked up behind and whisked the rifles from their hands. Over a dozen others grabbed spears. The Malays made a dash for their dinghy; but sank dead into the water literally pincushioned with spears.
>
> The crew and linguist were in danger of being kidnapped, so they abandoned the lugger and swam a considerable distance under water, and finally took refuge in some half submerged mangrove trees. From there they watched the plunderers ransack the camp, empty out trepang to get the sacks, and strip the wire off tubs (no doubt for future spear heads). The Lugger was then looted and away they paddled, triumphantly, with the dinghy and their own fleet of canoes loaded to the plimsoll mark with the pillage.
>
> The terrorised crew meanwhile scarcely dared to breathe, and were almost pumped bloodless by the swarms of mosquitoes and sandflies. They continued this vigilance in an adjacent dry jungle all next day, which was spent in almost crying their eyes out. Under cover of the first shades of night they swam out to the lugger, and sailed away for the nearest home of rescue, and after four days of subsistence on water alone they arrived at the Goulburn Island Mission Station. Here they were subsequently fitted up and equipped with a crew to the port in Darwin as aforementioned.
>
> These sort of murders are of late usually put down to interference with lubras. But in this case all witnesses and murderers and sympathisers

> declare that there were no arguments over 'gin trucking' or funny business with the sable maidens whatsoever.[11]

Ryko concluded with a promise that '"The murderers' den," or the "Myalls interviewed"' would be published in 'our next'.[12] But on 8 February the *Northern Territory Times and Gazette* reported:

> further publication of the interesting notes by 'Ryko'...has been temporarily postponed pending settlement of a point which has been raised as to inadvisability, in the interests of justice, of publishing certain allegations and comment associated with the recent murderous outrage by coastal natives which resulted in the violent deaths of two Malay trepang fishers.[13]

It seems likely that this embargo was imposed by Reverend Watson, as we explore further.

Six weeks later, around 29 March 1917, Ryko made 'a sudden exit' from Darwin by steamer to pursue copyright infringements of his work. Dramatically, 'he narrowly missed the steamer, which was just hauling off as he jumped aboard. His baggage was thrown after him by some friends, the while "Ryko" characteristically took a farewell snapshot of the crowd on the jetty.'[14] Ryko did not comment further on the event, but among the photographs he sold as postcards and souvenirs survives the remarkable image of the re-enactment of the murder (Figure 3).

AFTERMATH

'Big Billy' (Naindulka) and 'Yamoureece' (Yomurritj or Walavera) were sentenced to death for murder, but in November 1917 their sentences were commuted to life imprisonment at Fanny Bay Gaol in Darwin, 'on the grounds that they were Myall blacks and there was probably provocation over the matter of a Myall Lubra'.[15] Although Ryko denied that women were involved, this plea seems to have been a strategy of humanitarians such as Reverend Watson, considered to be more persuasive under British law at this time on the grounds of arguments for relativist treatment.

In July 1920 the Reverend James Watson of the Overseas Methodist Mission took the matter up, arguing that the 'blacks from Bowen Straits to Elcho Island are unanimous in declaring that these two men are innocent, and further, that Naindulka and Walavera were at Oenpelli at the time of the murder'.[16] In 1916

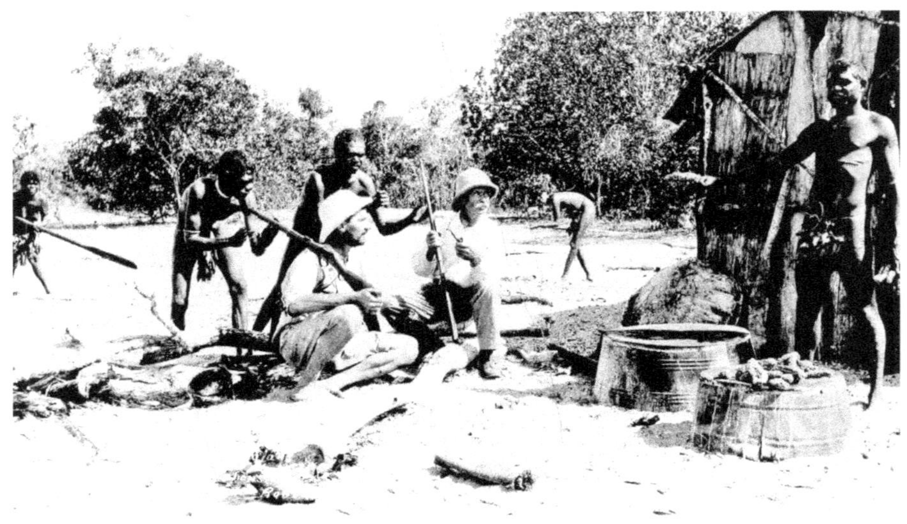

FIGURE 3: Edward Reichenbach. *Massacre series number 3 – how the murdered Malays lost their weapons.* National Archives of Australia, Canberra, M105, 42.

Watson had been sent by the Board of Missions to report upon the prospects of a mission to the Northern Territory, and following a five-month inspection it was decided to establish a mission to the Aborigines, with a base on islands 'adjacent to the coasts of Port Darwin'.[17] By late 1916 he had established a mission on Goulburn Island (Figure 4).[18] Watson's attempt to free the prisoners was unsuccessful, the authorities referring to their conviction 'on the clearest evidence'.[19]

Even at this early stage Watson omitted all mention of Ryko or his photograph, referring only to 'reconstruction' of 'their evidence' while 'on the spot'. Watson stated:

> I personally interviewed some of the murderers at Boucat Bay, a list of whose names I supplied to the authorities in Darwin, and neither of these names appear on that list. A second visit, two months later confirmed me in regard to these names. I may say that I examined the witnesses shortly after the murder, at Rabuma, on the spot where the tragedy was enacted, that the blacks might have the assistance of the surroundings in order to reconstruct their evidence.[20]

Watson's own view was very different from that of the Yolŋu (as relayed by Ryko), who specifically denied that their women had been ill-treated; rather, they objected to 'outsiders' invading their 'ancestral shores', and asserted their right to defend them, asking 'why should we run away from this our native land which we inherited from our fore-fathers?'[21] In this translation we can discern a fundamental element of the Yolŋu worldview, with its moral imperative to protect their ancestral inheritance, including its territory, people, religious property, language and all its ritual expressions. Typical of colonial officials, Watson was prepared to condone violence in defence of Aboriginal women, but not in defence of sovereignty.

REVEREND WATSON'S RECOLLECTIONS: THE 'OTHER SIDE'

Watson's own account differed fundamentally from that of Ryko and the Yolŋu: the photograph shows us beyond doubt that Ryko was present and he and his camera played a crucial role in 'reconstructing the evidence', as Watson put it.[22] Watson's memories infantilised the Indigenous people, and transformed their grievance from defence of autonomy and territory to the primal desire for men to control their women. Indeed, Watson's deeply gendered account shows how he saw himself as a muscular Christian who dared hardship and danger to take his message to the people.

Watson's own views about masculinity and race fundamentally reshaped this story when he told it again, in 1919 and 1927, emphasising his own manly behaviour, playing down the views and actions of the Indigenous people, and omitting Ryko's presence altogether. Watson had worked in New Guinea before the Territory, and was accustomed to giving lantern-slide lectures that emphasised the dangers of mission work and the primitivism of Indigenous peoples — such as in 1917 'Among the cannibals of New Guinea', which 'shed most illuminative side-lights on the arduous life of the missionary'.[23]

In February 1919 Watson was interviewed in Sydney by a reporter who described him as 'lean and tanned, with no spare flesh, but enough of it for hard work purposes', having spent several years in the wilds of the Northern Territory. He was asked, '[A]ny tight place adventures?', and responded with the story of the visit to Rapuma in February 1917. His account compared his role to the military heroism of soldiers braving enemy attack, and he termed the Aboriginal people the 'other side':

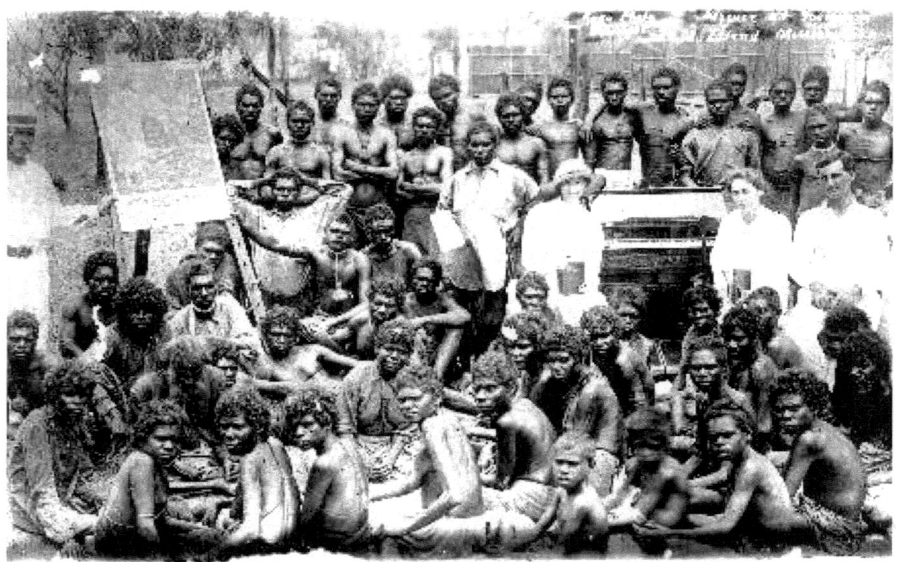

FIGURE 4: Edward Reichenbach. *A church service at Goulburn Island Mission Station.* 191? Karilyn Brown Collection, Northern Territory Library, Darwin, PH0413/0045.

> Yes, I think I may say that I have experienced something of the feelings of our splendid men when they went "over the top" on more than one occasion,' said the Protector, 'This was one event: Two Malay trepang fishermen had been murdered by the blacks, and I was instructed to report on the matter. It was near the mouth of the Goyder River that I expected to find them, and as my lugger neared the land blacks came pouring out from all sides over the sand hills and on to the beach, all of them armed with spears. Things did not look very promising for me, as my own blacks on the lugger were beside themselves with fear, and after they had besought me not to go ashore I had to forcibly prevent them from heading the vessel out to sea again. I knew that to turn back would be misunderstood by — let us not say the enemy, but the "other side" — and as I could not get my men to bring our little ship any closer I jumped overboard into a perfect inferno of pain among a description of poisonous jellyfish, and having swum and waded ashore walked up into the middle of the "other side", unarmed.[24]

The reporter concluded his account by noting that 'The blacks supplied Mr Watson, at his request, with an illustration of how the murder was carried out'. Several features of Watson's account strike the reader, particularly by contrast with Ryko's version (comprising his image and newspaper story). Watson makes no mention of Ryko, speaking as if he was the only white man present; he states only that the Aboriginal people had 'supplied' him, at his request, with 'an illustration' of the event, without explaining what form this had taken. Unlike Ryko's sympathetic (if sensationalising) stance, Watson also speaks as if the Yolŋu — whom he categorises in profoundly oppositional terms as the 'other side' — were, inevitably, structurally opposed to himself, and within this category he distinguishes between the 'myalls' (wild people) and 'his blacks' whom he infantilises as 'beside themselves with fear'. In 1927, a year after he had left the north and a decade after the event, Watson's version had become even more lurid: titled 'A missionary's ordeal', *The Register* (Adelaide) reported:

> To be the only white man among 300 hostile blacks was the unenviable position of the Rev. James Watson, the missioner of Arnhem Land. Murderers those people proved beyond all doubt, but whether the slaying of two others was justified according to their own standards was the problem with which the missionary was met. He was far away from any white habitation on a hostile shore in Boucaut Bay [Castlereagh Bay] with a few natives in a boat lying out on the waters as his nearest friends.[25]

By this time, a decade after the event, Watson's version, transformed by his unreliable memory into self-promotion, is almost unrecognisable as the event recounted by Ryko, and depicted by his photograph. Watson's views about Aboriginal people and their treatment become clearer if considered in light of his career overall. He spoke out strongly on their behalf, but in terms that were shaped by tightly defined limits on Indigenous behaviour and capacity; Aboriginal people were child-like and primitive, yet the victims of brutal settlers. Indigenous male ill-treatment of women was a recurrent theme, invoked to defend his own violent treatment of the offenders. He constructs himself as the daring, intrepid man of action, archetypal muscular Christian, omitting all mention of Ryko and distorting events. Watson's own code of masculinity prioritised protecting women, and justified his own brutality toward Aboriginal men, an attitude that formed part of a larger worldview. His white man's view of events contrasts with the Aboriginal view, evoked by the photo.

THE YOLŊU VERSION

The Yan-nhangu version of this history is now available to us through Laurie Baymarrwangga's account. Baymarrwangga is one of the last living Yan-nhangu speakers and descendent of the people of the Crocodile Islands (Figure 5). Born on Murrungga Island around 1919, she belongs to the Dhuwa Yan-nhangu group Malarra/Gunbirrtji (the mothers' mothers of the Gurryindi and Gamala\ga).[26]

Yan-nhangu is the language given to the people of the Crocodile Islands in the ancestral past. Yan-nhangu speakers are divided into six ba:purru or clan groups associated with distinct but continuous estates and distinct patrilectal varieties given to them by the ancestors. When the Dhuwa and Yirritja creation/ancestor/spirits brought into being the places and phenomena of the world, they named and bequeathed the distinctive language of this part of the world to the forefathers of today's Yan-nhangu people. Dhuwa and Yirritja are two halves, or semi-moieties, of an ideational system that divides the world into two categories, fundamentally classifying every aspect of the Yolŋu universe. Everything is either one or the other, so that every aspect of the physical and noumenal world, person or animal, is either Dhuwa or Yirritja, and is essentially/spiritually associated with a particular Dhuwa or a Yirritja clan group.

Yan-nhangu call themselves, and are referred to by other Yolŋu people as, people of the sea, people of the Crocodile Islands. In 1993 there were only 300 Yan-nhangu words recorded. Since then Baymarrwangga and the Yan-nhangu have worked with anthropologist/linguist Bentley James to record some 3000 words and the encyclopaedic knowledge of their environments held within.[27]

The two words *Yan* (lit: tongue), meaning 'language', and *nhangu* (proximal demonstrative), meaning 'this', together form the language of the Crocodile Islands.[28] For the Yan-nhangu-speaking people of the Crocodile Islands, the sea forms a backdrop for everyday activity, a space for action rich with the bounty of the seasons. The patterns of seasonal change formed a mental map governing the yearly round of inter-island travels. Yearly people followed the ripening fruits, return of fish, the mating of turtles and sea birds moving their camps in harmony with the seasons — the times and tides of the Crocodile Islands. The comings and goings of the seasonal winds also marked the yearly arrival of international travellers, the Macassans, who came each year to bring resources to the islands.[29]

The Yan-nhangu are responsible for the country, the people and the spiritual wellbeing of all aspects of their inheritance.

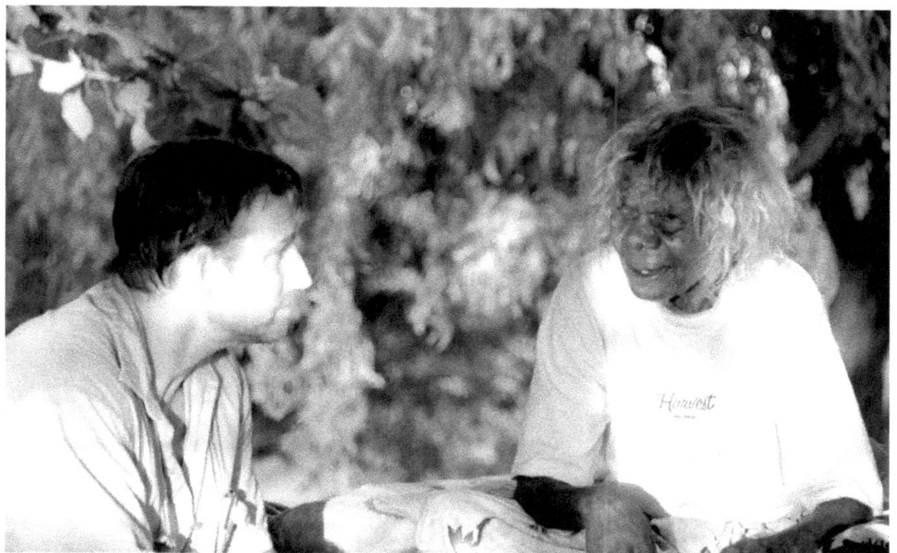

FIGURE 5: Chiara Bussini. Laurie Baymarrwangga talking to Bentley James. *Yan-nhangu atlas and illustrated dictionary of the Crocodile Islands*, Darwin, 2010.

In 1992 Ros Poignant made the intriguing suggestion that 'The Myalls' ultimatum' could be considered a petition, in the tradition of the 1963 Yirrkala bark petitions — the first traditional documents prepared by Indigenous Australians that were recognised by the Australian Parliament. But as Ravi de Costa notes, 'petitions not only recognise and appeal to authority; they are implicit descriptions of the moral worlds in which particular claims are sensible and legitimate. Thus petitions act to articulate the identity and status of the petitioner and that of authority in a shared moral order.'[30] 'The Myalls' Ultimatum' was not an 'appeal to authority' as much as an assertion of sovereignty, and there are few signs of a shared moral order. Perhaps Ian McIntosh's suggestion is more apt: that the Yolŋu vision of intercultural diplomacy is based on the notion of 'treaties' like those originally created with Macassans, which were based on reciprocity, not dissimilar to the way clans relate to one another within Yolŋu society.[31]

Nor have misconceptions of Yolŋu culture permitted much insight from the settler state. The Australian Government, for example, annexed the mission site at Milingimbi, largest of the inner Crocodile Islands, to the church in 1921 without acknowledgment or mention of the Yan-nhangu landowners.[32] This is an early example of a history of overlooking the rights of the traditional owners, right up to the present.[33] From the late 1880s until 1908 a number of pastoral ventures were attempted on the mainland adjacent to the islands, at the cost of many Yolŋu lives. In 1931 the Arnhem Land reserve was gazetted. The state maintained control over the reserve by continuing to provide leases and licences for mining exploration, pastoralism, trepang fishing, pearl shell collecting and crocodile hunting inside the reserve.[34] Coincident with the international human rights era, the *Aboriginal Land Rights (Northern Territory) Act 1976* (Cth) remains the apex of state recognition of Indigenous rights, rights that have been steadily eroded with barely a twinge of conscience by the settler society.

Yan-nhangu people made application for sea closures under the 1976 *Aboriginal Land Act* to protect their sea country and resources. However, these closures gave little protection from commercial fishermen.[35] The Yan-nhangu, like other coastal Indigenous groups in Australia, are the descendants of those Argonauts who made the first intercontinental journey to the great southern continent some 50,000 years bp (before the present). According to their laws they have husbanded the land, seas and knowledge of their ancestors, passing down the paintings and designs that specify the difference and connections among the people and places.

For the Yan-nhangu, their language and culture is associated with a complex of land, sea, totems, songs, ceremonies and sacred sites in the Crocodile islands. This is the sea country where they have lived from the beginning, and where Baymarrwangga has lived for ninety-six years.[36]

In Baymarrwangga's discussion of the specific events at Rapuma, she goes to great lengths to describe the authority of those who have rights to speak, those who own or manage the rights to tell, and to hear, aspects of this story. This strict and continuing adherence to the edicts of ancestral laws is a necessary prerequisite to the proper performance of Yan-nhangu history, and Yolŋu history more broadly.

Baymarrwangga tells that Yomoritj (Yomurritj), whom she knew, jailed for murder in 1917, was a senior estate manager for the Gurryindi holdings on Rapuma Island and the legal protector of its interests.

Yomoritj's Djinang-speaking Batjimurrunggu people share estates on Milingimbi. Yomoritj and his Batjimurrunggu brothers Dju\gun, Bandika and Gundjalk, and his sister Laylayun-guburryur, called the Yan-nhangu-speaking

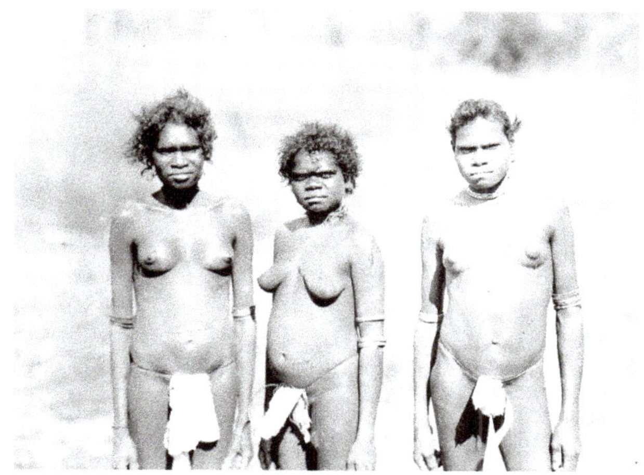

FIGURE 6: DF Thomson. (Left to right) *Sisters Gularrbanga #1, Gadayurr and Baymarrwangga #1 at Murrungga, central Arnhem Land, Northern Territory, Australia, c.1935.* Courtesy of the Thomson family and Museum Victoria, TPH1340.

Gurryindi people *Yothu/Yindi* (child and mother) and had responsibilities to protect and look after Gurryindi people, places and ceremonies. Yothu Yindi *(Nga:mu\u Manydji)* refers to ceremonial managers of the opposite moiety who have certain rights and responsibilities toward their mother's sacred inheritance. The Gurryindi people are the mother's group of the Batjimurrunggu, looking after their rituals, estates and the proper enactment of the ancestral law of their child group long before the coming of the mission.

The law of the islands is unequivocal; the people of the islands have a moral duty to care for their people, sea, land and environment. 'The Myalls' ultimatum' resonates consistently with the edicts of local ancestral law. Baymarrwangga, aunty to Yomoritj, explains that they were not only justified 'to punish by death', but also showed moderation in not killing the other shipmates for their failure to restrain their comrades.[37] These co-exploiters did not escape by skill and stealth but were spared despite their continued breaches of proper behaviour. The kinsmen and family members, fathers and brothers, were acting on their moral duty to protect kin and country in the face of armed provocation by strangers, and asked, in their ultimatum, 'Where can we lodge complaints against such unscrupulous invaders and abolitionists of our race? Who can we ask for protection from these invaders?'

In explaining exactly how Yomoritj and his kin's actions are consistent with ancestral laws, Baymarrwangga powerfully reaffirms her absolute conviction, and that of the law, to protect kin and country. She is talking from experience; her parents had good trading relationships with the Macassans who came each year to bring resources to the islands.[38] Australian anthropologist and photographer Donald Thomson, who photographed Baymarrwangga in 1937 at Murrungga, described the intricate and robust systems of local and regional trade and relations linking groups for thousands of miles — part of a historic global network that preceded the coming of the settlers.[39] Through their relations with Macassans, Yolŋu were accustomed to deal with outsiders, and to assert their sovereignty over their land in accordance with ancestral law.

CONCLUSION

Living history consists of a dialogue between past and present. Baymarrwangga's report is remarkable not only because she is a living part of this history, but because her view of this history was very nearly lost from the record forever. In the powerful settler view, there was little record of Yan-nhangu culture or history and no need for it. The imminent and terrible loss of Yan-nhangu language and history, like so many languages, was shrugged off as the price of civilisation, the price we all pay for a modern and more convenient world. This is the bare face of settler power, the desire to assimilate, normalise and appropriate the coastal and marine resources of Indigenous people and relegate their histories to oblivion.

None of this is inevitable. Since 1993 Baymarrwangga's struggle to document the Yan-nhangu language has been denied adequate resources by the state in spite of its rhetoric of reconciliation. Yan-nhangu language is the repository of the knowledge of the seas, the product of thousands of generations of intimate co-existence with the marine environment. Without resources, Baymarrwangga has started a family of projects aimed at sustaining the cultural and linguistic and biological diversity of the islands as a basis for sustainable livelihoods. These positive activities support residence on the islands' homelands: the very heart of Indigenous language transmission. This heroic struggle to retain country, in the face of continuing state suppression and misrecognition, resonates powerfully with Yomurritj's fight to save his community. This is the enduring moral imperative: to take up arms, to resist with whatever you have to protect your family and country from the fierce and brutal oppression of outsiders.

The great war of colonialism has not ended for Baymarrwangga. In 2007 the Northern Territory Emergency Intervention suspended racial discrimination provisions to compulsorily acquire her land, quarantine her pension and, among other indignities, pave the way for the repression of bilingual education in Northern Territory schools. In 2009 the Northern Territory Department of Education issued a directive that the first four hours of schooling in all bilingual schools must be in English. This highly repressive assimilationist device was not overturned until 2011, by which time the machinery of the bilingual schools was damaged and the momentum of community members further routed. New directives make it practically impossible to run a proper bilingual program without enormous outside funding support. In 2012 the federal government passed legislation that will enshrine the (so-called 'Emergency') Intervention: the *Stronger Futures in the Northern Territory policy statement*.[40] Of special concern to Baymarrwangga is that the Stronger Futures policy proposes to disband the more than 500 living homelands and move approximately 10,000 people into twenty overcrowded 'growth towns'.

We fear that the consequences of such a barbarous policy include the disintegration of local political and social institutions — of culture, language, local religion, family ties — and undermine the micro-economic opportunities of disadvantaged groups. Let us then re-examine the ultimatum put forward by the murderous Myalls in light of new evidence. Nearly a hundred years ago the Yan-nhangu landowners asked, 'Why can't strangers coming to our shores give us a square deal? We have enough sense to discriminate between fair play and foul play.' But for non-Indigenous Australians, the question is, 'Do *we*?'

NOTES

1. Yolŋu is a term increasingly used since the 1970s to describe an Aboriginal person of Arnhem Land. Many of the north-east Arnhem Land languages are called collectively Yolŋu-matha (literally 'people's tongue') and refer to a population of some 7000 people. Earlier anthropological literature referred to these people as *Murngin* WL Warner, *A black civilization: a social study of an Australian tribe*, Harper, New York, 1937, *Wulamba* RM Berndt, *Gunapipi*, Cheshire, Melbourne, 1951; RM Berndt, *Djanggawul*, Routledge and Keegan Paul, London, 1952; RM Berndt, *An adjustment movement in Arnhem Land*, Mouton, Paris, 1962 and *Miwuyt* W Shapiro, *Miwuyt marriage: the cultural anthropology of affinity in northeast Arnhem Land*, Institute for the Study of Human Issues, Philadelphia, 1981.

2. 'Arrival of overland cyclist', *Northern Territory Times and Gazette*, Darwin, 18 June 1914, p. 18.
3. 'Latest telegrams: trading with the enemy', *Northern Territory Times and Gazette*, Darwin, 17 June 1915, p. 8.
4. 'To all whom it may concern' (classified advertising), *Northern Territory Times and Gazette*, Darwin, 23 December 1915, p. 8.
5. R Poignant, 'Ryko's photographs of the "Fort Dundas riot": the story so far', *Australian Aboriginal Studies* 1996/2:24–41.
6. 'Murder by blacks', *Northern Territory Times and Gazette*, Darwin, 16 November 1916, pp. 10, 13.
7. Ryko, 'Territory jottings: primeval justice in the N.T.'s "top-knot": the crocodile massacre', *Northern Territory Times and Gazette*, Darwin, 1 February 1917, p. 17.
8. ibid.
9. ibid.
10. ibid.
11. ibid.
12. ibid.
13. 'News & Notes', *Northern Territory Times and Gazette*, Darwin, 8 February 1917, p. 10.
14. *Northern Territory Times and Gazette*, Darwin, 29 March 1917, p. 12.
15. Big Bill is a European name still used by Yan-nhangu people of the Gorryindi and Gamalangga clans as an English pseudonym for important men; National Archives of Australia, series A3 NT1921/55, 'Big Billy and Yamoureece convicted murder charge', Barcode 50647 (26 pages).
16. J Watson, formerly Protector of Aborigines, to The Administrator, 27 July 1920; National Archives of Australia, above n 15.
17. 'The Methodists. New mission station. Annual conference', *Sydney Morning Herald*, 3 March 1916, p. 8.
18. Watson also chose Milingimbi as a mission site in 1916 and building commenced in 1923; 'Aboriginal Mission, Goulburn Island Station', *Brisbane Courier*, 8 November 1916, p. 6.
19. But the Secretary Territory Melbourne telegrammed the Acting Administrator in Darwin (6 December 1920) and was told by return telegram, 24 December 1920, that Charles Williams, who had taken the arresting constable in his lugger, had testified that 'both prisoners told me they assisted with others'. Hunt wrote back to Watson (29 December 1920) informing him of this and that, according to Inspector Waters, 'the prisoners were convicted on the clearest evidence'; National Archives of Australia, above n 15.
20. J Watson, formerly Protector of Aborigines, to The Administrator, 27 July 1920; National Archives of Australia, above n 15.
21. Ryko, above n 7.
22. J Watson, formerly Protector of Aborigines, to The Administrator, 27 July 1920; National Archives of Australia, above n 15.
23. 'Darwin Methodist Church', *Northern Territory Times and Gazette*, Darwin, 27 September 1917, p. 6.
24. 'Adventure and work among the blacks', *Sydney Mail*, 19 February 1919.
25. 'A missionary's ordeal', *The Register*, Adelaide, 5 August 1927, p. 11.
26. The Yan-nhangu also comprise the Yirrijta Walamangu, Bindarrarr and Ngurruwulu groups, altogether responsible for estates on seas and islands of just under 10,000 square kilometres and including some 250 square kilometres of sacred sites in the sea. The group estate, or Yirralka (*ngaraka wa:nga, luku wa:nga*), is commonly glossed as spiritual home or bone country from which one's animating essences arise and bestow emotional attachment to land (L Hiatt, *Kinship and conflict: a study of an Aboriginal community in northern Arnhem Land*, Australian National University Press, Canberra, 1965; N Peterson, 'Totemism yesterday: sentiment and local organization among the Australian Aborigines', *Man*, New Series 7(1):12–32, 1972; H Morphy, *Journey to the crocodile's nest*, Australian Institute of Aboriginal Studies, Canberra 1984; J Rudder, 'Yolngu cosmology: an unchanging cosmos incorporating a rapidly changing world?', unpublished PhD thesis, Australian National University, Canberra 1993, p. 29).
27. The sociolinguistic title Yan-nhangu represents the Yolŋu people inheriting the estates and languages endowed by the Yan-nhangu ancestors. Yan-nhangu means literally the language of this place. The word *yan* denotes tongue or

language, and the word *nhangu* is the proximal demonstrative meaning 'this' or 'here'. So the language title Yan-nhangu literally denotes the language of 'here', the language of the Crocodile Islands, B James, 'Time and tide in the Crocodile Islands: change and continuity in Yan-nhangu marine identity', PhD thesis, Australian National University, Canberra 2009, pp. 7, 105.

28. B Schebeck, 'Dialect and social groupings in North East Arnhem Land', Australian Institute of Aboriginal Studies, MS 351, 352, 1968, p. 29; I Keen, *Sites of significance in the vicinity of the proposed Arnhem highway extension: a report to the Northern Land Council*, Australian National University, Canberra, 1978.

29. Macassan sailors from Celebes (Sulawesi) had been visiting the islands of the Yan-nhangu long before 'Krokodillen Eÿlandts' appeared on Tasman's chart (in 1644). Seeking *bêche-de-mer* or trepang, the Macassans brought with them new technologies. Arriving with the north-east monsoon in December and leaving in March when the wind turned to the south-east, relations with the Macassans were amiable, as they respected Yolŋu rights with regard to land, seas and resources within trading relations; Warner, above n 1, p. 458; DF Thomson, *Economic structure and the ceremonial exchange cycle in Arnhem Land,* Macmillan, Melbourne, *1949,* pp. 1–106, *p. 52;* FG Rose, *The Indonesians and the genesis of the Groote Eylandt society*, Museum fur Volkenkunde, Veroffentlichunger, hft. 11, 1961, pp. 524–31*;* CC McKnight, *The voyage to Marege: Macassan trepangers in northern Australia*, Melbourne University Press, Melbourne, 1976, *pp. 153–4, 158.*

30. R De Costa, 'Identity, authority, and the moral worlds of Indigenous petitions', *Comparative Studies in Society and History*, 48(3):669–98, 2006.

31. I McIntosh, 'A treaty with the Macassans, Burrumarra and the Dholtji ideal', *Asia Pacific Journal of Anthropology*, 7(2):153–72, 2006.

32. Northern Territory Archives Reference Section Box 473, ML Milingimbi collection, no. 12.

33. K Cole, *The Aborigines of Arnhem Land,* Rigby, Port Melbourne, 1979, p. 58.

34. State policy toward Indigenous people has had four overlapping phases: subjugation, segregation and protection, assimilation and, recently, self-determination. In 1911 the Commonwealth Aboriginal Ordinance Act and associated protectionist policy created reserves and missions to make sedentary the 'nomads' and 'smooth the dying pillow' (Cole, above n 33, p. 165).

35. I Keen, 'The Alligator Rivers Aborigines — retrospect and prospect' in ed. R Jones, *Northern Australia: options and implications*, Research School of Pacific Studies, Australian National University, Canberra, 1980, pp. 171–86; I Keen, 'An evaluation of the NT legislation providing for the closure of seas adjacent to Aboriginal Land', *Anthropological Forum* 5(3):421–39, 1985.

36. Significantly, this important feature of Yan-nhangu specificity continues to be overlooked by non-Indigenous researchers; M Langton, O Mazel & L Palmer, 'The "spirit" of the thing: the boundaries of Aboriginal economic relations at Australian common law', *Australian Journal of Anthropology*, 17(3):307–21, 2006.

37. Many anthropologists have noted over many years that failure to observe the laws of behaviour governing the moral order are expected to be punished by sorcery or death NM Williams, *Two laws: managing disputes in a contemporary Aboriginal community*, Australian Institute of Aboriginal Studies, Canberra, 1987, pp. 72–3; *see also* WEH Stanner, 'The Dreaming: an Australian world view' in PB Hammond (ed.), *Cultural and social anthropology: selected readings*, Macmillan, New York, *1964,* pp. 288–98*;* N Munn, 'The transformation of subjects into objects in Walbiri and Pitjantjatjara myth' in RM Berndt (ed.), *Australian Aboriginal anthropology*, Nedlands, WA, *1970,* pp. 141–63*;* N Peterson, 'Hunter-gatherer territoriality: the perspective from Australia', *American Anthropologist*, 77(1): 53–68, *1975;* I Keen, *Aboriginal economy and society: Australia at the threshold of colonisation*, Oxford University Press, South Melbourne, 2006; James, above n 27.

38. WCH Robert, *The Dutch explorations, 1605–1756, of the north and northwest coast of Australia*, Extracts from Journals, Log-books and other Documents Relating to these Voyages, Philo Press cv, Amsterdam, 1973, p. 175; Warner, above n 1, p. 458; Thomson, above n 29, p. 52.

39. Thomson, above n 29.

40. Department of Social Services, *Stronger Futures in the Northern Territory policy statement*, Australian Government, 2013, viewed 18 November 2013, <www.dss.gov.au/our-responsibilities/indigenous-australians/programs-services/stronger-futures-in-the-northern-territory-policy-statement>.

INDEX

Note: page references in bold type are to images or captions; those in italics are to note pages.

Abdula, Auntie Alice, 177, 194, 196
Abdula, Bill, 177
Abdula, Ian, 198
Aboriginal and Torres Strait Islander Commission, 226
Aird, Michael, 7, 9, 10, 11, 133
Aiston, George, *17*
Allen, James, 37, *50*
Allen, Maria, 37, *50*
Andrew, Brook, 12
Archer family, 144, 145
Aritcheuka, Dolly, **248**, 249
Australian Institute of Aboriginal and Torres Strait Islander Studies, 7

Baily, Henry, 36
Bamblett, Lawrence, 10
Batman, John, 103
Baymarrwangga, Laurie, 16, **232**, 254, 264, **265**, 266, **267**, 268–9
Beattie, JW, 42, 43, 44–5
Becker, Ludwig, 41, 111
Beembarmin (Tommy Farmer), **112**, 113
Benbow, Annie, 43
Berndt, Catherine, 182, 221
Berndt, Ronald, 182, 221
Bevan, Agrippa, 142
Bevan, Thomas, 138, 142–3, 144
  Kirwallie Sandy and others in fight scene, **143**
  Women photographed in Brisbane, **143**
'Big Billy' (Naindulka), 259
Billiamook (Larrakia man), **238**, 239
Bishop, Mervyn, 6
Bock, Alfred, 45
Bock, Thomas 25–6, 46
Bonney, Frederic, 69–70, 72
  Jacob and Mary sitting in a winter camp, with daughter Doughboy, **71**
Bonwick, James, 43
  The daily life and origins of the Tasmanians, 45
  The last of the Tasmanians, 45
Bostock, George, 61, **64**, **65**
Bostock-Smith, Shauna, 60–1, 63, **64**, **65**
Bowdler, Sandra, 22
Brady, Vincent (Qawanji Ngurku Jawiyabba), 7
Briggs, Maxine, 105
Bringing them home report, 26
Broughton, Frank, 83
Brown, Daisy, 190
Brown, Ellen Edith (née Sumner), 183–4, 187
Brown, Patrick Joseph Robinson, 185, **186**, 187, 188, **189**, 190, 202, 203
Brown, William Charles, 183, 185, **186**, 187, 188, **189**, 190, 202, 203
Browne, Thomas, 36, *48*
  Walter George Arthur, Maryann and David Bruny (daguerr.; attr.), **23**, 25, 26, 27, 28–9, 31, 32; coloured version, 29, 32
Bunce, Daniel, 110
Burnell, George, 169
  Aboriginal canoe building, **169**
  Stereoscopic views of the River Murray, 169–70
Bussini, Chiara
  Laurie Baymarrwangga talking to Bentley James, **265**
Butler, Rex, 12, *18*

Calder, JE
  The native tribes of Tasmania, 44
Camfield, Anne, 116
Camfield, Henry, 116
Carter, Paul, 240
Chauncy, Philip, 116–18
Chevalier, Nicholas, **110**
Cleary, Thomas, 66, 68
Clifford, Samuel, 36, 45
Clifton, William, 213, 214–15
  An Aboriginal family, **213**
  A seated priest, two small children ..., **214**
  Studio shot of two girls ..., **214**
Cole, EW, 169
colonial period in Australia
  colonial encounter and conflict, 2, 4
  and excision of Aboriginal people from national story, 12
  Indigenous dispossession and loss, 9
  racial theories, 3
  see also the various colonies/states
Colotoney (Indigenous man), 160
Conwillan (Kandwillan), Samuel, 161, 162, **163**
Copia, Jacques Louis
  Homme du Cap de Diemen; Enfant du Cap de Diemen (engraving), **31**
Cotton, John, 103–4, 105
Cotton, William, 105, 107
Cowan, Alice, 63
  descendants of, 63, **64**
Cowan, Elizabeth, 63
Cowan, Herbert, 61, 63
Cowan, John Thomas
  descendants of, 63
Cowan, Jonathon, 63
Cowan, Mary Ann (Williams) ('Mary Ann of Ulmarra'), 60, 61, **62**, 63, *74*
Croft, Brenda L, 6, 237
Crossland, John, 162
  Portrait of Samuel Kandwillan ..., **163**
Cullen, Janet, 61
Cullen, Sam, 61, 63
Cumpston, Zena, 70, 72
Cunningham, Peter, 3

Daintree, Richard, 138, 148–9, 151
  Men and boys ..., 151, **153**
  Studio portrait of girl holding fishing rod, 151, **152**
Daintree, Richard, and Antoine Fauchery
  Aboriginal camp, **112**
  Beebarmin ... and his wife Norah ..., **112**
  Sun pictures of Victoria series, 113
Dallwitz, John, 8
Dalton, Edwin, 57, *73*
Damery, Sally
  Walter George Arthur ..., 23
Dandridge, John, 38–9
Dandrige, Matilda, 38–9
Darwin, Charles
  The origin of species ..., 3, 57, 118
  see also evolutionary theory
David, Jacques Louis
  The intervention of the Sabine women, *49*
Davidson, Mrs Letitia, 44–5
  Two women (attrib.), **46**
Davis, Henry, 167

Davis, Uncle Ron, 197
de Costa, Ravi, 265
Denison, Lady Caroline, 27, 28
Denison, William, 26, 27, 32
Dietrich, Amelie, 146, 147
Diggles, Sylvester, 134
Doolan (Wiradjuri man), 14
Dowling, Henry Junior, 25
Dowling, Robert, 25, 26
Duwun, Minnie, **238**, 239
Duryea, Sanford, 216
Duryea, Townsend, 167, 170, 216
  James and Mary Jane Wanganeen, **166**
Duterrau, Benjamin, 46, *49*
  The conciliation, 24, **25**, 26, 27; as etching, 27
  The national picture, 27
Dwyer, JJ, 217
  Aboriginal man, Kalgoorlie, **220**
  An Aboriginal man of the Kalgoorlie region, **219**
  The belle of Kanowna, **218**
  W.A. Aboriginal, **206**, **218**

Edwards, E, 225
Ellen (Koori girl), **112**, 113
Elliot, Gilbert, 140
Elliott, Frederick, 242
Evans, Samuel, 216
Everett, James, *50*
evolutionary theory
  and images of Indigenous Australians, 57–8, 119, 246–7, *251*
  and narratives of extinction, 13–14, 58, 119, 217
  and racial difference, 161, 170, 236, 247, 261
  rationalisation for ill effects of invasion, 3, 58
  social evolution, 3, 4, 118–19, 167, 170, 236, *252*
exhibitions
  in Australia, 45, 118, 236, 237, 239, *251*
  international, 36, 43, 118, 149; and photographs (and artefacts) of Indigenous Australians, 57, 60, *74*, 118, 149, 168, 327
Eyre, Edward John, 157

Fauchery, Antoine, 108, 113
Fels, Marie, 120
Flick, Joe, 69
Foelsche, Paul, 234, 235, 236–7, 239, *251*
  Iwaidja people in camp, **237**
  Trepang Fishery Station, **235**
Forster, Edward
  Woman with possum skin cloak, **141**, 142
Foster, Wilton, 8
Franklin, Lady Jane, 46
Franklin, Sir John, 46
Frazer, James
  The golden bough, 246
Freeman, James, 138–9
Friday, Kate, 66
Friday, John, 66
Frith, Henry, 36, 45

Gadayurr (Aboriginal woman), **232**, **267**
Gale, Frank, 57
Gazard, J
  Aborigines from Central Australia, **244**
Gibson, Jason, 250
Giglioli, Enrico, 116, 119–20
  Group portrait ..., **123**
  Portrait of Maggie, **125**
  Tommy Hobson ..., **122**
  Voyage around the globe, 126
Gillen, Francis, 1, 11, 217, 246, 247–50, *252*, *253*
Ginzburg, Carlo, 69
Glover, John, 41, 46
Goode, Bernard, 167, 168
Goodman, George, 105
Goyder, George, 239, *250*
Green, John, 116, 118
  and family, 122
Green, Neville, 207, 208
Grosse, Frederick
  Portraits of an Aboriginal woman ... and Simon ... (engraving), **110**
Gularrbanga (Aboriginal woman), **232**, **267**
Gunlarnman, Jackey, **158**, 159, 160
Gunlarnman, Jemima, 159, 160
Gunn, Ronald, 29, 30, *49*
Gwynne, SC, 93, 94

Hale, Arch. Matthew, 161, 162, 163, 164
  The Aborigines of Australia, *172–3*
Hall, Robert, 167, 216
Hall, Stuart, 84
Ham, Thomas, 138, 140
Hamilton, William (Billy), 104
Hammond, Octavius, 160, 164
Haselden, Hubert, **110**, 111
Hawkes, Rev, 164
Hemings, Sally
  and Thomas Jefferson, 180
Hetzer, William, *73*, 217
Hill, Fitz W, 69
Hobson, Edward, 120
Hobson, Tommy, 119–20, **121**, **122**, **123**, **126**
Hodson, S, 211
hooks, bell, 85
Hughes, Karen, 176, **202**
Hunter, Ruby, 194, 195
Huxley, Thomas, 118, *251*
Hyllested, Peter, 138
  Katie, Lilly and Clara Williams, **135**

Indigenous activism and protest
  and the bicentenary, 7
  in colonial period, 28, 30, 31, 32
  Day of Mourning and Protest, 5
  and 1967 referendum, 5, 215
  land rights movement, 5, 6, 126; Mabo case, 194
  use of photography to promote reform, 5; *After 200 years* project, 7
Indigenous groups/clans
  A̲nangu (Pitjantjatjara and Yankunytjatjara), 8, 245
  Arrernte (NT), 1, 11, 247, 249–50
  Arrindinya (NT), 243
  Bandjalung (NSW), 58, 60
  Barngarla (Pangkala) (SA), 159, 167, 194
  Ben Lomond (Tas.), 32
  Boonwurrung (Vic.), 110
  Bunurong (Vic.), 119
  Dharawal (NSW), 56
  Dhudhuroa-Waywurru (Vic.), 119
  Dja Dja Wurrung/Djadjawrung (Vic.), 111, 113; Yung Balug clan, 126
  Eora (NSW), 55; Cadigal, 55
  Gumbaynggirr (NSW), 58, 60
  Gurindji (NT), 6, 237
  Iwaidja (NT), 236, 237
  Kauna (SA), 158
  Kokatha (SA), 159
  Kulin confederacy (Vic.), 3, 113
  Kurnai (Vic.), 16
  Larrakia (NT), 236, 237, 239
  Maraura (SA), 165
  Nauo (SA), 159, 167
  Neenbullock (Vic.), 104
  Ngaiwong (SA), 157
  Ngarrindjeri (SA), 168–70, 175–203

Noongar (WA), 15, 116, 207–8, 210, 223
Nuenone (Tas.), 26
Paakantyi (Barkindji) (NSW), 69–70
Pinjarup (WA), 210
Pitjantjatjara/Ngaanyatjarra (NT), 242
Taungurong (Vic.), 103, 105, 111, 113
Tjurabalan (WA), 245
Wailwan (NSW), 69
Warruwi (WA), 226
Wiradjuri (NSW), 10, 14, 76–99
Woolna (NT), 236
Wotjoballuk (Vic.), 113, 113
Wurundjeri (Vic.), 110, 111, 113, 118
Yaegl (NSW), 61
Yamatji (WA), 11
Yolŋu (Batjimurrunggu, Gurryindi, Nhangu, Yan-nhangu) (NT), 1, 254–69, *270–1*
Yuin (NSW), 55; Walbunja dialect, 55, 56
Yuwaalaraay (NSW), 69

Indigenous people and culture, 32, 246, 248, 268
artists, 6, 12–13, 66, 198, 237, 239, *251*; and old photographs, 12, 238, 239
connection to country, 4, 56, 60, 64, 69, 97, 103, 126, 134, 154, 175, 215, 240, 261
cultural heritage, 247, 261; and restitution, 1, 7–9, 11, 13
intellectual property, 9
loss, 268
and mobility, 4, 113, 116, 120, **169**
oral tradition, 225, 228
Stolen Generations, 193, 225, 226; apology, 194
traditional practices, 8, 249
see also Northern Territory; photography from an Aboriginal perspective

Indigenous photographers
availability of cameras, 5, 9, 76, 79
documenting life and developments in Aboriginal communities, 6, 7, 177, 194–8, 202
exhibitions: *Australian graffiti*, 12; National Aborigines Day show (1986), 6
Indigenous photography movement, 6
making Aboriginal people visible, 5–6, 68
and protests, 7
see also photography from an Aboriginal perspective

institutions, cultural
and access/return to Indigenous people of holdings, 225–7; Ara Irititja Project, 8–9, 227, 245; *Globalisation, Photography and Race* project, 227; *Storylines* project, 221, 227
Anthropology museum (Univ. of Q.), 143
Australian Museum (Sydney), 60
Battye Library of Western Australia, 221
Berndt Museum of Anthropology (UWA), 221–2, 226–7
British Museum, 141–2, 144
collections of remains of Aboriginal people in, 36
Grafton Regional Gallery, 60, 61, 63
John Oxley Library, 141
Museum Godeffroy, 146
National Gallery of Australia, 107, 140
National Gallery of Victoria, 107
and objects of Aboriginal heritage, 7–8, 36, 237, 242, 247; photographs, 47, 58, 59, 60, *75*, 107, 139, 140, 141–4, 146, 149, 160, 163, 164, 165, 221–4, 225
Pitt Rivers Museum, 12, 145, 146, 165, 227, 246
Powerhouse Museum (Sydney), *75*
Queensland Museum, 133, 149
Royal Geographic Society, 240, 242
South Australian Museum, 237, 243
State Library of Queensland, 140, 142, 144
State Library of Victoria, 144
State Library of Western Australia, 226, 227
University of Bristol Library, **163**, **164**, **165**
Western Australian Museum, 223–4

Jagga Jagga (Koori chief), **110**
James, Bentley, 264, **265**
Jeanneret, Henry, 31
Jemmy (Koori man), 110
Jevons, William, 4, 55–6
Group of three Aboriginal people at Jembaicumbene, **56**
Johnson, Dalrymple (nee Briggs), *50*
Jones, Philip, 169, 239, 240, 247
Judy (Pollerrelberner), 37, *50*

Karpany, George, 181
Karpany (née Kontinyeri), Queen Louisa, 178, 179, 180, **181**, 182, 183, 185, *204*
Karpany, Manuel (Old Dardle), **184**, 201
Kartinyeri, Aunty Dorrie, 182
Kerr, James Hunter, 111
... Aboriginal man standing, with rifle ..., **117**
Glimpses of life in Victoria ..., 111
Prince Jamie and his friend, 111, **114**
Young stockman, **115**
Kerry, Charles, 68, 69, *75*
Kerswell, Aunty Joyce, 198, **199**, 200
Kilborn, J, 67–8
Kilburn, Douglas, 3, 24, 105, 107, 110
... (Group of Koorie men), **108**
South-east Australian Aboriginal man ..., **102**, **106**
King, Henry, 68, *75*
Kleinert, Sylvia, 239
Knight, William, 138, 140, 142
Group in ... studio, **141**
Koolmatrie, Isabel, **195**
Koolmatrie, Ruby, 194

Lampard, Aunty Thora, 178, 196, **197**
Langton, Marcia, 2, 9, 236
La Trobe, Charles, 103
Lear, J, 88
Lee, Gary Mura, 239
Billiamook and Shannon, **238**
Mei Kim and Minnie, **238**
Nice coloured boys series, *251*
Nymgololo series, *251*
Lee, Shannon, **238**, 239
legislation
Aboriginal Land Act 1976 (Cth), 266
Aboriginal Land Rights (Northern Territory) Act 1976 (Cth), 5, 266
Aboriginal Lands Trust Act 1966 (SA), 170, *203*
Aborigines Act 1905 (WA), 210

Aborigines Act 1911 (SA), 170, 188
Aborigines Protection Act 1886 (Vic.), 119
Aborigines (Training of Children Act 1923 (SA), 186
Native Administration Act 1936 (WA), 211
Native (Citizens Rights) Act 1944 (WA), 211
South Australia Act 1834 (UK), 158
Lerimburneen (King Billy Logan), 128
Le Souef, William, 104
Lindsay, Aunty Rita, 192, 194, 196, 198
Lindt, John William, 58, 72
Australian Aboriginals series, 58–60, 61, **62**, 63, *73*
Livingstone, David, 240
Long, C, *48*
Long-Alleyne, Margaret, 187
Lorde, Audre, 94, 96
Lucas, Augustin, 3
Lucashenko, Melissa, 92
Lyon, RM, 207–8

Macarthur, Elizabeth, 56, *73*
Macarthur, John, 56, *73*
McCrae, Tommy (Yakaduna), 66, **67**, 68, *74–5*
drawings of Aboriginal people, 66
Macdonald, Gaynor, 10, 78, 79, 87
McIntosh, Ian, 265
Mack, Margaret (Pinkie), 180, **181**, 182, *204*
McKenzie, Peter, 7
Maggie (Koori woman), 119, 120, 122, **123**, **124**, **125**
Mannalargenna (Aboriginal Tasmanian), 37
Marquis, Daniel, 138, 144, 151
...frontal portrait of two young women, **145**
Group with painted backdrop ..., **145**
Kirwallie Sandy, **132**, **148**, 149
Man posing with club and shield, **147**
Woman and child, **146**
'Mary Ann of Ulmarra', *see* Cowan, Mary Ann
Mason, Auntie Annie (later Koolmatrie), 199, **200**, *204*
Mason, GE, 180, 181, 182, 201
Mason, Pat, 63, **64**, **65**
Massola, Aldo
Journey to Aboriginal Victoria, 23
Matthews, Daniel, 119
Maulboyheener (Robert), 32
Maurice, Richard, 242–3, **244**
Sturt Creek – catching and branding calves, **245**
Sturt Creek – cattle breeding, **245**
View in Musgrave Ranges, 242, **243**
'Wild Dog' Police station, 242, **243**
Maynard, Ricky, 7
media
representations of Indigenous people in, 5, 14
television: ABC: *Australian story*, 61, 63
see also newspapers
Mei Kim (Larrakia woman), **238**, 239
Metcalfe, Daniel, 144
Michaels, Eric, 7
Milerum (Ngarrindjeri elder), 180
Milligan, Joseph, 29, 37, 38, 46, *49*
Mira, John, 37
missionaries and Indigenous people, 8, 116, 119, 165, 169; respect, 160, 161–4, 166, 214
missions/reserves, 5
mission life, 92, 96; conditions, 212–13
NSW: Brungle, 83; Erambie, 10, 14, 80, 82, 83, 86, 88, 90, 92, 93, 94–8, *100*; Maloga, 119
NT: Goulburn Island, 258, 260, **262**; Milingingbi, 16, 265, *270*
as places of contact and exchange, 4, 116, 119, 170–1
SA, 170; Point McLeay, 167, 168, 169–70; Point Pearce, 167; Poonindie, 4, 160, 161–7, *172–73*
Vic: Coranderrk, 4, **104**, 113, 116, 118, 119; Ebenezer, **104**, 113, 116, 246; Framlingham, **104**, 113; Lake Condah, **104**, 113; Lake Tyers, **104**, 113; Mount Franklin, **104**, 113; Ramahyuck, **104**, 113, 116; Yelta, 169
WA, 210–12; Beagle Bay, 212; Moore River, 212, **222**, **223**; New Norcia, 15, 214
see also Tasmania
Mitchell, Ernest, 223–4
Aboriginal men in traditional dress ..., **224**
Mitchell, Jessie, 107
Moffatt, Tracey, 6
Monaghan, Esmay, 63, **64**, **65**
Mortlock, William Ranson, 159, 160
Mortlock, William Tennant, 159
Morton, Christopher, 13
Moseley, Henry, 58
Mulvaney, John, 252
Munjena (Arrindinya man), 243, **244**, 245
Munro, Keith, 7
Murray, Doolan, 83, **85**, 86, 87–8, **89**, 90, 96, 98
Murray, Ethel, **85**
Murray, Gary, 126, 128
Murray, Harry, 83, 90, **91**, 92–6, **97**, 98
Murray, Jane, **54**, **80**, 81–4, 87, 90, 97
Murray, June, **77**, 78, 81, 82, 83, 85, 86, 87, 89, 93–4, 96, **97**, **98**, 99
Murray, Margaret, 76, **77**, 78, **79**, 81, 82, 84, 85, 86, 87, 88–9, 93, 96, 97
Murray family, 82, 83, **85**, 86, 95, 97
Myetye, Bessy, 37

Nakata, Martin, 9
Nanultera (Indigenous man), 162
native tribes of Central Australia, The (Spencer and Gillen), 246, 250
Neville, AO, 222–3
New Guinea, 261
New South Wales
Aborigines Welfare Board, 82, 95, 96
colonisation, 69–70; invasion and dispossession of Indigenous peoples, 55, 93; conflict, 56
goldfields, 55–6; Indigenous people in, 56
government policy: assimilation, 92–3, 94
lives of Indigenous people: colonial period, **57**, 68, 99; culture and identity, 55, 69, 72, 93, 99
and narrative of colonial progress, 57
photography as hobby, 55
race in public discourse, 81, 82, 84, 86, 90, 94, 95, 99
Sydney, 55
New South Wales: photographs of Indigenous people, 4

Bandjalung people, 58
Clarence River series, 14, 58–60, 61, **62**, 68, *74*; importance for Indigenous community today, 60, 61–4, 69, 70–2, 76
and negative representations of, 14, 66, 68, 81, 84, 85, 90
Dharawal people, 56, **57**
encounters between Indigenous subjects and photographers, 56, 57, 58, 66, 69, 70, 84, 85, 86
Gumbaynggirr, 58
Paakantyi (Barkindji), 69–70
as staged narratives, 58, 59, 66, 72, *74*
and traditional lifestyle, 55, 58–9
Walbunja people, **57**
Wiradjuri (at Erambie): photographs, family, (racial identity, 79, 80–1, 82, 83, 84, 86, 88, 96–9; photographs and leadership narratives, 80, 81, 84, 85, 87, 90–3, 94–9; photographs and teaching, 85, 87, 88; reading photographs and oral history tradition, 76–81, 84, **85**, 86–90, 99; snapshots as social capital, 79, 81, 86
newspapers
Advertiser (Adelaide), **200**
Argus, 113
Clarence and Richmond Examiner, 60
Cowra Free Press, 81, 82, 83, 94
Illustrated Melbourne Post, 110
Lachlan Leader, 83
Launceston Examiner, 28
Northern Territory Times and Gazette, 254, 259
Perth Gazette, 207–8
Register (Adelaide), 162, 179–80, 263
and representations of Indigenous people, 58–9, 94, 168
South Australian Register, 168
Sydney Morning Herald, 59
Town and Country Journal, 68
Newton, Gael, 216
Nicholls, Pastor Douglas, 126, 128
Nixon, Bishop Francis, **20**, 37–8, 39, 41, 42, 43, 45, 46, *51*
The cruise of the Beacon (book), **20**, 42
Mary Ann and Walter George Arthur, **30**
after Tasmania, 44
Tippo ..., 41
Nora (Koori woman), **112**, 113
Northern Territory
Central Australia, 240, 242, 247
Crocodile Islands, **256**, 264–6
(Port) Darwin, 236, 237, 239, *250*
European settler–Aboriginal relations, 236, 239, 269; employment, 245, 248–9; and Indigenous rights, 261, 265–6, 267; and justice system, 259, 260; violence, 236–7, *253*, 255, 263, 266
exploration and European settlement, 234, 235, 236, 240, **241**, 242–3, 245; and Aboriginal assistance, 240, 245
and government policies, 265–6, 268, *271*; 'emergency' intervention, 269
(Macassan) traders and Indigenous people, 16, 233–6, 264, 265, 268, *271*; conflict with Yolŋu, 255–65, 267–8
mass tourism, 240, 242
photographers in, 1, 15, 16, 234, 235, 237, 239, 242, *250–1*, 254–5, 259, 260, 261
and theories of race, 236, 246–7, 261, 263, 268
Yolŋu (Yan-nhangu) culture, 264, 265–8, *270–1*; and loss, 268, 269
Northern Territory: early photography in
anthropology and visual and data, 246–7, 249–50
of Aboriginal people, **241**, 243; in Central Australia, 246–7, **248**, 249; Iwaidja, **237**, 239; Larrakia, 237, **238**, 239; Melville Islanders, 255; in pastoral industry, 245; as prisoners, 245; traditional life, 242
photographers and Indigenous people, 240–1, 242, 247; agency of Aboriginal subjects, 239, 242, 249, 250, 255, 259, 260
significance to descendants today, 237, 239–40, 245, 247
Trepang Fishery Station, **235**
and the Yolŋu people using photography, 16, 254, 259, **260**, 261, 263
Noye, RJ, 216
Orchard, Ken, 170
Oxenham, Donna, 11

Parker, Chief Quanah, 92, 93
Pepper, Nathaniel, 116, *172*
Peter (Napparinnya Kallatinya), 243, **244**, 245
Peterson, Nicolas, 144
photography of Aboriginal people in Australia: colonial
Aboriginal people as subjects, 1, 2, 13, 118; popular/commercial appeal of, 2, 58, 59, 69, 105, 167; in studios, 3, 4, 11, 59, 72, 105, 134, 151
and agency of Aboriginal people, 1, 2, 118, 203, 239
attempts to record 'primitive' Aboriginal subjects, 3, 4, 5, 59, 126; and recording 'disappearing' race, 58, 59, 60, 68, 157, 167, 168, 228
and European culture in Australia, 60; narrative of civilisation, 118
interactions of photographers and Indigenous people, 2, 16, 25, 46–7, 66, 69
mass reproduction of images, 42, 45, 58
see also institutions; science
photography from an Aboriginal perspective, 6
as evidence of events, 1
collaboration with subjects and communities, 7, 8, 9, 10
cultural meaning of, 9–10, 11, 12, 13, 14, 15, 69, 87, 225–6, 228; Indigenous identity, 13, 72; and memory, 12, 116
importance of visual archive, 6, 9, 224–9
photographs and family and cultural heritage, 1, 2, 7–9, 60–4, 99, 166–7; access/return, 8–9, 225–7; exhibitions, 10–11
see also Indigenous photographers; New South Wales; Northern Territory; South Australia
photography after federation
and Aboriginal agency, 11, 13, 92–3, 94, 96, 243
representations of Aboriginal subjects, 9, 11; as part of nature, 12–13
photography: history (in Australia), *16*

arrival in Australia, 2–3, 14
cartes de visite and portraiture, 4, 15, 142, 167, 217
and exploration, 240, 242, **243**, *252*
invention, 2
and mobility, 4, 234
technology, 247; ambrotypes, 57, 159, 160, 163; daguerreotypes, 2–3, 24, 25, 26, **102**, **108**, 110, 160, 216; digital technologies, 8; enlargement, 149; mass reproduction, 42; wet-plate collodion process, 4, 113, 139
Plomley, NJB, 26, 31
Poignant, Ros, 265
Poole, Rev F Slaney, 166
Preston, Margaret, 12
Princep, Henry, 22
Prout, John Skinner, 26, 28, 33, 45, 46, *47–8*, 107
Family group, Australia Felix, **106**
King Tippoo from Hobart Town V.D.L., **40**, 41
Mary Ann, Kings Island, **29**

Queensland
Brisbane: early photographers, 134, 136, 138, 140, 142, 144, 151
as frontier, 14
lives of Aboriginal people, 134; changes in culture, 151; and European commodities, 136
promotional exhibitions, 149, **150**
settlers and Aboriginal people, 136
Queensland: early studio photographs in Brisbane of Aboriginal people, 4, 10–11, 139–40, 141, 142–7, 151, 153–4
and Aboriginal agency, 133, 136–7
exhibitions: *Portraits of our elders*, 10, 133
leading a traditional way of life, 14–15
importance for communities today, 133, 134, 153–4
relations between photographers and Aboriginal subjects, 136, 138, 143; profit motive, 136
Queensland Aboriginal people in photographs (identified)
Buckner, **135**
Lucy, **135**
Maria, **135**
Mickey, **135**
Nancy, **135**
Nikki, **135**
Nudla, **135**
Sandy, Alexander, 136, **137**
Sandy, Kirwallie, **132**, **139**, 140, **148**, 149
Tundarum, **135**
Weerum, **135**
Williams, Katie, Lilly and Clara, **135**

Rankine, Aunty Daisy (née Brown), **181**, 182, 188
Rankine, Deborah, 182–3
Read, Peter, 83
Reibey, Arch. Thomas, 43–4
Reichenbach, Edward (Ryko), 1, 15, 254, 255–9
A church service at Goulburn Island Mission Station, **262**
Cyclist/Ted Ryko, **255**
series of photographs in collaboration, 16; *Massacre series number 3* (re-enactment), 259, **260**, 261, 263
Richards, Auntie Charlotte, 194, **197**
as photographer, 194, **195**, 196, **197**, 198, **199**, 202
Richards, Irene, **195**, 196
Richards, Nulla (Uncle Walter), 194, 195–6
Rigney, Thelma, 170–1
Riley, Michael, 6
Roberts, Alfred, 60
Robinson, George A, 24, **25**, 26, 28, 37, 40, 46, *50*
Roheim, Géza, 250
Rolepa (King George), *49–50*
Rollinson, Robert, 190
Roth, Henry
The Aborigines of Tasmania (album), 45
Roth, Walter
Royal Commission of, 210

Sally Sally (Koori woman), 110
Salvado, Bishop Rosendo, 214
Schrauder, Hermann, 171
science
anthropology, 180, 182, 221, 224, 246, 250, 268; and fieldwork, 246, 247–8; modern, 264, 265
collection of Tasmanian Aboriginal remains, 36
expeditions in Australia, 217
and interest in photographs visual data of Aboriginal subjects, 57, 60, 118, 119, 126, 146, 243, 246–7, *252*
and photographic collections of Indigenous Australians, 4, 69, 250
see also evolutionary theory; institutions
Searcy, Alfred, 233–4, 235
Short, Bishop Augustus, 161–2, 163, 165, 167, *172–3*
Shreeve, Noah, 167–8
A short history of South Australia, 168
Simpkinson De Wesselow, Francis, 41, 45
Smith, Christina, 165
Smith, Tim, 23
Solomon (Arrernte man), 249
Solomon, Emanuel, 167
Solomon, Polly, **248**, 249
South Australia
Aboriginal Protection Board, 192, 193
Aborigines' Friends Association, 169
Adelaide, 158; established photographers, 167; St Peters College, 162, *173*
Anglican Church in, 160, 161, 163, 166
Camp Coorong, 192, *203*; museum and education centre, 175, 176, 178, 179, 182, 203
established as colony, 158; and Aboriginal rights, 158
government policy, 170, 198; assimilation, 181, 188, 198; defining Aboriginality, 188; exclusions, 190, 191; removal of children, 185, 186–7, 188, **189**, 190, 192–3
impact of colonisation on Aboriginal people, 165, 170, 176, 180–1, 187, 188, 190; abductions, 160; accommodation, 157, 158; collaboration,180, 182, 191; conflict, 157, 158, 159–60, 167, 175; cross-cultural relationships, 180, 181, 182, 188, **200**
Ngarrindjeri nation, 168–70, 175–6, 194; country of, 175, 181, 192; culture, 175, 178, 180, 182, **183**, 195, 196; female leadership, 180, 182,

185, 202, *204*; lives of, 168–9, 170, 176, 190–2, 195, 198, *204*, (annoyances), 192
Point McLeay (Raukkan) Mission, 169, 170–1, 190
Poonindie Mission, 160; narrative of transformation, 162–3, 167, *172–73*; respect for residents, 161–2, 164, 166; outcome for residents, 167
Port Lincoln district, 159–60
Report of the South Australian Chief Protector of Aborigines (1910), 185
South Australia: photographs of Indigenous people
Aboriginal photographers, 171, 176, 177, 194–8, 202
importance to descendants and communities, 157, 166–7, 168, 171, 188; change and memory, 201
mapping Indigenous–settler relations, 158–9, 160
Ngarrindjeri photograph collections: connecting generations, 175–8, 181, 182, 185, 188, 199, 202, *204*; cultural and spiritual knowledge, 178, 180, 182–3, 202; healing relationships, 202–3; and loss, 192, 193, 201; photos, stories, history, 176, 177, 184–90, **191**, 194, 196, 198, 203
portraits of, 168–9, 170, 171; *cartes de visite*, 168; popular market for, 167, 168
portraits at Poonindie, 160–1, **165**, **166**; as missionary propaganda, 162, **163**, **164**, 165
Spencer, W Baldwin, 217, 246–7, 250, *252*
Stanley, Hazel, 190
Steele, John
Aboriginal pathways, 145
Stirling, Edward, 182
Strutt, William, 108
Stuart, John McDouall, 240

Taplin, George, 169, 170
The folklore ... of the South Australian Aborigines, 170
The Narrinyeri, 170
Tasmania/Van Diemen's Land
Aboriginal Tasmanians in, 24, 37, 44, 47; culture, 32; dispossession, 32, 44; fall into anonymity, 46; renamed, 40, *50*; and white authority, 28, 30, 31, 32
arrival of British, 22
Bass Strait Aboriginal community, 36, 37, 42, 43, 44, *51*
colonising culture in, 27, 28; Black War, 42; colonial injustice, 32; conflict and violence, 22, 32, 41, *49*
fine arts in, 39; representations of Aboriginal people, 24, **25**, 26, 27, 28, **29**, 33, **40**, 41, 45
government policy on Aboriginal Tasmanians, *51*; forced residency, 33, 44; exile of, 24, 25, 26, 30, 33, (ended), 26–7; refusal of recognition as legitimate Aborigines, 37, 42, 44
Hobart, 25; entertainment in, 27, 28
Oyster Cove Aboriginal station, 14, 21–2, 26, 30, 32, 33, 35, 38–9, 41, 43, 44, 45; conditions, 37; deaths, 38, 42, 44; and isolation, 36–7, 42; residents seen as 'tamed', 39; wish to leave, 37
Wybalenna (Flinders Inland), 30, 32, 33, 37, 39
Tasmania: first photographs of Tasmanian Aboriginal people, 13, **20**, 22, **23**, 24–8, 33, 34–6, 39, 41–3, 44–5
alternative perspectives, 14, 37–8, 42
and Aboriginal community today, 13, 21, 37, 45
mass reproduction of, 42, 45; digital reproduction, 46
misidentification, 46–7
photographs as public representation of Aboriginal people, 45
photography as dehumanising and tool of science, 36
as reminder of invasion and loss, 21, 22
reproduced as etchings, 45
Tasmanian Aboriginal people in early photographs (named)
Arthur, Mary Ann, **20**, **30**, 39, 43, 44, 45
Arthur, Walter George, **23**, 24, 26, 28, 30, 31–2, 43, 44
Bruney, David (Myyungge), **23**, 24, 25, 26, 28, 31, 34, 36
Bruney, Mary Ann, **23**, 24, 26, 28, 31
Calamarowenye (Tippo), **20**, 39, **40**, **41**, 42, 43
Coonia (Patty), **20**, 43
Drayduric (Sophia), **20**
Drunameliyer (Caroline), **20**, 42, 43
Lanne, William, 39, 43, 44, 45
Lennimenna (Jack Allen), 36
Meethecaratheeanna (Emma), **20**, 37, 42, 44, *50*
Pangernowidedic (Bessy Clark), 39, 43, 44, 45, **46**, *50*
Plowneme (Flora), **20**, 39, 42, 43
Trucanini (Lalla Rookh), **20**, 24, 36, 39, 43, 44, 45
Wapperty, **20**, 35, 37, 43, 44, **46**, *50*
Taylor, James, 242
Two Aboriginal men, standing ..., **241**
Taylor, Penny, 7
Tenberry (Ngaiwong man), 157, **158**, *171*
Tennant, Andrew, 160
They stole our land and took our children (collaboration), 186, 194
Thompson, Christian, *18*
We bury our own (series), 12, 13
Tindale, Norman, 180, 182
Tolbonco (Indigenous man), 164
Thomson, Donald F, 268
Sisters Gularrbanga #1, Gadayurr and Baymarrwangga #1 ..., **232**, **267**
Toussaint, S, 211
Trevorrow, Bruce, 192, **193**, 194
Trevorrow, Choom (Joe Junior), **156**, **191**, **200**
Trevorrow, Auntie Ellen, 175, 176, 178, 180, 182, 194, 199, 201, **202**
Trevorrow, George, **195**
Trevorrow, Hank, 192, **202**
Trevorrow, Jim, 200
Trevorrow, Uncle Joe, **156**, **191**, 193–4, **200**
Trevorrow, Tanya, 180, **183**
Trevorrow, (Uncle) Tom, **156**, 176, 178, 182, 190, **191**, 192, **193**, 195, 196, 198–9, **202**
Trevorrow family, 190, 194, **195**, 196, **197**, 198, 199
Tunnerminnerwait (Jack), 32

United States, 180
Native Americans in, 92–4

Victoria
artists' depictions of Indigenous (Koori) people, 107–8, **109**, **110**
Central Board for the Protection of Aborigines, 113
colonisation/settlement narrative, 111; and race, 111, 119
European audience for representations of Indigenous people, 107, 111, 118
gold rushes, 107; impact on Kooris, 107
government policies relating to Indigenous people: 'Aboriginal Protectors', 103, 104; assimilation, 66, 103; removal of children, 66–8; reserves, 103, **104**, 113
issues of race, 104, 105, 107
Koori interest in photography, 103, 116; and family/ community connections, 104–5, 118, 126; sensitivities, 118
Koori presence in: curiosity about Europeans, 107; at the goldfields, 56, 107, 108; and impact of invasion, 4, 32, 103, 111, **112**, 113, 116, 119; on traditional lands, 119, 126, 128; travelling, 107; visibility to settlers, 107, 108, 110
Koori–white photographic exchange in, 14, 103, 104, 111, 118, 119
Melbourne, 14, 103; Intercolonial Exhibition, 45, 118
missions/reserves, 4, **104**, 113, 116; as destinations for visitors, 116, 118, 119; and friendships, 122; as places of transformation/adaptability, 113, 119, 120, 122
photographs of Kooris, 4, 24, 102, 103, 106, 107, **112**; as evidence of adaptability, 119; mocking, 66, 68; portraits, 108, **110**, 111, **112**, 116, 118, **121**, **122**; subjects as celebrities, 111, in traditional garb, 111, **114**; use by descendants, 126
Vietnam War
Indigenous Australian soldiers in, **64**, **65**
von Guérard, Eugene, 107, 108
Series 01: Australien Reminiszenzen, **109**

Wagner, Conrad, 58, *73*
Walker, Alice, **200**
Walker, Joe (Uncle Poothie), **195**
Wallaston, George, *172*
Walpole, Edward, 43
Walter, Charles, 118, 119
Maggie ..., 124
Tommy Hobson, **121**
Tommy Hobson's residence, **126**
Wandin, Jemima, 118
Wanganeen, Elva, 167
Wanganeen, James, 165, **166**
Wanganeen, Lynnette, 166–7
Wanganeen, Mary Jane, 165, **166**
Warndekan, Rachel, 116–18
Washbourne, Thomas, 119, 126
Watson, Queen Ethel Whympie, 178, **179**, 180, 182, 185
Watson, Rev James, 255, 259–63, *270*
Watson, John, 138, 140
Group from Durundir, **135**, 136, 140
Kirwallie Sandy and others ..., **139**
Kirwallie Sandy in fight scene, **139**
Webster, Emily (née Brown), 185, 188
Western Australia
churches and Aboriginal people, 213
colonisation, 207, 209–10, 215
European views of Aboriginal people, 208
government policies: assimilation, 215, 223; control and violence, 210, 215; racialist, 15, 211; role of Aboriginal Protectors, 210, 222–3
impacts of invasion on Aboriginal people, 208–9; disease, 209; dispossession and desecration, 209, 215, 223; mixed-descent children, 209; violence and massacres, 209, 210
Institution for Native and Half-Caste Children, 116
lives of Aboriginal people: culture and skills, 208, 212, 223, (breaking down of), 211; government power over, 210, 211, 215; resistance, 210, 215; segregation, 210, 212
missions in, 210–12; conditions, 212–13; and cultural genocide, 211, 212; as tool of control and dispossession, 211
settler relations with Aboriginal people, 15; friendly, 207–8; rift in, 208; with women, 209
theories of race, 211, 215, 218
Western Australia: photographing Aboriginal Australians
documenting Indigenous people, 207, 217, 223, **224**; in Kalgoorlie, **206**, **218**, **219**, **220**
early photographers, 213, 215, 216, 217, 223
on missions, **212**, **213**, **214**, **222**, **223**; narrative of transition, 215
photograph collections, 207, 221–4, 226–7
as prisoners (in chains), **209**, 215
significance of early collections today, 215, 224–5; visual repatriation, 226–7
Westgarth, William, **109**
Australia Felix, 107
Wheeler, John, 138, 139
Whitlam, Gough, 6
Wilder, Joseph, 146, 147
Willshire, WH, *253*
Wilson, Ellie, **202**
Wilson, Aunty Hilda, 176
Winter, Alfred, 36
Wonga, Simon, 110, 111
Woolley, Charles H, 36, 45
Wooradi (Nuenone man), 26
Woretemoeteyenner (Bung), *50*

'Yamoureece' (Yomurritj or Waavera), 259, 266, 267, 268
Yarrie (Karruninnya), 243, **244**
Yerrebulluk (Dicky), **112**, 113
Yirrkala bark petitions, 265

www.ingramcontent.com/pod-product-compliance
Lightning Source LLC
LaVergne TN
LVHW052350100826
845147LV00013B/805

* 9 7 8 1 9 2 2 0 5 9 5 9 8 *